# QUESTIONNAIRE DESIGN, INTERVIEWING AND ATTITUDE MEASUREMENT

To
Betwyn

# QUESTIONNAIRE DESIGN, INTERVIEWING AND ATTITUDE MEASUREMENT

**New Edition**

## A.N. Oppenheim

Pinter Publishers
London and New York

distributed exclusively in the USA and Canada by ST. MARTINS PRESS

© A.N. Oppenheim, 1966, 1992

First published as 'Questionnaire design and attitude measurement' by
Basic Books, Inc., New York in 1966. This totally rewritten and recast
new edition first published in 1992 (reprinted 1993 and 1994) by
**Pinter Publishers Ltd**
25, Floral Street, London WC2E 9DS.

Distributed exclusively in the USA and Canada by St. Martin's Press,
Inc., 175 Fifth Avenue, New York, NY 10010, USA.

**British Library Cataloguing in Publication Data**
A CIP catalogue record for this book is available from the British Library
ISBN 1 85567 043 7 (HBK)
      1 85567 044 5 (PBK)

**Library of Congress Cataloging in Publication Data**
A CIP catalog record for this book is available from the Library of Congress

Typeset by DP Photosetting, Aylesbury, Bucks.
Printed and bound in Great Britain by
Biddles Ltd, Guildford and King's Lynn

# CONTENTS

# PREFACE

## From the preface to the first edition:

The world is full of well-meaning people who believe that anyone who can write plain English and has a modicum of common sense can produce a good questionnaire. This book is not for them.

It is intended to help all those who, for one reason or another, have to design a questionnaire. It could serve as a textbook for research students and undergraduates in social psychology and sociology and for practitioners of market research. It could also help doctors, personnel officers, civil servants, criminologists, social anthropologists, teachers, and many others whose curiosity or need for information may impel them into the quicksands of social research.

Questionnaire design cannot be taught from books; every investigation presents new and different problems. A textbook can only hope to prevent some of the worst pitfalls and to give practical, do-it-yourself kind of information that will point the way out of difficulties. It is not meant to be a work of scholarship, nor is it exhaustive. The number of references has been kept to a minimum, though some annotated readings have been provided with each chapter. Throughout, clarity and basic ease of understanding have been my guidelines; in each case, an attempt has been made to present the main lines of the argument and, while not shirking weaknesses in underlying assumptions, to omit some of the more esoteric controversies.

## Preface to the new edition

At the suggestion of many colleagues the book has been greatly expanded, as well as revised and updated. There are two new chapters on research design and sampling, two new chapters on interviewing, a chapter on questionnaire planning, a chapter on statistical analysis and a special chapter on pilot work. Other chapters have been changed and expanded, and a special set of Workshops has been introduced to offer practical experience. From having been a specialized text dealing with the design of questionnaires and attitude measures, it has broadened out and become a general survey research handbook. But its objectives have not changed. It still aims to reach those who have little or no background in the social sciences, and those who lack the facilities which many Western academics take for granted, as well as research students starting their first project and the junior staff of social research agencies. Teachers of courses in survey methods may find the book particularly useful because of the wide variety of examples spread through the text. It is my hope that many will find this not just a book to read but to keep.

In trying to make this text clearer, more accurate and better-written, I have sought the help of colleagues and graduate students. I owe much to their incisive critique and generosity of spirit and so does the reader. It is a pleasure to acknowledge my particular indebtedness to Neville Postlethwaite, Roger Thomas, Margaret Guy, Jennifer Marsh, Colin Taylor, Ronaldo Laranjeira, Julie Parker and Dan Wright. The responsibility for the book's remaining faults must be mine.

Bram Oppenheim
London, January 1992

# ACKNOWLEDGEMENTS

I wish to thank a number of people for their kind permission to use material from their works, as follows:

A.L. Baldwin, J. Kalhorn, and F.H. Breese, 'The Appraisal of Parent Behaviour', *Psychological Monographs*, XXIV (1949), No. 299.

E.S. Bogardus, 'Measuring Social Distances', *Journal of Applied Psychology*, IX (1925) No. 4.

William Caudill, *The Psychiatric Hospital as a Small Society* (Harvard University Press, 1958).

H.T. Himmelweit, A.N. Oppenheim, and P. Vince, *Television and the Child* (Oxford University Press, 1958).

Michael Shepherd, A.A. Cooper, A.C. Brown, and G.W. Kalton, *Psychiatric Illness in General Practice* (Oxford University Press, 1981).

The Open University. (Course DE.304)

# 1
# INTRODUCTION TO SURVEY DESIGN

## The need for good design

Suppose you want to find out why some people keep pets such as dogs, cats, fish or cage-birds. You may have jotted down some questions and handed these to forty-two pet owners in your neighbourhood or you may have conducted forty-two interviews. Assuming that your questions are well formulated and that all your respondents have answered truthfully, would you be able to draw any conclusions from your findings? Probably not, unless by 'conclusions' you mean those which apply only to these particular forty-two people. Such very limited conclusions are likely to be of little interest since it would be quite unwarranted to draw any wider inferences from the responses. Your little survey would tell you nothing about pet owners in general, and the results obtained in your neighbourhood might be quite misleading not only about pet owners in general but even about the majority of pet owners in your neighbourhood. You might nevertheless be tempted to study your findings more closely, for instance to see if the motives of dog owners differ from those of cat owners, but again the findings would tell you nothing about dog owners versus cat owners in general or even those in your own neighbourhood.

Nor could you test out the hypothesis that a pet is often a child substitute. It would, for example, be quite unwarranted to claim that your hypothesis had been supported because two-thirds of your sample were childless. It might be that more childless people answered your questions because you happened to know them or because they had the time or the inclination to do so. And besides, just because people are childless and have pets, this does not prove that they own pets *because* they are childless: associations do not establish causality. As before, it would also be wrong to draw any inferences from your findings which might apply to the childlessness of pet owners in general. Nor is it simply a question of numbers, for the same strictures would apply even if you had questioned many thousands of people. Moreover, there may be many reasons for keeping a pet; we should always avoid thinking in terms of simplistic monocausal models (see below and Chapter 2).

In short, the need for an appropriate research design arises whenever we wish to generalize from our findings, either in terms of the frequency or prevalence of particular attributes or variables, or about the relationships between them.

It is true, of course, that there are occasions when we wish to study a finite, special group, for example all the women in Dr Z's practice who gave birth to a baby in year Y, or all the employees who left firm X in a given month. But even in these circumstances research design problems arise. Quite probably, we wish to study these particular mothers, or job leavers, because we want to generalize about them; or compare them to other such groups; or predict what may happen this year, or next; or use their responses in order to improve our procedures. But unless our study is designed appropriately and is aimed at the correct target population, we will be unable to draw any such conclusions or comparisons. There may also be non-response problems (see Chapter 7) so that some of the necessary information will be missing, and the remainder of the responses may be biased. These matters will present us with further research design problems.

The need for good design becomes even more acute when we wish to undertake a more ambitious study. Suppose, for example, that we are asked to evaluate some social intervention such as the use of road paints to warn motorists to slow down before an intersection or the institution of a telephone helpline for children who are being abused. We might be asked to say, on the basis of survey research, whether such interventions are achieving their goal/ are cost-effective/should be discontinued or changed and so on. How would we go about this? How would we try to make sure that our conclusions are valid and could form a sound basis for generalization and further action?

It might be helpful at this point to make a rough-and-ready distinction between research *design* and research *techniques*, although each influences the other to some extent.

The term research *design* here refers to the basic plan or strategy of the research, and the logic behind it, which will make it possible and valid to draw more general conclusions from it. Thus, the research design should tell us how our sample will be drawn, what sub-groups it must contain, what comparisons will be made, whether or not we shall need control groups, what variables will need to be measured (when and at what intervals), and how these measures will be related to external events, for example to social, medical or other interventions. Research design is concerned with making our problem researchable by setting up our study in a way that will produce specific answers to specific questions. Good research design should above all make it possible for us to draw valid inferences from our data in terms of generalization, association and causality.

Research *techniques*, on the other hand, are the methods used for data generation and collection. Shall we gather our data by interview, by telephone or by postal questionnaire? How shall we measure attitudes, purchasing behaviour, social integration, conservatism or friendship patterns? Can we put questions together in groups to form inventories and scales (see Chapter 9)? How shall we analyse the contents of the replies to our questions? How shall we deal with missing data? Essentially, research techniques are concerned with measurement, quantification and instrument building and with making sure that our instruments are appropriate, valid and reliable.

This distinction between research design and research techniques holds true for all scientific disciplines. Moreover, the principles of research design are applicable quite generally to experimentation, the requirements of sampling and the logic and standards of inference in any discipline. However the creation and application of measuring instruments and data collection techniques tend to be specific to each discipline or group of disciplines. Cross-disciplinary research, such as doctors conducting social surveys of their patients' smoking habits, requires familiarity with measuring techniques in more than one discipline.

Here we shall be concerned primarily with the *design* of social surveys, the planned architecture of inquiry. In later chapters we shall deal with measurement and instrument building, that is with research *techniques* such as scales and questionnaires. However, as we have indicated before, these two aspects of research are often interlinked. The design of the research will determine whom we should question and what questions we should ask, while technical and fieldwork problems may set constraints on the research design.

## First steps in survey design

Too often, surveys are carried out on the basis of insufficient design and planning or on the basis of no design at all. 'Fact-gathering' can be an exciting and tempting activity to which a questionnaire opens a quick and seemingly easy avenue; the weaknesses in the design are frequently not recognized until the results have to be interpreted — if then! Survey literature abounds with portentous conclusions based on faulty inferences from insufficient evidence misguidedly collected and wrongly assembled. Not everyone realizes that the design of a survey, besides requiring a certain amount of technical knowledge, is a prolonged and arduous intellectual exercise in the course of which we are continuously trying to clear our own minds about our goals. We often find that, as the research takes shape, our aim undergoes a number of subtle changes as a consequence of greater clarity in our thinking (see Chapter 2). Such changes may require a new and better design, which in turn will lead to a better specification for the instruments of measurement.

The drawing up of the research design takes place at the very beginning of the research process, though the plan may have to be changed later. A social research study may last from a few months to many years, but most surveys go through the same stages or cycles of stages.

We may distinguish the following:

1. Deciding the *aims* of the study and, possibly, the theories to be investigated. General aims must then lead to a statement of specific aims, and these should be turned into *operationalized* aims; that is, a specified set of practical issues or hypotheses to be investigated. This should lead directly to a statement of the *variables* to be measured, and for each of these a set of questions, scales and indicators will have to be formulated.
2. Reviewing the relevant *literature*; discussions with informants and interested organizations.
3. Preliminary *conceptualization* of the study, followed by a series of exploratory or 'depth' interviews; revised conceptualization and research objectives (see below).
4. Deciding the *design* of the study and assessing its feasibility within the

limitations of time, costs and staffing. Abandon the study at this point, or reduce its aims, if the means to carry it out are insufficient.

5. Deciding which *hypotheses* will be investigated. Making these hypotheses specific to the situation (that is making the hypotheses operational). Listing the variables which will have to be measured. For instance, if we have some hypotheses about political participation, then how shall we operationalize this behaviour, and what variables shall we need to measure: party membership, fund-raising activities, going to political rallies, watching political events on TV, displaying a window poster or bumper sticker?

6. Designing, or adapting, the necessary *research instruments* and techniques such as postal questionnaires, interview schedules, attitude scales, projective methods, check lists or rating scales.

7. Doing the necessary *pilot work* (see Chapter 4) to try out the instruments, making revisions where necessary and trying them out again. Piloting other aspects of the research such as how to gain access to respondents.

8. Designing the *sample(s)*. Will the sample need to be representative (that is, a probability sample, see Chapter 3) and, if so, of whom? Are there lists or other sampling frames from which to draw a sample? Shall we need a control group? Shall we need a follow-up sample? How shall we cope with non-response and missing data, that is with differences between the designed sample and the achieved sample? Pilot work on the techniques of drawing the sample.

9. Drawing the sample: *selection of the people* to be approached.

10. Doing the *field-work*. This will involve the actual data collection process through interviewing or the sending out of the postal questionnaires; the day-to-day control of these complex operations; and the collection and checking of the returns. Contrary to expectations, the field-work stage is often shorter than the preliminary stages.

11. *Processing the data* (see Chapter 14): coding the responses, preparing the data for analysis and entering them into a computer if available.

12. Doing the *statistical analysis* (see Chapter 15), simple at first but becoming more complex; testing for statistical significance.

13. Assembling the results and *testing the hypotheses*.

14. Writing the *research report*: describing the results in words and tabulations; relating the findings to previous research; drawing conclusions and interpretations.

It should be clear from the above that a social survey is a complex operation, and a first requirement is therefore the development of a clear plan or over-all research design. It is the research design which must hold all the parts and phases of the enquiry together. The design must aim at precision, logic-tightness and efficient use of resources. A poorly designed survey will fail to provide accurate answers to the questions under investigation; it will leave too many loopholes in the conclusions; it will permit little generalization; and it will produce much irrelevant information, thereby wasting case material and resources.

Much will depend on the quality of the research conceptualization (see (3) above). 'Conceptualization' here refers to an improved and more detailed statement of the study's objectives, preferably with theoretical underpinnings. If, for example, we intend to study the buying of home computers, should we question both owners and non-owners? What about ex-owners? And what should we ask them about: their income, the availability of computers at their place of work, various aspects of home computer use (domestic accounts, word processing, computer games), the way people make decisions about major domestic expenditures? Later, a re-conceptualization might add to this list, for example educational use (if they have children); 'keeping up with the Joneses' (prestige factors); typing skills; fears about new technology (which might be gender-related); leisure pursuits; health-related fears; and so on.

Here is an example of a poor design. The research took place in a major conurbation in a developing country which was attracting large numbers of migrants from distant rural areas. The researchers found that many of the more recent arrivals in the city were suffering from psychosomatic and stress-related disorders. They concluded that this was due to the new migrants being adversely affected by the problems of urban living. However, the researchers did not present any data about comparable samples of long-established city dwellers to show whether they were experiencing higher, lower or similar levels of stress-related disorders compared to the new migrants. Moreover, assuming the findings to be valid, they do not constitute proof that the stresses arose from city life. It is equally possible to suggest that these migrants were suffering from long-standing stress-related disorders which had been present before they came to the city. It may also have been the case that the migrants were motivated in part to move to the city because they found the difficult living conditions in the rural areas too stressful! Thus, in failing to incorporate a control or comparison group, the design left loopholes for at least two alternative interpretations of the findings: a pre-existing condition and selective migration. Also, the researchers were too uncritical in assuming certain disorders to be necessarily due to stress and urban living conditions. We should always remember that association is not proof of causation.

One way of testing the adequacy of a research design in advance of the field-work is to run through the natural sequence of survey stages *in reverse order*. For example, let us assume that in our final report (stage 14, the Research Report) we expect to be able to show whether men differ from women in the ways in which they are politically active. To demonstrate this we shall need some statistical tables and cross-tabulations, for example a check-list of political activities reported by our respondents, cross-tabulated by gender (the statistical analysis stage). At this point we must draw up some dummy tables, showing the relevant variables in cross-tabulation with certain sub-groups, for example gender. In order to generate such tabulations we must have asked questions about political activism and we must have administered such a check-list; we must also know the sex of each of our respondents (the research techniques and pilot work stages). To be able to generalize from our findings, we must have established an accurate relationship between the members of our sample and the target population (the sampling and sample design stages). And to be meaning-ful, the limited topic of gender differences must be part of a wider conceptual-ization or theoretical framework (the literature review and conceptualization stages).

Thus, by running backwards through the survey stages we can try to ensure logic-tightness, so that nothing is left out and we shall have measured everything that needs to be measured.

The formulation of any questionnaire to be used in a survey must be an integral part of the research design stage. A questionnaire is not just a list of questions or a form to be filled in. It is essentially a measurement tool, an instrument for the collection of particular kinds of data. Like all such instruments, the aims and specifications of a questionnaire stem directly from the overall research design. Such objectives and specifications are not always obvious from a perusal of the questions. However, we cannot judge a questionnaire unless we know what job it was meant to do. This means that we have to think not merely about the wording of particular questions but, first and foremost, about the design of the investigation as a whole.

Thus it is essential for any researcher to draw up a statement (a) of general aims for the proposed study and to develop these into (b) a set of specific aims; these should be further developed into (c) a set of operationalized aims; that is, specific issues or hypotheses, which should point directly to (d) a list of variables, scales or indicators which will be needed: for example, how shall we measure parental education or strictness of upbringing? Dummy tables for the proposed analysis should also be drawn up at this point.

# An actual case

In the early fifties, when television-viewing was rapidly gaining ground in Great Britain, a survey was commissioned to supply answers to two broad questions: (1) what kinds of people were buying television sets? (2) How was the new medium affecting them? The large-scale survey that eventually took place used two samples. The first was intended to be representative of television-owners and was drawn from the lists of television licence holders. This sample was bound to be incomplete since it failed to include set owners who had not applied for a licence, but by and large it could give reasonable estimates of the income, family size, social and educational background, religion, consumer habits, and so on of law-abiding television owners at that time.

The second sample was assembled by asking the interviewers to question an adjacent non-television householder for each set owner in the first sample. It was reasoned that by interviewing the people next door a sample could be obtained, for purposes of comparison, that would be similar to the television owners in socioeconomic background, consumer habits and so forth.

The faults in this design were only realized toward the end of the investigation. Let us consider the logic of it step by step. The research had two purposes. The first was to find out what kinds of people were buying television sets. This implied something more than a purely descriptive study of a representative sample of set owners, since to state that such families had an average income of X pounds a week or that Y per cent of them had telephones or washing machines would be almost meaningless unless it could be put into some kind of context; in other words, it had to be compared to other figures. It might then become possible to conclude that television buyers more often came from the lower income levels, or had larger families, were less religious and so on. For a few points of comparison, data were probably available for the nation as a whole (including the television owners), but most of the questions had to be asked afresh. In order to show how television buyers differed from non-buyers, the second sample would have to be a representative sample of all the people who had not bought a television set. That a sample of people living next door to set owners would accurately represent the non-buying public was clearly too much to hope for, since in any case they had been chosen on the grounds of similarity in environment and socioeconomic background to the set owners. As the figures subsequently showed, the second sample, not being representative of the non-television buyers, was useless for purposes of comparison. Consequently, the accurate figures obtained from the first sample could not be made to reveal any social change or pattern.

And what of the second purpose of the investigation; how was the new medium affecting set owners? Here there were many difficulties, since it is often hard to disentangle the effects of *one* variable, such as television, from the effects of many others operating at the same time. A comparative study can try to do this by choosing a control sample as similar as possible to the television sample in every relevant respect, so that we can see what the people in the television sample would have been like if they had not bought television sets. There are still weaknesses even then because of pre-existing differences, matching problems and effects of guest-viewing, but the sample design failed to produce sufficient similarity between the two groups. Consequently, there was no way of telling whether or in what way changes had been produced in the television sample.

The second sample, that of the neighbours, turned out to be useless. It was neither a representative sample of non-television buyers (as required for the first purpose) nor a closely comparable control sample (as required for the second purpose). It should have been realized from the beginning that, since the inquiry had two objectives, two *different* comparison samples were required. This may seem obvious in retrospect, but the professional survey organization that carried out the research realized too late what had happened. Mistakes like this occur every day and can only be prevented by making the greatest possible effort to clarify our objectives before we start.

## Surveys versus experiments

How do we decide which of the many types of research design to choose for our particular purpose? This is a difficult question to answer since every research project presents its own particular design problems. Still, it is possible to discuss some basic types of research design in general terms and to make some rough-and-ready distinctions. In the next chapter we shall discuss cross-sectional designs, longitudinal designs, intervention designs, factorial designs and regression designs. All of these (and several others) can be grouped together under the heading 'analytic designs' (see Chapter 2) because, in one way or another, they attempt to deal with associations or with cause-and-effect relationships in ways analogous to lab experiments. They try to explain things, they seek to answer 'why' questions, or 'what determines X' questions and, in this way, they are to be distinguished from the other broad category, the 'Descriptive' designs. (See Chapter 3.)

Beyond the world of survey research, the scientific endeavour is characterized by another type of analytic design, the controlled laboratory experiment. This method, which involves the systematic manipulation of variables, is not usually available to the survey researcher who cannot, say, make people want to adopt a pet to see what effect this will have on them or cause them to be burgled to see how this will influence their attitudes towards the police. While it is sometimes possible to conduct simple experiments with people involving the manipulation of several variables, it should not be assumed that the controlled laboratory experiment is the 'ideal' design. Experiments and surveys are often contrasted with each other. Those who favour surveys criticize experiments for being unrepresentative, for dealing with artificial situations and for often failing to achieve the degree of precision and control that might justify them. Experimentalists are critical of surveys because of their reduced ability to control or manipulate important variables, for following events rather than making them happen and for their inability to prove causal relationships. Nevertheless, the survey researcher using an analytic design will have taken many a leaf out of the experimentalist's book. It would be more helpful to suggest that choosing the best design or the best method *is a matter of appropriateness.* No single approach is always or necessarily superior; it all depends on what we need to find out and on the type of question to which we seek an answer. Indeed many research enquiries have employed surveys *and* experiments at different stages, using the result of the one to inform and refine the other, and so producing conclusions that are both precise and representative.

## Descriptive versus analytic designs

As stated above, it is possible to make a broad distinction between two types of survey: (1) the descriptive, enumerative, census-type of survey; and (2) the analytic, relational type of survey.

The purpose of the descriptive survey is to count. When it cannot count everyone, it counts a representative sample and then makes inferences about the population as a whole. There are several ways of drawing a sample, and the problems of sampling, sampling bias and sampling error are dealt with later (see Chapter 3). The important point to recognize is that descriptive surveys chiefly tell us how many (what proportion of) members of a population have a certain opinion or characteristic or how often certain events occur together (that is, are associated with each other); they are not designed to 'explain' anything or to show causal relationships between one variable and another.

Descriptive surveys are well known and important. Any form of census falls into this category, as do many public-opinion polls and commercial investigations. Such surveys provide governments, manufacturers, economists and municipalities with information necessary for action. The job of such surveys is essentially fact-finding and descriptive — although the data collected are also often used to make *predictions*, for instance by comparing the results of similar surveys at different times and producing a trend, or by trying to forecast election outcomes or the number of homes that will be required in ten years' time and so on. Representativeness (or sometimes full enumeration) of a defined population is a first requirement.

There are many questions that actuarial surveys cannot answer or can answer only inadequately. Such questions usually start as 'why' questions and then proceed to examine group differences from which relationships between variables can be inferred. For instance, in comparing the results of election polls, we may find a rise, over a period of time, in the percentage of people choosing a particular party. We may wonder why this is happening and wish to explore the suggestion that, say, this party's policies with regard to old-age provisions makes it very attractive to older voters. We go back to our data and arrange the results according to age to see whether there are marked age-group differences in the expected direction. We could go further and try to find out whether low-income groups, or childless elderly couples, or young couples with elderly dependents are more prone to vote for this party, but clearly there is a limit to what we can do in this way: we may not have obtained the necessary information about income or elderly dependents; there may not be enough low-income voters above a certain age in our sample; we may not have asked any questions bearing on pensions and so forth.

We have now moved from questions about 'how many' to questions about 'why', from enumeration and description to an analysis of causality, and so we shall require a different type of survey, a survey with an *analytic* design.

## Problems of causes and effects

Many current ideas about causality have their origin in what we think of as 'science' or the scientific method. All science is concerned with relationships or co-variation between variables, but some of our ideas about relationships or associations have to undergo subtle changes as we move from the physical and biological sciences to the social sciences. We may start with the *'monocausal' model*, suggesting that a single cause can have a specific effect. Thus, if we put a kettle of water on a fire it will get hotter and eventually it will boil; similarly, the harder it rains, the higher will be the level of a river and, eventually, it will overflow its banks. In the 'heroic' early years of microbiology the thinking among researchers was often monocausal: one disease, caused by one strain of bacteria, to be cured by one vaccine or other anti-body. Associated with these monocausal or 'A causes B' models were several other ideas. For example, causality of this kind was assumed to be linear, proportional and incremental: the stronger the cause, the bigger the effect. In many cases this type of causality was also expected to be reversible: if the cause were weakened or removed, the effect would decline and disappear.

However, the monocausal model often does not tell the full story, and sometimes it can be seriously misleading. For example, the level of the river Thames at London Bridge is not determined solely by the amount of rainfall in the Thames valley. It can also rise or fall with the tides, with the phases of the moon, with the state of the flood defences on the river banks and the position of locks and weirs up-river, and with the direction of strong winds from the

North Sea. Each of these causes will have a greater or lesser effect depending on its strength and timing and so we have to learn to think in *multi-causal* terms. Not only that, but the effects of these causes may be singular or *cumulative*: when adverse conditions of wind and tide, moon and rainfall combine at the same time, we may well get an exceptionally high water level and even flooding. Likewise, though the cholera bacillus is present in small numbers in most communities, it does not usually become a dangerous epidemic unless certain other conditions obtain: poor hygiene, contaminated water supply, lowered resistance among certain members of the population.

Let us also note that, in a multi-causal model, the several causal factors may be independent or *interrelated*. Thus, the twice-daily tides and the phases and diurnal orbits of the moon interact with each other, as well as with the water level in the Thames. In developing countries or under disaster conditions, poor hygiene, lowered resistance and water contamination often go hand-in-hand to create the conditions in which cholera flourishes.

Nor is it always necessary for these interactions among causes to happen simultaneously. Their accumulation may take many years and form a succession of influences, for example the silting up of a lake due to industrial effluent, followed by the proliferation of algae and the death of fish and other forms of marine life. Or the death of an individual from lung cancer may be due to a degree of genetic predisposition followed by a stressful lifestyle and prolonged heavy smoking. This is sometimes called a *causal pathway* or, in people, a 'career'. Thus, a young person does not become a delinquent in a monocausal way, for example, by coming from a 'broken' home. Other factors, successively or simultaneously, help to create a delinquent career: upbringing factors, educational factors, friends and the 'delinquent sub-culture' and so on.

When trying to disentangle problems of causality we often find *associations* or *correlations*, but of themselves these are no proof of causality. We might find, for example, that people who have acquired a microwave oven also have poor dietary habits, or that children with access to a computer at home are also better at mathematics in school. Does this mean that possession of a microwave or a home computer *caused* the dietary habits or the maths performance? On the basis of such associations alone we cannot say. It might be true that A caused B; or it might be that B caused A; that is, that people with poor eating habits are more likely to buy a microwave and that children who are good at maths try to get their parents to buy a home computer. Or it could be that another determinant, factor C, was the cause of both A and B. People with a busy lifestyle might have poor eating habits and also need a microwave; children from better-educated families might both be good at maths and have access to a home computer. We note, therefore, that associations may or may not denote causality; that such causality might run from A to B, from B to A or from C to both A and B. And often there is an interactive network of several causes.

Some mothers score higher than others on a measure of strictness. We may find that they are more often working class; that they have larger families, on average; that they have completed fewer years of full-time education; and that they are less likely to read women's-magazine articles about child upbringing. It would be quite possible to map out these associations and then speculate about causal interpretations. However, we shall also find that working-class women are less well educated, on average; that people with less education tend to read less; that in large families there is often neither the time to read nor the money to buy magazines containing articles about upbringing and so on. Each of the associations is not just linked independently with maternal strictness; it is also likely to be linked to the other associated factors and co-vary with them, as well as with strictness. It would take quite a complex research design and statistical analysis to disentangle these strands and to establish causal links from such a network of associations.

The nineteenth-century British statistician Sir Francis Galton once conducted an inquiry into the 'Objective Efficacy of Prayer'. He operationalized his inquiry by trying to find out whether clergymen lived longer than members of other professions. (So far, by making a few assumptions, he appears to have followed a monocausal model: more praying causes longer life.) His data did indeed show a small association: a difference of between one and two years in favour of the clergy. But at this point Galton seems to have adopted a multi-causal model of longevity. He expressed the thought that such a small difference in average age attained might well be accounted for by easier life circumstances, concluding that 'the prayers of the clergy for protection against the perils and dangers of the night, for protection during the day, and for recovery from sickness, appear to be futile'.

Strictly speaking, though, even if Galton's data had shown a very large difference in the average age attained by clergy compared to other professions, this would not have constituted proof of a causal connection between prayer and longevity. Some pre-existing, self-selective factor might well account for the results; for example, it might be that in those days the clergy attracted exceptionally healthy recruits with a predisposition to longevity. Or the results might be explained by another, more current, association; clergymen might be sustained into old age by exceptionally supportive wives!

We must also consider time, or rather temporal sequence, when seeking to establish causality. Our understanding of causality includes the strong presumption that causes must antecede their effects. Since it is implicit in this view that *earlier* causes are likely to be more important, this may lead us to discount later causes. Thus, some women suffer from post-natal depression; but was the baby's birth the cause of the depression, or was the woman suffering from episodes of depression long before the pregnancy? We must not assume that just because B followed A, therefore B was *caused* by A. The baby's birth may, or may not, have been the significant event that caused the mother's depression. We merely picked up this association because the two events happened at about the same time.

To establish causality with any certainty is difficult; to establish associations is often easier but leaves us to speculate about causality. It sometimes happens that association patterns can give us a strong hint about causality, and perhaps suggest an effective intervention method, even though the cause remains unknown. John Snow, the London physician who worked in Soho in the nineteenth century, was the first to show the connection between cholera and a contaminated water supply. He meticulously mapped the addresses of those who died from cholera during an epidemic at a time when micro-organisms were unknown and the beliefs about the causes of cholera were mainly superstitions.

His data showed that all those who had contracted the disease had taken their drinking water from the Broad Street pump. When he eventually persuaded the parish council to remove the handle from the pump, the epidemic stopped. All Snow had, by way of evidence, was an association; discovery of the cholera bacillus still lay in the future. However, disjoining the association had the desired effect — though it has been argued that the result was only partly causal because the epidemic was on the wane anyway!

Even today in medicine it is not unusual to find health measures being recommended for the cure or prevention of ills whose causes are as yet unknown. The expected efficacy of these measures rests on the disruption of patterns of association, for example between coronary heart attacks and various dietary factors. Sometimes, too, the reverse happens: we may find an effective remedy, even though we do not understand how it works, for example quinine and malaria.

The laboratory experiment, if properly conducted, is the classical tool for establishing causality. It does so partly by systematic manipulation of particular causal factors (to show changes in causal factors being accompanied by changes in effects) and partly by eliminating as many other factors as possible. Thus, pre-existing causes may be eliminated by allocating subjects *randomly* to the various experimental conditions; co-variation of causes may be explored systematically and interaction effects observed; and measures such as a double-blind design can reduce the risk that human experimental subjects will influence the results by their own expectations, or that the experimenters or their assistants will unwittingly convey their expectations to their subjects. But critics of human experimentation will often point to the difficulties experienced in creating true experimental manipulation of psychological variables and to the fact that causes are not always what they seem: in survey research we can develop complex analytic designs to establish patterns of associations, but we can hardly ever prove causality because the experimental method is not usually open to us. However, we can sometimes participate in, or even help to plan, so-called natural experiments or social interventions or intervention programmes which, if properly conducted, can permit us to draw causal inferences.

Taking part in social intervention programmes confronts us with the fact that most societies have strongly held world views and many systems of causal attribution. For example, many religions have built-in assumptions about the causes of poverty, ill-health, crime and depression, and other assumptions about what makes a good marriage or a happy childhood. Similarly, the authorities responsible for law and order hold strong assumptions about the causes of criminal acts, traffic accidents, football hooliganism or prostitution. Typically, they will adopt a monocausal model, usually one embracing the personal responsibility of an individual. Thus, the responsibility for a car crash will be attributed to the driver with traces of a drug in his bloodstream. That the accident occurred on a notoriously dangerous bend, that the car crashed into a poorly sited telephone pole, that the road was made slippery by rain or ice, that the car's tyres were almost bald, that visibility was very poor at that time of night, that the driver was blinded by the lights of an oncoming vehicle are all facts that are often ignored, requiring a multi-causal model which the legal system would find difficult to handle. Societies often indulge in scapegoating: if a prisoner escapes from gaol, the prison governor is sacked, although he probably had no knowledge of the prisoner and no direct influence on the events of the escape. This is done in the name of an attributional system called 'accountability'. If a child commits a dangerous or criminal act, we demand restitution from the parents although they were not directly involved; we do this in the name of 'responsibility'. Such attributional systems have little or nothing in common with valid cause-and-effect analysis, but simplistic mono-causal models and punitive attributions are easier to use than more appropriate but more complex causal models, and they are culturally sanctioned and widely available. More appropriate multi-causal models, on the other hand, would demand resources, time and skills for their validation and further research to examine the effectiveness of appropriate intervention programmes. Thus the social researcher who seeks to establish appropriate causal models and to validate them not only faces the daunting problems of research design but also encounters much societal resistance.

## The future of causal attribution

Social research is trying to move from intuitive causal attributions (such as can be found in scapegoating, collective representations, stereotypes, health-belief systems, magic, folklore) to more objective kinds of causal attribution which are capable of verification and generalization. We have come part of the way with the aid of the research designs and strategies discussed above, but we still have a long way to go. This is partly because many of our ideas about research design and statistical analysis have come to us from other branches of knowledge, for example from the natural sciences, where other processes of causality predominate and where the linear approach to measurement has often been of good service. But societies and human beings are in important ways different from agricultural plots or biochemical reactions, and so we often feel that to apply some of these research designs to them is rather like putting our subjects on Procrustean beds.

For example, we rightly seek to distinguish between 'mere correlates' (associations) and 'actual causes', but the reason we cannot give associations the status of causes is because we do not know their place in a complex network of causality. The very word 'network' is a metaphor. It implies assumptions about the ways in which multi-causality works but, in fact, *we often cannot say what the correct causal model would be*. Take, for example, the long-term stability of belief systems and attitudes. Research shows that older people are often more religious than younger people and strongly believe in the hereafter. Does this mean that they had a more religious upbringing because they were educated long ago and have not changed since? Or have their religious ideas been subject to many influences and changes throughout their lives? Or have they recently 'found' religion because a strong belief system helped a close friend to come to terms with impending death? Our models of attitude measurement and change seem too linear to reflect such processes. Again, we often find that liking a school subject and being good at it go together, but by what means or metaphors can we describe and measure how such an association develops? The same might apply to alcoholism and drink-related occupations; or to the stages of becoming a criminal. Such processes are ill-served by our traditional causal models.

We seem to have inherited notions of causality which imply a linear, additive progression, a kind of geological or 'layered' causality in which bounded one-way influences are brought to bear on people at successive times causing them to change. Our designs and our statistical techniques predicate us to think in this way because we know how to apply them; this kind of causality we can more or less handle. But in social research we often come across what might be called 'spiral reinforcement' processes. A small success at school, or a word of praise from a teacher, may make a child just that little more interested in a particular school subject, the child tries harder and develops its interest in that subject, which in turn may lead to more praise and more success and so on. The process is incremental but not additive, influential but also interactive. The same may apply to the drinker who becomes a barman. A pre-existing liking for drink may lead by mutually reinforcing steps — a self-selective job choice, easy availability of drink, increased liking, membership of the drinking scene — to the development of problem drinking and so, ultimately, to dependence and alcoholism. As yet we have no models that can display, nor research designs that can reveal and predict, the workings of such causal processes.

In choosing our research strategy, our research design and statistical analysis, we should therefore remain aware that these contain implicit assumptions about causal links and causal processes in people. Indeed, such assumptions may long ago have insinuated themselves into our own research interests and into our thought processes about causal attributions. While we can make good use of existing research methods in the service of replicability, data disaggregation and representativeness, we must not forget that human lives and human causality are not composed of layers of regression coefficients. We need a fundamental re-think of the nature of the social influencing processes themselves. This may lead to the development of more appropriate analytic designs and to better models of human causality.

# Selected readings

## GENERAL TEXTS ON RESEARCH METHODOLOGY

Rossi, P.H., Wright, J.D. and Anderson, A.B. (eds), 1983, *Handbook of Survey Research*, Academic Press, New York.
   A good, comprehensive collection.

Kidder, Louise H., Judd, Charles M. and Smith, Eliot R., 1986, *Research Methods in Social Relations*, Holt, Rinehart and Winston, New York.
   Published by the SPSSI as a successor to the earlier text by Selltiz, Wrightsman, and Cook (see below), it is a comprehensive text at the undergraduate level.

Kidder, Louise H., Judd, Charles M. and Smith, Eliot R., 1986, *Research Methods in Social Relations*, Holt, Rinehart and Winston, New York.
Published by the SPSSI as a successor to the earlier text by Selltiz, Wrightsman, and Cook (see below), it is a comprehensive text at the undergraduate level.

Moser, C.A. and Kalton, G., 1972, second edition, *Survey Methods in Social Investigation*, Heinemann, London.
A well established, statistically orientated general text in survey methods, especially strong on sampling methods but also good on interviewing, questionnaire design and scaling methods.

Hoinville, Gerald and Jowell, Roger, 1978, *Survey Research Practice*, Gower, Aldershot, Hants.
Straightforward and practical general text on survey methods. Especially good on organizing fieldwork and postal surveys.

Babbie, E., 1989, second edition, *Survey Research Methods*, Chapman & Hall, London.

Kerlinger, F.N., 1964, *Foundations of Behavioural Research*, Holt, New York.
A comprehensive research methods text, especially strong on measurement and statistical problems.

Hippler, H.J., Schwarz, N. and Sudman, S. (eds), 1987, *Social Information Processing and Survey Methodology*, Springer Verlag, New York.

Maclean, M. and Genn, H., 1979, *Methodological Issues in Social Surveys*, Macmillan, New York.

Schuman, H. and Kalton, G., 1985, 'Survey methods' in Lindzey, G. and Aronson, E. (eds), *Handbook of Social Psychology*, Vol. I, third edition, Random House, New York.
An extensive textbook chapter touching on all the main points of survey research.

Altreck, Pamela L. and Settle, Robert B., *The Survey Research Handbook*, Richard Irwin Inc., Homewood Ill.
An easy to read undergraduate text.

Singer, Eleanor and Presser, Stanley, 1989, *Survey Research Methods*, University of Chicago Press, Chicago.
A reader dealing with sampling, non-response problems, validity, interviewer bias, telephone interviewing and related topics.

Przeworski, Adam and Teune, Henry, *The Logic of Comparative Social Enquiry*, Wiley (Interscience), Chichester, Sussex.
Deals with the logic of comparative studies and the problems of equivalence of measures. For advanced students.

Sage University Papers Series: Quantitative Applications in the Social Sciences.
An expanding series of small paperback volumes dealing with every aspect of social research methods.

The Open University, Course DEH 313, 1993, *Principles of Social and Educational Research*, The Open University, Milton Keynes.
An excellent set of self-study course books, available separately and supported by exercises and by collected readings.

Fink, Arelene and Kosecoff, Jacqueline, 1985, *How to Conduct Surveys*, Sage, London.
A text for beginners.

Selltiz, C., Wrightsman, L.S. and Cook, S.W., 1976, third edition, *Research Methods in Social Relations*, Holt, Rinehart and Winston, New York.
Still generally useful.

Hyman, Herbert, 1955, *Survey Design and Analysis*, Free Press, Glencoe, Ill.
A major older research text full of useful applications. Helpful on descriptive versus analytic designs.

Bynner, John and Stribley, Keith M. (eds), 1978, *Social Research: Principles and Procedures*, Longman and The Open University Press.
A useful collection of original papers on research design and methods of data collection.

ON PUBLIC OPINION POLLS

Bradburn, Norman M. and Sudman, Seymour, 1988, *Polls and Surveys*, Jossey-Bass, London.

# 2
# ANALYTIC SURVEY DESIGNS

The analytic, relational survey is set up specifically to explore the associations between particular variables. Its design is in many ways similar to that of the laboratory experiment. However, like experiments in the laboratory, it is usually set up to explore specific hypotheses. It is less orientated towards representativeness and more towards finding associations and explanations, less towards description and enumeration and more towards prediction, less likely to ask 'how many' or 'how often' than 'why' and 'what goes with what'.

## Four types of variables

In designing an analytic survey, it is helpful to distinguish four different kinds of variables:

1. *Experimental variables.* These are the 'causes' or predictors, the effects of which are being studied. They are sometimes referred to as 'independent' or 'explanatory' variables. The analytic type of survey, like the lab experiment, is set up to vary these factors systematically so that their effects can be observed. Often several such variables working both in isolation and in various combinations are of interest.
2. *Dependent variables.* These are the results, the effects–variables, the gains or losses produced by the impact of the experimental variables, the predicted outcomes. These variables have to be measured particularly carefully and group differences tested for statistical significance.
3. *Controlled variables.* As a source of variation these should be eliminated in order to fulfil the condition of 'other things being equal' when the effects or correlates of the experimental variables are stated. Variables can be controlled by *exclusion* (for example, by having only males in a sample, gender is excluded as a source of variation); by *holding them constant* (for instance, by interviewing all respondents on the same day, thus eliminating day-of-the-week effects); or by *randomization* (for instance, in the case of a multiple-choice question, by systematically randomizing the order in which the alternatives are presented to the respondents, thus eliminating ordinal and serial effects as a source of variation).
4. *Uncontrolled variables.* These are 'free-floating' variables and can theoretically

be of two kinds: (a) *confounded variables* and (b) *error*. The confounded variables, sometimes called 'correlated biases', have hidden influences of unknown size on the results. For example, in medical research the results of treatment may be affected by a hitherto unknown allergy or by unsuspected side effects; in some psychological research, genetic influences may play a much bigger part than anticipated; in advertising, public reaction to a new product or campaign may be unexpectedly volatile. Essentially this means that knowledge and understanding of the phenomena under investigation are still incomplete in important ways; there are variables, other than the experimental and controlled ones but confounded with them, that can affect the results and hence can produce serious misinterpretations. On the other hand, such uncontrolled variables can lead to the development of new hypotheses so that, eventually, their impact may be controlled.

Inevitably, any research design also suffers from error. Such error variables are (or are assumed to be) randomly distributed or, at any rate, distributed in such a way as not to affect the results.

In practice it is not usually possible to distinguish between confounded variables (that is, hidden additional causes) and 'pure error'. In analytic surveys, as in experiments, the influence of uncontrolled variables is made as small as possible. If the presence of confounded variables is suspected, a good deal of statistical analysis may be required to uncover their identity, and ultimately their impact must be studied systematically in a new enquiry.

An example may help to clarify these terms. Let us assume that we are trying to understand some of the determinants of children's bedtimes. We have decided to study the effects of age, which will be our experimental variable, and the survey will obtain information from a sample of children for every day of the week. Our dependent variable will be the children's bedtime, in all its variations. There are many variables that we will have to control in order to observe the effects of age. For instance, children who have recently been ill may have to go to bed especially early; we will probably control this variable by excluding such children from the sample. Children go to bed later in the summer and during school holidays; we may control these variables by holding them constant, by collecting all our data during one short period in the school term. Children go to bed later if they have older brothers or sisters; we can try to take care of this by making sure that children with older siblings are randomly distributed through our sample.

There remain a considerable number of uncontrolled variables, some of which are very likely to be confounded. For instance, socioeconomic background is likely to be an important influence on bedtimes; if we realize this in advance, we may be able to control it, but otherwise this factor can easily introduce a bias in our conclusions. It may, for instance, happen that the older children in our sample also come from more well-to-do homes, where bedtimes tend to be earlier; in that case, we may wrongly conclude that increasing age is *not* a good predictor of later bedtimes because, unknown to us, the socioeconomic factor is counteracting the age factor. Again, the child's gender, membership in a youth organization, or a keen liking for television may be important determinants of bedtimes in parts of our sample. Such uncontrolled variables, unless they are known to be randomly distributed, can bias the results to an unknown degree. The 'ideal' design would contain no uncontrolled variables.

For our design to be effective, each of the four types of variable must be measured as carefully as possible. This is of particular importance with regard to our dependent variable(s). It often happens that, in designing a study, people become so involved with the problems of the experimental variables (the 'causes') or the controlled variables, that they give insufficient attention to the dependent variable — or even forget to measure it altogether! Thus, in the earlier example about children's bedtimes, they may simply forget to ask any questions about bedtimes — without which all the other questions are useless. It will also soon become clear that 'bedtime' is not a precise concept: does it refer to the 'official' bedtime (if any) laid down by the parents, to the time the child actually gets into bed, to the time the child falls asleep? Do we ask the child, do we ask the parents or perhaps an older sibling, if any?

In deciding how to measure such a variable, we first have to define it and then define it further in operational terms. This process of defining should take us right back to the initial aim or purpose of our research. If we are, say, conducting some kind of medical enquiry about the need for rest and sleep in children, then 'bedtime' might well be defined as 'falling-asleep time' (to be followed by 'waking-up time' and questions about interrupted sleep). But if we are interested in, say, social-class differences in parental standards, then 'bedtime' might be more appropriately defined as the 'official' bedtime (if there is one). Thus, the definition of a variable will not depend on a dictionary but on the internal logic of the inquiry.

Further pilot work will then show how a variable, as defined for our purposes, can best be measured in the field. The pilot work may even show that we need still further refinement in our definition. We should never shirk any effort to make our dependent variable more precise and more robust. If we had simply asked a sample of parents about their children's usual bedtimes, then it would be very difficult to draw conclusions about differences in age, gender, school term versus vacation, week-ends etc. because parents may have interpreted our question in several different ways — with such an ill-defined dependent variable the rest of the study becomes almost meaningless.

Often there are difficulties in trying to define and measure a dependent variable. Imagine, for example, a study of the determinants of recovery from alcoholism; the term 'alcoholism' is difficult enough in itself, but to define 'recovery' from it is more difficult still. Or suppose you have been asked to measure the effects of a health education campaign, say with regard to the prevention of coronary heart disease. What exactly would be your dependent variable? A measure of knowledge? A measure of 'acceptance' or 'awareness' of the campaign's message? A set of cause-of-death statistics? Data from all the local hospitals?

Or again, suppose you have been called in by a municipal transport authority to find out whether the painting of bus lanes on certain busy roads (into which cars are not allowed between certain hours) is doing any good. What would be your dependent variable(s)? Average bus speeds before and after? Accident rates? Delays to motorists? Police expenditure? How, furthermore, would you try to measure each of these variables free of bias? And how would you make allowance for different times of day, different days of the week, different classes of road users, inbound versus outbound traffic flows and the novelty impact of such an intervention?

# Cross-sectional designs

Earlier we compared the bedtimes of different children at different ages, on the assumption that these comparisons could tell us what would happen to children over a period of time. We did not actually take the *same* group of children and follow them over a number of years. We hoped that the groups of children were comparable and that we could thus in fact observe the relationship between age and bedtimes. This type of design is known as cross-sectional to distinguish it from longitudinal or 'before-and-after' designs.

Suppose that in our example we had obtained a probability sample of children, say, between the ages of five and fifteen. What often happens is that such a sample is collected for a descriptive or actuarial purpose and that a kind of cross-sectional design is imposed on it afterward. First, we obtain the over-all average bedtime. Next, we compare the different age groups and find that bedtimes get later with increasing age. Then, we decide to compare the sexes, and we find that boys, on average, go to bed a little later than girls. We go on in this way, comparing bedtimes against a number of variables in turn such as social class, size of family, urban/rural differences and so on. Suppose that each time we find a difference in bedtimes. We now want to go further; we want to know, for instance, whether the age differences still remain if we hold social class constant. This means that for each of our social-class groupings, we have to compare the bedtimes of children in their different age groups separately. We could go still further and try to study the effects of three variables in combination, say, social class, urban/rural and size-of-family differences. However, to do this we need to have a sufficient number of cases in each of our combinations or 'cells' (unless our predictions refer only to *part* of the sample). Some of these cells will be readily filled, for instance those for children from large families in urban districts with working-class backgrounds. Other cells will be difficult to fill or may remain empty, such as those for children from small working-class families in rural areas. This is because a sample selected to be representative of the child population as a whole will not contain sufficient numbers of these rarer combinations to make comparisons possible.

We have moved to a different kind of research problem. Now we no longer ask 'How many?' but 'What goes with what, and why?' We have moved from a descriptive to an analytic type of survey that tries to answer questions about relationships and determinants, and therefore we shall need a different type of sample, a sample that is primarily geared to making comparisons.

Upon re-examining the preceding example, we note that our difficulties arose partly from running out of cases to fill the cells representing rare combinations and partly from the fact that some of our experimental variables were related to one another as well as to the dependent variable (bedtimes). Thus, in finding differences between children with urban or rural backgrounds, we wondered whether this difference would disappear if we held social class constant because the proportion of working-class children was much higher among the urban part of our sample. Perhaps, if there had been as many middle-class children as working-class children in both the urban and the rural parts of our sample, the urban/rural differences would have been negligible.

Another point we note is that it becomes necessary to *plan in advance* the comparisons we wish to study and to make them part of our research design; we cannot usually apply this kind of analysis to a sample which has been collected for some other purpose.

## Factorial designs

The problem of interrelated independent variables has led to the development of factorial designs, whose particular function is to disentangle complex sets of interrelationships. They are analogous to the 'agricultural plots' type of design which led to the development of analysis-of-variance techniques. Analysis of variance is, however, chiefly applicable to quantitative variables, whereas surveys deal mostly with categorical variables (see Chapter 9).

This type of analytic survey design is one of the ways in which we can approximate laboratory conditions. However, in laboratory experimentation we create or introduce our experimental variables and, while controlling for most other variables, observe the concomitant changes in the dependent variable. In survey research we are not normally in a position to impose experimental factors or to manipulate the lives of our respondents, for instance by allocating them at random to an experimental or a control group. Instead, we select respondents who already have the characteristics required by our design and compare them in their groupings. This makes it impossible to give causal interpretation to any pattern of associations we may find. Instead of dealing with just one experimental variable and controlling all others, the factorial design enables us to study several experimental variables *in combination*. Not only does this provide us with more information but also with greater confidence in predicting the results under various circumstances.

At the outset, we have to decide which are going to be our experimental variables — we will want to vary these systematically and in combinations with each other. We must aim to control all other variables by exclusion, holding constant or randomizing. The choice of experimental variables predetermines what we can hope to get out of our study; if we decide, later on, that some other variable should have been chosen, it may not be possible to show its effects except by selecting a new sample. This means that we must have an adequate general idea beforehand of the lay of the land in our particular area either through previous studies or from the pilot work.

The choice of our experimental variables will be limited by practical considerations. We might start off rather ambitiously by choosing, say, sex, age, class, urban/rural and size of family in our bedtime study. Let us assume that we have ten age divisions, seven socioeconomic grades and five family-size groupings, while sex and urban/rural are dichotomies. This would give us a design containing $10 \times 7 \times 5 \times 2 \times 2 = 1,400$ cells, which, even at no more than ten cases per cell, would require 14,000 children. If this is unacceptable, we can either cut down the number of experimental variables, or make them cruder (for example, by reducing class from a seven-point scale to a dichotomy), or probably both. In this way we can reduce the number of cells and, thus, the number of cases required, to more manageable proportions. Even so, a design requiring three dozen cells and forty cases per cell would not be at all unusual. Equal (or proportionate) numbers of cases are required in each cell in order to disentangle the experimental variables from each other. Respondents in each cell should be a probability sample (Chapter 3) of all those eligible to be in that cell.

A disadvantage of the factorial design is the need for careful selection of cases. Sometimes this will mean that a special *enumeration stage*, using only a short questionnaire, will have to precede the main inquiry (the much larger enumeration sample being used to supply the respondents to fit each cell of the factorial design). At other times, the number of respondents in some cells will unavoidably remain below requirements, and in that case, some method of statistical extrapolation or 'randomized replication' will have to be used.

The factorial design makes no pretence of being representative. Indeed, in its final form it is often markedly unrepresentative, owing to the need to incorporate equal or proportionate numbers of respondents in each cell, so that very rare combinations of determinants may be encountered as often as the more popular or typical ones. (However, it is sometimes possible to extrapolate and adjust the figures afterwards, using 'correction factors', to make this kind of sample yield population estimates also.)

The factorial design permits us to vary our experimental variables systematically and in combinations of two or more, though such patterns of multiple association cannot be interpreted as causal. We also need to introduce measures to control the remaining variables and to eliminate as many uncontrolled variables as possible. Some of this can be done, as before, by exclusion, holding constant and randomization, but inevitably some confounded variables may remain. In the later stages of the analysis, various hypotheses concerning these confounded variables will be explored by means of special cross-tabulations, matching of subsamples (see below), and by multivariate analysis. While a confounded variable may turn out to have an unexpected effect on the results, upsetting the regular pattern of the design as planned, it can also be stimulating to further research and the discovery of new relationships.

## Designs using regression and other multivariate analyses

As we have seen, in social research we rarely deal with monocausal phenomena, that is with a single cause having a specific effect. Almost invariably we have to deal with multi-causal models, so that any effect is the outcome not of one cause but of a complex network of determinants. Quite possibly many of these will not only be related to the dependent variable but also to each other: they will form a network of *interrelated determinants*.

Suppose that we are interested in some aspect of school achievement: why do some children do better than others at, say, arithmetic? We shall soon find that this is not merely because some children are more intelligent than others, but because their performance is also related to several aspects of teaching at school, to parental support with homework, to size of school class and so on; it is easy to think of two dozen or more possible determinants — far more than a factorial design could cope with. Each of these variables contributes to the outcome (the dependent variable 'achievement in arithmetic', as tested) to a different degree and in a different way. Also, we shall find that each determinant (experimental or independent variable) may be related to others; there may be more effective teaching in smaller classes or more parental support for more intelligent children. This makes it difficult to find out what influence each independent variable, of itself, has on the outcome or what would be the effect of changing a particular independent variable.

There are advanced statistical procedures, such as the various kinds of multivariate analysis (for example multiple regression analysis, path analysis), which are capable of disentangling this kind of associational network. Ideally, they can do three things for us. First, they can give us a firm idea of the total variance accounted for by our independent variables (that is, how much of the variation in our dependent variable we can 'explain' with the aid of the independent variables we have chosen and how much variation remains unexplained). Second, they can tell us which are the most important determinants and which are less important or insignificant. Third, they can tell us how powerful each determinant is after its links with other variables have been discounted (for example, do brighter children still do better at arithmetic, even when we 'allow' for parental help with homework?). In other words, they can tell us how powerful each determinant is, 'other things being equal', or 'holding everything else constant'. Sometimes, too, these statistical techniques can show what additional influence or strength each successive independent variable has added during the emergence of a causal network or what its unique explanatory power is.

These multivariate techniques are not always applicable. They rest on statistical assumptions which may be hard to fulfil and generally they require interval-type variables; that is, quantitative integers such as scale scores. Nominal or categorical data such as eye colour or marital status are more difficult to handle (see Chapter 9).

Moreover, even these more powerful techniques do not, strictly speaking, allow us to make causal references. Rather, they help us to disaggregate the variance (the fluctuations or differences) in the dependent variable according to the *relative* importance of the independent variables which we have entered into the design and to do this by statistical rather than by experimental means.

Multivariat analysis is not for the beginner. You will need access to a reasonably powerful computer, to the relevant computer software and to sound statistical advice. These techniques are best applied in well-researched domains such as education, in which it is possible to generate precise hypotheses and potential causal models about interrelationships between variables as well as adequate measures by which to test them.

One technique of multivariate analysis is called *multiple regression*. What will this technique do for you? First, having listed all your hypotheses and constructed your measures of the dependent variable(s) and of, perhaps, several dozens of (potentially interrelated) independent variables, you will need to obtain your data. You will not need a preliminary enumeration survey such as might precede a factorial design study; but you will need substantial numbers (or perhaps even a national sample of the relevant groups) to obtain adequate variability on your measures and to enable you to show that any group differences you may find have not arisen by chance (that is, are statistically significant), and are large enough to be socially relevant and useful. After processing and analysing the data the computer program will produce a table which lists all your independent variables one by one and will give a figure for each such variable to indicate how much it contributes to the 'explanation' of your dependent variable. A total will also be given, showing how much of the variance is explained by all your independent variables put together. If your measures and hypotheses have been strong, then together they might account for, say, 80 or 85 per cent of the total variance. In the social sciences we are more likely to have poor predictors, so a total of 40 or 50 per cent is more probable — leaving about half the variance unaccounted for. Left to its own devices, the program will produce this first table showing your independent variables in order of the size of their explanatory contribution. Thus, this first pass through the data will give you two things: (a) the total proportion of the variance accounted for; and (b) a list of coefficients, starting with a handful of significant ones and ending with a larger list of variables which have virtually no 'power', that is which at first sight contribute little or nothing to an 'explanation' of the dependent variable.

You may, however, wish to go further. An advantage of multiple regression is that you, the researcher, can determine the order or sequence in which your variables will enter the analysis. You may have testable hypotheses about the relative importance of each independent variable and feed them into the analysis in this order. Or you may wish to test a general model. For example, in educational research you might wish to determine the order of entry of your independent variables according to the developmental stages in a child's life: first, the pupil variables (such as IQ and quality of the home); then, the school-related variables (such as average expenditure per pupil); after that perhaps the teacher-related variables (for example, proportion of teachers with relevant specialist training), and finally the classroom-related variables (such as size of class, availability of equipment) — all depending on how the research design has been set up and what questions it is trying to answer.

While there are advantages in this flexibility, a word of caution is needed. This is because many of your variables are likely to be interrelated, and so the impact of any given variable may be shared by that of others. This makes the results more difficult to interpret. It all depends on the type of associational network you are studying and on the degree of independence of your variables.

This discussion of regression analysis has taken us rather far afield, yet it is only one of a number of multivariate analysis methods. We might, instead, have chosen to use analysis of covariance, factor analysis or some form of discriminant function analysis. These all require more advanced statistical knowledge (as well as the availability of appropriate computer software), and your choice will depend on the kind of problem you are investigating. For example, cluster analysis or discriminant function analysis are probably most appropriate when you are seeking to develop a typology, a way of classifying your subjects into a few distinctive sub-groups. Factor analysis (see Chapter 9), on the other hand, would be appropriate when you are trying to discover the main underlying determinants of your data or to test a set of hypotheses about them.

In choosing the appropriate statistical technique much will depend on previous research, on how well understood the particular domain of enquiry is. In some fields we have a number of reliable quantitative measures, some precise theories and some useful causal models and so we may be able to apply multivariate techniques of analysis with advantage. In other fields we would hardly know where to start, and the use of such analytic techniques would be premature. What would we do, for example, if we were asked to find out why some people become amateur clarinettists or start to invest in the stock market, while others do not?

## Before-and-after designs

We have noted repeatedly that cross-sectional, factorial and multivariate types of design cannot determine true cause-and-effect relationships; they can only give us information about associations or correlates — though some of these are very suggestive! *Before-and-after designs* (sometimes referred to as pre-test/post-test designs) have been developed in an effort to overcome this disadvantage.

The form of the simplest before-and-after design is indicated by its name: a set of measurements (base-line measures) is taken of a group of respondents, who are then subjected to an experimental variable and afterwards measured again — once more or perhaps several times. The difference between post-test and pre-test results or observations is said to be the 'effect' of the experimental variable, though this is misleading.

At first sight it may appear that this design will present far fewer problems in respect of controlled and uncontrolled variables and error because the respondents in the experimental group 'act as their own controls'. They provide the 'other things being equal' conditions that enable us to isolate the effects of the experimental variable on the dependent variable so that we can draw valid causal conclusions about the process.

But can we? We cannot legitimately attribute all the before-and-after differences to the effects of the experimental variable we are investigating until we are sure that, without it, such changes would not have occurred or would have been smaller or different. Depending on the time interval between pre-test and post-test (a few hours, a day or two or perhaps many months), it is always possible that some changes in the expected direction may take place even without the impact of the experimental variable. For example, some of the people whom we have subjected to an advertising campaign to buy a certain product or brand might have done so anyway; some patients who have been given an experimental treatment might have recovered even without this intervention. This may be due either to concurrent influences (for example a price reduction) or to pre-existing ones (for example a strong immune system). Moreover, if people are aware that they are participating in a survey or an experiment, this in itself will often produce certain changes — they become more aware or alert, they develop expectations about the outcome, and with all the attention they are receiving they may try to 'respond' extra-well. In medical research this is known as the 'placebo effect', where patients may respond positively even when given an inert substance.

It is therefore necessary to have, in addition to the experimental group, a matched *control group*. Indeed, sometimes we need more than one control group. To return to our earlier example, if we are investigating the effects of a new medical treatment for a particular illness, we cannot simply count the number of recoveries and attribute all of them to the new treatment; we need to know how many of our treatment group of, say, fifty-three patients would have recovered anyway, and it is the function of the control group to tell us that. By subtracting the number of recoveries in the control group from the number of recoveries in the experimental group, we obtain the *net effect* of the treatment.

We have now arrived at the basic outline of the classical 'effects' design. To start with, we need two matched groups as similar as possible. One will be designated the experimental group, the other the control group. At the beginning of the study, both groups are given base-line measures (the 'before' condition or pre-test). Next, the 'treatment' or 'intervention' is applied only to the experimental group. The control group is given nothing, or only a placebo, and is allowed to get on normally with its life. At the end of a suitable time period, both groups will be given the same measures again (the post-test measures). Next, we calculate the before-and-after differences for each group. Let us say that we find eighteen recoveries in the experimental group, and six recoveries in the control group. By subtracting the latter number from the former we arrive at the net effects of the intervention; that is, twelve recoveries which would not otherwise have happened.

But the results of such a design are not always what they seem, and great care is needed in interpreting the outcome. One problem is that of the placebo effect. In early trials of an experimental medication the psychological effect of being given a new drug is often very positive, making it difficult to isolate the effect of the medication itself. Therefore, to make them feel part of the experiment, members of the control group are given some inert substance (a placebo) which they believe to be the new medicine. Even this may not be sufficient. It has sometimes been found that the nurses or doctors unwittingly make patients aware that they are getting either the 'real' medicine or a placebo and so, nowadays, we adopt a 'double blind' design, in which neither the patients nor the medical staff know who is being given the new medication and who is getting the placebo, thus enabling us to isolate the drug's effects from those of other variables.

There are other problems with before-and-after designs. How, for example, can we be sure to get rid of pre-existing determinants? We might, say, wish to find out the impact of a particular video presentation and so we get two similar groups and show the experimental group the video in question, while the control group is shown some other tape. But how exactly did we obtain the two groups? Could there have been a 'volunteer bias', where subjects allocate themselves to the experimental or the control group, perhaps because they are more, or less, interested in the topic?

In such a case, this pre-existing interest factor might bias the results, probably by exaggerating the effects of the video tape. Volunteer error must therefore be strictly controlled during the allocation of people to groups: preferably subjects should know as little as possible about the topic in question, they should not know until later which of them was in the experimental group, and the allocation to each group should be done with the aid of a table of random numbers (see below). In real life this is not easy since people often object strongly to random allocation procedures. For example, if we need to evaluate the amount of social work and probation service care needed for ex-prisoners, we might well decide to allocate subjects at random to a high-care and a normal-care (that is control) condition, but some ex-prisoners might have strong objections to being allocated to the control group if they become aware that they are part of an experiment. There may also be ethical objections.

Special attention will need to be paid to the choice and measurement of the dependent variable. Even in medical research it is not always clear what constitutes a 'cure' or for how long a patient needs to be followed-up before we can be sure that there will be no relapse. If we decide to study the effects of 'stress', what measures should we use: psychosomatic illness episodes, subjective stress assessments, psychiatric breakdown symptoms, or what? If we decide to run a campaign to combat the spread of sexually transmitted diseases by trying to persuade people with certain symptoms to come forward for treatment, how can we measure the success or otherwise of our campaign? An obvious measure might be the number of new cases that come to the clinics, but this might be a short-lived effect. A subtler measure of 'success' might be the proportion of cases who are willing to give names and addresses of sexual partners — which might suggest that the campaign's 'message' has got through and might indicate a longer-lasting effect (though this would need checking). If necessary our design will have to incorporate several different measures of effect and might also need to incorporate repeated effects measures over a long period of time, that is a *long-term follow-up design*. The longer the time period, the harder it becomes to assign changes to causes because of the many intervening variables that might affect the dependent variable — and, of course, there may be significant case losses during the follow-up period. If this happens, then the loss of numbers is less important than the possibility of *bias*, for example that we lose touch with our treatment 'successes' while the 'relapses' remain with us.

Even when we have a straightforward and readily measured dependent variable, care needs to be taken in assessing effects. To take a hypothetical case, suppose we are conducting a political campaign to persuade an electorate to vote for party X in a two-party system, and suppose further that voting intent or party preference both before and after our campaign is 50–50. Does this mean that our campaign has had no effect? Not necessarily. It might just be that *every* voter in our sample has changed to the other party, leaving the distribution of party preferences still at 50–50! This leads us to the important observation that comparisons between overall distributions before and after an intervention leave us in the dark as to the amount of change that has actually taken place. In the above example, if party X preferences had gone up, say from 50 per cent to 65 per cent, does that mean that 15 per cent of our respondents changed their minds? Such a finding might be a serious under-estimate of the amount of change that has actually taken place. For example Party Y might have lost 20 per cent of its initial supporters but gained 5 per cent of new supporters who had come across from Party X — so the actual movement or change in party preferences might be greater than the overall figures suggest. To overcome this problem we should not rely on before versus after overall distributions; we should calculate a *change score for each individual*. Although change measures are often unreliable and difficult to manage statistically, they will give us a better indication of the amount of change that has taken place.

Sometimes we may become involved in assessing change processes beyond our control. For example, administrative or political reforms are often introduced with scant regard for the requirements of accurate research design, and their assessment and evaluation is fraught with both experimental and political difficulties. Changes are typically introduced for the country as a whole, leaving no comparison or control groups; and they are often introduced without taking base-line measures before the start, making comparisons even harder. Some years ago a national education authority decided to introduce a moral education programme in its schools. A curriculum was prepared, textbooks were written and teachers were given special training courses. Shortly before the introduction of the new programme in the schools it was realized that the conventional type of school examination would be difficult to apply, since moral education is less a matter of knowledge and more a matter of attitudes. Hurriedly some social psychologists were commissioned to produce a set of attitude scales to be used in assessment, but this took time, and meanwhile the schools had begun teaching the new programme. This made it impossible to obtain base-line measures, though some 'half-way' measures could have been taken. In the event, a full attitude measurement programme was only undertaken at the end of the school year. The social scientists were disappointed because, having taken part in a 'natural experiment', they had no 'before' measures with which to compare their 'after' measures. The government and the education authorities were, however, delighted with the results since they showed the nation's youth to have high moral attitudes — which were mistakenly attributed to the new teaching programme!

## Matched-samples designs

We have left to last what is perhaps the most difficult aspect of before-and-after designs, namely, the problem of obtaining two identical groups, an experimental and a control group. Let us remind ourselves of the requirements for a control group: *the function of a control group is to show what would have happened to the experimental group if it had not been subjected to the experimental variable.* In principle, therefore, the two groups should be as similar as possible, but what exactly does 'similar' mean here, and how is this objective to be achieved?

Sometimes it is possible to draw both samples in exactly the same way from a larger population, such as two probability samples (see Chapter 3). Another method is to split one sample into two by random allocation to each of the two conditions. These two techniques should equalize the two samples for any relevant pre-existing attribute or determinant, such as the *volunteer error* or the *self-selection error*. At other times all we can do is to equalize the two groups in their overall distributions on a few relevant variables, for instance by making sure that both groups contain the same proportion of women, that their average age is about the same, that the proportion with post-secondary education is the same and so on *(group matching)*. An improvement on this is *individual matching*: for each member of the experimental group we select another, very similar, individual to act as control. Since we obviously cannot match pairs of individuals on everything, we should match them on those variables which are relevant; that is, are likely to be related to the dependent variable. In a well-studied field we should know on what attributes to match (though there may still be practical difficulties), but in other domains we have only common sense and perhaps some pilot work to guide us. The situation becomes even more difficult when, as often happens in surveys, we have numerous dependent variables. If we are studying, say, the effects of moving to a new address, then our dependent variables may include emotional effects, changed journey to work, shopping habits, friends and visiting behaviour, and leisure activities, each of which has a different set of determinants. This would mean that we would need to match on different criteria for each type of effect in turn! In practice, matching is usually only possible on four or five variables together, and within fairly crude limits, so that investigators tend to choose matching attributes with the widest relevance to the different types of effects to be studied. Inevitably, some variance remains uncontrolled, for we remain victims of the *matching paradox*: if we knew beforehand on which variables we needed to match, we would not need to do the research!

In large-scale studies it is sometimes possible to conduct a preliminary *enumeration survey*, to collect a subject pool for matching purposes. While this is costly in terms of subjects, it enables us to find many more suitable matches, which in turn adds to the precision of the results.

When we are dealing with larger groups or whole towns or villages (for example, to study the impact of a new by-pass road), the best we can probably do is to find another town or village as similar as possible but some distance away, and use this as a control (or rather, comparison) sample.

One final point to bear in mind about matching is that the implications of case losses from either sample are quite serious: for each lost case, we also lose its match.

## Longitudinal survey designs

The before-and-after designs discussed above are really part of the larger family of 'longitudinal' designs, so named to contrast them with cross-sectional designs. In cross-sectional designs we compare unrelated groups and we take all our measures at more or less the same time. In longitudinal designs we take *repeated measures of the same respondents* at several time intervals.

Longitudinal designs tend to be somewhat weaker in terms of causal attribution. This is because typically there may be months, or even years, between the time the base-line measures are taken and the final measurement stage. During such a lengthy interval many intervening variables may influence the effects we are studying. Also, longitudinal surveys often lack control samples, and they tend to suffer from case losses and consequent biases.

Longitudinal studies may be prospective or retrospective. Examples of typical *prospective* longitudinal studies are long-term follow-up studies of groups of children or of major social interventions; or the study of the long-term effects of advertising or of other communication campaigns. In *retrospective* longitudinal studies there may be only one data collection point, for example when studying a group of alumni, or there may be several. Sometimes respondents are asked to furnish base-line data about themselves, as far as that is possible, for example about pub-going behaviour before and long after becoming unemployed. In some longitudinal studies the results are fed back to the intervention agency (for example, the hospital, the educational institution, the market research office) as soon as possible at every stage of the follow-up so that remedial action may be taken. This may help to make the intervention more effective, but it compromises the causal interpretation of the longitudinal design.

In longitudinal surveys case losses become a serious problem, since they will almost certainly introduce a bias in the results. This is a major hazard in retrospective follow-up studies; that is, situations where the follow-up was not planned as part of the initial intervention but is instituted years later. If we decide this month, say, to undertake a long-term reverse follow-up study of all those who graduated in nursing from college Z twenty-five years ago then we might, with some difficulty, obtain a complete list of names, addresses at the time, ages, college grades and anything else on record. But if we now send out a follow-up questionnaire to those addresses we can still find, who will be most likely to reply? More men than women because women often change their name when they marry; those who are still active in the profession; those who have not gone abroad or moved to a succession of different addresses; and those who think of themselves as 'successful' or who have positive memories about their college years . . .

## Panel studies

A panel study is a particular kind of longitudinal study which involves a set of base measures followed by a succession of follow-up interviews or other measures. For example, this is how a social trend, or the impact of a political campaign, can be evaluated. Panel studies do not aim at great precision and frequently do not have control groups. More often their function is to throw light on processes of slow, informal influence and change or to illustrate the changes through which people go in adapting themselves to a new variable in their lives.

Inevitably panel studies suffer from the twin problems of volunteer bias and contracting sample size. As each interviewing wave follows the next, it becomes more and more difficult to locate all the panel members and to maintain their interest in the study; replacements are only a partial answer to this. Another risk is that panel members may begin to take a special interest in the problems at issue; they become more knowledgeable and more critical and, to that extent, less representative. Or members of a panel may change their behaviour as a result of the greater awareness produced by repeated questioning. Nevertheless, successful panel studies can make contributions to knowledge which are obtainable in no other way.

# Choosing the appropriate design

First of all, the decision must be made as to whether an analytic or a descriptive study will be undertaken (descriptive designs are the subject of Chapter 3). A great deal follows from this choice, and it is often risky to try to combine elements of both — especially if the data have already been collected! For an analytic study, two issues must be carefully considered before starting:

1. How much is already known about the main causal variables and processes in the chosen area of enquiry?
2. How much control will there be over events; for example, the timing of the introduction of an experimental variable; the allocation of subjects to groups or conditions?

By dichotomizing each of these issues we arrive at four groups:

A. Little is known, and the researcher has no control over events.
B. A well-researched domain, but the researcher has no power to influence events.
C. Little is known, but the researcher has power to control events.
D. A well-researched domain, and the researcher can control events.

There are appropriate designs for each of these categories (see Table 2.1).

Table 2.1. Survey designs for analytic studies

|  | Little is known | Well-researched domain |
|---|---|---|
| No control over events | Cross-sectional designs<br>Natural experiments<br>Retrospective follow-up<br>Panel studies | Factorial designs<br>Multivariate analyses<br>   including multiple<br>   regression |
| Power to control events | Planned prospective follow-<br>   up with control sample | Before-and-after designs<br>   (matched groups)<br>Effects and intervention<br>   studies |

## LITTLE IS KNOWN; RESEARCHER HAS NO CONTROL OVER EVENTS

No causal inferences possible, only associations. Here we find the simple *cross-sectional* design studies. In this category are also the so-called *natural experiments*, in which the 'effects' of a newly introduced variable are confounded with pre-existing and (self)-selective factors; the *retrospective long-term follow-up* study without a control group and suffering from biases due to case losses and pre-existing factors; and *panel studies*, which can throw light on change processes over time — though not in causal terms — but are likely to suffer from case losses and volunteer behaviour.

### A WELL-UNDERSTOOD DOMAIN, RESEARCHER HAS NO POWER OVER EVENTS

Here we can hope to formulate precise hypotheses and distinguish between the dependent variable and the independent, controlled and uncontrolled variables. No causal inferences possible, but designs featuring complex multivariate analyses (for example, multiple regression, analysis of variance) and *factorial designs* all help to disaggregate the variance. Associations no proof of causality, and direction and sequence of causality often remain uncertain because designs basically cross-sectional.

### LITTLE IS KNOWN IN THE AREA; RESEARCHER CAN CONTROL EVENTS

Here is the *planned, long-term, prospective follow-up* of two or more near-identical samples (one of which acts as the control sample) to which individuals have been randomly assigned. Nature and timing of the intervention controlled by the researcher. Causal inferences possible.

Random allocation hard to achieve, but is essential in order to control for pre-existing factors. The longer the time period, the harder it becomes to exclude influences which might affect the causal process between experimental and dependent variable: causal identification becomes a problem, as does bias due to case loss. Basically an *extended before-and-after design* with control group is needed. Such designs often vague, not sure of their objectives; few clear, measurable hypotheses.

### A WELL-RESEARCHED AREA; RESEARCHER CAN CONTROL EVENTS

Domain of the classical *before-and-after* design with a matched or randomly allocated control group. Precise, measurable hypotheses possible about out-come. Matching may be a problem; sometimes requires an enumeration study beforehand. Random allocation to control or experimental group necessary to control for pre-existing factors. Instead of a control group, may use a comparison village or town which is as similar as possible to the experimental area.

Generally permits short-term causal inferences. Typical would be *effects* studies, for instance of the impact of a persuasive communication; and *intervention* studies, for example of social reforms, provided the researcher really is in control. If this is not the case, the design becomes defective (for example no pre-test; no control group) and causal inferences become invalid to varying degrees.

# Selected readings

Mitchell, Mark and Jolley, Janina, 1988, *Research Design Explained*, Holt Rinehart and Winston, New York.
A practical and clear undergraduate text.

Kish, Leslie, 1987, *Statistical Design for Research*, Wiley, Chichester, Sussex.
Highlights the statistical considerations that enter into the research design process.

Bernstein, I.N., 1976, *Validity Issues in Evaluative Research*, Sage, London.

Himmelweit, Hilde T., Humphreys, Patrick, Jaeger, Marianne and Katz, Michael, 1981, *How Voters Decide*, Academic Press, New York.
An example of a complex series of causal research designs.

Blalock Jr, H.M. (ed.), 1985, *Causal Models in the Social Sciences*, Aldine, New York.
For advanced students.

Campbell, D.T. and Stanley, J.C., 1966, *Experimental and Quasi-Experimental Designs for Research*, Rand McNally, Chicago.
A famous and still relevant early text, concerned with evaluation studies and social experiments.

David, James, A., *The Logic of Causal Order*, Quantitative Applications in the Social Sciences No. 55, Sage, London.

## ON LONGITUDINAL STUDIES

Goldstein, Harvey, 1979, *The Design and Analysis of Longitudinal Studies*, Academic Press, New York.

## ON MULTIPLE REGRESSION

Pedhazur, E.J., 1973, *Multiple Regression in Behavioural Research*, Holt, Rinehart and Winston, New York.
For the advanced student.

Achen, Christopher H., 1982, *Interpreting and Using Regression*, Quantitative Applications in the Social Sciences No. 29, Sage, London.

# 3
# DESCRIPTIVE SURVEY DESIGNS

As we have seen, descriptive surveys such as opinion polls, market research studies and censuses are widely used and demand high standards of precision. Usually such surveys are concerned with large populations. In the present context the term 'population' is used to denote all those who fall into the category of concern, for example all electors in constituency C or all subscribers to telephone exchange T. The term 'sample' is used to indicate a smaller group, usually but not always a representative one, within a population. A key issue in designing a descriptive study is the relationship between a sample and its population. Most readers will be familiar with the idea of a 'representative' sample; that is, one that has the same characteristics as its population but is much smaller in numbers. However, it should be understood that samples are not *necessarily* representative or may only be representative of part of a population. For some research studies we have to over- or under-sample on certain variables (for example, to include an extra proportion of pensioners for special study).

In order to state the relationship between a sample and its parent population we must be able to describe them in terms of characteristics which are common to them both. For example, in many types of market research certain demographic characteristics, such as the distribution of age, socioeconomic status, sex and marital status, are used to describe both populations and samples in order to show the 'success' or accuracy of a sampling operation. However, it often happens that we need to study a population whose size and demographic characteristics are largely unknown, and so it is impossible to 'draw' a sample from it because we have no 'sampling frame'. Examples of such 'unknown' populations might be divorcees, ex-psychiatric patients, pipe smokers, lesbians, cyclists or amateur gardeners. We have no idea how many of them there are in the country, where or with whom they live, what jobs they hold or how their ages are distributed. In practical terms, we have no way of contacting them without doing some large and costly enumeration surveys, and some of these groups are difficult to define, for example pipe smokers and amateur gardeners. No doubt it would be possible to find and interview a few such people, but these would not constitute a 'sample' because we cannot state what their relationship is to their relevant populations since these are unknown. Without this knowledge, we cannot draw any more general conclusions from such interviews because they represent no one but themselves.

In many countries there are some large, nation-wide sampling frames readily available, such as the electoral registers, postcode address files or zip-code areas, telephone books and other directories. Depending on how we define the population we need to study, a little ingenuity can usually uncover some sort of sampling frame. Most professions and many occupations have lists or registers; there are school records, hospital records, motor car records, marriage and divorce records, company records etc. In addition, there are privileged records (for example, social security, tax, medical, criminal, banking and credit records) from which it is sometimes possible to draw a sample if the study has been commissioned by the relevant authorities.

The appropriateness of any sampling frame has to be evaluated in terms of the particular needs of the study at hand. For example, in the United Kingdom local electoral registers are always a little out of date. This is because on average some 10 per cent of electors move to new addresses in any one year (and this rate of movement differs quite sharply from area to area); the registers omit certain categories of people such as prisoners and those of non-British nationality; they do not contain the names of those who, for whatever reason, have not entered their names on the electoral register; and, assuming a voting age of eighteen, they will not contain anyone below the age of seventeen, and only some of the seventeen-year olds. Thus the electoral registers only offer a sampling frame of those adults who are eligible to vote, have registered their names and addresses and have not moved house recently! On the other hand, these electoral registers are particularly useful because they contain addresses as well as names. This makes it easier to select named individuals for our sample or to sample households or addresses. Such a sampling frame might be adequate for a political poll or for a study dealing with percepts of citizenship, but it is of dubious value to a research dealing with ethnic minorities or with young people.

A national *census* attempts to give us a complete enumeration of an entire population in a given country on a given day, but this is an expensive and cumbersome operation which can only be conducted by governments, and then only at fairly lengthy intervals. Therefore, in practice, for most social surveys we rely on *representative samples*; that is, on a study of usually fewer than 2,000 carefully chosen people who, together, can give us an accurate picture of what would have emerged from a study of an entire population of many millions — a study of the nation in microcosm. There is, or should be, an exact correspondence between sample characteristics and population attributes. Once a representative sample has been questioned we shall want, first of all, to compare its characteristics with the known population statistics to see if any errors have crept into the sampling operation.

## Drawing a representative sample

How should a representative sample be drawn? In principle, a representative sample of any population should be so drawn that every member of that population has a specified non-zero probability of being included in the sample. (This is why it is often referred to as a *probability sample*.) Usually this means that every member of the population has a statistically equal chance of being selected.

The best way of ensuring this is by means of a completely random sampling method. Randomness, in this context, does not mean some sort of arbitrary process. It is a statistically defined procedure that requires a table or set of random numbers which can be generated by a computer, or can be found at the back of most statistics textbooks. If we are dealing with a small population — for example a register of a few thousand members of a particular association — then this might become a desk-top operation. We can number the names on the register from 1 to, say, 7,500 and then use a random numbers table to select a random sample of, for instance, 300 names for our survey sample. The division of 300 into 7,500 is called the *sampling fraction*. In this case the sampling fraction is twenty-five; that is, a random selection of one name in twenty-five. However, as we shall see, this does not imply that we can run our finger down the list of names and choose every twenty-fifth name. The selection must be truly random. Such a sample would be called a *simple random sample* and should be distinguished from a *cluster sample* (see below).

To carry out such an operation for a population of millions, or for a whole nation, would be extremely cumbersome and expensive. There are also practical considerations related to the geographical location of our respondents. Even drawing a small sample of 300 names from a population of 7,500 might yield addresses that are spread far and wide and might greatly increase the cost of interviewing or might require a postal questionnaire. Even if we succeeded in drawing a truly random sample of, say, 1,600 names and addresses from a nationwide population of many millions, the geographical spread would increase the interviewing costs to prohibitive levels.

We might therefore resort to a modified sampling method which is called the *cluster sampling* method. This takes advantage of the fact that most populations are structured in some way, or could be divided into sub-sections according to certain characteristics; that is, they can be clustered. Thus, a large national labour union will have numerous local branches which, in their turn, are grouped by state, province or county; a national electorate will be subdivided into local constituencies, which fall into regions, which form parts of a state or province and so on. The small cluster of addresses that share the same postal or zip code are part of a nation-wide mail distribution system which is hierarchically structured according to zones, sectors, districts, regions and provinces. Cluster sampling is designed to make use of these structured hierarchies. As we have seen, random sampling requires that each member of the population should have an equal chance of being chosen. In cluster sampling this principle is applied to each stratum in turn. Suppose we have a population which is stratified into three levels: local section, region and state; and suppose further that there are thirteen states each containing from 25 to 40 regions which, in turn, might each contain 120 to 260 sections. What we have to do is to work systematically from level to level with our table of random numbers. First we choose, say, four of the thirteen states at random; from each of these four states we choose, say, six regions at random; from each of these twenty-four regions we choose, say, eight sections at random; and finally, from each of these 192 sections we choose ten people at random for our sample. This procedure would give us a sample of just under 2,000 names and addresses which, in theory, is as accurately representative of the population as a completely random selection would be — with the advantage that the addresses will be 'clustered' geographically, thus greatly reducing interviewing costs and travel expenses. (In reality, the sampling procedure is more complex, because we have to take account of the relative sizes of each unit within strata and of the intended sampling fraction, but here we are concerned only with the basic rationale.)

There are various other methods by which we can draw a representative sample, though these may not meet the exacting standards of a probability sample. One of these is called the *quota sampling* method. A 'quota' in this context is a cell within an overall sample, designed to have the same sociodemographic characteristics as its population; that is, the sample should have the same sex ratio as the population, the same ethnic and socioeconomic status groupings, the same proportions of married, single, divorced and widowed members and so on. (In practice, fieldwork agencies tend to use rather fewer sampling variables.) A 'cell' might then be allocated to a particular interviewer or group of interviewers. Instead of being given a list of names and addresses (for example, from an electoral register) the interviewers are given a quota: they must find and interview, say, twenty-five single, white working-class women aged thirty-six to forty-five. When all the cells, or quotas, are put together they will form a sample which should have the same sociodemographic characteristics as the population, and the sample's responses to questions about a forthcoming election, TV programmes, frozen foods or children's toys are expected to be a faithful reflection of the answers that would have been given by the population as a whole. In principle this quota sampling procedure is applicable also to any other defined population, for example divorced non-white Methodist home-owners, just so long as we have accurate population statistics (probably from the latest census) to enable us to draw up our sampling quotas.

The main advantages of the quota sampling procedure are speed and low costs. The interviewers have to use their initiative and local knowledge in order to fill their quotas and must tactfully decline to interview people whom they approach but who turn out to be outside the quota; that is, who turn out not to be divorced, not to be home-owners, not to be Methodist and so on. The procedure has often been criticized because interviewers tend to have their favourite locations (a bus or railway station forecourt, a shopping mall), favourite times (week-day late afternoons, week-end early evenings) and their own expectations of what makes 'a good respondent' on sight — any of which may introduce biases. (Such biases may, however, be purely local within-cell effects, and the quota stratification is expected to minimize such sources of error.) Interviewers may also, after a long and disappointing day on the streets, be tempted to 'stretch' a category, for example by including a respondent whose age falls just outside their assigned quota. Yet detailed comparative research has shown that the results from quota samples are often closely comparable to those from other kinds of representative samples. Certainly the method is widely used, especially in situations where speed and costs are important.

The costs of an interview survey are strongly influenced by *contacting time*, the time an interviewer has to spend in order to find a respondent to interview. It has been estimated for the United Kingdom that achieving a 70 per cent successful interview response rate in a probability sample requires an average contacting time of about forty-five minutes, and this time increases rapidly if a higher response rate has to be achieved. On average, this means that an interviewer using a probability sample will successfully complete fewer than five thirty-minute interviews per day, compared to nine interviews per day and an average contacting time of less than ten minutes using a quota sample, and an even higher completion rate for telephone interviews.

The importance of a relevant and accurate sampling frame cannot be overstated. We often read impressive reports in newspapers or magazines who have polled their readers by means of a questionnaire printed in their own pages. Since virtually nothing is known about the target population (other than, perhaps, some kind of readership 'profile'), and since the returns are likely to be highly biased and their representativeness unknown, no valid conclusions can be drawn from the results, either about the readers of that newspaper or magazine or about the nation as a whole, no matter how many questionnaires have been returned.

When we are drawing a probability sample from a complete population list, for example members of a trade union or a list of subscribers to a periodical, and if we have a known sampling fraction, it is always tempting to run down the list and choose every Nth name. The dangers of this approach are illustrated by the following anecdote. A sociologist was conducting a study of pharmacists. He was interested in their urban/rural spread, their training and social background, the extent to which sons followed in their fathers' footsteps, their ethical codes and so on. He designed and piloted a postal questionnaire to be sent out to a representative sample of pharmacists. He obtained the most recent annual register of pharmacists, a bound and printed volume. By coincidence, he found that his sampling fraction corresponded exactly to the number of names on each page, so he sent a questionnaire to the first and last names on every page of the register. Only when it was too late did he realize his mistake. Since the list was in alphabetical order according to surname, the first surname on each page was often the same as the last surname on the preceding page. Not only had he, therefore, unwittingly sampled by pairs, he had also thus increased ('over-sampled') the probability of finding father/son pairs in his sample. And if, to avoid the consequences of his error, he had arbitrarily discarded one member of each pair, he would have 'under-sampled' for the prevalence of father/son pairs.

So we note that the only safe way to draw a probability sample from an alphabetical list is by simple random sampling with the aid of a table of random numbers. Even if the names are not in alphabetical order it is wiser to use a random numbers table to avoid any unknown bias.

## 'Snowballing' and judgement samples

As we have seen, problems arise when we wish to sample a population with unknown characteristics. For example, how would we obtain a sampling frame for football supporters, amateur saxophonists or homosexuals? Even if we could operationally define such people, how would we sample them in a way that permits generalizations? And how would we know whether, or to what degree, our sample is representative, since we have no accurate parameters for the population? One approach that has been used is the *snowballing* technique, where a few appropriate individuals are located and then asked for the names and addresses of others who might also fit the sampling requirements. If this approach is repeated a number of times it might yield substantial numbers, but it is difficult to know how accurately these represent the population of concern.

For preliminary investigations and for some parts of the pilot work, researchers sometimes draw a *judgement sample*. This description really means that accurate parameters for the population are lacking but that the investigators have done their best to obtain as wide a spread of individuals as possible. There is the risk, however, that the sample will represent only a particular sector of the population and that only very roughly. For example, if we interview a judgement sample of the homeless, of the elderly demented or of drug addicts, then these are probably individuals who for one reason or another have come to the notice of the authorities or of certain charitable organizations, or who have sought help or been made to seek help by their families or friends. It would be very misleading to generalize from these cases to the wider populations of drug addicted, demented or homeless people. Indeed, those who come forward for help or treatment are likely to be quite atypical.

Since these kinds of samples do not meet the requirements of probability sampling, statistical assumptions about sampling errors and estimates of population parameters do not apply.

## Sample size and sampling error

The field of sampling is in some ways highly technical and full of statistical pitfalls for the beginner. Often it requires compromises between theoretical sampling requirements and practical limitations such as time and costs. Consider, for instance, the question of sample size. Common sense suggests that a larger probability sample will give a better estimate of population parameters than a smaller one, but will also be more costly. Yet the size of a sample is, of itself, not very important: a national sample of many thousands might still be very poor — if, for example, it consisted solely of readers of a particular newspaper who had returned a questionnaire. A sample's *accuracy* is more important than its size. A properly drawn sample of fewer than 2,000 adults can give us more reliable estimates on a population of many millions, for election polls or other types of social research, than a huge sample of a quarter of a million which is poorly drawn. Statistical tables exist which will show the degree of precision (the *sampling error*) which is theoretically obtainable for samples of different size; thus, the accuracy of a given percentage result might be plus-or-minus 2 per cent for a sample of 2,000 or 6.5 per cent for a sample of 200. A finding that 30 per cent of our sample said 'yes' to a particular question must therefore be interpreted to mean that the true figure for the population will most likely lie between 28 per cent and 32 per cent, or between 23.5 per cent and 36.5 per cent, depending on sample size, with important implications for the statistical significance of group differences. These figures are optimum theoretical estimates, based on the somewhat unrealistic assumptions that we have an accurate and up-to-date sampling frame, that we have conducted the sampling operation faultlessly (or have been able to compensate for any biases), that the fieldwork has been error-free, that there is no non-response and so on. Obviously, the true sampling error will in practice be larger and will depend greatly on any deviations from the ideal sampling procedures.

But sampling error is only one of several reasons for choosing a given sample size. Perhaps more important is the number of sub-groups we wish to compare. If there are only two, or three (say, two sexes, or three age groups), then having some 200–300 respondents in each might suffice. But if we have many sub-groups (for example twenty-three areas, or firms, to be compared with each other individually), then a much larger sample will be needed to reduce error and to attain statistical significance. Another important determinant of prospective sample size will be the nature of the dependent variable. If this is an interval scale (see Chapter 9), then we can hope to deal with group averages in our comparisons and our sample need not be larger than a few hundred. But if the dependent variable is nominal or categorical, for example sixteen different types of crime, or a dozen consumer behaviour patterns, then reaching statistical significance would probably require over a thousand respondents. If we have more than one dependent, variable, as might easily happen if we have an analytic design, then this further compounds the problem.

In short, sample size will be determined by theoretical requirements (such as sampling error, cluster size, required accuracy of population estimates), by the precision of the sampling operation, by the number of sub-group comparisons we aim to make and by the nature of the dependent variable — and ultimately, by constraints of time and costs.

## Choosing a survey design for a descriptive enquiry

The first question to ask is: is it possible to study a complete population (for example, all the employees of a particular firm) or will a sample have to be drawn? For a complete *population* study, defining that population may be a problem: where to draw the line? Case losses or non-response owing to absence, illness, refusal etc. are often a problem because they may cause biases. Refusals should be counted and studied separately from non-contacts (using whatever interviewer observations or background data are to hand). Where possible, biases should be countered by statistical weighting. Successive population censuses may reveal changes, but no valid causal interpretations are possible.

For a *sample* study, the question is: should it be representative; that is, should it be possible to obtain population estimates from the sample? Or should it aim at representing certain special sub-groups, for example non-voters in a particular election? Or some kind of mixture, for example a population sample in which groups of special interest have been deliberately oversampled, such as families with twins?

For a *representative* sample, is there access to any kind of *sampling frame*? Are there records, address lists or data banks from which a representative sample may be drawn? A sample cannot be drawn if almost nothing is known about the population, for example women who have had any kind of miscarriage. Can population parameters be operationally defined, for example above/below a certain age, subscribers to X magazine, people who regularly ride a bicycle to work?

If some population parameters or an accurate sampling frame are available, what method should be used to draw a sample that is truly representative? The *simple random* or *equal probability sample* is often regarded as ideal, but may be too costly or impractical. Various kinds of *cluster random samples* may be possible, and offer savings, but may increase the sampling error. *Quota sampling* is frequently used where constraints of time and costs apply; the quality of a quota sample will depend on the number of attributes used for clustering the interviews which, in turn, depend on the sampling frame. Sampling from *lists* should be done with the aid of a table of random numbers.

What about *sample size*? This will depend, first, on statistical considerations such as the accuracy of the estimates required and the problems of statistical significance; second, on the proposed comparisons between sub-groups: the more sub-groups, the larger the sample needs to be; third, on the complexity of the dependent variable(s); and fourth, on time and resources.

Finally, a few words of warning. The *achieved* sample will be less accurate than the *designed* sample. What steps should be taken to anticipate and reduce non-response bias in the results, especially in mail surveys (see page 106)? People sometimes draw *predictions* from descriptive studies, for example public opinion polls at election time. How may over-interpretation of the findings be avoided? For a 'trends' study using repeated probability samples (for example for market research purposes), each successive sample will need to be as similar as possible to the first achieved sample. It is not sufficient to repeat the sampling process as before. Any sampling procedure should be tried out for feasibility and completeness in a *pilot* exercise.

# Selected readings

Dillman, D.A., 1978, *Mail and Telephone Surveys*, Wiley, Chichester.

Hoinville, Gerald and Jowell, Roger, 1978, *Survey Research Practice*, Heinemann, London.
   Straightforward and practical general text on survey methods. Especially good on organizing fieldwork and postal surveys.

ON SAMPLING

Rossi, P.H., Wright, J.D. and Anderson, A.B. (eds), 1983, *Handbook of Survey Research*, Academic Press, New York.
   See chapters 2 and 5 on sampling.

Henry, Gary T., 1990, *Practical Sampling*, Applied Social Research Methods Series No. 21, Sage, London.
   A practical guide to the sampling of both general and special populations.

Moser, C.A. and Kalton, G., 1972, *Survey Methods in Social Investigation*, Heinemann, London.
   See chapters 4-8 on sampling theory and methods.

Kalton, Graham, 1983, *Introduction to Survey Sampling*, Sage University Paper No. 35, Sage, London.
    A clear introduction to probability sampling.

Kisch, L., 1965, *Survey Sampling*, Wiley, New York.
    For the advanced student.

Cochran, W.G., 1977, *Sampling Techniques*, Wiley, London.

Hess, Irene, 1985, *Sampling for Social Research Surveys 1947–1980*, Survey Research Center, Institute for Social Research, University of Michigan, Ann Arbor, Mich.
    Detailed account of ISR sampling practices.

## ON VALIDATION

Belson, William A., 1986, *Validity in Survey Research*, Gower, Aldershot, Hants.

Brinberg, David and McGrath, Joseph E., 1985, *Validity and the Research Process*, Sage, London.

# 4
# PILOT WORK

Questionnaires do not emerge fully-fledged; they have to be created or adapted, fashioned and developed to maturity after many abortive test flights. In fact, every aspect of a survey has to be tried out beforehand to make sure that it works as intended.

It might be thought that once the main decisions about the design of the proposed research have been taken the researcher would soon be able to make a start with question writing and data collection. This, however, is very unlikely. If we think of any survey as having to pass through a number of stages — from the initial formulation of basic ideas to the specification of the research design, followed by the fieldwork, then the data processing and statistical analysis and so on to the writing of the final report (see Chapter 1) — then we must allow a substantial period of time for the construction, revision and refinement of the questionnaire and any other data-collection techniques. Questionnaires have to be composed and tried out, improved and then tried out again, often several times over, until we are certain that they can do the job for which they are needed. Sometimes we can borrow or adapt questionnaires from other researches, but there still remains the task of making quite sure that these will 'work' with *our* population and will yield the data we require. This whole lengthy process of designing and trying out questions and procedures is usually referred to as *pilot work*.

Each survey research presents its own problems and difficulties, and expert advice or spurious orthodoxy are no substitutes for well-organized pilot work. Piloting can help us not only with the wording of questions but also with procedural matters such as the design of a letter of introduction (and from whom it should come), the ordering of question sequences and the reduction of non-response rates. We should realize from the beginning that pilot work is expensive and time-consuming, but avoiding or skimping on pilot work is likely to prove more costly still.

The length of time taken by the pilot work can differ greatly, and should not be underestimated. If an enquiry follows a well-known path, using adaptations of tried-and-tested instruments, a few weeks of pilot work may be sufficient for an experienced team, though even then short-cuts may cause fatal errors. It should not, for example, be assumed that an American or Australian questionnaire will work equally well in Britain, or vice versa, nor even that a questionnaire already used in an earlier British study will suit another British project, while the translation of questionnaires from one language to another is akin to entering a series of minefields. But if the questionnaire is lengthy, and especially if new attitude scales or scoreable inventories have to be constructed (see Chapters 11 and 13), and when we add to this the need to pilot the *administrative processes* required to put a survey into the field, then the pilot work will take many months — and sometimes more than a year. This often comes as an unpleasant surprise to inexperienced researchers and may well produce budgetary pressures and time constraints. However this early period of development work really is essential to prevent later problems for, once a fault has found its way into the main field-work, it will almost certainly prove irretrievable.

For example, in a recent international study of various health problems it was decided to include a set of factual questions about domestic facilities available to respondents. These questions had been used successfully before, in several countries. One of the items listed was 'running water'. Pilot work for the new study showed that respondents in developing countries often interpreted the item to mean a river or a brook near their home. So the item wording had to be changed. It now became 'piped fresh water supply' and this new wording, too, had to be piloted — just to make sure.

Let us note that if the pilot work had not uncovered this unintended interpretation, the item might well have been used in the main field-work, since respondents found it easy to answer the question. Only much later, during the analysis phase, might an observant data processor have noticed a remarkably high proportion of respondents who apparently had no piped fresh-water supply — but by then it would have been too late. We must realize that a poorly worded item is not necessarily one that causes respondents difficulties in answering; far more dangerous are apparently unproblematic items which, unwittingly, produce spurious negatives or positives.

## What should be piloted?

In principle, almost anything about a social survey can and should be piloted, from the detailed method of drawing the sample to the type of paper on which the interviewers will have to write (is it too absorbent or too rough?), for almost anything that can go wrong, will go wrong! It is dangerous to assume that we know in advance how respondents or fieldworkers will react, and it is a mistake to ask an 'expert' (see page 62). When in doubt — and especially when *not* in doubt! — do a pilot run. In a mail survey, should you send respondents a reply-paid envelope or should you take the trouble to send out envelopes with real stamps on them? In the former case your questionnaire may be regarded as too 'official' or too 'commercial' and perhaps suffer from a lowered response rate; in the latter case, some respondents may steam off the stamps and keep them, while others may be more strongly motivated to reply because they feel that they have been trusted (see page 105). Will the colour of the paper affect the response rate? Will the type-face make a difference? Does having a sector marked 'for official use only' (perhaps for data-processing purposes) put respondents off? Will a student questionnaire that looks amateurish invoke sympathy and a higher response rate or should students be encouraged to produce a 'professional-looking' appearance with the aid of a word processor and a laser printer? What will be the effect of promising anonymity to respondents: will it make them give franker replies, or will it put them off because they find it too impersonal (see page 105). A good deal of research has been devoted to these and many similar issues, and many divergent orthodoxies have grown up in the field of survey methodology: for example, that mail questionnaires must never be longer than two (three, four) pages or that they should never (always) be sent out so as to arrive at the week-end. But to what extent can we safely generalize from these researches or from the verdicts of experts? There is only one way to make sure and that is to do your own pilot work.

It is essential to pilot every question, every question sequence, every inventory and every scale in your study. (There are special procedures for the piloting of scales (see Chapter 11)). If the pilot work suggests improved wordings, you need to pilot those, too. Take nothing for granted. Pilot the question lay-out on the page, pilot the instructions given to the respondents, pilot the answer categories, pilot even the question-numbering system. Some years ago an academic study of a group of doctors who gave contraceptive advice both in public hospitals and in private clinics included a question about fees: 'How do the fees you receive from your hospital work compare with the fees you get in private clinics?' The question had been piloted and was found to be well understood, it was not regarded as too intrusive and respondents experienced few difficulties in answering it. But here are some of their answers: 'very poorly', 'quite well', 'not at all', 'much lower' and so on. The fact that these responses could not be classified or processed in any way only became clear long after the data had been collected on the main sample, and the question had to be abandoned. Moral: in the case of open-ended questions, pilot not only the question itself but also the coding and quantifying of the responses.

Sampling aspects of the study can and should also be piloted. If, say, you are proposing to draw a random sample (see Chapter 3) from a set of employee records, health records or court records, how exactly will this be carried out? Will you take every umpteenth record card or folder, working your way steadily through a set of filing drawers or lists? Will a computer be asked to extract these records? Will a table of random numbers be used, which will necessitate irregular intervals between 'cases' and much more movement within the data base? And how good is the data base, anyway? Is it seriously incomplete? Does it still include many individuals who have long since left or have died? Are certain categories excluded or filed elsewhere; for example, part-time workers, notifiable infectious diseases and so on? How long will it take to draw your sample of, say, 2,000 cases? How long will it take to get formal permission to draw a sample from the records and approach individuals? What is the refusal rate likely to be? All these aspects of the study can and should be piloted.

And what about the statistical treatment of the results? It is a very useful exercise to 'write the report before you have the data'; that is, to prepare a set of dummy tables for which the statistical analysis will have to provide entries (see page 50). Thus, if your study of children's cigarette smoking contains the hypothesis that children pick up the habit from older brothers or sisters, then your final report will need to contain a table (or perhaps a series of tables) to show how true or partly true this is. Presumably such tables will have headings across the top such as 'older brother, non-smoker', 'older brother, light smoker', 'older brother, heavy smoker' and 'no older brothers'; and the same for older sisters; and some headings for those who have more than one older sibling of one or both sexes. This could get quite complicated if we sub-divide the sample further according to whether any such older role models live at home or not; and what the age difference is between each older sibling and the respondent. Presumably we shall want to do this analysis separately for boys and for girls, perhaps divided into age groups as well. And what would the entries in such tables be? The respondents' claimed number of cigarettes smoked per week? Smoking expenditure figures? Over what period? It can be very useful to construct such dummy tables long before the fieldwork is started; they will highlight the need for special questions (for example, the age interval between the respondent and each older brother or sister, if any); the need for summary statistics (for example, expenditure averages over certain periods); and probably the need for a larger or differently chosen sample for the exploration of this particular hypothesis — or the decision to give up the whole idea!

Altogether, as we saw in Chapter 1, it is often very useful to run through the sequence of a survey enquiry *backwards* as part of the pilot work. In order to draw conclusions about certain hypotheses, the relevant tabulations must be available, which will depend on certain questions or scales or other measures having been given to samples that are precisely relevant to this enquiry. If questions have been left out or forgotten, if the answer categories do not bear on the hypotheses, or if the sample is inappropriate to the issues, the statistical analysis will be meaningless, and the intended hypotheses cannot be examined. From start to finish every stage of a survey must be linked to what is to follow and to what has gone before. The whole set of operations must be coherent and integrated, and a reverse pilot exercise will show up any weaknesses. It must always be possible to justify the inclusion of every item; it is simply not good enough to say that 'we shall see what to do with the responses later' or to include a number of items just for luck — these are signs of sloppy design and inadequate pilot work and will most probably lead to wasted effort and misleading results.

## Organization of pilot work

Since almost every aspect of a survey enquiry can be made the subject of pilot work, a line has to be drawn somewhere and some issues will receive greater priority than others. The greatest amount of pilot work will usually be devoted (a) to the measurement of the dependent variable and (b) to those problems that, at least at the outset, are expected to be the most difficult. If the survey is to contain inventories, projective techniques or attitude scales, these are likely to require separate and quite substantial pilot work (see Chapters 11, 12 and 13).

Yet the pilot work should also be seen as an effort at condensation of the main fieldwork. If the survey instrument is to contain groups of items that are to form an index, a scale, or an inventory which will yield a score, then one would need to start with an item 'pool' of perhaps as many as a hundred items or more, to be administered to a substantial sample (say, 250 respondents or more), in order that the 'best' items can be selected by statistical means (see Chapter 9). It is possible to administer such item pools to the main fieldwork sample and to conduct the scaling procedures afterwards, but this might overburden respondents with a survey instrument of prohibitive length. It is therefore preferable, and less wasteful, to conduct any scaling procedures in advance of the main fieldwork on separate pilot samples. In this way, the length of each scale may be reduced from an item pool of many dozens to a short and more effective scale of perhaps fifteen or twenty items. When finalised, such scales can then be included in the main fieldwork without making the questionnaire too long.

This principle of separation can often be applied quite generally. The midphase of the pilot work, after all possible questions have been generated, is likely to have produced a questionnaire that is much too long. It is therefore good practice to divide the items up into separate booklets that are relatively short and contain roughly similar items which can be tried out on separate pilot samples. Thus, one booklet might contain 'factual' questions on the respondent's behaviour (say, with respect to toothbrushing in a dental health study or videotape borrowing in a mass media survey); another might contain 'awareness' questions; a third might be concerned with opinions and attitudes (including scales where relevant); a fourth booklet might ask about demographic aspects of the household (ages of children, size of the home, job history, education and so on). Each of these booklets will follow its own journey of pilot development, from the initial 'drawing board' phase, through several improved and shorter versions, to the final text which will be included in the main fieldwork.

An added advantage of having such 'sub-assemblies' is that it will break up the later phases of the pilot work into a number of smaller operations without overburdening the respondents. It will also give the researcher valuable experience in the relevant administrative proceudres: drawing small samples, contacting respondents, explaining the purpose of the survey, timing each operation and so forth. When ready, several subsections may be piloted together (perhaps experimenting with different question sequences), and eventually we will need to pilot the questionnaire as a whole.

## Exploratory pilot work

The earliest stages of the pilot work are likely to be exploratory, and will be primarily concerned with the *conceptualization* of the research problem (see Chapters 1 and 5). They might involve lengthy, unstructured interviews; talks with key informants; or the accumulation of essays written around the subject of the enquiry. For example, suppose we are doing a study of attitudes to the police. After looking at published research on this topic, and bearing in mind the objectives of our study, how do we make a start with our questionnaires? How do people 'see' (perceive) the police? Are they seen as a threat, as enemies? Or as helpers and protectors? Or a bit of both? How do people feel about police uniforms, and are these feelings linked to attitudes to other uniforms (military, nursing, firemen, prison staff)? Are the police seen as authority figures and perhaps subconsciously linked to parental authority? How do people form their attitudes to the police: from the media? from experience of traffic police? from having been the victim of a crime? Do people believe the police to be biased against certain minorities? Are they seen as corrupt and likely to tamper with evidence? How would a respondent feel if his or her son or daughter wanted to enter the police force? These are but some of the issues that might emerge during a free-style, exploratory interview. (How to conduct such 'depth' interviews will be discussed in Chapter 5). A couple of dozen such wide-ranging, unstructured interviews might give us the beginnings of a conceptualization of the problem, and this will enable us to develop what is sometimes called a 'hidden agenda'.

A *hidden agenda* is a flexible list of topics (not actual questions) to be covered in an exploratory interview. It will be shared among the several depth interviewers concerned, but it is not expected that each interview will cover all topics nor will topics always be approached in the same order. Whenever a topic proves itself to be productive with a particular respondent, the interviewer will 'flow with the tide', even at the risk of missing out some topics. In the same way, new topics may be added to the agenda: for example, a respondent may have a lot to say spontaneously about the police in connection with drink-driving offences. Perhaps this topic had not been considered for inclusion initially, but after discussion it might now be added to the hidden agenda.

From these early, exploratory interviews (which should always be tape-recorded, and listened to by the depth interviewer afterwards, as well as by other members of the team), a rough shape of the enquiry will emerge. For example, it is likely that a set of questions will be needed to obtain people's direct, personal experiences with the police — in different roles and contexts: as a speeding motorist; as the parent of a young delinquent; after being burgled, living next-door to a police officer. Another likely set of questions will deal with mass-media preferences, with special attention to crime serials, law-and-order issues, road-safety items and so on. Drink-driving issues may also require a special set of questions. And there will probably be a need for several attitude scales, the dimensions of which can already be sketched, even at this stage.

Once this exploratory stage has given us a 'feel' for the problem we are investigating, the rest of the pilot word can proceed in an organized form, not unlike an assembly line. Within the overall plan certain sections may be developed further, perhaps by particular team members, piloted as separate booklets and eventually put together as a coherent whole.

## Piloting factual questions

A useful way of making a start with question wording (see Chapter 8) is to consider some of the factual questions that will be needed. These often take the form of *multiple-choice questions* (see Chapter 7). As we shall see, all multiple-choice questions should start their lives as open-ended ones. We should *never* just 'jot down a few questions', invent some answer categories and then insert them in the later stages of the pilot work without first piloting them in 'open' form.

When we design multiple-choice questions we have two problems: the wording of the question and the design of the answer-categories — and these two problems interact: if the respondent knows the answer categories (either by reading them on a self-completion questionnaire or on a show card, or by having the interviewer read them out as a 'running prompt'), this will influence the meaning given to the question and may constrain the response, while the interviewer, too, is influenced by the answer categories (even if they are not read out). By first experimenting with the question in 'open' form we can discover how respondents spontaneously interpret the question (their frame of reference); we can then either modify or 'sharpen' the question in accordance with our purpose, or 'guide' the respondent by offering additional answer categories which the respondent might not have considered. We might also include categories dealing with popular misconceptions that we might wish to explore.

Suppose, for example, that we are interested in the ways in which people save money. A wide-open question about savings will yield a variety of responses which could be used to form answer-categories later. However, typically some respondents will use a 'pot' system (that is, setting aside small sums of money for a special purchase) which they may not regard as 'savings', while some may fail to mention mortgage repayments or insurance policy premiums because these, too, may not be considered 'savings'. It all depends on how the term 'savings' is interpreted, but clearly, as it stands, the question may yield a considerable under-estimate, and we might not have realized this if we had not piloted the question in open form.

So what to do? It depends, first of all, on the *purpose of the question*. If we are interested in the subjective meanings attached to the concept 'savings' then clearly we should not 'lead' respondents by suggesting additional categories to them — or at least not in the initial question but perhaps later, in the form of follow-up probes. But if the purpose of the question is to obtain as complete a picture as possible of any forms of savings behaviour (the scope of which will have to be carefully defined in the planning of the research), then we can either sharpen the question by offering a definition which includes mortgage repayments, insurance premiums, etc., or we can add these to the list of answer categories — or perhaps we may do both. It will depend on subsequent pilot work with the revised question, trying out the question in several different forms and comparing its 'yields' in parallel pilot samples. (See page 61.)

How do we know when a question needs rewording? In principle, we always try to see whether the responses tell us what we need to know but, in addition, there is always the problem of inadvertent biases. A poor question will produce a narrow range of responses or will be misunderstood by part of our sample; the question may be too vague, or it may ask for information which the respondent does not have or cannot remember; it may be a leading question ('Do you generally refrain from dropping litter in the street?') which biases the answers, or a question that operates at the wrong level of intimacy for its purpose. A question may be too wide or too narrow in scope; it may require an introductory sentence or a supplementary question (a 'probe'); it may be too colloquial or too technical, too intimate or too abstract, too long or too short. As we have seen (see p. 49 above) some questions are well understood and seem perfectly reasonable but produce answers that cannot be classified.

If they concern variables that are of special importance, some questions may

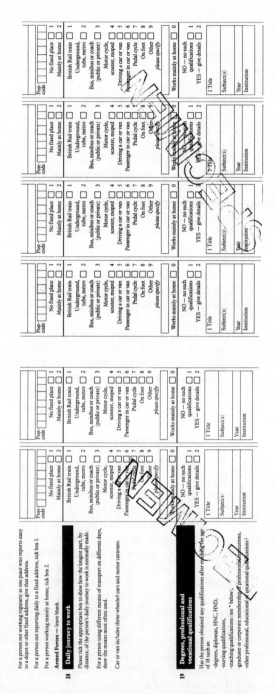

*Source:* From 1991 Census, England. Crown Copyright.

go through as many as eight or more revisions before producing satisfactory results, and it is not uncommon to 'use up' several hundred respondents in pilot work. Even questions that are 'borrowed' from other surveys need to be piloted to ensure that they will work as required with our kind of respondents. This is particularly the case with surveys of school children and with questions that have been translated from other languages.

By the time a self-completion question is in its final form it may have undergone many changes since it was first designed. On page 54, for example, is question 18 from a recent British national census.

There was room on the census form for responses concerning six members of the household, so the answer categories were repeated six times across the page, each preceded by a question about the address of the person's workplace. Note that this was a question about the journey *to* work, not about the journey home or elsewhere.

It is obvious that this question must have been piloted many times and has undergone some changes since it was used in the preceding census. The question appeared in a block of questions about the respondent's current or most recent paid job within the last ten years. Its form must have been decided to meet one or more specific purposes; for example, if the aim of the question had been to ascertain the *costs* or the *duration* of the journey to work, then the wording of the question would have been quite different. The question is preceded by a heading, which is often a useful way to focus the respondent's mind on the issue, and this is followed by several definitions and guide-lines. Thus, the phrase 'the longest part of the daily journey' was clearly understood to mean either time, or distance, by respondents in the pilot sample; to make sure that all respondents understood the question in more-or-less the same way, a qualifying clause was added: '. . . the longest part, by distance, of the daily journey. . .' In the pilot work it must also have emerged that some people go to work by different means of transport on different days, hence the guide-line 'show the means most often used'.

Category 5, 'Driving a car or van', must have seemed simple enough; yet evidently people driving three-wheeled vehicles or motor caravans ('campers') to work must have been uncertain how to answer, so another guide-line was included. We note that there are separate categories of driving a car or van, and being a passenger in such a vehicle; this distinction must have been relevant to the purpose of the question. We also note that several of the categories contain more than one mode of transport, for example 'Bus, minibus or coach (public or private)'. We must, in making such combinations, not only be guided by some form of logic (for example two-wheelers; three-wheelers; four-wheelers; and so on) but, most importantly, by the *purpose of the question*: why do we need to know these things? How important will it be for the users of the information to be able to distinguish between each and every mode of transport? Against this must be set the general desire to keep questions relatively short: we have ten answer categories here, which is about the most that an average respondent can use or distinguish. So for every combined answer category there must be some rationale, some justification, based partly on pilot work and partly on the purpose of the question.

We might think that, by now, the question had exhausted all possible means and modes of transport, but we must never become complacent: almost invariably we shall need the 'Other (please specify)' category. Not only will this help respondents who come to work by unusual means, for example by water bus or on a horse; it will also show, if such frequencies remain low, that the principal categories cover virtually the entire domain of answers and that the pilot work has been effective. Should, however, a substantial number of respondents make use of this category, then these responses will have to be classified and coded as part of the data-processing stage (see Chapter 14), using additional categories, so not all is lost.

And finally, what about the respondents who do not have a journey to work at all? For them, there is a special category: 'Works mainly at home.' Now we may hope that every paid job holder in the country will be able to answer this question but, until all the results have been processed, we cannot be sure. That is one reason why the Office of Population Censuses and Surveys conducts what are called 'post-enumeration surveys' (see Selected Readings). They send out interviewers to hundreds of addresses from which census forms have been received to conduct meticulous quality checks. In respect of a very similar journey-to-work question used in the 1981 census they found more than 8 per cent disagreement between what was stated on the form, and what turned out to be the case at the interview. A third of these disagreements were due to mistakes by the form filler, 43 per cent were due to misunderstandings of the instructions, 7 per cent were because the respondent's personal travel circumstances were not catered for on the census form and the remainder were due to other causes. Thus, despite extensive pilot work, the question did not always work as intended, with consequent error-variance in the final results.

## Exploring percepts and attitudes

Questions of this kind call for a subtler approach. Here we can make use of the *sentence completion* technique (see Chapter 12). Thus, in the previous example concerning percepts and attitudes about the police, we may proceed from pilot interviews using deliberately vague, exploratory questions, such as 'Do you think the police can be trusted, on the whole?' to self-completion questionnaires using open-ended sentences such as the following:

Sometimes I wish the police would . . .
Without the police . . .
The police are always trying to . . .
A uniformed policeman makes me feel . . .
When I am out alone at night . . .
When I hear a police siren I feel . . .
People who trust the police . . .

and so on. Thus it becomes possible to move from the time- and effort-consuming technique of personal interviews to a written approach: sets of such incomplete sentences may be given to single respondents, or to groups, who can be asked to complete each sentence in writing with whatever spontaneous ending occurs to them. It should be emphasized that at this stage we are not trying to obtain some kind of 'true measure' of each respondent; we are still in the pilot stage and so we are trying to obtain ideas, concepts, forms of words and material for future questions. The approach is 'projective', in the sense that we are trying to get respondents to reveal something of their own thought processes and feelings.

The way to handle these responses, obtained from small pilot groups, is to take each item in turn and then to list or type out all the responses to each item. For example, here are some responses to the pilot item A YOUNG WOMAN WHO DRINKS TOO MUCH...

*Male respondents:*
    is nice to have a date with if she pays
    is an easy lay
    is no worse than a young man who drinks too much
    is trying too hard to mix in
    shouldn't
    is probably oversexed, frustrated, or having a period
    — unhappy, I think
    isn't really my type
    occasionally is normal; frequently is neurotic
    usually ends up wishing she hadn't
    is undesirable
    is easy
    is worse than a young man who does, by far
    is OK
    must be careful of the company she does it in.
*Female respondents:*
    can end up being sick
    is sad
    is fine, if she has control of certain situations
    is likely to lose her friends' respect
    is a hateful sight
    should be helped
    is not worse than a man who does
    is on the road downhill
    is trying to forget something
    tends to be looked down on
    might eventually lose some of her own self-respect and that of her friends
    usually has a problem
    is perfectly entitled to if she wishes
    ought to stay at home!!

In conceptual terms, these responses raise the issue of 'double standards': do the same standards apply to young women and to young men? Do male respondents apply different standards compared to female respondents? This might well be an issue to be explored further, in the research as a whole. Conceptually, we also notice that some male respondents link too much drinking by a young woman with sexual behaviour, whereas some female responses make a link with the loss of self-respect and the respect of friends (though one wonders whether there is also a hidden link here with sexual behaviour). Should this be followed up and form the basis of a hypothesis? But some respondents avoid moral comment and focus on more practical issues: cost; being sick; social mixing. Still other respondents try to suggest causes: frustration, having a period, social striving, neurosis, trying to come to terms with a problem. Should we perhaps explore these causal attributions further? Ought we perhaps to think of making up an inventory of perceived causes of drinking too much? Or are these attributions merely covert forms of disapproval? Or part of a broader set of stereotypes about women?

Such a set of responses is also useful in terms of question wording. There are spontaneously used terms here which we might use in formulating questions: 'an easy lay'; 'trying too hard to mix in'; 'oversexed'; 'be careful of the company she does it in'; 'a hateful sight'; 'on the road downhill'; 'trying to forget something'; 'lose her self-respect'. One could readily see how some of these responses could be turned into *attitude statements*, for example 'a young woman who drinks too much is perfectly entitled to do so' (agree/?/disagree). Such attitude statements have the added advantage that they have not been made up by the investigator (see p. 179).

Another approach which is particularly useful in the early stages of pilot work on attitude questions is the apparently simple but actually *projective* (see Chapter 12) question. Often, it can be made to look like a factual question, and the respondent may not be aware that the response also reveals values and attitudes. For example, a study of the attitudes of psychiatric nurses used, in the early stages, the question: 'Why do patients sleep together in dormitories?' To many nurses in traditional hospitals the question seemed easy and slightly absurd. Some gave historical explanations, others said that it was for ease of observation by the night staff, but one middle-aged ward sister wrote: 'Because it is the correct way to sleep.'

Here are some responses by 13–14-year-olds who took part in a political socialization enquiry. The question was: 'Why do all births, deaths and marriages have to be officially recorded?'

It is something you are very happy about and something you are very sad about.

We must know how many people die, have married and have just been born.

Because of accidents, then they could contact the parents.

Marriages have to be recorded because of certain reasons about ages and parents' consent.

So that no-one can pretend they are someone else or say they have been married when they aren't.

So that the government can tell how many people have been born, married or have died.

So that the mother cannot change the baby's name.

So that they can be shown to the family.

A policeman might want to trace someone.

So the churches know how many deaths, marriages and so on.

They have to be recorded because they are very special.
Because they want to know how many people are in the country.

This seemingly innocuous question, which looks very much like a 'knowledge' item, was designed to elicit the extent to which these young people had advanced beyond the mainly concrete, personal level and could give explanations in terms of broader system needs. A set of multiple-choice items could readily be based on the responses to such pilot questions, and scores could be derived for each pupil to show the level of political development reached. As before, this technique has the added advantage that it uses the adolescents' own language and expressions.

## Piloting other aspects of the study

Question wording is but one of many aspects of pilot work. To refer once more to the journey-to-work question above, *layout* is of paramount importance, especially when dealing with a self-completion questionnaire. We note, looking at the census question again, that all the categories have been 'justified to the right', so that all the answer-ticking boxes are one above the other and on the right-hand side of the page. We might, perhaps, have put these boxes on the left, and justified the categories also to the left — pilot work can show which is best here. Nor should we only be concerned with the convenience or comprehension of the respondents; we also need to think of the data processors, who will have to enter the data on their computers. Next to each response box there is a number, located in such a way as not to irritate or confuse the respondent and yet making it very easy to enter (and to check) the numerically coded answers using a computer keyboard — imagine the scope for errors if, say, the categories had been justified to the left, yet the numbers had remained where they are, on the right!

On the actual census form, colour and contrast were used to good effect, and such aspects can and should be piloted, too. Thus, the heading 'Daily journey to work' was set in white lettering on a dark-green background rectangle; the guide-lines were printed in dark brown on a pale green field; and the answer categories were not printed, as here, below the guide-lines, but alongside them, to the right — using dark-brown lettering on a contrasting, pale-brown background. These are not matters that should ever be left to the printers, or to the artistic licence of the designers; only systematic pilot work can determine how such aspects influence respondents and help or hinder the survey. Often such techniques subtly guide and clarify the respondents' task, though they may not be aware of this. On the census form, to give a further example, all the answer boxes were in white, thus gently helping respondents to put their ticks in precisely the right place — some respondents can be remarkably careless in the way they place their ticks! And they were told to *tick*, not to ring, underline or place a cross by the chosen response category.

On another point of detail, the frequently used 'escape' category 'Other (please specify)' must always be followed by a space, or some lines, to accommodate the answer — and this, too, should be piloted. A large space suggests that a lengthy response is expected; a small space makes the response seem unwanted. So how much space is neither too much nor too little, but just right?

There are many other aspects of an enquiry that can and should be piloted. The actual procedures for drawing our sample have already been mentioned. Letters of introduction should be piloted: how effective will endorsement by a prestigious source be in securing widespread co-operation by respondents? How 'official' should it be? Will some people be put off by it? We should pilot various other methods of reducing non-response in postal questionnaires. For example, if we need replies from parents in a study of school children, should we (a) send letters accompanied by a self-addressed envelope to the parents' homes by post; or (b) hand each child in a classroom a sealed envelope addressed to his/her parents, the response envelopes to be brought back to the school and collected by the class teachers; or (c) sample only a few children in each classroom, and have the parental returns mailed back to the research team separately by each parent? Each method has advantages and disadvantages, and the best way to decide which method to use is to conduct three parallel pilot runs.

We can pilot the effects of the age or sex or ethnicity of our interviewers on the responses, the quality of the paper we use, the ordinal position of multiple responses (do people tend to pick the first and the last categories?) and the timing of each section of the questionnaire to avoid making it too long.

It should be clear from the above that, if these issues are important, pilot studies of some size, frequency and complexity will be needed. Sometimes it is sufficient to send out three or four experienced interviewers to collect data on some fifty cases and suggest improvements. Their purpose is not the collection of findings but the testing out of questions and procedures. They must put themselves in a critical frame of mind, thinking also of difficulties that less experienced interviewers might encounter. Their job is to make sure that the questions make sense to the respondents (including problems of translation and the use of vernacular) and that the categories provided for multiple-choice questions or field coding are mutually exclusive and comprehensive. When the interviewers encounter problems in the field they should be encouraged to try to design better questions or alternative categories — and in this they can often secure the assistance of respondents. ('How do you think this question should be asked?') They should also be encouraged to be critical of layout, routing instructions ('If Yes, go to Question 24'), space for verbatim recording, fieldcoding issues, and of anything else that might impede the study.

In the case of small samples, all the answers to each question should be copied out on sheets of paper, one sheet per question. In this way one can quickly see whether the question has any obvious faults and whether the answers seem to bear on the issues required. Sometimes it helps to group the questionnaires before copying, in terms of socioeconomic status, gender, age or some other relevant variable. Such copied-out, grouped sets of responses are of great help in determining the sensitivity of questions and in devising coding categories or multiple-choice answer categories.

Though pilot samples tend to be small, some of the anticipated group differences (for example between people who have, or have not, been burgled) should emerge and can be given greater scope and precision.

Sometimes an organization has to repeat a set survey many times over the years, for instance a household expenditure survey or a mass media survey. A standard questionnaire may be evolved in which only the details are changed to correspond with the relevant day, week or month. Such a situation is sometimes used for *split ballot* type of pilot work. The whole pilot sample is divided up into two or more matched sub-samples, and two or more versions of the same questionnaire are produced, for instance on different-coloured paper or with a change in question order. Studying the results of such a rigorous comparison will show the effects of such variations in technique, which can be utilized in subsequent surveys.

## Processing the pilot data

During the pilot work we should also think well ahead towards the analysis stage (see Chapters 14 and 15). For instance, suppose we are doing a survey of the adjustment of foreign students in this country and that we propose, as important variables for assessment, their pattern of friendship choices, their leisure-time activities and their contacts with home. We shall of course be thinking of ways to question students on these points in some detail, but we should repeatedly ask ourselves exactly why we need these answers and what we propose to do with them later on. For instance, with regard to friendship choices, do we want to obtain an estimate of the extent to which respondents chiefly make friends with members of their own nationality? If so, we shall have to ask for the nationality of each friend mentioned and compute some kind of ratio. Do we want to investigate in what ways various social contacts have influenced their attitudes towards this country? If so, then we shall have to get an evaluation of the 'satisfactoriness' of each relationship. If we ask them about their leisure-time activities, perhaps we shall wish to compare these to their previous leisure-time activities in their home country. Have we remembered to ask about those, and is the information in comparable form? Are we, at a later stage, going to want to calculate an over-all 'adjustment index' or a 'loneliness quotient'? If so, now is the time to work out exactly how this should be done, using the pilot data.

This kind of thinking ahead does not necessarily mean added questions and greater complexity; sometimes it helps to simplify questions. A well-known example concerns asking respondents for their age. This can sometimes cause a certain amount of embarrassment, and so we must consider what we are going to do with this information. Very likely we shall use it in our tabulations in condensed form, such as 'forty-five and over' versus 'under forty-five', or in steps of ten or fifteen years at a time. If this is so, then we need not ask respondents for their exact age; they should merely be asked to state whether they are forty-five or over, or under forty-five, or else whether they are in their twenties, thirties, forties and so on, thus causing less embarrassment. There is little point in burdening respondents and risking reduced response rates by asking for detailed answers when the results are going to be treated in highly condensed form in the analysis. Each time we should ask ourselves: what is this question doing here, and how do we propose to analyse it later?

Due attention should be given to the statistical and data-processing techniques to be used in the analysis. A well-phrased question emerging from careful qualitative pilot work may produce responses that are hard to quantify. The calculation of an index or scale score may produce computational and scoring difficulties. The introduction of probes and the production of multiple answers to the same question each produce problems of quantification to which attention should be paid during the pilot stages (see Chapter 14). There is no point in asking 'interesting' questions that produce responses which cannot be analysed.

## On whom should our questions be tried out?

In principle, respondents in pilot studies should be as similar as possible to those in the main enquiry, that is they should be a judgement sample (see page 43). If the main enquiry is meant to highlight certain group differences (such as between people who have and people who have not had a surgical operation), then such groups should also be available for comparison in the pilot samples, to test the questions for relevance and sensitivity. The practice of habitually trying out questionnaires on samples of university students is to be deprecated most strongly (unless, of course, the questionnaire is intended for use with students) for differences in educational and social background, literacy, social values and average age may produce very different levels of understanding and capacity to respond compared to a general population sample. It is important to cover the full age range of respondents as well as different degrees of literacy. Where relevant, members of special groups who might not readily appear in a pilot sample (for example pensioners, ethnic minorities) should be sought out, to make sure the questions work for them. However, in the rare instances in which our total population is very small and highly specific so that we cannot afford to 'use up' any part of it for pilot samples, we must seek some alternative samples that should be comparable in their knowledge and ways of thinking.

Should the respondents be asked to help? Yes. Wherever possible the respondents should be told that they are taking part in a try-out study and that we want them to be critical, to ask about things they don't understand and to help us to make a better question schedule. When difficulties arise, say 'How would you ask a friend about this?' and engage their co-operation. People are often very good at simplifying questions or putting them in their own words.

Can experts help? There is always the temptation to avoid doing a lot of tedious, expensive and time-consuming pilot work by submitting the question-naire to an expert. This temptation should be firmly resisted, mainly because it is based on illusions. Of course, if you submit a question such as 'How much money do you save on average and how much money do you have in the following savings accounts? (a) __ short-term; (b) __ long-term', it will hardly take an expert to advise you that this question is really two questions, that it is much too vague, that terms such as 'on average' and 'short/long-term' need defining and that it does not allow for people who do not save or save without using (bank) accounts. But even an expert cannot compensate for the fact that you have not thought enough about the purpose of the question (which the expert cannot know) and that you have not allowed for the many different ways in which people save and for the many varied meanings of the term 'save'. Nor must you imagine that an expert could simply sit down at a desk and draft the best possible set of questions. An expert may make fewer technical errors (such as using overlapping categories; for example, age 20–25; 25–30; 30–35; etc.) and may have experience in specialized domains (for example, asking questions about delinquent behaviour), but experts would be the first to use pilot work for their own surveys and would insist on much greater precision in the design and purpose of any question. So it may be interesting to have an expert 'pick your questions to pieces', but you will learn more from doing the pilot work yourself, and it will produce new and better questions as well as a reformulation of question objectives. An expert should never be used as a short-cut.

## What about scaling?
### (For scaling procedures, see Chapter 9.)

For scaling purposes we generally use a separate questionnaire booklet at first and a separate and larger sample, say 100–150 respondents. The text will consist of an *item pool*; that is, a set of several dozen or more attitude statements, knowledge questions (true/false) or checklist items (see Chapter 13) which have been compiled from earlier pilot interviews in line with a conceptual framework (for example, a set of knowledge items dealing with stocks and shares). The objective of the pilot work is to reduce the size of the item pool by statistical means; for example, Likert scaling, factor analysis. To achieve this, each item will have the same set of response categories (Agree–?–Disagree; true–?–false; or others) which will be scored numerically by computer, after which all the items will be correlated with each other. Subsidiary objectives will be to make sure that the items are understood by the respondents and are meaningful to them; to suggest possible rewordings; and to experiment with layout and answer categories. If respondents are sufficiently literate, this kind of pilot work is best done in groups, using a self-completion booklet. The procedure should produce a set of around a dozen or more items with *known statistical characteristics*, which may be said to form a scale, and which will yield a reliable score for each respondent. Simply writing a set of items and then scoring these without subjecting them to scale construction techniques is unlikely to yield reliable scores.

After the pilot work, the new scale(s) can be incorporated in the final questionnaire.

## Report on the pilot work

In larger studies it is good practice to produce a detailed question-by-question report on the pilot work. Any response frequencies should not be interpreted as 'findings', since the pilot samples are unlikely to be representative. Frequencies can, however, be used to eliminate or rephrase questions which produce undesirable response distributions. The pilot report should deal primarily with the comprehensibility of the various techniques, and the proposed modifications to items that require them, together with the results of further pilot work to show how effective the changes have been. The questionnaire or interview schedule can now be amended and standardized for fieldwork application.

## The benefits of pilot work

Pilot work may be costly, but it will actually save time and money in the end. Studies which have been inadequately piloted or not piloted at all, will find that a great deal of effort has been wasted on unintelligible questions producing unquantifiable responses and uninterpretable results. Moreover, dozens of administrative matters concerned with sampling and fieldwork that 'could not possibly go wrong', *will* go wrong.

Pilot work can also be immensely rewarding. There is an intellectual challenge in conceptualizing and re-conceptualizing the key aims of the study and in making preparations for the fieldwork and analysis so that not too much will go wrong and nothing will have been left out. There is satisfaction in seeing the emergence of a short, reliable scale from the mass of pilot data. And there is gratification in finally producing a really effective set of multiple choices which respondents can use and which neatly embody the purpose of the question. Pilot work can produce some nasty surprises, but it is never dull.

## Selected readings

*1981 Census Post Enumeration Survey Report*, HMSO, 1985.

# 5
# THE EXPLORATORY INTERVIEW

## Types of interviews

Probably no other skill is as important to the survey research worker as the ability to conduct good interviews. No amount of sophisticated scale-building or statistical analysis can rescue a research project in which the conceptualization and instrumentation have been built on poorly conducted exploratory interviews; this is one phase of a research project which it would be unwise to leave to someone else. The interview, unlike most other techniques, requires interpersonal skills of a high order (putting the respondent at ease, asking questions in an interested manner, noting down the responses without upsetting the conversational flow, giving support without introducing bias); at the same time the interviewer is either limited or helped by his or her own sex, apparent age and background, skin colour, accent etc. When taken seriously, interviewing is a task of daunting complexity.

First, let us make a few distinctions. Interviews may be used for many different purposes — we have press interviews, therapeutic interviews, employment selection interviews, interviews making requests or stating demands and so on. But the interviews with which we shall be concerned are different from all these. They are essentially of two kinds:

(a) *exploratory interviews*, depth interviews, or free-style interviews (including group interviews);
(b) *standardized interviews* such as used, for example, in public opinion polls, market research and government surveys.

As is evident from their titles, and from the list of research stages we considered in Chapter 1, these two types of interviews generally enter the research process at different points: first, the exploratory interviews and later (if at all) the standardized interviews. They also have quite different purposes and have to be carried out in quite different ways.

An interview is not an ordinary conversation, although the exploratory interview appears similar in some respects. In some societies the concept of a social research interview either does not exist or is vigorously resisted precisely because it is not an ordinary conversation. Until it is accepted as a socially approved phenomenon, with its attendant roles and expectations, it may well outrage potential respondents for many reasons: they resent the intrusion by a complete stranger; they do not want to be so accurate or attentive in their responses; they want to share in the control of the interview and ask questions of the interviewer; and they fear the potential use to which their responses might be put. Or, conversely, they may feel enormously flattered at being interviewed at all; engage in elaborate displays of friendship and hospitality; involve the interviewer in personal or family matters; and seek to strike up a lasting relationship. Every interviewer must realize that these problems exist and that people have a perfect right to feel this way; indeed, the ethics of conducting interviews are a continual topic of lively controversy. Every interviewer must also learn how to cope with the biases and distortions which these problems create — always assuming that some kind of interview eventually takes place! For many people, being interviewed requires the learning of a new social role (the 'good respondent' role) in a new social exchange setting and the interviewer, too, has to learn and adopt a social role which may be quite unlike his or her normal persona.

If an interview is not a conversation, then what is it? The purpose of all research interviews is to obtain information of certain kinds. This information may be in the form of factual replies to factual questions, or responses to attitude scale items, or ideas and feelings, or percepts and expectations, attitudes and the like. The respondents may, or may not, 'have' this information, or they may 'have' it but be unable, or unwilling to communicate it. Although words and sentences are exchanged in both directions, an interview is essentially a one-way process. Indeed, if it should become a two-way process of communication (more like a genuine conversation), it will lose much of its value because of the biases introduced by the interviewer. Respondents get very little out of a standardized interview — perhaps a gift, a slight degree of interest, a little ego-boosting and a general feeling that they have been of help. Interviewers in a standardized interview also get very little out of it; the data will go back to research headquarters and, at the most, they will see a report on the study, perhaps months later. There is (apart from money) only the intrinsic interest in meeting many different people and in a job well done. The depth interviewer probably gets rather more out of it since he or she will be more deeply involved in designing the research and developing hypotheses and instruments. But in order to do their job, both kinds of interviewer must 'switch off' their own personality and attitudes (this can be very exhausting) and try to be unaffected by circumstances, by their attitude to the topic or the respondent, or by personal involvement.

## Standardized interviews versus depth interviews

The purpose of the standardized interview in the typical large-scale survey is essentially that of data collection. We are at this point in what might be called the 'mass production' stage, as distinct from the 'research and development' stage. The various research objectives and hypotheses have long since been formulated; the interview schedule and the wording of the questions have been exhaustively tried out in pilot work; the sample has been drawn; the field force recruited (possibly); and arrangements made for coping with refusals and otherwise unobtainable respondents, with fieldwork checks and the return of the completed schedules for data processing.

We now come to the actual interview, with the interviewer and the interview schedule in interaction with the respondent. The crucial assumption here is that of 'equivalence of stimulus'; that is, we have to rely on the interviewer's skill to approach as nearly as possible the notion that every respondent has been asked the same questions, with the same meaning, in the same words, same intonation, same sequence, in the same setting and so on. That is why we call these interviews 'standardized', though to achieve this kind of psychological 'sameness' is a manifest impossibility. What is needed, rather, are ways of making the question *mean* the same for each respondent even if this should require somewhat greater flexibility in the role of the interviewer. Finding this balance between flexibility in reacting to the respondents' answers and standardization in the question asked is the particular skill of the good interviewer.

The purpose of the *exploratory* interview is essentially heuristic: to develop ideas and research hypotheses rather than to gather facts and statistics. It is concerned with trying to understand how ordinary people think and feel about the topics of concern to the research.

Often these are emotionally 'loaded' topics and only a highly-skilled depth interviewer can get people, over the period of an hour or longer, to talk freely and with some degree of insight about their thoughts, feelings and formative experiences. Here nothing is standard. At most the interviewers will have a 'hidden agenda', a handful of headings or topics around which they will seek to direct the interview as unobtrusively as possible. In the main fieldwork stage, many hundreds of respondents will typically be interviewed in a standardized way; by contrast, at the earlier exploratory stage, perhaps no more than thirty to forty free-style interviews will take place. It would be very foolish even to try to quantify so small a number and, besides, these respondents are unlikely to be properly representative of the survey population; nor will they all have received the same questions, let alone been asked the same questions in the same way.

The job of the depth interviewer is thus *not* that of data collection but *ideas* collection. The primary objective is to maintain *spontaneity*; the ideal free-style interview would consist of a continuous monologue by the respondent on the topic of the research, punctuated now and again by an 'uhuh, uhuh' from the interviewer! The interviewers will seek to reduce their own role to an absolute minimum, to avoid leading the respondent. If something is not clear a 'non-directive' prompt will be used such as 'yes, yes' or 'I see, yes, do go on', or summarizing what the respondent has just said, or maintaining a pleasantly expectant silence. Depth interviewers must, as the saying goes, 'listen with the third ear'. They must note not only what is being said but also what is being omitted; must pick up gaps and hesitations and explore what lies behind them; and must create an atmosphere which is sufficiently uncritical for the respondent to come out with seemingly irrational ideas, hatreds or misconceptions.

It is essential for the exploratory interviews to be recorded on tape. In this way they can be analysed in detail afterwards, for there is much that will have escaped the busy interviewer in the stress of the actual interview; also the tapes can be examined by more than one person. A useful set of exploratory interviews can greatly broaden and deepen the original plan of the research, throw up new dimensions to be studied, suggest many new ideas and hypotheses, important differences between groups of respondents and so on. As an added benefit the interview tapes will produce a rich store of attitudinal and perceptual expressions, on which questions and attitude items can be based. Thus, depth interviews help in the formulation of the research problem, in the articulation of dimensions and hypotheses and in the details of instrument building. Only in the eventual full-scale study will it be possible to test the validity of the hypotheses thrown up in the exploratory interviews.

## The depth interview

Let us now enter a little further into the problems of the depth interview.

First, whom should we interview? In principle, we should wish to interview a judgement sample, a small sample that is typical of the respondents whom we aim to question in the main survey. Exact representativeness is not usually necessary, but we need a good spread of respondent characteristics so that we can reasonably hope to have tapped probable respondents of every kind and background. Sometimes we may aim to set up two contrasting sub-samples; for example, when interviewing widows about their husbands' death and funeral or cremation (a subject that obviously calls for great skill and delicacy), we might wish to make a distinction between widows whose husbands died suddenly or unexpectedly and those whose husbands died after a long and serious illness, and so we may divide our intended sample of depth interviewees accordingly. In consumer research, we might wish to compare users and non-users of a particular product or service. Sometimes, too, we might wish to conduct depth interviews with 'key informants' such as the works manager and the personnel officer in a factory, or funeral directors in the above example.

How many depth interviews should we conduct? There can be no definitive answer to this question but thirty or forty interviews is probably typical. In the process of conducting a series of depth interviews, in which usually only two or three especially experienced and trained interviewers are involved, it generally becomes obvious when the series has reached the point where no new ideas are emerging; a quick consultation will then bring the series to a close. Obviously depth interviews are costly and time-consuming, and so there are usually extraneous pressures to reduce numbers to a minimum. But quality, rather than quantity, should be the essential determinant of numbers.

How should the respondents be obtained? Ideally each respondent should be recruited by a field interviewer. One or more field interviewers should be sent out with something like a quota sample to fill (for example, five middle-class women over sixty who have lost their husbands in an accident or in some other sudden way within the past six months). They should explain to potential respondents that the interview will last about an hour or perhaps longer; that the interviewer will be an experienced professional who will maintain confidentiality and high ethical standards; that the questions will not be of the market-research type but will range widely over many topics; and that their expenses will be paid, together with a modest fee (if any) for their assistance. If possible, the respondents should be given only a vague idea of the central topics of the interview (for example 'it's about the ways people spend their leisure'); it is *spontaneous* reactions that are wanted, not carefully thought out positions.

If the respondent is willing and can spare the time, details can then be settled about time and place, possible child-minding and other arrangements, special means of transport and so forth. Recruitment interviewers, like all others, must carry identifying letters and offer respondents some printed information about their organization and an address and phone number in case they have further questions.

Recruiting people for depth interviews often meets with difficulties such as shift work, busy people being unable to spare the time, reservations about being 'probed' by a psychologist and so on, which may all lead to bias in the sample. It would be unrealistic to expect a depth-interview sample to be a precise microcosm of the intended sample in the main survey. What we need is a sample whose outlook, attitudes, percepts and experiences are likely to cover a similar range and variety in order to avoid unanticipated responses later, when questioning the main sample.

Where should depth interviews take place? It is possible to conduct depth interviews in the interviewer's home, in the respondent's home, or at the respondent's place of work, but it is unlikely that a long enough period without interruptions and distractions will be available. Home interviews are unavoidable with some groups of respondents, but it is generally preferable to conduct depth interviews in a meeting room in a local hotel (to reduce travelling distance), in an office hired for the purpose in a nearby district, or at rooms of the research company or academic department. It is best to avoid settings that may be perceived as unpleasant or threatening by respondents; for example, a school head's study, a hospital, a room above a pub or a betting shop. Potentially noisy settings should also be avoided in case this causes interference with the tape recordings.

There should be an ante-room, where a receptionist can regulate the flow of interviewees, deal with children and with the payment of fees and expenses, phone latecomers, arrange for transport and so on. Refreshments should be available.

The setting for the actual interview should be private, quiet and comfortable and not intimidating. Some thought should be given to the positioning of easy chairs, coffee table, recording equipment, lights and so forth and to the question of smoking or non-smoking. If there is a desk in the room it should not form a barrier between the interviewer and the respondent. Everything should be done to create a comfortable, unhurried and relaxed setting for a private, confidential talk; anything that might upset or disturb respondents or make them feel pressed or intimidated should be avoided. The respondents should come away with a vague feeling of pleasure at having been of help and having had an interesting conversation with an attentive professional, though preferably without a clear idea as to the exact purpose of the interview; they should never go away angry or upset, or feel that they have been the subject of a painful inquisition.

By whom should depth interviews be conducted? Formal training or academic qualifications in one of the social sciences are no guarantees of competence in this field. The ability to present a somewhat neutral presence, a friendly and interested manner, extensive experience and insightful 'traffic management' are probably more important than a degree in social psychology. The interviewer should be able to maintain control of the interview, to probe gently but incisively and to present a measure of authority and an assurance of confidentiality. Tone of voice, a pleasant and polite manner, deportment, choice of dress, the management of personal space, an acceptant and non-judgemental attitude and a willingness to listen should be among the interpersonal skills; these will encourage respondents to talk freely on personal matters, while not giving the impression that they can get away with trivial insincerities or waste the interviewer's time. High ethical standards should prevail; no respondent should be afraid to produce self-incriminating or embarrassing feelings or information, and if a respondent gets angry or tearful the interview should be gently discontinued and the respondent helped to regain composure.

What is the 'hidden agenda'? As we have seen, the purpose of the depth interview is to collect percepts and ideas and to improve the conceptualization of the research problem. Interviewers must be well briefed so that they fully understand the objectives of the research. Since there are no fixed questions, each depth interviewer will be equipped with a list of general topics or areas around which the interview should be conducted; these topics will be derived from the first attempts at conceptualization and will be added to from time to time during the course of the interviews. For instance, if we may return to the earlier example of a study of recent widows, it is obvious that we shall need to ask a number of factual questions to do with the cause of death, cremation or burial, religious affiliation and so on. We shall need to explore ideas about death and 'after-death', memories of the deceased, responses of the extended family, other sources of social support, and (more delicately) causes of anger, hostility or disappointment, loneliness and fears, perhaps a sense of relief, financial matters and the costs of burial or cremation and many others. These might constitute the initial hidden agenda. During some of the early interviews we may also find that the counselling sometimes offered by the funeral firm seems to be important to some, that there are interesting attitudes to the formalities required after death, such as obtaining the death certificate, and that matters of appropriate funeral dress, floral tributes and the disposal of the deceased's clothes are all 'productive' areas to probe in an effort to conceptualize more fully what the death of a husband and the sudden acquisition of the new status of widow 'mean', in a given society. Such topics will now be added to the hidden agenda.

The hidden agenda is only 'hidden' in the sense that it should not be too obvious to the respondent. The interview should move naturally from topic to topic, maintaining the fiction of an interesting conversation. The interviewer may start with any of the topics on the agenda and proceed in any order. It is often not possible to cover all the topics in a single interview; it is better, therefore, to obtain some rich material on a handful of topics, rather than to press on at a relatively superficial level in order to cover every point.

As conceptualization and re-conceptualization proceed, it is most helpful for interviewers to exchange ideas and tape recordings; for research students or other aspiring depth interviewers to have frequent meetings with their supervisors; for all concerned to exchange short notes, write-ups or quotations from interviews. This should help to expand and sharpen ideas about which variables will need to be measured and how; about possible connections between variables, about underlying, unspoken issues within the person and about the wider implications of the research for such topics as gender roles, social change, media impact and so forth.

What does the depth interviewer actually do? The depth interviewer is often frantically busy, without being allowed to show this. Having welcomed and thanked the respondent after being introduced, the respondent must now be seated and put at ease, perhaps with the help of some refreshment and the offer of a cigarette (or not, depending on smoking policy). The interviewer will next produce an agreed and rather vague statement of purpose such as: 'well, as you may have been told already, today we are conducting some discussions about people's opinions on the media (health foods/the trades unions/the causes of unemployment). We are planning a major survey on this topic, and we have asked you along today so that we can benefit from your views and experiences in planning our research. The interviews are entirely private and confidential, your name will not be linked to anything you say here, and I have not been told anything about who you are or where you come from. Most people find these interviews very interesting.'

Before going any further, the interviewer must now, if possible, secure the respondent's permission to record the interview on tape. Usually, there will be a microphone in plain view (turned towards the respondent, not the interviewer) and the recorder will be under the interviewer's control. In industrialized countries most respondents will be familiar with sound recorders and readily give their consent when asked, 'do you mind if I tape our conversation? It helps me to remember afterwards what you said, and' (disarmingly) 'it saves me taking notes.' In less-developed countries more explanations may be needed and various suspicions may have to be allayed. The recorder must not be turned on until permission has been obtained. If the respondent refuses to consent to a tape recording, the interview may proceed with the aid of some ultra-rapid note-taking, or the interviewer may decide to terminate the interview as soon as politely possible. (If this happens repeatedly, this may cause a bias.) Most respondents soon forget all about the microphone, though some may ask to hear a portion of the tape played back to them.

The interviewer has already been busy up to this point, gaining 'first impressions', planning how to start the interview proper, perhaps pouring coffee or coping with a recalcitrant tape recorder while going through the above introductory phases. To gain a few moments of respite, and to get the respondent settled into a 'question-answering mode', the interviewer may open the next phase with a wide-open, highly projective general question ('projective' in the sense that the question means whatever the respondent chooses to make it mean, which in turn may be interesting or significant) such as: 'Now, first of all, would you like to tell me a little about yourself?' Such an opening question should sound chatty rather than intrusive. In general the first few questions should be spoken quite slowly, to help the respondent to get used to the interviewer's voice and manner.

Such a broad opening question may produce a small flood of information at several levels. Up front will be something, perhaps, on occupation, marital status, children (if any) or dwelling area. Immediately behind this may be noted the 'presentation of self' aspects. (Is the respondent nervous? Trying to impress us with status or possessions? Resistant or secretive? Has something obviously been left out; for example, ethnicity, physical handicap?) Deeper still are other domains such as how (at this point) the task of being interviewed is perceived by the respondents; perhaps what they think the interviewer wants to hear or know about; how they construe their own identities, at least for now; and what systems and language of social categorization they use, for example: 'We live in a council flat across the river.'

It is worth mentioning that this opening question, 'Now, first of all, would you like to tell me a little about yourself?' can be answered, even by a co-operative respondent, with the monosyllabic answer, 'Yes'. This gets us no further; the question violated one of the elementary rules of depth interviewing, namely to avoid asking questions that can be answered by simply saying 'Yes' or 'No'. Moreover, instead of gaining the busy interviewer a few moments' respite and perhaps some good jumping-off points for further questions, it suddenly requires the formulation of further questions. Or worse, the respondent may smile helpfully and say, 'Yes — what would you like to know?' So now the interviewer has fallen into the trap of role reversal and will have to 'project' some of the interests of the research while trying not to get flustered! Or else deflect the question back onto the respondent by playing a further projective card: 'Well, tell me anything about yourself that you think I might need to know.' Oh dear! Our interview has not got off to a good start.

Assuming, now, that the respondent has given us a few personal details, we next have to engage in a spot of rapid mental traffic management. We cannot follow up every piece of information at once, so we have to make a choice. However, we also have to remember most of the other items, to follow up later; perhaps we should jot these down. This is a situation that will recur throughout the interview; the respondent touches on more than one topic (or more than one idea occurs to us, while listening), so we have to choose what looks most likely to be a productive topic, realizing all the time that we might have done better to choose a different topic from the respondent's reply, one that we are now hoping to remember and to slip into the conversation naturally at some future moment. A co-operative and voluble respondent can leave the interviewer with a wide mixture of leads to follow up.

This type of 'traffic management' goes on throughout the interview. It need not always remain hidden below the surface. Sometimes we can say: 'Now you will remember telling me a little earlier that you disliked XYZ. Can we now come back to that? I wonder what makes you feel this way?' and thus deliberately switch topics. The reverse may also happen. A male respondent may, for example, talk about his business and add an aside such as: 'But of course you can never trust the banks.' Clearly he is throwing the interviewer a 'lead' and hopes that it will be picked up. The interviewer may wonder, and then decide to test the strength of feeling behind the throw-away remark by *not* asking a question about the banks. Sure enough, several exchanges later the respondent may say again: 'But of course, we all know that the banks can't be trusted.' The interviewer may, quite deliberately, decide once again not to rise to the bait until the same sequence is repeated once more. Having ascertained the strength of feeling in the respondent on this topic by observing his attempts to divert the interview to the topic of 'the banks', the interviewer may now, at last, raise a quizzical eyebrow and say: 'The banks? Well, what about the banks? Tell me more.'

Besides this kind of 'traffic management', the interviewer is also following parts of the hidden agenda in what will hopefully seem like a natural order. Here again, judgement has to be used when a promising lead opens up: to follow the lead or to stick to the agenda? In an interview on self-medication (buying non-prescription medicines at a chemist's) a young woman was asked what she would do in the case of a sore throat. She started to answer, then stopped herself and said, a little pompously: 'No, I would do nothing, for *the throat must take care of itself*'. In the rush of the moment some interviewers would have missed the cue, but it turned out that this young woman perceived her body as largely divided into two zones: organs and areas of which she had to take care, such as the hair, the skin, the nails; and parts that had to 'take care of themselves', such as the kidneys, the lungs, the intestines. Then there was a third, borderline zone of organs which might, or might not, take care of themselves; this zone contained most of the body's orifices, including the throat. Thus, her buying behaviour at the chemist's was determined by her perceived obligation to care, or not to care, for different organs of her body. The throat seemed to be in a borderline category, and when she felt that 'the throat must take care of itself', she would not buy any remedies for it. It took some time to tease these ideas out of the respondent, who was well aware that these were unorthodox notions, but this diversion from the hidden agenda proved worthwhile when, in many subsequent interviews, other respondents also came up with variations on the same set of ideas.

This example also illustrates the third main below-the-surface activity of the interviewer, besides traffic management and following the hidden agenda: maintaining *rapport* at the right level so that the respondent will keep talking. In the above example, if the interviewer had manifested surprise, ridicule or had merely raised an eyebrow, the respondent might have closed up. Only by maintaining a receptive, permissive and non-judgemental attitude throughout can the interviewer hope to obtain insights into motives, ideas and percepts which respondents know to be 'irrational' or self-incriminating but which nevertheless guide their behaviour.

Interviewers must not only try to get the respondents to 'flow' freely by encouraging them and by rewarding them with comprehension; sometimes the flow has to be stopped, or diverted, when the respondent is spending too much time on issues which are far removed from the purposes of the research. This is not easy to do without upsetting the respondent, but an attempt could be made by saying: 'Shall we come back to this later, after I have finished my questions?' At other times the respondent may try to turn the interview into a conversation by asking the interviewer questions; these could likewise be deflected by suggesting, 'shall we come back to that later?' while noting and responding to any of the respondent's immediate anxieties such as 'who else is going to listen to these tapes?'

How are questions formulated during a depth interview? Part of the answer is that, in a depth interview that is going well, there should hardly be any need for questions as such. The interviewer may merely suggest a topic with a word, or an unfinished sentence left trailing, and the respondent will 'take it away' and will produce a rounded and personalized response, punctuated by sounds of encouragement from the interviewer. A depth interviewer has to engage in a little bit of acting from time to time rather than try to ask 'correct' questions. Thus, there is probably no need to ask: 'Now what about your children? Do you have boys, or girls or some of each? How old are they? And how do you feel about them? Do you have a favourite?' The interviewer could merely look up and say, quietly, 'Children . . . ?' and await a reply as construed by the respondent. This also avoids the danger of leading, of putting ideas into the respondent's mind or pre-determining the lines of response.

When questions *have* to be asked, they should be as open and as projective as possible. We should try to avoid formal and leading questions such as: 'What do you consider to be the appropriate role for the Church when someone has died?' or 'do you keep a bottle of disinfectant in the cupboard under the sink?' but explore each area more obliquely to allow the respondent maximum spontaneity. We might start by asking, say: 'Now what about funerals? Let's discuss how you feel about them.' This formulation is designed to let the respondent, not the interviewer, determine which aspects of a funeral arouse strong feelings; also to see if the role of the Church is mentioned without prompting. In the case of the disinfectant question, we might start by getting the respondent to say what is meant by the term 'disinfectant' and to mention some brand names; then discuss family responsibilities and see if a specific member of the family is held 'responsible' for the supply and use of disinfectants, and where they are kept and why. Some men, for example, will not use bath salts because they think they are 'sissy' and will use quantities of disinfectant instead. Thus, the use and location of disinfectants in some homes is closely linked to symbols of manliness.

In depth interviewing, every effort is made to get respondents to express their own ideas spontaneously in their own words. It is only too easy for an inexperienced interviewer to ask questions which are subtly leading (or sometimes not so subtly!) and so make respondents aware of what may be expected of them. Thus, the question 'do you think that a clergyman has no role at a modern funeral?' is highly leading (note especially the word 'modern' and its implications); but so is 'how do you feel about abortion on demand?' or 'do you think our country should go to war to save its oil supplies?' The best way to learn to avoid leading questions is to listen to your own tapes — this can be quite mortifying but is a much healthier corrective than criticism from colleagues. Yet under the stress and immediacy of a difficult depth interview even the most experienced interviewers will occasionally lapse into leading questions.

Depth interviewers therefore need to practise the *non-directive approach*. They must exercise great patience, they must try to interfere as little as possible and let the interview 'run itself'. Above all, they must cultivate the art of the non-directive probe. Suppose the respondent has just come to a momentary halt, saying: 'And so I don't believe that women should go into politics.' We should avoid the temptation to disagree with the respondent or to enter into an argument. Our job is to get the respondents to reveal their inner thought processes — but how are we to do this? Here is where we need the non-directive probe. For example, we might merely offer a tentative 'uhum, uhum', implying that the respondent should continue to develop this line of thought. Or we might just say nothing, and merely smile expectantly. Most respondents find silence in an interview unbearable and feel that they have to continue talking —

indeed, silence is often a very effective yet non-directive press to go on. Or, taking more of a risk, we might *repeat back* to the respondent what has just been said. This may seem odd, at first: will the respondent not get angry if we just repeat 'mmm, you say women should not go into politics?' However, it seems that, if done naturally, respondents experience this as evidence that they are getting across and as a signal to develop their views further. But there is always the risk that in repeating a view we distort it: for example by saying 'I see; you say women should be kept out of public life' or worse: 'I see; you say women should stay at home and mind the kids' — which is not at all what was said! The incomplete sentence can also be used as a non-directive probe, for example 'I see; so you feel that women and . . . politics . . .' (on a rising note), leaving the respondent to complete the sentence and carry on. A less oblique probe which is still non-directive is the use of a gentle inquiry such as 'what makes you say that?', 'could you explain further?' or 'please tell me more.'

In some kinds of depth interviews real objects (for example consumer products; toys; car badges), or pictures of faces, scenes or objects can be introduced for discussion and for sorting into categories (for example, alcoholic versus non-alcoholic drinks; modern versus traditional). Often the same topic is approached more than once during an interview, in different ways or from different angles.

Very occasionally, after a topic has been explored in a free-style manner, a deliberately directive probe will be used; for example, 'some people say that more goods should be carried by road. How do you feel about this?' When driven to use such directive questions, it might be better to offer two or more points of view, such as 'some politicians are campaigning to have more goods carried by road, while others want more goods carried by rail. What do *you* think?' But the question remains leading, in that it assumes the respondent must have a point of view and that it can only be one of the two choices offered in the question.

If the interview has gone fairly 'deep', perhaps bringing up old resentments, painful memories or hurtful experiences, then the interviewer should offer acknowledgement: 'I appreciate that talking about things like this is not easy' or 'knowing something about your personal experience of X will be very valuable in guiding our research.' It might also be advisable to take a few minutes to soothe the respondent by discussing more superficial topics, in order to ease the stress of the situation and make the respondent feel more comfortable.

How should a depth interview be concluded? Eventually, the interviewer might indicate that the interview is over, for example by saying, 'well, I think we have covered everything I needed to ask you. Thank you very much, you have been most helpful,' perhaps followed by 'is there anything you would like to ask *me*?' or 'do you have any questions?' After answering these, the interviewer might get up, formally switch off the tape recorder, thank the subject once more for attending and move towards the door. Sometimes, at this very last moment, the respondent will make a revealing comment or offer a confidence, perhaps out of relief that the interview is over. The interviewer should be mentally prepared for this and not hustle the respondent to the door, for often these less-guarded 'off the record' remarks can be especially valuable. They should, of course, be noted down as soon as the respondent has left.

How should the interviews be processed? The interviewer should take a few minutes after each interview to jot down ideas and suggestions that have been stimulated by the interview as well as anything that might have affected the interview, for example any intervention by a third party in a home interview.

As soon as possible, the interviewer and any available colleagues should listen to each tape, for different people note different underlying themes in an interview tape. Usually this takes considerably longer than the duration of the interview because the tape will be frequently stopped and sometimes re-wound a small distance to go back over a passage. First, attention has to be paid to operational matters; for example, should new topics be included in the hidden agenda(s)? Should more vegetarians be interviewed, or some other group? Are new ideas no longer emerging, in which case should the depth interviews be discontinued?

Next, a short resumé of each interview should be prepared, highlighting some of the key topics discussed. After that, an attempt should be made at interpretation, both at the personal and at the theoretical level. For example, silences and omissions might suggest painful or very personal issues. Insight and intuition are important at this stage, but the 'correctness' of any particular interpretation is irrelevant. Remember that the prime purpose of these interviews is heuristic: to generate further ideas about topics and variables that should be included in the research plan, links that should be explored, attitudes and motives that might determine some behaviours.

What further use may be made of the depth interviews? The tapes can be an invaluable source of useful question wordings and attitude statements. Research workers tend to become too intellectual, and to develop the language of specialists; it is generally much better if attitude questions and statements (see Chapter 10) can be put in the respondents' own, every-day language. Therefore the tapes should be combed for expressions and sayings that could be used as attitude items in a questionnaire — or in a subsequent depth interview. Depth interviews should not be regarded as arcane or esoteric, bordering on the psychoanalytic and of use only in research that is highly 'academic'. They can be very useful in such conventional and practical areas as market research, opinion polling, product development, patient follow-ups, architectural research or transport studies.

Depth interviews can often lead directly to a useful conceptualization and the building of pilot instruments. Here is an extract from a depth interview with a south London woman in her fifties who had been an alcoholic and was now taking part in a follow-up study:

I ain't gonna say I haven't been frightened. I'll tell you one experience I had.

I'd started work in my place in January, and in June every year we have a Savoy 'do'. Now, that's laid on just for the staff — no husbands, no boyfriends, only the staff. Well, I went, and that was my *first* social gathering off the bottle. I'd only come out of hospital at Christmas. Well, I goes in there and, as you know — well, I don't know if you do, but it's all la-di-da, you know, top-hat-and-tails sort of thing. Well, I went in style. I had a Mercedes to take me and I had a Mercedes to fetch me. Well, that's my husband. 'You're going in style. You're going to be the same as everybody!'

Now, when I get in there, all the bosses are there, all the VIPs from the firm, and who should walk up to me but one of the senior partners. 'Oh, glad to see you, Doreen.' I was shaking from head to toe. 'Got here all right? Now, what would you like to drink?' I said, 'I *don't* drink, but I'll have a bitter lemon.' I think I was the only non-drinker there. So I said, 'Excuse me, Sir, there's Patricia over there,' and off I goes. I goes up to them and it's

'Where's your drink, Doreen?' I said, 'I think I've left it over there. I've had enough. I must have had one or two before.' Now, I'm lying, ain't I? Two! I'd had bleedin' *none*. All of a sudden, a waiter came up to me. 'Oh, *there* you are,' he said, 'I've been looking for you. Here's your bitter lemon.' So, right, I takes the bitter lemon. 'What's the matter?' says Emily. I said, 'I don't drink. I don't want to make myself look like a fool. If I start drinking I'll do the strip tease in here.' So, out we goes into dinner.

Now, each table has got so many staff and so many partners, two partners to a table. Who should be on my bloody table but two senior partners. I thought, Jesus bloody Christ! So, as we sit down, this one started into me. I hadn't been at the firm long, so he didn't know a lot about me. 'Are you settling in here?' he said. 'Yes, I'm enjoying it,' I said, 'and I think this is lovely.' I thought, if I could get out of here I would, but I couldn't, could I? So, I'm sitting there. This is my first big 'do' and look at the 'do' I'm at, and it's all bitter lemon.

You have different drinks with every bit of the meal, you know, and I thought, Jesus Christ, how much more of this are they fetching round! Each time I'm having bitter lemon. This bloke, at the side of me, out of the blue he said to me — words to the effect that do I not drink, or do I not drink for a reason. Now, that bloke could have been genuine, but straight away I think 'I'm an alcky, ain't I?' I had the shakes from top to bottom. I said, 'Oh no, I've never drunk. It doesn't appeal to me. Other people like it, but I couldn't care less, as you can see.' 'Well,' he said, 'it surprised me to see that you don't take a little wine with your meal.' 'Well, it's not being used to it,' I said, 'I'm not in your class. I'm married to a greengrocer, not a lawyer.' I thought, right, I'm what I am and you can't alter me. I'm a Battersea girl. He thought this was funny, but I was shaking.

Now, after we moved from our tables, this bloke that was sitting near me, he went up to two senior partners. Now, he could have been talking business, but now and again they looked round at me. Knowing what he'd said to me, I thought, maybe they're talking about me. Now, when I go in Monday, I ain't got a job!

At 12 o'clock, when the car came for me, I got in and I broke down and cried. When I got home, I woke up me husband, and next morning I rang up my doctor, and I was still shaking and crying. My first words to him were 'I went to a "do" last night, but I haven't been drinking!'

This is, admittedly, an unusually vivid and fluent account, told without any prompting. The incident had taken place some five years earlier, yet it was fresh in the respondent's mind, perhaps because her adjustment was still somewhat fragile. The purpose of this series of depth interviews was to develop further ideas about this kind of fragility and the dangers of relapse. How do ex-alcoholic patients manage to stay off drink? What are their subjective experiences, their fears and perceived risks, their coping styles, their social supports? This series of initial interviews, together with ideas from the relevant literature, eventually led to a conceptual framework and the decision to measure a number of variables by means of structured inventories. One of these was an inventory of 'dangerous situations' (dangerous to sobriety, that is). The actual items were obtained from interviews such as the above and from pilot work using a sentence completion technique (see Chapter 4). After editing and further pilot work, two dozen items were randomly arranged in a structured inventory of which the following is an extract:

Here are situations which some people have experienced as being dangerous to their staying off drink. Which of these may have been dangerous for you *during the past four months*? There are four boxes. 'Very dangerous, Quite dangerous, A little dangerous, Not at all'. Please tick that box which comes closest to your feelings about those situations which may have been dangerous to your staying off drink *during the past four months*. There are no right or wrong answers or trick questions. We want to know how *you* feel. PLEASE BE SURE TO ANSWER *EVERY* QUESTION. Please put only one tick for each question.

### 'SITUATIONS DANGEROUS TO MY STAYING OFF DRINK'

| | VERY DANGEROUS | QUITE DANGEROUS | A LITTLE DANGEROUS | NOT AT ALL |
|---|---|---|---|---|
| 12. When I pass a pub or off-licence | | | | |
| 13. When I'm with other people who are drinking | | | | |
| 14. When I feel no one really cares what happens to me | | | | |
| 15. When I feel tense | | | | |
| 16. When I have to meet people | | | | |
| 17. When I start thinking that just one drink would cause no harm | | | | |
| 18. When I feel depressed | | | | |
| 19. When there are problems at work | | | | |
| 20. When I feel I'm being punished unjustly | | | | |
| 21. When I feel afraid | | | | |
| 22. When I'm on holiday | | | | |
| 23. When I feel happy with everything | | | | |
| 24. When I have money to spend | | | | |
| 25. When I remember the good times when I was drinking | | | | |
| 26. When there are rows and arguments at home | | | | |
| 27. When I'm full of resentments | | | | |

This inventory was twice subjected to factor analysis (see Chapter 9) and yielded three independent factors:

*Factor 1* — *internal situations (moods and feelings)*, for example when I feel tense/ depressed/very angry/tired;
*Factor II* — *external situations (social occasions, holidays)*, for example when I'm on holiday/on special occasions/at Christmas;
*Factor III* — *lessened cognitive vigilance*, for example when I start thinking that just one drink would do no harm.

In this way, when this inventory was administered in the main study to over 300 ex-patients, each respondent could be given three scores which, in turn, could be related to other variables.

Thus the depth interviews supply the ideas and the conceptualization of the problem, they help to identify the variables to be measured and they provide many of the items for new scales. The process helps to ensure that, despite the requirements of reliable measurement, we retain the subjective framework of our respondents.

## Group interviews

Clearly, individual depth interviews are expensive and time-consuming and are not easy to arrange. Some researchers prefer, therefore, to conduct sessions with *groups* of respondents. The requirements for sampling and recruitment of respondents are much the same as for individual depth interviews; those who agree to take part are brought together with an experienced group discussion leader in one room (possibly in someone's home) to conduct a round-table discussion. Care should be taken over the seating arrangements so that each group member can readily catch the leader's eye, and logistic arrangements have to be made beforehand about drop-outs, transport, payments, refreshments and tape or videotape recording. The leader's approach will, in principle, be much the same as in individual depth interviews: there is likely to be a hidden agenda, and the leader will try to be as non-directive as possible, while maintaining control of the group. However, there is the further intention that a lively discussion should develop among the respondents who, it is hoped, will spark off new ideas in each other. This could become a source of bias; for example, if one person tries to dominate the discussion or if the group splits into separate camps.

Provided the topic is relatively straightforward, such group sessions may provide us with all that we need, and in a more economical way. However, leading such group discussions requires special talents and experience. For example, some respondents feel uncomfortable if they sense that they disagree with the rest of the group and so may remain silent; it is the leader's job to 'bring them out'. If the discussion is suitably lively, there are likely to be recording problems; so, if possible, the group leader should get people to speak one at a time. And group discussions — say, eight or ten sessions with between eight and a dozen people in each — are likely to 'use up' more subjects than individual depth interviews.

Ultimately, the choice between group or individual qualitative interviews will depend on the degree of 'depth' required. This is not easy to assess before the start of the research — both approaches may be tried before making a decision. And, of course, constraints of time and expenditure will also apply.

## Selected readings

Banaka, W.H., 1971, *Training in Depth Interviewing*, Harper & Row, New York.

ON GROUP INTERVIEWS

Krueger, Richard A., 1988, *Focus Groups*, Sage, London.

# 6
# STANDARDIZED INTERVIEWS

## Interviews versus questionnaires: advantages of interviews

Let us now return to a consideration of standardized interviews. We may well ask: why use interviews at all? To this there are a number of answers, but let us remember the overriding condition of relevance or appropriateness: one cannot say that interviews are always good or always bad, but rather that interviews are preferable for some problems, or under some conditions, and not others — and often, it has to be admitted, the choice will eventually be made for quite extraneous reasons such as costs or pressure of time.

Interviewers come into their own when we need to ask numerous open-ended questions, or open-ended probes, and where the interviewer has to record verbatim the answers given by the respondents. Such open-ended questions are important in allowing the respondents to say what they think and to do so with greater richness and spontaneity. Obviously, interviewers have to be trained and instructed most carefully in the flexible use of probes, and the probes themselves may have to be standardized.

It is often suggested that another advantage of using interviewers is that of *improved response rates*. A postal questionnaire may easily produce a response rate below 40 per cent; interviewers can generally do much better than this, but not always. We have to distinguish between quota samples (trying to find, say, twelve middle-class men over the age of forty-five) and probability sampling, where the interviewer is given a list of names and addresses (for instance, from the electoral register). In the latter case a great deal of time and effort may have to be expended in repeated call-backs before a new name is substituted. Likewise, quota sample interviewers may readily meet a very high refusal rate as well as other difficulties in filling their quotas. However, in the final analysis what matters is not only the total number of completed questionnaires but, more importantly, the question of *bias* in the sample of respondents. In that respect, interview surveys based on probability samples offer a clear advantage over postal questionnaires.

A third set of advantages in the use of interviewers is that they can give a prepared explanation of the purpose of the study more convincingly than a covering letter can; will more easily reach less well-educated respondents; help the ones with reading difficulties; offer standardized explanations to certain problems that arise; prevent many misunderstandings; and maintain control over the order or sequence in which the questions are answered. These are some very down-to-earth, practical advantages. Generally, it can be said that *the longer, the more difficult and the more open-ended the question schedule is, the more we should prefer to use interviewers*.

Many research workers also like to use interviewers because they feel that interviewers are more 'valid' in some sense. 'After all,' they would argue, 'the interviewer has actually seen and talked to this person, has reported a written set of real responses made at the time and there cannot have been too many misunderstandings. Surely this is worth a whole lot more than little ticks in boxes returned by you-know-not-who!' This point of view is perhaps more an expression of research directors' anxiety at having become divorced from their subject material than a serious statement about validity. For interview results may be genuine and rich, yet they can also be biased and unreliable.

Perhaps the most important determinant both of response rate and of the quality of the responses is the subject's *motivation*. Data collection may be regarded as a transaction in which it is usually fairly obvious that the research worker stands to gain, in some sense, while the respondent is asked to give time, thought, privacy and effort; anything that will make this transaction less unequal and one-sided will help both the rate of returns and the quality of the responses. Thus it is important for the interviewer to be able to explain how the particular respondent came to be selected for the sample and why it is important that he or she, rather than someone else, takes part. Extrinsic motivators such as a preliminary postcard, a promise of a reward, the payment of 'expenses' or a gift of a 'free sample', may sometimes also be effective in persuading people to participate. Rewards intrinsic to the subject of the survey, such as parental interest in the health of their children or the belief that important changes will be made as a direct result of the survey, can also improve results very markedly — there may even be a danger of over-eagerness creating a bias. One of the most important parts of interviewer training and briefing is to develop instant ways of engaging the respondent's interest and attention, to create and sustain 'rapport' at just the right level, and to leave the respondent feeling that something pleasant, interesting and worthwhile has been accomplished.

One more advantage of using interviewers may be mentioned: in some studies, the interviewers are asked to make on-the-spot assessments; for example, of the state of repair of a dwelling, of the proximity of the nearest bus-stop. While once again raising the issue of the reliability of such assessments, it is clear that they can best be obtained by means of a personal home visit.

## Disadvantages of interviews

The disadvantages of using interviewers are to some extent a reflection of their advantages. Obviously, interviewers are much more expensive than postal questionnaires (which cost little more than the expense of paper and printing or duplicating, the cost of two envelopes and two stamps per subject). The larger or the more dispersed the sample, the greater the total cost of the interviewing operation. Travel costs and call-backs add to this.

The cost factor also enters the data-processing stage: since interviewers are used particularly where many open-ended questions have to be asked, there will be a major and costly coding operation allied to any study that uses interviewers. Coding, which we shall be considering in Chapter 14, is the name given to the process of developing and using classifications for the answers to each question. The costs have to be assessed in money terms but also in *time*: unless a large, permanent interviewer force is engaged, most studies using interviewers will take weeks if not months to complete — and the coding may take longer still. But postal studies may also take time. We have to wait for the responses to come in, then send out two or three reminders at, say, fortnightly intervals, and extend the deadline to capture the final trickle of returns.

Inherent in the use of interviewers is, or ought to be, the problem of *briefing*. One Thursday afternoon a group of interviewers who had for many years been part of a widely dispersed national field-force conducting consumer surveys, were shown the following typical question from one of their own recent schedules: 'In the past week, which of the following goods have you bought?' followed by a list. The interviewers were then asked: 'What is meant here by the phrase "in the past week"?' The first one replied: 'Well, today is Thursday, so I would ask from last Thursday till today.' The second one disagreed with this: 'The respondent might not yet have done her shopping for today,' she said, 'so I would ask her from last Wednesday until yesterday.' The third interviewer pointed out that a week had seven days and that Sunday was not usually a shopping day, so she would naturally ask 'from the preceding Tuesday'. The fourth interviewer said that 'in the past week' meant just the current week on whatever day the interview took place, so she would always ask 'starting from the previous Monday', and the results for the whole country would be ironed out statistically. The last interviewer said that she had been with the company a long time and knew what they really wanted, and so she always asked respondents to tell her what they had bought 'on your last big Saturday shopping expedition'.

This example shows, first of all, that even such a simple word as 'week' can have quite different meanings for different respondents and interviewers. Second, that because we think that everyone else means the same thing when they use the same word, it does not occur to us that it may need an explanation or a qualification. Third, that it is necessary to conduct pilot work on even apparently trivial matters. Fourth, that every question schedule has to be discussed with the interviewers, tried out by them, followed by further discussion and a firm briefing. And finally, that some of these problems might not have arisen if efforts had been made to maintain better contact with the interviewers.

## Ethical considerations

The basic ethical principle governing data collection is that no harm should come to the respondents as a result of their participation in the research. If, for example, a respondent has been upset by some of the questions in an interview, then the interview may have to be abandoned rather than risk upsetting the respondent still further. It goes without saying that data collection should not be turned into an attempt to sell things to the respondent — not only is this unethical but it gives social research generally a bad reputation. The respondent's right to privacy and the right to refuse to answer certain questions, or to be interviewed at all, should always be respected, and no undue pressure should be brought to bear. In the case of children, permission should always be sought from their parents, teachers, club leaders or whoever is in charge of them at the time.

## The interviewer with a clipboard

What actually happens during a standardized interview? The situation during a structured, standardized interview is radically different from that of a depth interview, and yet some of the same rules and cautions apply. For a start, the interviewer in a standardized interview is almost invariably a woman; this is presumably because in many societies potential respondents, especially women, find it easier to be approached by a woman than by a man, are more likely to establish rapport with her, ask her into the home and answer questions more frankly. Besides, survey agencies usually find that it is cheaper to take on women and that women can more readily be employed part time or on an hourly or daily rate. It has also been argued that, on the whole, women are more empathic and generally make better interviewers.

The interviewer-with-the-clipboard finds herself in a far less comfortable situation than the depth interviewer. Gone is the quiet office atmosphere, her respondents will not have been found for her by a recruiter, there will be few consoling offers of refreshments (or else too many, this time pressed upon the interviewer by hospitable respondents) and generally she will be working against the clock. The schedule-bound interviewer is on her own, out in the streets or at the bus station in all weathers or looking for some elusive address in an unfamiliar neighbourhood. She has to carry her own equipment and find and button-hole her own respondents, or else locate a hard-to-find address only to meet with refusal or perhaps with no response at all (in which case one or more call-backs may be required).

Interviewing can be interesting and rewarding (though it is usually poorly paid), but it can also be morale-sapping, very tiring physically and mentally, and sometimes dangerous. Not every respondent will have fascinating things to say, and interviews can be extremely tedious and repetitive. Some people are very rude or unpleasant, while others may voice provocative opinions, yet the interviewer must remain outwardly calm, pleasant and friendly, try to sustain good rapport and never show in her expression or behaviour what her own values are. Sometimes she will find it hard to maintain her composure and 'correct' social distance when the interview reveals circumstances that cry out for social justice.

Small wonder, perhaps, that there is a high rate of turnover in many interview forces. It is also said that, after a time, some interviewers become 'burnt out': they are no longer interested, no longer conscientious, they are only doing it for the money. For this reason, and of course to detect outright cheating, a reputable agency will conduct a proportion of check-interviews in every survey. To make this possible, respondents are usually asked for their name, address and phone number, which will be treated as confidential.

## The process of responding

Let us now look a little more closely at what we are asking our respondents to do when we ask them a question. What is going on in their minds? How do they formulate their responses? Suppose the interview is a standardized one and that the interviewer has just spoken the words: 'When did you last read a copy of *Punch* magazine?' Let us assume that the purpose of the study as a whole has been explained satisfactorily to the respondent, that a certain rapport has been set up between the two parties to the interview in reasonably congenial surroundings, so that the respondent is at ease and is perfectly willing to try to answer questions. Let us further assume that the interviewer has spoken the question correctly (reading errors do occur at times) and without particular emphasis, and has previously ascertained that *Punch* magazine is known to the respondent. We must also hope that the question will be heard and understood correctly by the respondent.

A search process of some complexity must now begin in the respondent's mind. First, a *search specification* or *mental template* must be formed: the essential meaning of the question is formulated as an instruction to the brain to start searching. At this point there are many possibilities that could cause unreliability: some respondents may, for example, interpret the word 'read' in the above question as 'read text and cartoons from cover to cover', some as 'idly leaf through it in a waiting room' and some as 'buy a copy'. Search templates will be formulated accordingly, obviously with very different results. The search now proceeds, through 'the attic of the mind', trying to find the relevant occasion on which *Punch* was 'read' and to date it. This process is likely to become very inaccurate unless the occasion is in the recent past or it can be placed accurately in relation to some other event, for example 'last week-end; I know, because my mother-in-law came to stay with us and she brought a copy with her that she had read on the train'. Otherwise, the respondent will continue to think back. The search will be terminated at a fairly early point because long pauses in an interview are difficult to sustain, and because the respondent may come to feel that there 'must be' a quick and simple answer to this question. Eventually some rather nebulous recollection may be 'made to fit' the template: 'I probably saw a copy at the dentist's; that was, well, let me see, *how* long ago? I know I should go every six months, so let's say: about three months ago, that should be near enough right.'

Having half-formulated an answer, this must now be passed through a number of filters. Was there a more recent occasion? Can anybody check up and find out you were inaccurate? Will the interviewer laugh at you if you admit that you do not read *Punch*? Is there anything self-incriminating in seeing it but not buying it yourself, or not going to the dentist more often, and so on? Having passed these various censoring filters the response now has to be formulated in terms of words that make a sentence, leaving out the ruminative 'hmmmm's' and 'ah, well let me see's' and such apparently irrelevant details as the visit to the dentist. In this particular case, there also has to be a subtraction process: three months ago was when? And so, in the fullness of time, the words 'it was last June' are spoken, hopefully heard and understood correctly by the interviewer and field-coded with a tick against the 'within the current quarter' box. If this whole process of responding seems potentially fraught with error, then let us ask ourselves how much worse it might be under less-than-ideal conditions, dealing with a non-factual topic (for example 'do you think we do enough for the mentally ill these days?') and with an embarrassed or resistant respondent.

## The interviewer's central task

As we have seen earlier, the job of the standardized interview is that of *data collection*; at this point in the study the interviewer does not have the luxury of using her own initiative by adding questions to the schedule or following up interesting ideas. She is bound by the requirement of *stimulus equivalence*, by the notion that every respondent should understand a given question in the same way as every other respondent. Deviation from the exact wording of the questions, from their pre-determined order, from the manipulation of prompt cards or from an even tone of voice can all play havoc with this process. The idea that we can ever actually obtain true stimulus equivalence is of course unrealistic, but it is something to be aimed at in principle because interviewer bias is probably the largest source of error in survey work of all kinds. To put it another way: ideally, when we look at our statistical results and find, say, that significantly more men than women said 'yes' to a given question, we want to be sure that we are dealing here with a genuine sex difference and not also with some greater or lesser degree of 'interviewer effect'. In short, we must strive towards obtaining data that are 'uncontaminated' by the interviewing process.

This aim has been attacked as wrong-headed in principle as well as unattainable in practice, and as denying the 'reality of the situation' while indulging in a positivist fallacy and misrepresenting the basically interactive character of the data being collected. These critics suggest that we are on a self-deceptive quest when we seek to apply 'data-collection tools' to human beings in order to obtain some pseudo-objective responses. They would see the situation as essentially subjective and interactive: any 'answer' can only be understood if we know how the respondent felt about the interviewer, about being interviewed, about the topic and the particular way it was perceived, and about the social and hierarchical relationship between interviewer and respondent at that particular moment. Our attempts at creating a standardized situation would be regarded as 'scientizing' and falsifying the information being collected which is essentially interactive in nature. The unit-of-analysis should not be some 'answer' to a question but rather a social episode, a culturally determined dialogue between two strangers playing roles.

While sympathetic to these concerns, to accommodate them would require an entirely different type of research process to which our present techniques are poorly suited. On the other hand, we should not think of the structured interview as too robotically standardized. It is part of the interviewer's job to take personal and situational variables into account, though not to the extent that they will constitute a source of bias. Any measure (see Chapter 9) will contain two kinds of errors: *random* errors, which we should seek to reduce for the sake of greater accuracy but which would not bias the results in one direction or another; and *systematic* errors, which are much more worrying and which would cause the final, accumulated results to be an indistinguishable mixture of 'true' answers and 'interviewer effects' or interviewer bias. Examples of systematic errors might be habitual attempts to hurry less well-educated respondents; regularly offering a one-sided explanation of a particular question; or failing to hand show cards to more 'intelligent-looking' respondents. Random errors, due to carelessness, inaccuracies, misunderstandings and the like, will cause our results to be distributed around an imaginary mid-point which constitutes the 'true' finding, rather like attempts to hit a bulls-eye. Much more dangerous are systematic errors or biases, since these would result in a substantial over- or under-estimate of the 'true' value, thus perhaps forecasting the wrong results in an election, exaggerating or minimizing ethnic differences, or over- or underestimating the prevalence of domestic violence. Because such systematic errors or biases generally go undetected, we cannot make allowances for them; we do not even know whether they have caused our findings to be too high, or too low, or are present only in part of our sample and to what degree. Our key effort must therefore be directed towards the prevention or reduction of hidden, *systematic* bias in the interviews.

How is this to be done? On first thought, the answer would seem to lie in absolutely rigid standardization of the interviewers' behaviour and of the interview schedule. Every interviewer training course, every briefing and every interview schedule should strive for precision and conformity in conducting an interview, so that all interviewers will do 'exactly the same thing'. However, this presents us with a problem because what we are seeking to produce is not 'stimulus equality' but 'stimulus equivalence' (see above, page 86); that is, that the respondent's understanding of the question or task will be the same as that of every other respondent interviewed by this or any other interviewer in the survey. This means that interviewers must also be trained to use their judgement in departing sometimes, and within certain limits, from the exact text of their schedules in order to offer an explanation, or some more familiar re-wording, to a respondent who does not comprehend, or has misunderstood the question — while always trying to remain non-directive and not 'putting the answer in the respondent's mouth'. This is not easy, and it is a test of the interviewer's skill to do this smoothly yet without causing a systematic bias.

In their interviewer training programmes, some agencies make a distinction between three types of questions: (a) *factual* questions, where the interviewer is expected to read out the question as printed on the schedule but has some latitude to offer explanations, correct misunderstandings or offer a previously agreed definition; (b) *attitude and opinion* questions, which interviewers are forbidden to explain or reword in any way; and (c) certain standard *classification* questions (for example, on household composition), where the interviewers are expected to devise their own probes to ensure that they have correctly obtained all the information required. This goes a long way towards resolving the contradictions between the requirement for standardization and the need for flexibility and 'equivalence'.

Let us take a simple factual question from a survey on behalf of the Notown private bus company. On the interview schedule, the question reads: 'Did you make a bus journey yesterday?' This question is not as easy as it looks. Some respondents may say 'well, my firm sends a coach to pick us up, does that count?' Or 'do you mean a Notown bus or a municipal one?' or 'no, but I did get a lift from my brother-in-law; he drives his mates to work in his van'. Or 'I'm a pensioner, and the ambulance came to take me to the day centre'. Or 'yes, I always go into town on a Friday to do my shopping' (evidently has not realized that the question refers to Sunday, 'today' being Monday). Indeed, if the interview does take place on a Monday, then the schedule will probably contain an instruction to ask about the preceding Saturday — which complicates matters still further! What is the interviewer to do in such situations? Of course, the question should have been more adequately piloted so that a better phrasing could have been devised, and she may have been briefed in respect of some of these queries. Also, a well-conducted survey would have instituted controls for the day of the week. But the interviewer should also be given the necessary background knowledge about the purpose of the study and of this particular question. For example, she should be aware that the reason for the question is that the Notown Bus Company wants to know its present market share; that is, what proportion of all bus journeys (defined, for example, as 'fare-paying week-day journeys by licensed public carrier') take place on its vehicles. On no account should the interviewer therefore be tempted, when answering the respondent, to say 'well, all we need to know is: did you catch a Notown bus yesterday?' which would be grossly 'leading' and would yield a falsely high estimate of the Notown market share. Nor should she re-word the question by saying: 'Yes, but yesterday, did you go to work on a local bus, a Notown one or a municipal one, maybe?' which provides unwanted prompts, emphasises journey-to-work and puts 'yesterday' at the beginning, any or all of which may produce systematic biases. Her repetitions and clarifications must be *non-directive* ones, but this is more easily said than done, and only training, good briefing and experience will enable her to satisfy the requirement that all respondents should understand the question in the same way, without bias and without having had an answer 'put in their mouth'.

These problems get much worse when we are dealing with *attitudinal questions*, for example 'in your view, could Party Z produce a credible government?' or 'Do you think we are doing enough to help people in poorer countries?' Respondents may ask the interviewer for clarification: what is the question getting at? But attitude questions are notoriously sensitive to wording and nuance problems, and so the interviewer is not allowed to expand on the question. She might well try something like 'Well, what's your opinion? What do you think? In your view, could Party Z produce a credible government?' (without emphasizing 'could'). If the respondent asks for the meaning of 'credible', the interviewer may first try 'Well, whatever it means to *you*', then perhaps offer 'Well, you know, a government that has credibility'. It is just possible that an alternative has been agreed at the briefing such as: 'It means a government that people can believe in', but by now we are in deep water. We should not expect the interviewers to compensate for the shortcomings of the questionnaire designer. The phrase 'a government that people can believe in' may, or may not, have the same meaning as 'a credible government' to every one of our respondents; hence we may, or may not, have resolved the equality=equivalence dilemma. Ideally, attitude questions and statements should be so well designed and so fully piloted that they can be read out and responded to without any variations, explanations or substitutions. In this instance, rather than offer a substitution at the briefing, the word 'credible' should have been recognized as problematic at the pilot stage and firmly excluded.

Let us now summarize the position we have reached, as far as the standardized interviewer's central task is concerned. Since respondents, questions and situations differ so much, it would be unrealistic to demand of the interviewer that she restricts herself rigidly and exclusively to reading out the questions on her schedule in the prescribed manner. This would not produce 'stimulus equivalence' and would also make it difficult to sustain good rapport; that is, a friendly willingness on the part of the respondent to answer further questions. What we require of the interviewer, and what good question phrasing and good briefing should help her to produce, is that each of her respondents should have an adequate understanding of every question and that she achieves this aim by non-directive means.

As we have seen, it is good practice to distinguish between different types of questions. *Factual* questions should be read out as printed, but — within strict limits — the interviewer is allowed to explain, to correct misunderstandings and to provide definitions. *Attitudinal* questions (see Chapters 8 and 11) are much more sensitive, and no deviations should be allowed. In the case of standard *classification* questions the interviewer can be given more latitude in order to obtain all the relevant information.

However, while she is working in the standardized mode, the interviewer should not be expected to compensate for inadequacies in question design and pilot work. Thus, the problem of ensuring equivalence really starts long before the field interviews, with the work of the questionnaire designer.

## The interviewer's principles of performance

If the above already seems like a tall order, there is more to come. Every fieldwork agency and every briefing manual will have its own guidelines, which will cover many additional points about the interviewer's task and the problems she may encounter. Here are some examples:

### RAPPORT

This elusive quality, which keeps the respondent motivated and interested in answering the questions truthfully, is one of the main reasons for employing interviewers. There can be too much or too little rapport, and either would be undesirable. If the interviewer creates too little rapport, or fails to sustain good rapport, then the respondent will be resistant, will start guessing or joking, will not take the task seriously and will try to cut the interview short. If rapport is too good, then the interviewer will find herself cast in the role of a helper or a social worker or a personal friend, the interview schedule may have to be abandoned half-way through, and the interview becomes unduly prolonged and difficult to terminate.

The interviewer must play a role, and must obtain the respondent's co-operation in playing the role of 'good respondent', so that the role-play of a standardized interview can be performed. The interviewer must at all times remain detached and professional in her attitude yet be relaxed and friendly; she must offer identification about herself and her organization but she must not get personally involved; she must promise confidentiality, she must explain how the respondent came to be selected and allay any misgivings the respondent may have about letting her into the home. Yet she must also appear open, friendly and trustworthy, not 'cold' or 'official', and she must avoid exerting pressure on respondents or arousing the thought that she may be trying to sell them something. During the interview she must avoid answering personal questions such as 'well, what would *you* say?' or 'do you vote for the X-party, too?' or 'don't you agree with me that . . .', so as not to bias the responses, though she may promise to have 'a general chat' afterwards. She will have to deal tactfully with personal comments or approaches from male respondents, yet maintain good rapport. Some respondents regard the interview situation as a licence to complain about everything that is wrong with the world, others are just naturally very slow and discursive, while still others are unresponsive, taciturn or too brisk.

With these, and with dozens of other problems, the interviewer must try to find a way of coping that will neither offend nor bias the respondents, while keeping them 'in role' in a good-humoured way and maintaining rapport at just the right level. At the same time she must deal unobtrusively but efficiently with her recording tasks, especially the verbatim taking down of answers to open-ended questions. Of course she must also thank respondents at the end of the interview and promise those who ask for the results of the survey that her research organization will send them an outline of the findings in due course.

PROMPTS AND SHOW CARDS

It often happens that a question has a number of prepared answer categories; for example, the names of all the local newspapers, or self-ratings such as 'strongly agree/agree/not sure/disagree/strongly disagree'. Sometimes, a short list of answer categories can be read out by the interviewer as part of the question (the so-called 'running prompt'), but in other cases she is equipped with *show cards*. These are cards on which the respondent can see the answer categories and keep them in mind while answering the question. The interviewer may have to manipulate several sets of prompt cards, help respondents who have reading difficulties or those who cannot locate their spectacles, and finally get all her cards back again at the end of the interview.

PROBES

This term is used to describe follow-up questions, after the respondent has given a first answer to the main question. They will be indicated on the interview schedule. Some probes will be quite general, non-directive and non-specific; for example, 'could you tell me a little more, please?' or 'any other points you'd like to make?' Other probes might be more specific; for example (after a No to the bus journey question): 'Could you tell me why that was?'. Still others may require several follow-up questions, and sometimes interviewers are instructed to probe for specific issues — costs, timing, uncomfortable seats, waiting periods. It is best, for the sake of standardization, to print such additional questions on the interview schedule rather than leaving them to be phrased by the interviewer.

Here is an example of a question with probes:

How would you say that this area differs from the others around it? (PROBE: WHAT KIND OF AREA IS IT? ARE THE PEOPLE ANY DIFFERENT?) (WRITE IN VERBATIM)

---
---
---

The interviewer is expected to write down verbatim on the interview schedule everything the respondent says (which may not be an easy task) for later coding and analysis. Unfortunately, it has been shown that some interviewers have strong expectations about what respondents 'really mean' or 'are trying to say', and so they 'hear' (and write down) things that were never said. For this reason, special attention should be paid to recording problems during interviewer training.

Probes are one of the main advantages which interviews have over postal questionnaires, but they are also one of the most serious sources of interviewer bias. Research has shown that many interviewers tend to be selective in their note-taking and often get into faulty habits which introduce a systematic error.

## FIELD CODING AND CALCULATIONS

On her schedule the interviewer will find many questions to which she has to record the response by putting ticks in boxes or by circling a response category. Sometimes these will be pre-coded answer categories which she has to read out to the respondent, but there will be others where she must immediately classify the response into one of a set of categories which the respondent will not usually see; for example, an occupational classification, a type of consumer product or brand, or a classification by religion or by country of birth. This approach sometimes goes further. For example, respondents may have to be taken day by day over the past seven days, to state for each day how many cigarettes they have smoked, pints of beer they have drunk and so on. The interviewer may then be expected to add up these figures and check them with the respondent; for example, 'Well, I make that sixteen pints in all, would you say that this is about right?' Obviously, these calculations are a potential source of error, but in most cases the figures can be checked again by adding them up later under easier conditions.

Some agencies expect their interviewers to do field coding of verbatim answers. Generally this tends to be very unreliable, unless the interviewers have received special training in a standard coding frame. Some interview schedules contain 'check questions', and it is left to the interviewer to draw the attention of the respondent to any inconsistencies and obtain a 'true' answer. Sometimes the schedule asks for interviewer *ratings*, for example of the socioeconomic level of the district; of the state of repair of the home; of the presence of certain items of furniture which constitute an index of some kind. Once again detachment, care and sensitivity are required of the interviewer.

## QUESTION ORDER

It can easily happen that a respondent, in answer to an early question, continues and perhaps digresses towards a topic which will be broached in a later question. If the interviewer tries to make the respondent stick to the point, there may be some loss of rapport; if the interviewer rapidly leafs through her schedule and there and then notes the answer to the later question, the correct sequence of questioning (which may be quite important, because of contextual effects of preceding questions) will have been lost; if she more or less ignores the additional information then, when she reaches the later question, the respondent may say 'but I've already told you all about that!' How to cope with such situations is very much part of the interviewer's training and briefing.

## ROUTING INSTRUCTIONS

These are directions to the interviewer to go to a different part of the schedule, depending on the respondent's answer. They usually take a conditional form, such as 'IF YES, go to Question 36' or 'If AGREE, or STRONGLY AGREE, offer List B and tick all that apply'. Routing instructions can get quite complex at times, and it is only too easy to leave out large sections of the schedule which should have been asked.

On page 93 for example, is a page from a British government survey on leisure and drinking.

## LANGUAGE

Despite efforts during the pilot work to eliminate phrases which are poorly understood, the interviewer must be alert to problems of alternative usage (see Chapter 8). We have already seen that even a simple word such as 'week' can have many different meanings; the same applies to words such as 'tea', 'book' (a word often used to denote magazines), 'immigrant', 'drink' and many others — every agency will have its own fund of horror stories. In some countries, language use is strongly linked with socioeconomic or ethnic status; in Britain, for example, the term 'dinner' has meanings which are quite different for middle-class and for working-class respondents. Guarding against the effects of

43. One factor which can affect people's leisure
activities is whether or not they have a car or
a motorbike.

Can I just check, does anybody in your
household have a car or a motorbike?

|  |  |  |
|---|---|---|
| Yes (either) ................ | 1 | ASK (a) |
| No .............................. | 2 | GO TO Q.44 |

(a) Do you personally
ever drive the
car/motorbike?

|  |  |  |
|---|---|---|
| Yes (either) ................ | 1 | ASK (i) AND (ii) |
| No .............................. | 2 | GO TO Q.44 |

IF YES, CHECK FLAP AND ASK FOR
EACH EVENING WITH MAIN ACTIVITY
NOT AT HOME

HAND CARD D TO INFORMANT

(i) Can I just check, on . . . . . . day
after spending most of the evening
at . . . . . . (ACTIVITY AT Q.10) which
of these methods did you use to get home?

| | (i) EVENINGS | | | | | | | (ii) BEFORE 14.00 | |
|---|---|---|---|---|---|---|---|---|---|
| | Sun | Sat | Fri | Thu | Wed | Tue | Mon | SUN | SAT |
| Walking all the way .................. | 1 | 1 | 1 | 1 | 1 | 1 | 1 | 1 | 1 |
| Public transport ......................... | 2 | 2 | 2 | 2 | 2 | 2 | 2 | 2 | 2 |
| Driving yourself by car or motorbike .......................... | 3 | 3 | 3 | 3 | 3 | 3 | 3 | 3 | 3 |
| Being driven by somebody else ..................................... | 4 | 4 | 4 | 4 | 4 | 4 | 4 | 4 | 4 |
| Bicycle ...................................... | 5 | 5 | 5 | 5 | 5 | 5 | 5 | 5 | 5 |
| Other (SPECIFY) ...................... | 6 | 6 | 6 | 6 | 6 | 6 | 6 | 6 | 6 |
| ............................................... | | | | | | | | | |
| CODE ALL THAT APPLY ON EACH OCCASION | | | | | | | | | |

IF DRANK AWAY FROM HOME
BEFORE 14.00 ON SUNDAY OR
SATURDAY ASK                    DNA ......    1    GO TO Q.44

(ii) Can I just check, on ................. day
after going out to ...........................
.......................... (FIRST DRINKING
OCCASION AWAY FROM HOME)
which of these methods did you use
to come home?

RECORD ABOVE

such group differences in usage is particularly important because they can become a source of systematic errors (see page 129).

(see page 129)

## 'PROBLEM' RESPONDENTS

The interviewer must know how to deal with respondents who have, or who present, particular problems. For example, the questioning of children requires very special skills, not least because they are so easily led. Elderly respondents may be reluctant to admit that they are deaf or forgetful. Some respondents may be illiterate, which will require a change in procedures. Members of immigrant groups may fear that they may get into trouble with the authorities and may be reluctant to answer questions about themselves. Some topics may turn out to be unexpectedly self-incriminating; for example, welfare or insurance pay-outs, car mileage claims, trips or holidays which may reveal extra-marital relations. 'Knowledge questions', that is lists of true/false statements which may reveal how much, or how little, factual knowledge the respondent has, say, about stocks and shares or about wines or the legal system, may cause considerable embarrassment to some respondents. *On no account must the interviewer show surprise at wrong answers*, or hint (by tone, gesture or pencil poised) what the correct answer might be.

## SITUATIONAL PROBLEMS

Interviews may take place almost anywhere: in the street, in a park, in a private home, in a hospital, a school, a prison, a factory. The interviewer has to be aware, and has to try to counteract, the influence which some of these situations may have on the responses. Interviewing workers on the factory floor, perhaps within earshot of the foreman, may produce far more guarded responses than interviewing the same people in the privacy of their own homes. But even in the home there may be situational problems: for example, how does the interviewer deal with the 'helpful' husband who insists on being present at an interview with his wife and keeps 'correcting' her or answering on her behalf?

## SPECIAL PROCEDURES

As a part of some interviews, the interviewer may be expected to carry out special procedures. For example, she may leave behind a trial sample of a new product and promise to return in a week's time to hear the respondent's comments; or she may leave a diary form behind (also to be collected later), in which the respondent is expected to record some form of recurrent behaviour, such as the family's TV watching or details of daily meals. Each of these procedures will require special briefing and try-outs, not least because such 'special' procedures can influence other parts of the interview.

In audience research, for example, some agencies used to send out interviewers with an extra questions schedule intended only for those who had seen or heard a particular programme. Oddly enough, it was found that this increased the audience figures for those programmes! What seemed to be happening was this: audience research, which takes respondents through the previous day to find out which programmes they had watched or heard, can get very tedious and many of the interviewers were looking forward to a chance to make use of the special questionnaire about Programme X — but this they could only do if the respondent had viewed it or listened to it. So the interviewers would probe and linger, perhaps more than otherwise, when dealing with the time when Programme X was on the air, in the hope of having an opportunity to apply their special schedule. When comparison studies were carried out on carefully matched samples, it was found that interviewers with a special schedule produced higher audience figures for Programme X than interviewers who did not have such a schedule.

IMPRESSION MANAGEMENT

Each interviewer must realize, as will her employers, that she creates an immediate impression on a potential respondent even before she opens her mouth, and that this impression may determine the success or failure of an interview or whether an interview takes place at all. If an interview does take place, then the first impression made by the interviewer will be augmented by further observations as the situation develops. Her mode of dress, her accent, her apparent age, her hair style, her ethnicity, any cues about her education and social background and, of course, her sex — in short, her whole 'presentation of self' will have an influence on her respondents. Different respondents will be influenced diversely and may draw different inferences from whichever aspects they notice. To some, for example, a regional accent may be attractive, to others it may not be, while some will not even notice it. Sometimes it is assumed that interviewers should, as far as possible, be 'matched' to their respondents, on the assumption that many people feel more comfortable when being interviewed by field workers of similar background. It might be counter-productive, for example, to send out a group of very young interviewers to question a sample of old-age pensioners. However, there are no hard-and-fast rules for such a subtle process: some elderly respondents might enjoy talking to a much younger person about their views and experiences, while others might resent such an encounter and find no common ground. Our own ideas about our self-presentation, the 'messages' we try to send, may not be the same as the ones that our respondents receive: 'attractive, mature woman' may be perceived as 'mutton dressed as lamb'. Each respondent has different expectations and receives different subjective impressions, and each fieldwork agency will have its own ideas about interviewer selection and self-presentation. The fact that these are subtle, even unconscious processes, on which it is difficult to carry out objective research, does not make them any the less pervasive or potentially biasing.

What is the interviewer to do about all this? First and foremost, it is important that she should be *aware* of the processes of impression management. She cannot hope always to make a uniformly favourable impression, but she should refrain, while on an assignment, from giving expression to her own distinctive style and personality and, instead, ask herself how she can best hope to make a positive impression on her potential respondents. Her professional role should be to the fore, she should avoid flamboyance and should subdue as much as possible her social class, ethnicity, age and educational background — in short, she should aim at respectable social neutrality. If she needs help in creating the right 'image', the agency will be able to assist her.

RESPONDENT SELECTION

Sampling (see Chapter 3) is very much part of the interviewer's job. She will have been given instructions for the selection of her respondents, and these will generally be of two kinds: either she is given a series of addresses, names-and-addresses or workplace locations; or she is given a quota, for example fifteen working-class married women aged between thirty-five and fifty, not in a full-time occupation. The addresses will have been chosen for her from existing records; for example, a professional body listing, or a follow-up sample of discharged bankrupts. Sometimes she will have to interview all adults living at a given address, at other times she will be instructed to make a choice according to certain criteria. She will be given further instructions about what to do in cases of refusal (substitution rules) or if there is no one at home (call-back rules). Departure from such instructions, for whatever reason, will impair the quality of the sample and hence affect the results of the research.

In the case of quota sampling the interviewer usually has more latitude. Most interviewers know from experience where, in their neighbourhood, they are most likely to find respondents who meet the day's requirements, but therein lie risks of bias, too: a preference for railway station forecourts may undersample the car- and bus-commuters and the stay-at-homes; a preference for department store exits may over-sample shoppers, and so on. Since they are under considerable time pressure, interviewers may sometimes stretch the limits of their quota categories, for example to include an otherwise co-operative respondent who is probably just too old or too young; or they may be tempted to include unmarried co-habitors in the 'married' category. Once again, any departure from instructions will cause error and may cause a systematic bias in the selection of the sample.

## To sum up: main causes of bias

We have looked at many potential sources of systematic error that attach to the standardized interviewing method of data collection and with which the interviewer must be trained to deal. While each source may overlap with others, we have noted the following categories:

*Before the interview:*
   departures from the sampling instructions, by the interviewer;
   adverse impression management by the interviewer.

*During the interview:*
   poor maintenance of rapport;
   rephrasing of attitude questions;
   altering factual questions;
   careless prompting;

poor management of show cards;
biased probes;
asking questions out of sequence;
unreliable field coding;
biased recording of verbatim answers;
poor management of 'problem' respondents;
inadequate management of situational problems or of
    'special procedures'.

To these must be added the imperfections and biases that may emanate from the structure and wording of the interviewing schedule itself; these will be dealt with in other chapters.

## Telephone interviewing

The most obvious advantage of conducting structured interviews by telephone is their *low cost*. It has been estimated that face-to-face interviewers spend only about one-third of their time in conducting interviews, the remainder of their time being taken up by travel and by locating respondents. Besides savings in travel expenses and travelling time, telephone interviews also offer savings in other ways. They are generally conducted at a noticeably faster pace than face-to-face interviews, and permit close and continuous supervision at a central facility. The results of a set of telephone interviews are usually available in much shorter time, while substitutions for refusals and not-at-homes can also be made very quickly. *Speed* is therefore a second major advantage of telephone interviewing — an important factor in fields such as advertising, media research and opinion polling. However, computer-assisted face-to-face interviews, using lap-top computers which can transmit their data nightly by telephone to a central processing computer, can offer turn-round times which are very competitive.

The most obvious draw-back of telephone interviewing is the problem of sample representativeness, especially in countries where telephone ownership is well below the 80–90 per cent found in some Western countries. This is not always the major handicap it might appear to be. Many studies do not require nationally representative samples: for instance, studies of professionals, of industrial managers or of commercial firms can safely assume that all their sample members will be accessible by telephone. Sometimes it is reasonable to define the sample as representative not of all school teachers/war veterans/private pilots but only of those who are accessible by telephone.

Given that not all households or individuals are accessible by phone (note that we are concerned here with access, not with telephone ownership), in what ways will our sample be biased? Not being accessible by telephone is usually linked with lower income, with being young and male, and with having moved house recently. In addition, some subscribers choose to go ex-directory (in Britain the proportion is currently some 25 per cent of all subscribers and rising), but these are unlikely to fit the above categories. On the other hand, in rural areas a widely distributed population can be sampled more easily, and perhaps more accurately, by telephone.

In principle, there are three ways of generating a random sample of telephone numbers: (a) from some other sampling frame, such as the computerized post-code address file (PAF), from a membership list, or from an existing set of records, in which case a phone number will have to be found for each name. (In Britain, telephone numbers are, in practice, likely to be found for about two-thirds of such a sample.); (b) by drawing a random sample from the most recent telephone directories themselves (this procedure will miss out ex-directory subscribers); and (c) by 'random digit dialling' (RDD), where a computer selects telephone numbers at random from within a set of stratified geographical regions which correspond to telephone area codes. (This latter method has the advantage of potentially including people who are ex-directory.) Since the same private telephone often serves several people, a sample drawn by telephone number is often more like a sample of households than a sample of individuals. So long as there is no country-wide, computer-accessible, comprehensive and up-to-date list of the names, addresses and (where appropriate) telephone numbers for the entire adult population, all these methods of sampling will remain relatively cumbersome — though probably no more so than other probability sampling methods now in use. As we have noted, in telephone interviewing it is quick and easy to make substitutions for refusals and for respondents who are not at home.

What other biases might we expect with telephone interviewing? For example, is the refusal rate higher, compared to conventional interviews? Despite some misgivings, this is not usually the case, and the telephone refusal rate is sometimes actually lower, perhaps because of the advantage of 'interviewer invisibility' to some respondents. But time of day is important: evening and week-end refusal rates can be high. For a longer interview it sometimes helps to make a preliminary call, to book a time at which the respondent can take an extended telephone call. In some countries there is increasing resistance against 'cold' telephone calling.

What kinds of questions can be asked over the telephone? Conventional interview schedules have to be specially adapted for telephone interviewing, but otherwise all but the most complex kind of question can be asked successfully over the phone, and the telephone often seems to reduce resistance to 'sensitive' items. Problems may, however, be experienced with respondents who are hard-of-hearing, with elderly respondents and those from minority groups — but probably no more so than with conventional interviews. Each interview schedule will have to be piloted and adapted to telephone use and computer assistance as necessary.

Some agencies operate a mixed-method model, using both conventional and telephone interviewing. This will require detailed research to show whether or not the two different modes produce comparable data on similar respondents within the same study; otherwise it might not be valid to merge the results of the two data sets. The mixed-method approach is also likely to reduce the speedy turn-around advantage of telephone interviewing. Some agencies have set up large pools of respondents who have agreed in advance to be interviewed by telephone; bias may be reduced by structuring each sample to be interviewed along demographic lines, while the interviewing of special sub-samples becomes a ready possibility.

In addition to conventional interviewer skills the telephone interviewer will obviously need an excellent telephone manner, especially when speaking to those who resent having their privacy invaded by a stranger, who fear for their personal safety, or who think the interviewer is trying to sell them something. Special skills will also be needed to make do without prompt cards and when requesting an interview with a member of the household other than the person answering the telephone. But in most ways the problems of telephone interviewing tend to be very similar to those that are encountered in structured interviews in general.

## Selected readings

Beed, Terence W. and Stimpson, Robert J., 1985, *Survey Interviewing*, Unwin Hyman, London.

Fowler Jr, Floyd J. and Mangione, Thomas W., 1990, *Standardized Survey Interviewing*, Sage, London.

Gordon, R.L., 1980, *Interviewing: Strategy, Techniques and Tactics*, Dorsey Press, New York.

Turner, Charles F., and Martin, Elizabeth (eds), 1984, *Surveying Subjective Phenomena*, Russell Sage Foundation, New York.
    Phrasing questions in interviews.

Sudman, Seymour, and Bradburn, Norman M., 1974, *Response Effects in Surveys*, Aldine, Chicago.
    About interviewing and question writing, recall problems and interviewer–respondent interaction.

Hyman, H.H., *et al.*, 1954, *Interviewing in Social Research*, University of Chicago Press, Chicago.
    Early experimental studies of interviewer bias.

Kahn, R.L. and Cannell, C.F., 1961, *The Dynamic of Interviewing*, Wiley, New York.
    An older text, very detailed on problems of bias and interviewer skills. Still useful.

### TELEPHONE INTERVIEWING

Frey, James H., 1989, *Survey Research by Telephone*, Vol. 150, Sage Library of Social Research.
    Very useful and practical, deals with sampling problems, computer-assisted telephone interviewing and administrative aspects.

Dillman, D.A., 1978, *Mail and Telephone Surveys*, Wiley, New York.

Groves, Robert, Biemer, Paul, Lyberg, Lars, Massey, James, Nicholls, William, and Waksberg, Joseph, 1988, *Telephone Survey Methodology*, Wiley, New York.
    A wide-ranging description of telephone-interviewing applications.

# 7
# QUESTIONNAIRE PLANNING

## What is a questionnaire?

The term 'questionnaire' has been used in different ways. Some practitioners would reserve the term exclusively for self-administered and postal questionnaires, while others would include interview schedules (administered face-to-face or by telephone) under the general rubric of 'questionnaires'. In a different way the word 'questionnaire' is sometimes used to distinguish a set of questions, including perhaps some open-ended ones, from more rigidly constructed scales or tests. There is, of course, some overlap between these techniques. For example, the problems of item wording or phrasing, and of ordering the questions in a particular sequence, are common to them all. In the present context we shall therefore use the term 'questionnaire' fairly loosely to cover postal questionnaires, group- or self-administered questionnaires and structured interview schedules (including telephone interviews). In this broader sense, a questionnaire may also contain check lists, attitude scales, projective techniques, rating scales and a variety of other research methods which will be discussed in later chapters.

A questionnaire is not some sort of official form, nor is it a set of questions which have been casually jotted down without much thought. We should think of the questionnaire as an important instrument of research, a tool for data collection. The questionnaire has a job to do: its function is measurement.

But what is it to measure? The answers to this question should be contained in the questionnaire *specification*. Many weeks of planning, reading, design and exploratory pilot work will be needed before any sort of specification for a questionnaire can be determined, for the specification must follow directly from the operational statement of the issues to be investigated and from the research design that has been adopted.

Well before we make a start with our questionnaire, we should have a rough idea of the pattern which our enquiry is likely to follow. Are we conducting a short, factual enquiry or are we conducting analytical research on a set of attitudes? How large is the sample likely to be? Shall we be dealing with adults or with children? If with adults, will they be housewives, company directors, relatives of prisoners, students or a probability sample of the entire population? Do we intend to approach the same respondents more than once? Are we dealing with phenomena that are subject to seasonal fluctuations? Do we intend to promise our respondents anonymity? All these, and many other issues, will affect our measurement specification and procedures.

The detailed specification of measurement aims must be precisely and logically related to the aims of the overall research plan and objectives. For each issue or topic to be investigated, and for each hypothesis to be explored, a precise operational statement is required about the variables to be measured. If a political poll is to include variables such as people's attitudes to a new tax, or the degree to which they identify with their local community, how are such variables to be measured? If we wish to examine the hypothesis that young children get their ideas about cigarette smoking from older siblings, then how shall we operationalize this issue in practice and what measures will we require?

To lay down such detailed specifications in itemized particularity for an entire research project is not an easy task; it requires painstaking intellectual effort, based on the depth interviews, the research design and the conceptualization of the research problem. The net result should be *a comprehensive listing of every variable to be measured* and of the way(s) in which this is to be accomplished. The priority and importance of each variable should also be taken into account. A relatively peripheral variable may require only a handful of questions, but measurement of the key variables that are central to the research design will need a more elaborate approach requiring, perhaps, inventories or scales composed of many items. Instrument building and questionnaire composition cannot proceed until we have a complete specification of the variables that need to be measured and of the types of instruments that will have to be built (scales, check-lists, open-ended questions etc.).

Each survey will have its own particular problems, but it is possible to present some general considerations that have to be borne in mind in most surveys and about which decisions will have to be made before we can begin to write our first question. These decisions fall into five groups:

(1) The main *type of data collection instruments* which we shall need, such as interviews, postal questionnaires, content analysis of records, observational techniques and so on;
(2) The *method of approach to respondents* (after their selection through the sampling procedures), including sponsorship, stated purpose of the research, length and duration of our questionnaire, confidentiality and anonymity; the special problems of research in schools;
(3) The *build-up of question sequences* or modules within the questionnaire, and the ordering of questions and scales or other techniques within a general framework;
(4) For each variable, the *order of questions* within each module, using approaches such as funnelling;
(5) The *type of question* to be used: for example 'closed' questions with pre-coded answer categories versus free-response questions.

Each of these topics will be discussed below in general terms under its own heading, but we should bear in mind that every survey is to a large extent unique. The best way to move from the general to the particular, in order to find local solutions for specific dilemmas, is through small-scale field trials. Guess-work, intuition, expert advice and spurious orthodoxy are no substitutes for properly conducted pilot work.

# 1. Main method of data collection

As we have seen, there are many methods of data collection in social research, but here we are concerned primarily with those methods that use a 'question-naire' in the broadest sense, namely the standardized, formal interview; the postal, self-administered questionnaire; and the group-administered question-naire. Each has advantages and disadvantages, and our final choice will depend on its appropriateness to our purpose and to the means at our disposal. We should also bear in mind some of the issues that have already been raised in Chapter 6 on standardized interviewing techniques.

## MAIL QUESTIONNAIRES VERSUS STANDARDIZED INTERVIEWS

The main *advantages* of postal questionnaires are:

(a) low cost of data collection;
(b) low cost of processing;
(c) avoidance of interviewer bias (but see below);
(d) ability to reach respondents who live at widely dispersed addresses or abroad.

The main *disadvantages* of the postal questionnaire are:

(a) generally low response rates, and consequent biases;
(b) unsuitability for respondents of poor literacy; for the visually handi-capped, the very old or for children below the age of, say, ten; often unsuitable for people with language difficulties;
(c) no opportunity to correct misunderstandings or to probe, or to offer explanations or help;
(d) no control over the order in which questions are answered, no check on incomplete responses, incomplete questionnaires or the passing on of questionnaires to others;
(e) no opportunity to collect ratings or assessments based on observation.

The advantages and disadvantages of the interview are almost a mirror-image of these points. Interviews often have a higher response rate; they offer the opportunity to correct misunderstandings and to carry out observations and ratings while controlling for incompleteness and for answering sequence; and interviewers can often succeed with respondents who have reading or language difficulties. But interviews are expensive and time-consuming to conduct and to process, there are always the risks of interviewer bias, and interviews are usually too expensive to reach a widely dispersed sample.

Incidentally, in the case of a postal questionnaire it may not be altogether true that since there is no interviewer, there can be no interviewer bias. In a sense, a ghost interviewer is still present because the respondent may conjure up an image or a stereotype of the organization which sent the questionnaire and of the kind of person who might be asking these questions. In other words, the respondents will interact with the questionnaire and may 'project' some kind of person or organization 'behind' the questions, and this may bias their responses.

## SELF-ADMINISTERED QUESTIONNAIRES

The self-administered questionnaire is usually presented to the respondents by an interviewer or by someone in an official position, such as a teacher or a hospital receptionist. The purpose of the inquiry is explained, and then the respondent is left alone to complete the questionnaire, which will be picked up later. This method of data collection ensures a high response rate, accurate sampling and a minimum of interviewer bias, while permitting interviewer assessments, providing necessary explanations (but *not* the interpretation of questions) and giving the benefit of a degree of personal contact. Research workers may in this way utilize the help of someone in an official capacity who is not a skilled interviewer. However, the greatest care is needed in briefing such persons or they may, with the best intentions, introduce fatal biases.

## GROUP-ADMINISTERED QUESTIONNAIRES

The group-administered questionnaire is also largely self-explanatory and is given to groups of respondents assembled together, such as school children or invited audiences. Depending on the size of the group and its level of literacy, two or more persons will see to the administration of the questionnaires, give help where needed (in a nondirective way), check finished questionnaires for completeness and so on. Sometimes, variations in procedure may be introduced. For instance, the audience may be provided with empty booklets; some slides or a film may be shown; and then a group of numbered questions might be read aloud, one at a time, while the respondents write their answers in the booklets next to the question numbers. This ensures that all respondents answer the questions in the same order and that they all have the same amount of time to do so. Groups of forty can readily be controlled in this way, but contamination (through copying, talking or asking questions) is a constant danger.

## 2. Approach to respondents

Most of the issues under this heading have already been touched upon in Chapter 6 on standardized interviewing; basically, whether by interview or by mail, we must find ways of gaining the respondents' co-operation and of motivating them to respond to our questions. The ways in which we approach respondents are therefore of paramount importance.

### INCREASING RESPONSE RATES

The whole area concerning the 'best' way to approach respondents has long been beset by myths and by controversy among practitioners. More recently these problems have been the subject of a great deal of systematic research in a number of countries, and it is now possible to draw some tentative conclusions. However, these cannot be regarded as hard-and-fast rules and pilot work remains essential.

The following factors have been found to *increase response rates*, either to mail surveys or to personal interviews or to both:

*Advance warning* — a letter or postcard informing the respondent of the study in advance, and inviting participation.

*Explanation of selection* — explaining the method of sampling used, and how the respondent came to be chosen.

*Sponsorship* — this may take the form of an interviewer identification card plus a pamphlet describing the research organization, or it may be a covering letter or a letter of introduction from someone expected to be influential. Sponsorship can be a powerful motivator (for example, if a postal questionnaire to members of a trades union is accompanied by a letter of support from its general secretary), but it can also go horribly wrong! (If, say, the general secretary is thoroughly distrusted by a section of the membership; this would not merely reduce the response rate but would also introduce a powerful bias.)

*Envelope* — this refers to the appearance of the *first* envelope in a mail survey (that is, not to the return envelope). It has a better chance of being opened and read if it is addressed to the respondent personally, if it has a stamp on it (that is, not commercially franked) and if it 'looks professional' rather than like junk mail. The class of postage and any special delivery method seem to make little difference, though these effects may differ from country to country and from time to time.

*Publicity* — advance publicity in the local media can be helpful to some surveys, provided it is favourable! Negative local publicity, or generally negative publicity about all surveys can be very damaging to response rates.

*Incentives* — small incentives have generally proved helpful, but larger incentives often are not. Future incentives, for example the chance to win a major prize if the questionnaire is returned or the interview completed, are generally helpful. Interviewers may also be more persistent if they know they can offer a reward, thus reducing non-contacts.

*Confidentiality* — all survey data must be treated as confidential, in the sense that only the researcher(s) will have access to them, and steps must be taken to ensure that no information will be published about identifiable persons or organizations without their permission (see also under ethical considerations, Chapter 6). Here we refer to an explicit statement or promise made to potential respondents in order to overcome possible apprehensions. For example, the following may be displayed prominently on the front of the question schedule:

THE CONTENTS OF THIS FORM ARE *ABSOLUTELY CONFIDENTIAL.* INFORMATION IDENTIFYING THE RESPONDENT WILL NOT BE DISCLOSED UNDER ANY CIRCUMSTANCES

*Reminders* — mail surveys tend to suffer from low and slow response rates, so reminders may be sent out when the rate of returns begins to drop, and perhaps again after a week or two, to those who have not returned the questionnaire. This becomes impossible if we have promised anonymity (see below), unless we send out reminders to the entire sample, which might be too expensive.

*Anonymity* — this is not the same as confidentiality and can be promised only in certain circumstances, for example to the members of a quota sample (though even here names and addresses are sometimes requested so that a check interview or phone call can be made). Respondents who have been sampled from a list of names and addresses are clearly *not* anonymous, though they can be promised that any identifying information will be destroyed at the data-processing stage. Identifying respondents by a code number rather than by name may be reassuring to some extent. In the case of mail questionnaires, complete anonymity (so that returned questionnaires cannot be identified) may increase the response rate, but it then becomes impossible to send out reminders to the non-respondents (unless we sent out reminders to the entire sample which might be too costly and will annoy those who *have* responded). Anonymity is especially important in surveys that involve 'sensitive' topics.

*Appearance* — there have been many experiments with general layout, type face, colour and quality of paper etc. in the case of postal questionnaires. No clear general conclusions have emerged; it is best to aim at a relatively 'conservative' but pleasant appearance.

*Length* — thickness of the question booklet, number of pages, and time required to complete have all been investigated many times; generally these variables tend to interact with

*The topic, and its degree of interest* to the respondent — long and complex interviews or questionnaires will often be completed successfully if the topic is of intrinsic interest to respondents (for example, if it is about their children), or if they believe that their responses will have a direct influence on policy.

*Rapport* — this does not really apply to postal questionnaires. In respect of interviews, it is part of the interviewer's skill to establish and sustain rapport, so that the respondent remains motivated and will complete the interview (see Chapter 6).

*Return envelopes* — it has often been alleged that non-respondents will steam the stamps off return envelopes, thus reducing response rates, while others have suggested that a 'real' stamp (rather than a business reply envelope) indicates trust and will increase response rates. The evidence seems to favour the latter.

The above determinants of response rates can be classified as (a) extrinsic (for example sponsorship; incentives) and (b) intrinsic (for example, the topic; length of time required). Obviously there may be other factors that will influence response rates. Among these are *situational* variables. Efforts have been made to get in touch with people who have been listed as 'refusals' or as 'non-contacts' by field interviewers, in order to find out if these are a cause of systematic bias; that is, whether their unavailability or refusal to take part was in some way related to the subject matter of the survey. If there was no such relationship, for instance if the interview was refused because of illness or because the respondent was just going out, then these non-responses are classed as 'situational'. In such cases, an appointment for a call-back interview can often be successful. However, call-backs are expensive and have diminishing rates of return.

DEALING WITH NON-RESPONSE

Despite increasing sophistication in the approach to respondents, some steps have to be taken to deal with non-response in any survey and especially in a postal survey. These steps have to be anticipated and planned; it is simply not good enough to find, eventually, that only 38 per cent of the questionnaires have been returned and then try to do something about it. First, let us note that a low response rate can usually be overcome without too much difficulty by sending out some more questionnaires or by conducting some further interviews. The issue here concerns *not the number or proportion of non-respondents, but the possibility of bias*. We need to find out whether the reasons for the non-response are somehow connected with the topic of our research; for example, in a general study of attitudes to unemployment, have many of the unemployed in our sample been unwilling to respond? In other words, is there a confounding bias?

To reduce this possibility, first, many steps can be taken to boost the over-all rate of response in our sample, as we have seen, and any such steps should be tried out in the pilot work. Next, having done our best to maximize the response rate, we have to attend to the question of bias. Some simple sociodemographic checks are often possible. For instance, if we have names and addresses for our sample and for those who have replied or been interviewed, then we can run some comparisons to see if, say, there are too few northerners among our returns, or if people whose surnames begin with J or T are under-represented. In other situations we may be able to find out if we have a disproportion by gender, or by age, in our returns.

What is to be done about such a bias? Some survey practitioners would engage in statistical weighting; that is, they would statistically boost the cells in the sample that are deficient due to low response rates. This, however, assumes that within each cell the non-respondents have the same attributes or experiences as the respondents, so that the reasons for their non-response are purely situational or at any rate are unconnected with the topic of the survey. But can we be sure of this? After all, our checks for non-response can usually be conducted on the basis of only a few demographic variables and these may, or may not, be associated with our topic of interest. Thus, in a study of newspaper-reading habits it might not matter that we have too few northerners among our returns, provided that there is no association between newspaper-reading habits and living in the north — but this may have been one reason for conducting the survey in the first place! In principle, therefore, we can often ascertain a bias in our returns along demographic lines (such as those we have used to draw our initial sample), but this will not tell us much about a bias in the opinions or behaviour with which our survey is concerned.

Sometimes we can try to do something more complex. We can undertake a multivariate analysis (see Chapter 15) of our returns and discover what are the strongest correlates of our dependent variable(s). If these correlates are variables for which we have information about our non-respondents (typically, these would again be the demographic variables which we have used to draw our sample), then it might be possible to produce estimated values for our non-respondents, at least on some of our dependent variables. This is a hazardous procedure, which might best be confined to populations about which we know a good deal already, such as medical practitioners or school children. In other cases, it might be safer to do no more than to indicate the direction of the bias due to non-response; that is, we might report that our results concerning newspaper reading among northerners are likely to be an under-estimate (or an over-estimate) due to non-response problems — and leave it at that.

## ACCESS TO SCHOOL CHILDREN

In recent years there has been an increase in the number of surveys and other large-scale investigations among school children. The structure of the educational system provides a ready-made sampling frame in terms of age and often sex, in terms of educational level, geographical area and so on. If access can be obtained to whole school classes, then data can be rapidly obtained by means of self-administered questionnaires completed in the classroom; such procedures have obvious advantages over home visits or mail questionnaires, though self-completion questionnaires for children are more difficult to design and require more intensive pilot work than questionnaires for adults.

However, parents and schools are (like many organizations) very sensitive to the presence and activities of social researchers. School authorities have special responsibilities to the children and their parents and, moreover, some schools in recent years have been almost over-run by research students. It is important, therefore, to take particular care when we seek access to samples of children in schools.

For a start, even though we may know some teachers or school heads in a particular area, it is always best to write first to the director of education or the chief education officer of the appropriate municipal education authority. The letter will seek permission for an approach to be made to the head teachers of the local schools in order to conduct research among their pupils (and staffs, if the latter are also to take part). Accompanying this formal request will be a statement which outlines the aims, design and methods of the research, and includes some justification for doing it, usually expressed in terms of its relevance to education, child health etc. This may well require brief reference to previous research in the field and to the researcher's experience, indicating his or her qualifications and status. Any measuring instruments to be employed should be listed, especially if published tests are involved. The researcher must also be prepared to submit copies of questionnaires and texts for approval. When approval in principle is given to a researcher to approach individual head teachers (with whom a meeting is generally requested), an assurance of the confidentiality of any data obtained is usually required. This confidentiality applies to the responses of individual children, the names of participating schools and often the education authority itself, none of whom should be identifiable in any published report or thesis. Likewise, no data from individual children should be made available to anyone outside the research team, not even to their parents or class teachers. The exact terms of confidentiality will be agreed with the officer of the education authority concerned. Finally, in the approach to authorities and to the schools, the timing and duration of a study must be considered and mentioned.

The timing of the fieldwork in a research study is an important issue for the researcher; the schools, too, will want to know how much classroom time the study will require. For example, a prolonged study will have to take account of the structure of the school year, and the holidays between the terms, especially in summer. Half-term holidays, school outings etc. also can upset or delay data collection arrangements. School examinations are a constraining influence, for however interesting or important a research study may be, examinations form a vital stage in the education of adolescents, and head teachers will be most reluctant to upset the teaching of examination classes. After examinations, however, children are often much more readily available. It must be borne in mind, however, that with the end of the school session classes are often reorganized within a school, or children moved to other schools in the system so that a particular group of pupils involved in a study may no longer be available as a group. A more usual problem of data collection in schools is the absence of children due to illness or the loss of children who move away from an area during a research study. This problem is less serious where school classes are large, consisting of over thirty children, so that adequate numbers of subjects remain. But if children have been matched in pairs in the research design, the loss of one can mean the loss of both members of the pair from the study, since rematching to preserve numbers is often impossible.

In some schools the head will wish to obtain parental permission for the research. The best approach in this case is to offer to draft a circular, to be signed by the head, briefly explaining the research and giving the proposed starting date. The children concerned can be asked to take such a circular home to their parents. In the second part of the circular the parents will be told that their child has been chosen (among others) to take part in the proposed research and that parental permission will be assumed *unless the parents object* before the proposed starting date. Thus the onus is put on the parents to withdraw their child from the research, if they wish.

## 3. The build-up of question modules

Typically, the novice starts to design a questionnaire by putting a rather forbidding set of questions at the top of a blank sheet of paper. These are likely to ask for name, address, age, marital status, number of children, religion and so on. However necessary, questions of this kind (*classifying* or *personal data* questions) tend to be very offputting to respondents. We must put ourselves in their place. Having had the purpose of the study explained to them in a cover letter or by the interviewer, and having agreed to co-operate, they now expect some interesting questions dealing with the topic of the study; for example, their journey to work or their children's education. Instead, they are being steered in a different, rather 'personal', direction by being asked a series of questions about their private life! To us such questions as 'are you single/married/living as a couple/widowed/divorced?' would be no more than routine classifying items, but to the respondents they may well refer to highly sensitive aspects of their lives. We have little enough 'right' to intrude on them as it is, and if we start off with questions of this kind we should not be surprised if we get no further response. Unless there are very good reasons to do otherwise, personal data questions should always come near the end of a questionnaire and should be preceded by a short explanation such as 'now, to help us classify your answers and to make our statistical comparisons, would you mind telling us . . . how old you are?' and so on.

Towards the end of the pilot work our questionnaire will consist of a series of question *modules* or sequences, each concerned with a different variable. We must now consider the order in which these modules should appear on the final questionnaire. In this, we shall want to bear two sets of considerations in mind: the internal logic of the inquiry, and the likely reactions of respondents — often these will have conflicting requirements!

Consider, for example, a readership study. We might start with a set of 'awareness' questions, which are designed to tell us what newspapers and magazines the respondent has seen or has heard of. These might be followed by some 'factual' questions, dealing with the respondents' own behaviour; for example, what daily paper(s) they read (if any), what they read in the week-end and so forth. Next, there might be a module on magazines and, after that, a module on book reading and library borrowing. We hope that, so far, the respondents have not found the questions too difficult and that co-operation is readily forthcoming. We might now offer a module on likes and dislikes in newspaper contents; the next modules might ask about preferences for different content areas such as sports, stock-market news and so, eventually, we might come to political attitudes and the political orientation of newspapers. By now, we shall have moved also from simple question-and-answer sequences to check-lists, ratings and perhaps to attitude statements. Finally, we shall need to ask some personal data questions and come to the end with a 'thank you'.

We hope that, from the respondent's point of view, this has seemed an interesting, sensible and non-threatening experience. Piloting the questionnaire as a whole may, however, show us that some respondents become very embarrassed by the 'awareness' questions at the beginning because they feel it puts them 'on the spot', whereas they would not mind answering some questions about their own reading behaviour right at the beginning. The pilot work might further show that questions to do with book reading and library borrowing cause difficulties because respondents tend to over-claim (prestige bias) — but then cannot remember the titles of the books or the names of the authors. Perhaps it might be better to continue with more newspaper questions and save the library questions till last? Or, if people are irritated by these, would it be better to end with an easier module, say, about the part of the paper which they like best? Perhaps we should also give some more thought to the placement of the political-attitude scales. Will they be influenced by the immediately preceding module dealing with the preferred sections of a newspaper? Will the respondents be too tired by then? Should we try, among the personal data, to ask for political party affiliation or preference? Or if not there, then where else can we suitably ask about this?

Meanwhile, how are we getting on with the *balance of question types*? Have we got too many open-ended questions, which are time-consuming and require a lot of writing? Should we put all the pre-coded questions together at the beginning, irrespective of logic or content, so as to leave all the open-ended questions to the end? And should we perhaps treat the attitude scales separately as a self-completion technique?

Consider now a somewhat more ambitious study, say, a survey of criminal victimization and perceptions of crime. We shall need to ask respondents about any personal experiences of crime which they may have had — burglaries, car thefts, assaults, pickpocketing — but we shall also want to ask about their perceptions of crime in general and in their area, and about their attitudes to the degree of seriousness of different crimes, as well as their attitudes to the police and to the courts. Which of these modules should come first, or last, and why? Crimes are often not reported to the local police, or there may be a problem with an insurance claim, or with ethnic prejudice, or two youths may fight over a girl, or a child may steal from its parents. These are very *sensitive areas*, and people's ideas about crime may not fit the appropriate legal categories, nor will their ideas about the relative severity of crimes necessarily correspond with the sentencing policies of the courts. Yet often people have extremely strong attitudes in respect of such matters as self-defence, child abuse, exceeding the speed limit, drugs and the behaviour of the police. To make the final decisions on the order in which modules dealing with each of these topics should appear on a question schedule will not be easy.

## 4. Order of questions within modules

We now come to a consideration of the order of the questions within each module. Let us assume that we have a detailed specification for our module and that we have some suitable questions from the pilot work, some 'open' and some 'closed', with which we are trying to construct part of an interview schedule. In what sequence can we best approach the issue? Should we ask about attitudes first, or begin by asking about personal experience and then 'broaden out' towards more general attitudes? Or perhaps the other way around?

The *funnel approach*, preceded by various 'filter' questions (see below), is one well-known type of sequence which is often used — though for our particular purpose some other sequence, suggested by further pilot work, may turn out to be better. The funnel approach is so named because it starts off the module with a very broad question and then progressively narrows down the scope of the questions until in the end it comes to some very specific points.

WORKSHOP I: FUNNELLING QUESTIONS

Suppose we want to know whether some people avoid boiled sweets because they are said to be harmful to the teeth. It would not do to ask them a question such as, 'do you believe that boiled sweets are harmful to the teeth?' or, 'do you avoid eating boiled sweets because you feel that they harm the teeth?' These would be grossly leading questions, and, besides, the respondent may never eat boiled sweets, or may avoid them for some other reason. Obviously, it would be valuable if we could get some of the respondents to say spontaneously that they avoid boiled sweets because they are damaging to the teeth, before we suggest it to them and before they become aware of what the questions are really about. Therefore, we may start off with some very broad questions such as: 'What is your opinion of boiled sweets?' 'What do you think of people who eat boiled sweets?' Each question provides the respondent with an opportunity to mention the issue of dental decay spontaneously. Next, we might ask more restricted questions, such as: 'Do you eat boiled sweets at all?' 'Did you eat boiled sweets when you were a child?' 'Do you allow your children to eat boiled sweets?' Each should be followed up with 'why is that?' if the reply is negative, thus providing further opportunities for the dental issue to emerge spontaneously. After that, we may narrow the questions still further: 'Do you believe that boiled sweets can be harmful in any way?' 'What would happen if you ate too many boiled sweets?' 'What are some of the disadvantages of eating boiled sweets?' Note that the dental problem still has not been mentioned directly. Finally, we bring up the problem as nondirectively as possible: 'Some people say that eating boiled sweets is bad for your teeth, but others say that it makes no difference. How do you feel about this?' Or, 'Do you believe that eating boiled sweets is bad for your teeth, or do you think that most people's teeth will not be damaged by eating boiled sweets?' And so on. By proceeding in this way we not only increase our chances of obtaining what we are seeking through a spontaneous reply, we also place the whole issue of boiled sweets and tooth decay in the context of some of the other factors that determine the eating of boiled sweets. This context can be very important; it may well be that other reasons for not eating boiled sweets are mentioned far more frequently than the possible danger to the teeth.

A *filter* question is used to exclude some respondents from a particular question sequence if those questions are irrelevant to them. Thus, in the above example, we might wish to ask for some factual information about sweet-buying behaviour and boiled sweet purchases. Obviously, if the respondent never buys these sweets then there is no point in asking about frequency, weight, type of shop, type of container, colour preferences and so forth. Therefore, our illustrative question sequence will be preceded by a filter question such as 'do you buy boiled sweets from time to time?' or, 'have you bought any boiled sweets within the past two weeks?' If the answer is negative, the interviewer will be instructed to skip the next few questions and proceed to the beginning of the next question sequence (a routing instruction).

Each survey produces its own problems of question order, which makes it difficult to offer general principles. We try, as much as possible, to avoid putting ideas into the respondents' minds or to suggest that they should have attitudes when they have none. Therefore, with regard to any issue, we may want to start with open questions and only introduce more structured or pre-coded questions at a later stage.

Some researchers prefer to start each question sequence by asking a few factual, multiple-choice questions about the respondent's own habits, background or experience. Further questions follow naturally about the respondent's attitudes concerning these points and about wider issues. For example, we may ask the respondents how often they go to church, if at all, whether they went to Sunday school as a child, and then follow these questions with some broader ones on religious issues and attitudes. Other researchers prefer to start each module with wide-open questions and ask about the respondent's own behaviour or experience at the end. In both approaches there is the danger that inconsistencies and contradictions between attitudes and behaviour will emerge which the respondent may try to cover up.

Our final choice of approach and sequence must be determined by our own survey problems and by the results of the pilot work.

# 5. Question types

## Open and closed questions

Broadly speaking, most questions are either 'open' or 'closed'. A *closed* question is one in which the respondents are offered a choice of alternative replies. They may be asked to tick or underline their chosen answer(s) in a written questionnaire, or the alternatives may be read aloud or shown to them on a prompt card or a slide. Questions of this kind may offer simple alternatives such as Yes and No, or the names of five political parties in an election; or they can offer something more complex, such as a choice of ways of keeping order in a classroom or a choice of motives for smoking cigarettes.

*Open* or free-response questions are not followed by any kind of choice, and the answers have to be recorded in full. In the case of a written questionnaire, the amount of space or the number of lines provided for the answer will partly determine the length and fullness of the responses we obtain. Inevitably, some of this richness is lost when the answers are classified later, but it is useful to report a few such answers in full in the final report to give the reader some of the flavour of the replies. Statistical tabulations are important and must remain our first aim, but they make dull reading.

The chief advantage of the open question is the freedom it gives to the respondents. Once they have understood the intent of the question, they can let their thoughts roam freely, unencumbered by a prepared set of replies. We obtain their ideas in their own language, expressed spontaneously, and this spontaneity is often extremely worthwhile as a basis for new hypotheses. In an interview, however, there is the risk that we will obtain, not so much a rounded and full account of the respondents' feelings, but rather just what happens to be uppermost in their minds at the time. If this is true, then we may still ask whether what comes first to the respondents' mind is not also most important for them, and for us.

Free-response questions are often easy to ask, difficult to answer, and still more difficult to analyse. As a rule, we employ a classification process known as *coding* (see Chapter 14), which requires drawing up some system of categories, a *coding frame*. The design of such coding frames and the actual coding operation require trained staff and are extremely time-consuming; for this reason researchers have to curb their desire to have too many open questions.

Sometimes, if the first answer seems a little ambiguous or does not go far enough, we can instruct the interviewer to *probe*. This often takes the form of asking the respondent to explain further or to give reasons for something stated earlier; at times, a particular issue may be brought into the discussion deliberately, if the respondent has not already mentioned it. Such probes should be as nondirective as possible, thus: 'Could you say a little more about . . . ?' 'Why did you say just now that . . . ?' 'Now, what about the . . . ?' 'And how do you feel about . . . ?' The risk of interviewer bias is probably at its highest whenever probes are employed. They are 'safe' only in the hands of the most highly trained and experienced fieldworkers, and many survey organizations avoid probes altogether.

Closed questions can be attitudinal as well as factual. The alternatives offered are very much part of the question and should be reported as such, for they guide the respondent's answers. Suppose that we ask the question: 'Some people in this community have too much power. Who are they?' Left to their own thoughts, some respondents might think in terms of political parties, others in terms of criminals and racketeers, still others in terms of certain professional groups. Consider the different effects of offering either of the following lists of possible answers:

| Blacks | OR | newspaper owners |
|--------|----|------------------|
| Asians |    | landlords |
| Arabs  |    | the police |
| Chinese |   | big businessmen |

Each of these leads the respondents in a particular direction, which may or may not correspond with their own thoughts. Moreover, they are expected to express an opinion; very few people would insist on a response such as 'none of these'. Under these conditions, merely to report that X per cent of our sample stated that, say, landlords have too much power, would be grossly misleading unless the other alternatives offered to the respondents were also reported. On the other hand, the fact that we are directing the respondents' thoughts does not of itself make the question invalid or worthless. We may be particularly interested in comparing hostility toward landlords with hostility toward newspaper owners, and the pilot work may have shown us that these two groups are rarely mentioned in a free-response question. But we must be aware of what we are doing and make our choice suit the requirements of our research.

Incidentally, if we guide the respondents' thinking along particular lines in this way, it may also influence the answers to subsequent free-response questions (*contextual effects*).

Closed questions are easier and quicker to answer; they require no writing, and quantification is straightforward. This often means that more questions can be asked within a given length of time and that more can be accomplished with a given sum of money. Disadvantages of closed questions are the loss of spontaneity and expressiveness — we shall never know what the respondents said or thought of their own accord — and perhaps the introduction of bias by 'forcing' them to choose between given alternatives and by making them focus on alternatives that might not have occurred to them. Closed questions are often cruder and less subtle than open ones, although this is not necessarily so, and we do lose the opportunity to probe. There may also be some loss of rapport, if respondents become irritated because they feel that the choice of answers fails to do justice to their own ideas, so we ought to include an 'Other (please specify)' category.

Sometimes there may be good reasons for asking the same question both in open and in closed form. For instance, if we ask, 'what are some of the things that make a person move up in the world?' we shall get a pretty clear idea of the way in which the respondent thinks the social system works and the relative importance of several avenues of mobility, such as education, hard work, money, luck. We get a free, spontaneous sketch in the respondents' own language and containing their own ideas. This is most valuable, but it makes it difficult to compare one group of respondents with another. Also, we cannot be sure that such an impromptu sketch really contains all the factors that are important to the respondent. A momentary lapse, a feeling of reticence, or the inability to put ideas into words can cause the omission of significant points. Therefore, later in the interview we may ask the same question again, but this time we will produce a list which respondents may be asked to rate or rank (see Chapter 9), or from which they may be asked to choose the three most important factors. Having already obtained the spontaneous responses, there can now be little harm in introducing a set of ideas obtained in the pilot work, even though some of these might not have occurred to some of our respondents. By using a 'closed' approach we ensure that the results of several groups can readily be compared and that all respondents have considered the same universe of content before giving their replies.

Which type of question gives more valid results? When it comes to an enumeration of items of behaviour, such as newspapers or magazines read the previous week or programmes watched on television, the open type of question produces a lower yield than the prompt-list kind. This is partly due to temporary forgetfulness and partly to the fact that some papers or programmes have low memorability. Weeklies and monthlies are not recollected as well as dailies, when open and closed questions are compared. On the other hand, multiple-choice questions are subject to a small degree of spurious inflation; people confuse last week with some earlier week, or confound the names of programmes or publications. (Diary techniques (see Chapter 13) may give the most valid and precise estimates, but they cause some respondents to engage in duty viewing or duty reading.) It is clear, therefore, that caution must be exercised when we compare prompted results with those of free-response questions.

## SUMMING UP

Let us now try to compare the open type of question with the pre-coded or closed one (see Tables 7.1 and 7.2). Each has its advantages and disadvantages, and most surveys will deploy a mixture of the two.

Table 7.1. Open questions

| Advantages | Disadvantages |
|---|---|
| Freedom and spontaneity of the answers | Time-consuming |
| Opportunity to probe | In interviews: costly of interviewer time |
| Useful for testing hypotheses about ideas or awareness | Coding: very costly and slow to process, and may be unreliable |
| | Demand more effort from respondents |

Table 7.2. Closed questions

| Advantages | Disadvantages |
|---|---|
| Require little time | Loss of spontaneous responses |
| No extended writing | Bias in answer categories |
| Low costs | Sometimes too crude |
| Easy to process | May irritate respondents |
| Make group comparisons easy | |
| Useful for testing specific hypotheses | |
| Less interviewer training | |

## FIELD CODING VERSUS OFFICE CODING

Field coding is one of the functions of the interviewer (see Chapter 6). A question is read out to the respondent as an open question, and the answers are coded on the spot by the interviewer, by ticking or circling among the categories provided on the interview schedule (but these categories are *not read out* to the respondent). In a simple case, the respondent may be asked for country of birth; the interviewer listens to the answer, and then ticks the appropriate category, for example, Latin America, South West Asia, Eastern Europe and so on. This technique may cause considerable error, bias and loss of information, and needs to be used with discretion.

Note that this is not the same as asking a closed question: the respondent is not aware of the pre-coded categories which have been provided for the interviewer. Note also that the response itself is not recorded — it is lost, it cannot be retrieved for checking or correction, or for re-coding later. We are forced to rely completely on the skill and training of the interviewer, who must make instantaneous decisions (while preparing to ask the next question). It is easy to understand how errors, omissions and misclassifications may arise in the urgency of the moment, all the more so if the question demands a discursive answer (such as asking respondents what they think of keeping pets) — and the schedule contains a complex and subtle list of field-coding categories, such as 'make the house dirty', 'teaches children to take care of others', 'animals are better friends than people', 'too expensive', 'always good company, someone to talk to when lonely', all derived from the pilot work. Faced with such a very general question, most respondents will offer a considerable amount of comment, and it will be up to the interviewer to select and condense what seems most important, and tick or circle the most relevant categories. To do this well requires a great deal of briefing and training, and some bias and loss of information cannot be avoided.

By comparison, *office coding* (see Chapter 14) takes place under more tranquil circumstances. The responses will have been recorded in writing, the coding frame will have been derived in part from the hypotheses and the pilot work, and in part from a sample of responses obtained in the main fieldwork, so the categories are likely to be more appropriate. Any doubts or queries can be discussed with the coding supervisor; if necessary, re-coding can take place because the original responses are still available. Reliability checks can be conducted as desired. On the other hand, office coding is much more time-consuming than field coding, requires additional staff and facilities and adds greatly to the cost of the study.

## LOSS OF INFORMATION

The problem of loss of information, of condensation and compression, should be placed in perspective. The question is not how we can avoid loss of information but rather *at what point* we can best afford to lose information. At first sight, it may seem as if the open question causes the least loss. All the interviewer has to do is to ask the question and write down the reply. But already some loss of possibly relevant information has occurred: the facial expression and tone of voice of the respondent, the hesitations and reformulations, the little digressions and repetitions, not to mention large parts of a longer answer. All these will not be recorded, for most interviewers cannot use shorthand, and most interview schedules provide only a limited amount of space in which to write. Inevitably, even when attempting to get a complete record of an answer, the interviewer selects, and selection may reflect bias. Sometimes, she only hears what she expects or wants to hear. Nor is the interview situation the only point at which loss or distortion of information may occur. Further loss will take place when the questionnaire reaches the office and is coded, for the number of coding categories cannot be unlimited. At a still later stage, during the statistical analysis, more information loss may occur if coding categories have to be combined or when over-all scores or indices are calculated. Therefore, if we allow the respondent a free answer, we must ask ourselves at what stage the inevitable loss of some information will cause the least bias: during the interview itself, by asking for field coding; or later, if we ask for complete answers to be recorded first. The interviewer in the field generally has a better appreciation of what the respondent was trying to say, but the rushed circumstances of an interview may make it more difficult to fit the response immediately into the appropriate category. The coder in the office can ponder more carefully, but by then only the written record is available. The content of the question and the complexity of the answers will largely determine our decision, but the quality of our field force and of our coders will also have to be considered.

A further point in connection with loss of information is the question of relevance. Many surveys, regrettably, contain redundant or irrelevant questions, which have been put in for the sake of 'interest' but have no bearing on the problems at issue. Also inevitable are the many open questions that will — due to the freedom they give the respondent — produce a good deal of information that is not really relevant to the inquiry. In such instances, irrelevant information may be eliminated as early as possible by means of closed questions or field coding. However, we must be careful not to omit information that may be important as contextual or background material.

These comments about loss of information apply also to the use of closed or multiple-choice questions, with the added problem that the alternatives offered may bias the responses. All closed questions should start their careers as open ones, except those where certain alternatives are the only ones possible: the names of the candidates in an election, the daily newspapers on sale and so on. Careful pilot work (see Chapter 4) is very important here; only by trying out an open question in various forms and attempting to 'close' it afterwards, can we gain an appreciation of the loss of information involved. Also, the pilot work will provide us with a set of multiple choices that will really fit the range of answers to be expected and that will reduce, if not eliminate, the loss of information. Whether we choose to put the question in open or closed form will partly be decided by whether it is possible to provide a set of suitable multiple-choice answers. Surprisingly, the pilot work sometimes offers the possibility of closing quite subtle questions, thus avoiding the expense and possible distortion of coding.

## Selected readings

Sudman, Seymour and Bradburn, Norman M., 1983, *Asking Questions*, Jossey-Bass, San Francisco.
   A detailed, practical discussion of factual and attitudinal question design.

Hoinville, Gerald and Jowell, Roger, 1978, *Survey Research Practice*, Heinemann, London.

Converse, Jean M. and Presser, Stanley, 1988, *Survey Questions*, Sage, London.
   Some excellent practical advice from two experienced survey researchers.

Schwarz, N. and Strack, F., 1991, *Context Effects in Attitude Surveys: Applying Cognitive Theory in Social Research*, European Review of Social Psychology, Vol. 2, Wiley, Chichester.

Moss, L. and Goldstein, H., 1979, *The Recall Method in Social Surveys*, Studies in Education No. 9 (new series), University of London Institute of Education, London.

# 8
# QUESTION WORDING

---

WORKSHOP II: AN UNANSWERABLE QUESTION

What's wrong with the following question?

Do you approve or disapprove of people that go to football matches

1. Yes
2. No

Please comment on why:

Well, quite a lot. To begin with, it is a splendid example of an unanswerable question because the answer categories (Yes and No) are not appropriate to the form of the question. Perhaps 1. Approve; 2. Disapprove might be better. If a questionnaire or an interview schedule contained such a question, we might find that most respondents are perfectly willing to answer it. The problem lies with the *answer categories*: we cannot tell whether 'yes' means 'yes, I approve', or 'yes, I disapprove'. It might well be, to take the problem further, that many respondents would not even be aware of the ambiguity. Some might assume that '1' meant 'approve' and '2' meant 'disapprove'. To others, '1' might signify 'disapprove;', and '2' might indicate 'approve'. In any case, when it comes to the data-processing stage (see Chapter 14), how are we to know which means what? Thus, we have the unenviable situation in which the question is easily understood and answered by many, using one of the two alternatives — and yet we can do nothing with the responses because we don't know what they mean!

Now let us look at the question again. It is, of course, extremely crude and, as an attitude question, it does not even begin to do justice to the complexities of people's attitudes to football. It is also leading, in the sense that 'approve' precedes 'disapprove'. We might get quite different results if the question had been worded the other way around. It fails to offer any kind of middle position such as 'uncertain', or 'it depends'. Nor does it have a 'no answer' or 'not applicable' (N/A) position to cater for people who have had no experience of football matches (though some of them might, nevertheless, have opinions on the matter). For 'people that go' it might be better to have 'people who go' to football matches. The probe 'please comment on why' is also ungrammatical and might have been worded less curtly. Questions *will* sometimes need to be worded colloquially, but this should only be done with discretion and checked in the pilot work. Poor grammar may irritate some respondents and cause them to treat the whole questionnaire with contempt.

Let us also look at the *layout* of the question. For a start, there is no '?' after 'matches'. The probe at the end is located too far to the right and leaves no space for the requested comments (a few lines beneath the probe would help). But more important is the fact that no *instructions* have been given to the respondent. If, say, the 'yes' answer is chosen, then should it be ringed, or underlined, or given a 'tick' on the right, or on the left; or should the numeral '1' be ringed, or crossed — or what? Perhaps little response boxes should have been provided? To the left or to the right? These may seem pernickety criticisms, but failure to attend to such matters of layout can produce endless trouble at the data-processing stage and may cause much loss of information while the respondent, too, may at times be baffled. Such matters of presentation, instruction and layout should never be left to a typist. They require the systematic attention of an experienced researcher and should be part of the pilot work.

We now come to the most serious deficiency of this question and one that is not immediately apparent: what is the *purpose* of the question? The researcher who produced this question had been asked to design a simple, factual question to ascertain how often respondents attended football matches. Whatever we may think of the question we have just considered, in no way does it qualify as a factual question, nor will it allow us to infer how often the respondent goes to football matches! The question is, quite simply, inappropriate — it does not meet its stated purpose.

This problem is frequently encountered in questionnaire research, especially when we are asked to evaluate someone else's questionnaire. The questions may all seem quite reasonable, but without some knowledge of their purpose, that is of the research design and the questionnaire specification, we cannot state whether the questions will meet their objectives or not.

Some people still design questions as if the process of interviewing or of filling out a questionnaire were rather like unloading a ship, with every item of cargo labelled according to its contents and marked with a specific destination, so that it can be lifted out of the hold and set down as and when required. In reality, questioning people is more like trying to catch a particularly elusive fish, by casting different kinds of bait at different depths, without knowing what is going on beneath the surface! The function of a question in an interview schedule or questionnaire is to elicit a particular communication. We hope that our respondents have certain information, ideas or attitudes on the subject of our enquiry, and we want to get these from them with a minimum of distortion. If it were possible to do this without asking them any questions and without the respondent having to 'respond' that would be so much the better, for the questions we ask, the possible misunderstandings they provoke in the respondent, the choice or phrasing of the answers, and the recording procedures all have influences on the final result that we could well do without. Would that there were ways of looking into the minds of our respondents without having to ask them any questions at all!

However, for the time being we have to rely on some form of questioning, with all its attendant risks of bias and distortion, and on the fallibility of the respondent's own internal search processes. We must always remember that, however much we try to standardize our questioning procedures in order to create 'stimulus equivalence', there will always remain differences in the way in which questions are put to each respondent, and these may (or may not) have important influences on the results. Similarly, what is understood by the respondent and what starts off the 'process of responding' (see Chapter 6) will be different every time, while whatever is recorded or noted down from the respondent's answer will be selected and possibly biased. While our primary concern here is with question wording and design, we must not imagine that once questions go into the field they will constitute an absolutely standardized set of stimuli; nor will the responses reach us in 'pure' form. We must always bear in mind the difficulties the respondents may have in understanding the question and in forming an 'inner picture' of their own answers or reactions, and the degree to which these may be affected by inner curbs on private or self-incriminating information, by poor rapport, by the wish to maintain a social façade and by the response expectations which the question may suggest. In other words, it is difficult enough to obtain a relatively unbiased answer even from a willing and clear-headed respondent who has correctly understood what we are after, without making our task virtually impossible by setting off this 'train of responding' on the wrong track through poor question wording.

In a sense the problem of question wording is akin to a sampling process. We are sampling a particular universe of content in the respondent's mind: say, his or her attitude to Mexicans. We are not intending to obtain the whole of this universe of content but only enough of it to enable us to outline its salient features, general direction (positive or negative), its depth or intensity, and perhaps the presence or absence of specific beliefs. Our questions must be adequate for this sampling process; they must not be too one-sided, and they must make it easy for the respondent to answer fully. This means, first of all, that the focus and contents of the questions must be right; second, that the wording must be suitable; and third, that the context, sequence and response categories (if any) must help the respondent without unintentionally biasing the answers.

Each question also has a covert function: to motivate the respondent to continue to co-operate. A question that strikes respondents as rude, abstruse or inconsiderate may affect not only their reply to that particular question but also their attitude to the next few questions and to the survey as a whole. We must strive, therefore, to meet respondents half-way and to give and maintain the general feeling that they are being treated, not in an adversarial manner but with respect and consideration. We must never forget that the respondent is doing us a favour by taking time and trouble to answer our questions. In designing questionnaires it is not merely important for us also to look at things from the respondents' point of view; we must make them *feel* that we are doing so.

This can be done both by avoiding defects and by creating positives. Thus, we should avoid humiliating respondents, baffling them with terminology, patronizing them or making them feel in the wrong. Politeness helps: instead of staccato phrases such as 'marital status', 'length of residence' and so on, we should state such questions in full, not forgetting to say 'please', or 'would you mind'. Some questions will benefit from an introductory sentence or two by way of explanation, but we must neither talk down to respondents, nor talk over their heads by using technical terms or abbreviations. Keeping in mind that we shall probably be dealing with people of differing educational backgrounds, our questions should be clear to the less well educated while not seeming too vague or silly to the university graduates. The use of slang or street terminology, and the commission of deliberate grammatical errors in an effort to maintain rapport, requires the greatest care if misunderstandings or ambiguities are to be avoided.

Another way of maintaining the respondents' co-operation is by making the questionnaire and the answering process more *attractive*. In self-completion and mail questionnaires the layout, printing, choice of paper, spacing, answering directions and so forth should all be carefully considered, and piloted wherever possible. For example, the method of answering multiple-choice questions should be *consistent* throughout: either circling, ticking or underlining, and always either on the right or on the left. Open-ended questions, which require thought and writing on the part of the respondent, should be kept to a minimum. Since reading is so much quicker than writing, every effort should be made to save the respondent time and trouble by the appropriate use of lines, insets, different fonts, colours, headings, boxes and so forth.

It happens too often that, once the final draft of a questionnaire has been assembled, the general layout and appearance are left to a subordinate. This is a short-sighted practice. The person in charge of the study should personally review the over-all appearance and layout from the respondent's point of view and smooth out any remaining rough edges. One good way of doing this, in addition to pilot work, is to read the questions out aloud to see if they 'flow'.

Another hidden attribute of every question is its link with the conceptual framework of the study. There should always be a clear answer to queries such as 'Why are we asking this question? What is it doing here? How do we intend to use the responses?' In the course of much pilot work and revision it is only too easy to lose sight of the purpose of some of our questions and — as we saw in Workshop II above — to be left with questions that no longer meet their aims or, conversely and even more importantly, with aims that are no longer being met by appropriate questions. There should be continual discussion and reference-back to the specification document.

## WORKSHOP III: QUESTION CONTENT AND PURPOSE

As we have seen in the preceding chapter, we should have a questionnaire plan or outline giving the sequence of all the major and minor issues with which we are concerned. We must now decide, for each issue in turn, how thoroughly we will 'sample' it. Here, for instance, is a question from a survey dealing with dental services:

Have you heard of fluoridation of water supplies?

Yes .............................. 1
No ................................. 2
Don't know ............. 3

*If 'yes'*
How do you feel about fluoridation of water supplies?
Do you approve? ............................ 4
Do you disapprove? ...................... 5
Are you undecided? ...................... 6

*Probe all answers*
Why do you say this?

There were no other questions concerning fluoridation in the survey. Presumably the researchers concerned regarded this as an interesting but relatively unimportant issue on which they did not propose to spend a great deal of interviewing time. Or perhaps the pilot work had shown that very few people had ever heard about fluoridation. At any rate, the survey team must have made some decisions. First, they decided not to leave out this issue. Second, they decided to sample it only briefly. Third, they decided that one multiple-choice attitude question, preceded by a filter question, and followed by a 'why' probe, would suffice. They must have been tempted to ask more questions, perhaps designed to find out what information the respondent had on this subject. They might have considered the possibility of making the questions more specific, for instance by asking about the fluoridation of 'your' water supply. They did not assume that everyone would know what fluoridation is or would have a clearly defined attitude toward it, but they did not find it necessary to offer an explanation of this technical term before asking questions about it. The questions were kept as short as possible, using mostly familiar words.

Do we know why the question was asked at all? Very often problems of question construction make us realize that we are not clear enough in our own minds as to what the questions are about. Very likely, for instance, in the example just given, the main interest centred upon the reasons against fluoridation. If, instead, the main issue had been the amount of information possessed by respondents about the effects of fluoridation, different questions would have been asked.

Greater precision concerning the purpose of the questions will sometimes make it easier to avoid ambiguity in question wording. Consider, for instance, the meaning of the word 'read' in a factual question such as: 'Which magazines have you read in the past seven days?' Should 'read' here be regarded as synonymous with 'bought'? Or with 'bought and also read'? Or with 'borrowed but read'? Or could it include 'borrowed but only glanced at'? 'Picked up in a waiting room'? What about 'borrowed in order to read just one article'? What about exchanges of magazines? Annual subscriptions? 'Just looked at the pictures?'

It is obvious that we must stop thinking of the meaning of words in dictionary terms and instead ask ourselves what we are trying to find out. What are we going to do with the data when we have collected them? This will make it easier to decide which of many possible meanings of a word we wish to employ. For instance, if we were concerned with magazine sales or with personal expenditure, we might alter the question to: 'Which magazines have you bought in the past seven days?' However, if we were concerned with exposure to magazine advertising, a very broad definition of 'read' would be appropriate. It all depends on the purpose of the question.

# Factual questions

The adjective 'factual' is here used to distinguish this type of question from others, thought to be more difficult to design, that may deal with knowledge, motives or attitudes. However, factual questions are just as likely to present the research worker with awkward problems. Consider, for instance, the use of the word 'bought' (see above, Workshop III). Does this include buying for others? Does it include buying on credit? Does it include things paid for by and bought on behalf of someone else? Does it include presents?

Mealtimes are another example. In England, the word 'tea' as in the question: 'When do you usually have tea?' refers to a light meal (which may or may not include tea as a beverage) taken at almost any time after about three-thirty in the afternoon. Some families have 'tea' in the mid-afternoon. Others refer to the main evening meal as 'tea'. Some give their children 'tea' when they come home from school and then give them 'supper' later. In other families a meal given to children is called 'tea' but the same meal taken later by adults is called 'dinner'. Different customs exist in different social classes and in different parts of the country. The institution of 'high tea' further complicates matters. To say, therefore, that something happened 'at tea-time', or to hear that product X is always taken with one's tea, requires elucidation. When drawing up a questionnaire we tend to forget how circumscribed our own experience is, and we take for granted that whatever the word means to us, it will mean the same to everyone else.

In a housing survey it was found that many respondents reported fewer bedrooms than their houses actually contained. They simply did not think of a study, a playroom, a sewing room or a guest room as 'bedrooms' in the sense intended by the survey. Similarly, in a survey concerning coffee, many respondents failed to mention powdered or 'instant' coffee because they did not think of these products as 'coffee'. The last two examples point, first of all, to the need for definitions — both for the sake of the researcher and to help the respondent. 'Is the child afraid of one or more animals?' we may ask a sample of mothers, and add, 'that is, ordinary domestic animals, not lions, tigers etc.' More subtly, both examples also point to differences in frame of reference that may exist between researcher and respondent. A typical problem word might be 'family', a term which has widely different meanings depending on one's frame of reference. Or, to give another example, in a study of saving, insurance policies were often not mentioned: some people don't think of them as a form of saving.

We must not assume that people have the information that we seek. They may be reluctant to admit that they do not know or, being anxious to please, they may guess. We must avoid giving the impression that respondents ought to know. Such questions as 'what was the name of the author?' (of a recently borrowed library book) and 'what brand was it?' (of consumer goods) would be better worded: 'Can you remember the author's name?' and 'Can you remember what brand it was?' Or we may offer a face-saving phrase such as: 'For many people, life is so hectic nowadays that they often cannot remember small details from one week to the next.' If in doubt, and especially if technical terms or difficult words are part of the question, a filter question can be helpful. Recall is often poor even on quite important issues. For instance, it has been shown that parents are quite inaccurate in their recall of details about child-rearing practices and early developmental progress even if their children are only three years old, and the parents were part of a special panel study. In consumer surveys, to go back more than two or three days can be extremely misleading.

It is generally best to keep questions short — preferably not more than twenty words. If more than two or three alternative answers are possible, a show card should be offered on which the respondents can read the multiple choices; they should not be asked to keep too much in their minds. Every effort should be made to use familiar words. Even so, some of the simplest words can become problem words if they are too vague — words such as: *you, about, all, any, few, government, fair*.

If we offer the respondent a list or a set of multiple-choice answers, we run the risk that these may become subject to *ordinal biases*. For instance, when asked for a numerical estimate, people tend to choose a figure near the average or near the middle of a series. In a list of opinions or ideas, those at the beginning and those at the end may have a greater drawing power. Even when only two possible answers are offered, there may be a tendency to choose the latter. To overcome these problems, some investigators randomize the order so that each interviewer or group of interviewers (or each subsample of respondents in a mail inquiry) has the answers in a different order. Others use the *split-ballot* technique in pilot work, dividing the sample into two or more equivalent parts and presenting each part with a different answer sequence which makes it possible to measure the ordinal bias and to make allowance for it. Though such procedures are expensive and demanding, they should certainly be applied to questions which recur from one survey to another; only by drawing general conclusions from split-ballot and similar pretests in many investigations will we be able to arrive at a more precise principle that will enable us to minimize these biases.

The problems of the *double-barrelled* and *double-negative* questions are mentioned by many writers. 'Have you suffered from headaches or sickness lately?' (Would a positive answer refer to headaches, to sickness or to both?) 'Would you rather not use a nonmedicated shampoo?' (What does a negative answer mean here?) 'Do you know if the deadline has expired yet?' (A negative answer might mean that the respondent does not know, or knows the deadline has not yet expired.) Such confusing questions should be avoided.

Another type of question to avoid is the hypothetical one, whereby respondents are asked to make predictions about their own future behaviour or reactions. Planners and decision-makers often ask for hypothetical questions to be included in a survey, for example about a new road development, a new type of magazine, a new keyboard facility. Hypothetical questions of the 'suppose . . .' variety may reveal an intention or a state of mind at the time of asking, but have often been found to be poor predictors of people's future reactions or behaviour, especially to something they have not previously experienced.

As we have seen in the preceding chapter, respondents are influenced not only by question wording but also by the context of the question, the position of a response on a list of multiple choices, by the time available for responding, by postal versus interview method-of-questioning, by open- versus closed-question format and so on.

Making some rough generalizations we can sum up these effects, at least on factual questions, as follows:

Table 8.1. Effects of question format

| | Open | | Closed | |
|---|---|---|---|---|
| | interview | postal survey | interview | postal survey |
| Effects on: | | | | |
| (1) ordinal and contextual influences | fixed | variable | fixed | variable |
| (2) memory and periodical behaviour | lower frequencies | higher frequencies | lower frequencies | much higher frequencies |
| (3) social desirability bias | much more | less | more | less |

Thus, for recall items including periodical behaviour, closed questions and checklists generally yield higher frequencies than open-ended questions, especially so in postal questionnaires. Conversely, open-ended questions are generally more sensitive to social desirability bias, especially in an interview situation.

---

WORKSHOP IV: FACTUAL QUESTIONS

Let us start with what may at first appear to be a simple, factual question: the possession of a videotape recorder or VTR set. A first attempt at the phrasing of this question might read:

*Do you have a videotape recorder?*

The question as phrased will probably be found to be too ambiguous. The word 'you' is notoriously troublesome in questionnaire construction: who is the 'you' in this question? Is it the respondent, the whole family, the parent (if a child is answering), the landlord (if a lodger or tenant is answering) etc.? And the word 'have': what does that mean? Does it mean own, have on rental or buying on credit? And since 'do' seems to indicate the present, what does someone answer whose recorder is away being repaired? Let us rephrase the question:

*Is there a video recorder in the house where you live?*

This is beginning to sound a little offputting; in any case, what if you live in a flat or a bungalow? And if you live in a large house that has been sub-divided and a family upstairs rents a recorder but you, yourself, do not have one, how do you answer the question? Should we abandon the word 'house' and, instead, ask about 'your family'? That will create yet other problems: if grandmother (who is a member of what you think of as your 'family') lives far away but owns a VTR, do you answer 'Yes'?

When dealing with problems of this kind, it is often helpful to go back to fundamentals and inquire: why are we asking this question? What are we going to do with it? It may then transpire that we are interested only in *rented* VTRs or only in the question of *access* and not of ownership, and that will simplify the wording of the question. Likewise, as we saw in an earlier example, the word 'read' is open to many different interpretations, but we can narrow it down once we know whether, say, we are interested in the sales of and subscriptions to a magazine or in a person's 'exposure' to its advertising contents. A dictionary is no help in such situations: we first need to get the issues clearer in our mind and then do the pilot work.

## Can we lay down some rules?

It would be nice to think that question wording could be carried out in accordance with a short set of simple rules or principles. Many authors have tried to do this and have, at best, succeeded only in stating the obvious or in listing pitfalls to be avoided. But question design is also a creative process, emerging from brainstorming sessions, adaptation of earlier questionnaires, listening to the tapes of depth interviews or group discussions, and to the contributions of experienced interviewers and helpful pilot-work respondents. However, here are some basic rules:

*Length* — questions should not be too long; they should not contain sentences of more than, say, twenty words. If a longer sentence is needed, then it should be broken up, so that there will be several shorter sentences, each dealing with only one or two tasks or concepts. It is often helpful, especially when starting a new section of the questionnaire or interview, to have some introductory sentences which will give the respondent time to adjust and will slow down the interviewer. For example:

Now I am going to show you a number of descriptions of acts which are crimes. For each one I want you to indicate how serious it is. Of course, in one sense all of these acts are serious because they are all crimes, but they are not all equally serious. For example, most people consider murder to be a more serious crime than shoplifting. What I want to know is how serious you *personally* think each crime is, and not what the law says or how the police or the courts would act, or what anyone else would say. You indicate this by giving each crime a score from one to eleven. For example . . .

and so on, followed by thirty descriptions of crimes which the respondent has to rate according to seriousness.

*Avoid double-barrelled questions* — 'Do you own a bicycle or a motorbike?'; 'Do you think it is a good idea for children to learn German and Spanish at school?' In such instances, the respondents are left in a quandary if they want to say 'yes' to one part of the question but 'no' to the other and, if they say 'yes', we do not know whether they mean 'yes' to both, or to one (and if so, which one).

*Avoid proverbs* and other popular sayings, especially when measuring attitudes, for such sayings tend to provoke unthinking agreement. Instead, try to make the respondent think afresh about the issue by putting it in other words.

*Avoid double negatives* — for example 'Cremation of the dead should not be allowed', followed by agree/disagree. Here, the 'disagree' response is likely to create difficulties because respondents who favour cremation have to engage in a double negative (that is, they do *not* agree that cremation should *not* be allowed). Try to put the issue in a positive way.

*Don't Know and Not Applicable* categories are too often left out, both in factual and in non-factual questions. If we ask 'Who is the owner of the home in which you live?' we should allow for the possibility that the respondent does not know, or that there are legal complications (because a house sale is in progress or because the landlord has died recently). Similarly, in the case of an opinion question such as 'Do you think, on the whole, that the government is doing a good job?', a 'don't know' response makes good sense. It has been argued that some people give a 'don't know' response in order to avoid thinking or committing themselves; but do we really want to obtain 'forced' responses which are virtually meaningless? Indeed, sometimes 'don't know' responses can be very important. For example, before mounting a health education campaign dealing with sickle-cell anaemia, should we not first find out how many people have heard of it or know what it is?

*Use simple words, avoid acronyms, abbreviations, jargon and technical terms* or else explain them. Respondents who do not know what the terms mean may feel intimidated and may guess or pretend to know the answers. There is an old story about a survey dealing with the Metallic Metals Company; many respondents had strong views on its labour relations, the quality of its products, the dangers to the environment and so forth when, in fact, the company did not exist! *You* may know what UNCTAD is or does, or the meaning of HIV, or BMW, or benzodiazepines or an exhaust catalyst, but do not assume that your respondents do. When in doubt, use pilot work.

*Beware the dangers of alternative usage* — this applies to even the simplest words which 'could not possibly be misunderstood'. As we have seen (see Chapter 6), there is much disagreement as to the meaning of the word 'week'. A child's age may be given as his age *next* birthday. To some people, the word 'dinner' indicates an evening meal, but to others it means a cooked meal, as in 'Usually I give him his dinner at lunch-time'. Words such as 'read' or 'tea' have many meanings. In some nutritional surveys it was found necessary to send the interviewers out with plastic models and pictures of certain foods or meals in order to avoid ambiguities.

*Some words are notorious for their ambiguity* and are best avoided or else defined; for example, the words 'you' and 'have' as in 'do you have a car?' Is this a question of ownership or of use or availability? What if the respondent has the use of the family car but does not own it? Who is this 'you' — the respondent, the household, the entire family or the firm? And what if the respondent has access to two cars? Other notoriously ambiguous words are 'family', 'bought' and 'neighbourhood' — every survey agency will have its own list of dangerous words and associated horror stories.

*All closed questions should start their lives as open ones* so that the answer categories will be based as much as possible on pilot work (see Chapter 4). Even then, always consider the inclusion of an 'Other (please specify)' category.

*Beware 'leading' questions* — 'When did you last borrow a video tape?' It assumes (a) that all respondents have access to a videotape player; (b) that they generally borrow tapes; and (c) that it is not done by someone else on their behalf.

Similarly, 'how often do you take a foreign holiday?', or 'do you generally buy the brand that is least damaging to the environment?'

*Beware loaded words* such as democratic, black, free, healthy, natural, regular, unfaithful, modern.

*Don't over-tax the respondents' memories* by asking questions such as 'in the past thirteen weeks, which of the following branded goods have you purchased?' A period of thirteen weeks may be thought of as a 'quarter' by planners and economists but it is meaningless to most respondents and, in any case, far too long for the recall of relatively trivial items of shopping. For recurrent items of behaviour it is risky to go back more than a few days. For more important events such as major acquisitions, periods in hospital, or being mugged, the respondent has first to be taken through the preceding few months with the aid of 'anchoring dates' such as public holidays, family birthdays, school holidays and the like, followed by an attempt to locate the event(s) in question in an individual time frame.

*Pay due attention to detail* such as layout, show cards and prompts (note especially the danger of overlapping categories, as with 'age 25–30', '30–35'), the wording of probes (follow-on questions), routing or skip-to instructions and even question numbering. Your data processors will not thank you if, for example, you start every new section of the questionnaire with question (1)!

It is worth reiterating that questionnaires are not created by following rules such as the ones above. Each questionnaire is unique (even if it is mostly composed of questions that have been asked before but which are now being applied in a new context) and presents its own special problems. The way to check on the wording of questions and, where necessary, to make improvements, is through the pilot work. In the later stages of the pilot work, if doubts still persist regarding the best way to word a particular question, we may need to use the split ballot technique: we obtain two or more comparable samples and administer our question(s) in alternative forms to see the effects of different forms of wording (see page 61).

# Special problems

### QUESTIONS ON PERIODICAL BEHAVIOUR

Typical of the many areas that can cause difficulties is the problem of measuring *items of recurrent behaviour* such as going to church, drinking whisky, visiting the cinema or going to the dentist. We shall pass over problems of definition of terms, boasting, and the vagaries of memory, and concentrate purely on the study of periodical behaviour sampling. We could start by asking:

*Did you go to the dentist/cinema/etc. yesterday?*

This raises a behaviour sampling problem. We want to end up with some statistic about the typical frequency of this kind of behaviour. Are we assuming that, if we had a large and representative sample, the percentage we obtain would be typical of this kind of behaviour? Not, surely, if all our respondents were interviewed on the same day, for different days of the week probably would show a different pattern.

Shall we ask:

*Have you been to the dentist/cinema etc. within the past week?*

We have already seen how different the definitions of the word 'week' can be; we now ask: how do we know that this past week is representative of all the weeks in the year? Perhaps we happen to be interviewing during a holiday period or in the coldest part of winter. So should we then extend the period, and ask over the past fortnight/the past quarter? That produces problems of recall inaccuracies. It would be better if we could stick, perhaps, to one week but spread the interviewing period over the best part of a year to allow for seasonal variations, though this may not be practical.

Another approach is often used:

*When did you last . . . ?*

If the behaviour is at all infrequent, this obviously creates memory problems. It also assumes that the 'last' occasion was somehow typical of habitual behaviour patterns so that we can arrive at a meaningful average; but is this true? On a mail questionnaire this question is also open to anchoring problems: responses such as 'I remember, it was the day after our neighbour's dog got run over' or 'when my brother and his wife came to stay with us' — which cannot be converted into days or weeks. (The alternative to this wording, 'how long ago is it since you last . . . ?' requires, in effect, *two* tasks of the respondents: fixing the occasion and doing a subtraction. Even if they get the former right, they may err in the latter respect.)

Or shall we dispense with all these time (and behaviour) sampling problems and simply ask:

*How often do you usually . . . ?*

Here we have asked the respondents to do the time sampling for us. We shall never know how far back in time they have gone in order to do their calculations, how many exceptions they allowed themselves before they recognized that a change in a habitual pattern had taken place, and what the word 'usually' means to them.

Yet another procedure that is sometimes used is to request respondents to keep a *diary* of particular kinds of behaviour over a period of, say, a fortnight. Apart from the expense and the problems of low response and delay in filling-in, we also find that people then start to engage more often in the behaviour they are asked to note, in order 'to have something to write'.

So we see that it is really not at all easy to 'get at' such 'simple, factual' material

— even with co-operative respondents, on unembarrassing topics, where a 'true' answer can be thought to exist and to be known to the respondent. Imagine the difficulties involved in finding out from a rather resistant wife what her husband's pay is — a touchy topic to which she may not even know the 'true' answer! (See Workshop V, p. 133.)

CLASSIFICATION QUESTIONS

*Classification* questions are a special type of factual question that asks about age, sex, marital status, income, education, occupation, family size and so on. These are of special importance in stratifying the sample and tend to recur from survey to survey; for both these reasons they are worth special attention. As we have already seen, unless there is some special reason to do otherwise (for instance, in quota sampling), such questions should come right at the end of the questionnaire, by which time we can hope to have convinced the respondent that the inquiry is genuine. Even then, we ought to use an introductory phrase, such as: 'now, to help us classify your answers statistically, may I ask you a few questions about yourself and your family?' With these questions, too, we must be particularly rigorous in excluding unnecessary detail. As mentioned before, there is no need to ask for the respondent's exact age, when all we really want to know is whether he or she is over or under forty-five. Or, to take another typical question, do we really need to know whether the respondent is separated, divorced or widowed? And must we go into quite so much detail with regard to household composition?

One need hardly stress that in gathering this kind of information, in particular, definitions are important, both for the interviewer and for the respondent. There must be clear instructions concerning stepchildren, mortgaged house ownership, part-time occupations and so forth.

The purpose of asking for the occupation of the main breadwinner is usually in order to grade it on some scale of social class or social prestige. People often give vague job identifications such as: clerk, engineer, businessman, farmer, secretary, civil servant; these terms require further information before they can be classified. One can ask supplementary questions or probe in various ways, but the information needed for each job is different. We have found, however, that the following two questions keep the 'unclassifiables' to well under 10 per cent: (1) 'What is the name of your job?' (2) 'Please describe as carefully as possible the work that you do.' Moreover, even in written questionnaires directed to husbands (about their wives' jobs) or to schoolchildren (about their fathers' occupations), enough information will usually be obtained to make classification possible.

It has been suggested that wives and children often do not know what their husbands or fathers do for a living. Nowadays, in Western societies, this is fairly rare and likely to be due to special circumstances. (Questions about earnings, though, are apt to be far less successful!) Even children of below-average intelligence can give job descriptions that are very clear and free of humbug. Here are some examples:

A constable in the M borough police. My father sees that shop doors are closed at night and gives advice to passing motorists.

Electrician. He cuts the light off of people who do not pay the bill.

A steel erector. My father erects steel and iron for buildings, factories and coal mines. He mostly works a lot of feet up.

District manager of a brewery. He looks after a certain number of public houses; he sees the right kind of people go into them and settles any disputes which may arise.

Barber. He cuts men's hair and small boys too and big boys.

Wives, on the other hand, will sometimes introduce prestige distortion, describing the husband as an 'engineer' when he is a garage mechanic, as a 'civil servant' when he is a street cleaner, or as 'manager' when he is a stall holder. Similarly, some husbands may exaggerate or trivialize the importance of their wives' job.

Occupational classification systems can present many difficulties. How, for example, should students be classified? What should be done about actors, some of whom may be more famous and prestigious than others? Or about farmers with different acreages? And how should a married couple be jointly classified when both partners are in full-time occupations that are classified differently? Also, in many countries such classification systems fail to cater for women. If they are married and running the home, they are often classified according to their husbands' job, and if they are in full-time work, the classification schemes often fail to provide for their occupations.

In general, classifying questions tend to be predominantly sociodemographic, but for some inquiries a psychological classification would be more relevant — for example, a score on a general-knowledge test, a do-it-yourself score, a romanticism score, a radicalism score or a frustration-resistance score.

---

## WORKSHOP V: SOME FIRST ATTEMPTS AT WORDING A CLASSIFICATION QUESTION

Below are listed ten attempts made some years ago by a group of British graduates to phrase a factual question, asking married women about their husbands' income. When reading these attempts, several points stand out. First, most of the questions are too blunt: there seems to be far too little awareness that this is a sensitive area, which may require a carefully worded introductory sentence or two, as well as some explanation of the reasons for asking the question. Second, it soon becomes obvious that the term 'income' is too vague and that the data will not be suitable for comparisons unless we specify whether, say, tax and other items have been deducted or not. Third, the types or sources of income need to be considered: weekly wages/ annual dividends/pension/freelance professional earnings? In turn, this suggests that the question needs to take account of wide variations in people's economic circumstances.

A. Is your husband
   — employed
   — unemployed
   What is your husband's average gross income per week?
   What is your husband's average net income per week?

B. Does your husband tell you what his income is?
   How much does your husband earn
   (a) each week?
   (b) in a year?
   Where did you get that information from?

C. Do you know what your legal husband's full income is?
   If so, do you know approx how much tax he pays?
   If so, do you know approximately how many other deductions
   he pays from his income, i.e. life insurance, house mortgages
   Do you know if he has other sources of income besides his
   job(s), i.e. share dividends, interest?

D. Housewives have difficulties in deciding how well their husbands are paid. Please tick the figure nearest to *your* husband's
   income and also tick whether you think it is satisfactory or not

   | | | |
   |---:|---|---|
   | 0 – | 3,999 | |
   | 4,000 – | 5,999 | |
   | 6,000 – | 7,999 | £ per year |
   | 8,000 – | 9,999 | |
   | 10,000 – | 11,999 | |
   | – | | |
   | – | | |
   | – | | |
   | 100,000 – | 100,499 | |

   Satisfactory          Unsatisfactory

E. Do you know how much your husband earns per week?

   Yes ☐    No ☐

   If your answer to question one was 'yes', could you now tick the
   appropriate box

   over £200 p.w.        ☐

   £110–199 p.w.         ☐

   £85–109 p.w.          ☐

   £60–84 p.w.           ☐

   £25–59 p.w.           ☐

   less than £25 p.w.    ☐

F. Please mark one box to show the annual income earned by your
   husband for 19 . . . When calculating income include wages/

salary, pensions and interest earned from bonds, shares and bank deposits

- ☐ No income
- ☐ less than £3,000
- ☐ £3,000 to £3,999
- ☐ £4,000 to £5,999
- ☐ £6,000 to £7,999
- ☐ £8,000 to £9,999
- ☐ £10,000 to £11,999
- ☐ £12,000 to £19,999
- ☐ £20,000 or more

G. Are you married? . . . . . . Yes/No
   If yes, does your husband have a source of income?
   
   Yes/No
   
   If yes, could you indicate how much your husband's income is each week
   
   . . . . . . . . . Pounds

H. Is your husband in receipt of an income? (irrespective of source)
   Yes/No
   If 'yes', do you know the amount of that income?
   Into which category would you place your husband's income?

   (a) up to £3,000 p.a.
   (b) £3,001–£6,000 p.a.
   (c) £6,001–£9,000 p.a.
   (d) £9,001–£12,000 p.a.
   (e) £12,001–£15,000 p.a.
   (f) more than £15,001 p.a.
       (please specify to within the nearest thousand pounds)

   Can you be more specific about the actual amount of your husband's income?

J. Does your husband earn
      less than £2,999 p.a.
      £3,000–£5,999
      £6,000–£8,999
      £9,000–£11,999
      £12,000–£14,999
      £15,000–£18,999
      More than £19,000?

K. How much money does your husband earn each month
   (use the preceding 12 months)

| | |
|---|---|
| zero ☐ | 1,001£–1,500£ ☐ |
| 30£–150£ ☐ | over 1,500£ ☐ |
| 151£–250£ ☐ | |
| 251£–500£ ☐ | |
| 501£–750£ ☐ | |
| 751£–1,000£ ☐ | |

The different question writers have different sets of assumptions and expectations, which are expressed in the ways they have worded their questions. These, in turn, force us to the most important point of all: why are we asking this question? What kinds of detail or degrees of precision are required? What use will be made of these data in the statistical analysis? If, for example, the purpose of the question is merely to divide a large sample into some three or four income categories, then it may suffice to offer the respondents a pre-coded question, using the limits of those income categories. But then again, the question may be the first in a series of questions concerned with savings and insurance, for which a good deal of detail may be needed about financial circumstances and income sources. As we have said before, question design has to be *integrated* with the survey's objectives and with the planned analysis. Pilot work will show how well the questions meet their aims.

Several other points of difference are worth commenting on, some of which you may have noted already. These students have clearly been warned against the dangers of having overlapping categories (for example £60–90 pw; £90–120 pw — the sum of £90 pw could go into either category) and gaps in category ranges (for example £60–90 pw followed by £100–120 pw); both of these are mistakes frequently made by beginners. Such gaps or overlaps would be obvious in numerical categories such as we have in this example, but would be far less obvious (yet equally troublesome) when we offer categories of, say, favourite types of reading matter. Example C, with its legalistic emphasis, nevertheless fails to ascertain any actual amount! Several attempts seem not to distinguish between income and earnings, and one (F) includes in 'earned income' those sources which are usually regarded as 'unearned' — this would obviously have to be sorted out and respondents would need to be instructed in writing, or else the interviewers would have to be briefed on this point. Some attempts (B, D) ask additional questions which may, or may not, be relevant. Husbands with irregular earnings (for example shopkeepers, professionals, salesmen) are poorly catered for, while the period covered by the question (*which* week, month or year?) is usually left indeterminate. (But note that F specifies a particular year and in a way so does K — though very few women could answer either question readily, even if their husbands are on regular incomes. K has the added disadvantage that, if the survey extends over many months, the twelve-month periods will not be comparable.)

None of the attempts really caters for the 'don't know' respondent, nor for the wife who only has an approximate idea; whenever we design a set of pre-coded responses we should always consider including a 'don't know' category. Routing instructions (for example 'if Yes, go to Question 29') are generally poor or absent, and not many attempts include precise answering instructions. Thus, in the case of 'Yes/No', what is the respondent supposed to do: ring? tick? cross out? underline? This can lead to confusion and unreliability when we come to use the data. Boxes are sometimes offered on the left, sometimes on the right, if at all. The approach of B and D is much gentler to the respondent than the bluntness of J. Evidently, the range of expected annual incomes differs widely (up to more than £100,000 a year!), while there are even preferences for the location of the £ sign (see K).

## LEADING QUESTIONS AND LOADED WORDS

Leading questions are so worded that they suggest what the answer should be or indicate the questioner's own point of view. Examples might be: 'You haven't forgotten to brush your shoes today, have you?' 'Most people nowadays believe in racial integration; do you?' 'Are you against giving too much power to the trade unions?' Generally, factual questions are less sensitive to 'leading' than attitudinal questions.

A 'loaded' word or phrase is one which is emotionally coloured and suggests an automatic feeling of approval or disapproval: for instance Nazi, bosses, interference, motherly, starvation, strike-breakers, British, intelligent, Socialist. Respondents are reacting not so much to the issue posed by the question as to the loaded phrase itself. Split-ballot trials will show considerable differences in the distribution of answers to a question using the phrase 'bosses' compared to one using 'leaders' — both are loaded phrases but loaded in different directions. Once we are aware of the problem, we can exercise our ingenuity in trying to find a less loaded term, but the trouble is that we often fail to realize the danger. Words and phrases that are more or less neutral in one context or to one group of people may be highly loaded in another context or to another group, for instance the term 'birth control'.

Here are some items from a questionnaire dealing with various aspects of job choice. Each item consisted of a pair of choices, only one of which could be selected by the respondent; this technique sometimes helps to overcome problems of loading. In the pilot work, strenuous efforts were made to reduce or eliminate loaded phrases:

(1)  A job in which you do a lot of    OR    A job where, once you have learned it,
     hard thinking                            you always know how to do it

(2)  Where somebody helps you    OR    Where you have to decide for yourself
     to decide what is to be done          how to do things

(3)  Where the pay is not very   OR   Where the pay is high, but you don't get
      high, but you get a pension             a pension when you retire
      when you retire

(4)  Where you work with your   OR   Where you work with your hands
      brain

The results showed that the items were, in fact, fairly evenly balanced in pairs
and that the respondents were expressing genuine preferences and were not
merely reacting to such loaded words as 'routine jobs', 'independence', 'security',
or 'manual job'.

Much inadvertent leading comes from a failure to state alternatives. The
possible alternatives are merely implied or assumed to be so obvious as not to
require stating; for instance, 'do you prefer being examined by a doctor of your
own sex?' instead of 'would you rather be examined by a male or by a female
doctor, or doesn't it matter which?' However, sometimes a question which is
leading because it fails to state alternatives becomes less so when the alternatives
are given or read aloud to the respondent as multiple choices; for example, 'how
much trouble have teeth and gums been to you throughout life?' (This is leading,
in that it assumes that the respondent's teeth or gums *have* been troublesome
and fails to suggest a negative alternative or to use a neutral filter question.) It
is followed by (1) 'A lot of trouble.' (2) 'Some trouble.' (3) 'Little trouble.' (4) 'No
trouble.' One cannot help feeling that the wording of the question still suggests
to the respondents that they must have had some dental troubles, but if the four
alternative answers were shown or read to them, they might well see that a
negative answer was acceptable, which would reduce the leading effects of the
question. As we have seen earlier, any multiple-choice answers offered to the
respondent become part of the question and should be reported as such.

Leading bias often creeps in when we are formulating probes and follow-up
or 'why'-questions; for example, 'how often do you go to your local supermarket?' followed by 'why don't you go more often?' — which suggests that the
respondent ought to go more frequently. If the formulation of probes is left
entirely to the interviewer, serious biases may result that will never be brought
to light. For instance, a question about voting intent might be followed by the
instruction, 'probe for importance of education policy, housing development,
and defence programme.' It is almost impossible to imagine how one could
phrase, on the spur of the moment, probes and follow-up questions that would
allow the respondents to indicate awareness of these issues and their bearing on
voting intentions without at the same time leading them. Even if we phrase a
neutral 'why'-question it may become a source of bias if different interviewers
read it out differently. In the well-known example: *'Why do you say that?'* (see
Payne, 1951) the stress can be placed on any of the five words it contains with
very different effects!

## SOCIAL DESIRABILITY BIAS

We should always be aware that many factual questions are loaded with
prestige. Some people will claim that they read more than they do, bathe more
often than is strictly true and fill more pipes from an ounce of tobacco than

would seem likely. They claim that they buy new tyres for their car when in fact they buy retreads; they deny reading certain Sunday newspapers of dubious repute; the clothes that they buy are expensive; they would seem to make donations to charity with great frequency and to visit museums almost every week! There is no simple answer to this problem, but, in addition to being aware that it exists, there are two general measures that may help. First, use filter questions, or word the main question in such a way that a low-prestige answer is equally possible; thus, instead of 'have you read any of the following magazines within the last seven days?', perhaps try 'have you had time to read any magazines at all within the past seven days?' The latter creates a more permissive situation for the non-reader. Second, brief interviewers to impress repeatedly on the respondents that *accuracy* is the prime requirement and that a negative response is just as good as a positive response.

As we have noted, classification questions such as occupation, income, education and even age lend themselves very readily to prestige bias, and we must be particularly on our guard with these. However, not all cases of overclaim are due to prestige factors. In some cases, especially where there is a long list of possible answers, respondents are too eager to please; they want to give the interviewer 'something' to put down so as not to disappoint her. Nor is overclaiming the only likely source of error; in respect of the consumption of certain goods, such as alcohol or tobacco, we often find persistent *under*statement.

People are reluctant to admit lack of knowledge. In straightforward knowledge questions we generally get a higher percentage of 'don't know' responses than in opinion questions dealing with the same issues. This is because people are reluctant to admit that they do not really understand the question or are unfamiliar with its contents. We must always keep this possibility in mind (if possible, sift out those people for whom the question is meaningless) and not assume that 'everyone' will know and will have an opinion on the subject of our inquiry. Similarly, if we start questions with phrases such as 'doctors say that ...', 'as you know ...', 'many people nowadays ...', 'research has shown ...' or with the mention of names of well-known personalities, we are inviting prestige bias.

People do not like to think of themselves as fools, and it is best to avoid questions that require the admission of foolish or reprehensible behaviour. Not many mothers would, for instance, reply affirmatively to the question: 'Are there any foods or drinks that your children have that you know are bad for their health?' In a survey dealing with oranges, greengrocers were asked whether customers often requested their advice on which brand to buy. This was followed by the question, 'and do they mostly act on your advice?' Not surprisingly, 98 per cent said 'yes.' If the question does contain some low-prestige alternatives, we should offer respondents a respectable 'out' — an opportunity to say that they intended to read the prestigous book mentioned (but had not actually done so) or that they had been too busy to become acquainted with certain political issues.

It has sometimes been found that the mode of questioning has an effect on the degree of social desirability bias: face-to-face methods such as interviews are more likely to provoke respondents to put themselves in a better light than anonymous self-completion or postal questionnaires — but this is not always the case. Similarly, telephone interviews may, or may not, be less prone to this kind of bias. Pilot work will help to overcome this problem, for example with the aid of the split-ballot technique (see page 61 and table 8.1).

QUESTIONS ON SENSITIVE TOPICS

It is not always obvious whether or not a topic is 'sensitive' to our respondents or to a particular sub-sample of respondents, and so we must define 'sensitivity' in subjective terms: a topic is sensitive if some respondents find it embarrassing and show reluctance to answer questions about it. A question can be embarrassing for several reasons: because it asks about socially 'taboo' topics (child abuse in the course of religious rites); because it asks for information about socially disapproved behaviour (extra-marital sex); because it could lead to self-incriminating answers (drug-taking); because it deals with matters which the respondent regards as highly personal or private (inheritance); or because it may put the respondent in a bad light (questions about dropping litter). Social investigators sometimes forget how sensitive some people can be about certain topics.

Such issues are really a special case of the social desirability bias discussed above, but they may require more drastic measures, since it seems unlikely that a nondirective question or a set of forced choices will suffice to obtain honest and complete answers. It is also worth mentioning that some of the embarrassment may be in the interviewers rather than in the respondents. There is the risk that some interviewers, fearing a pained or hostile reaction from the respondent, will find themselves sounding remorseful and making excuses instead of asking a plainly worded question. Pilot work will often show that respondents are perfectly willing to answer straightforwardly phrased questions about topics such as incontinence, a criminal record, abortions, smuggling, hit-and-run accidents, drug taking, and excessive alcohol consumption once they are convinced that the information is relevant, that it will be treated confidentially (and preferably anonymously) and that the interviewer is non-judgemental.

In this context there is a place, in the hands of the skilled investigator, for the deliberately leading question such as: 'How old were you when you first started to masturbate?' This puts the onus of denial on the respondents, the intention is to make them feel that this behaviour is quite common and well known and can be discussed in a matter-of-fact way. Great care, however, has to be taken in interpreting the results.

Another way of overcoming denial tendencies is to hand the respondent a show-card on which the responses to a sensitive question have been given numbers. All the respondent has to do is to call out the numbers of the applicable items or responses; this is considered to be less embarrassing than putting such 'admissions' into words. Belson (1975) has developed a very specialized technique whereby young delinquents can report self-incriminating information with the aid of a set of cards and a ballot box, so that the interviewer has no knowledge of the responses until after the respondent has left.

In milder instances of socially disapproved or private issues, merely offering the respondents a number of prepared categories can be sufficient. If such matters are printed on an official-looking form, respondents realize that they are not alone in engaging in this behaviour or in having these problems, and so these matters become more admissible. For instance, few mothers would admit that one of their sons was a thief, but such admissions become easier when they are offered the following alternatives: (1) 'Never takes anything that belongs to someone else'; (2) 'Has helped himself to someone else's things at least once or twice (including taking things belonging to other members of the family)'; (3) 'Has stolen things on several occasions.' Altogether, the creation of a permissive atmosphere in the questionnaire as a whole, together with a guarantee of anonymity, can do much to overcome this problem.

### QUESTIONNAIRES IN SCHOOLS (see also Chapter 7)

Both open and closed questions are also widely used in research in schools. Children tend to write much more slowly than they can read and they are often taught to start every answer by repeating the question. Thus: Q 'Why do policemen wear a uniform?' A 'Policemen wear a uniform because people would not know they were policemen if they didn't.' From the researcher's point of view this is a time-wasting practice and so we would be well advised, when using open-ended questions in schools, to print both the question *and the start of the answer* so that the child merely has to finish the sentence: 'They wear a uniform because . . .'

Altogether, survey work with school children requires additional care in piloting and fieldwork, and a different emphasis on some aspects. For example, interviewing children in a school presents not only the additional problems of overcoming the children's possible fear of strangers and getting some genuine and valid responses; but also there are the logistics of lessons and break-times to cope with, and after the third or fourth interview every child in the school will have heard a (probably inaccurate) version of the questions being asked! Group-administered questionnaires can overcome some of these problems, at least with children above the age of nine or ten in Britain. Even then, very great care is required in the pilot stages, and it is best to have several fieldworkers present in each classroom to help with spelling, to answer questions and to distribute and collect questionnaires. Bearing these precautions in mind, and with a promise of confidentiality, excellent results can be obtained quite rapidly from large numbers of school children with the use of pre-coded questionnaires and many other closed techniques.

### INSTRUCTIONS (SEE ALSO CHAPTER 6)

Every questionnaire will contain instructions to the respondent, while interview schedules will in addition contain instructions to the interviewer.

On self-administered questionnaires, instructions to the respondent will usually include answering procedures ('Tick one'; 'Put a circle or ring around the number of the item you prefer'; 'Underline all that apply to you') and routing directions or skip-to instructions ('If NO, go on to question 26'; 'If you do *not* have access to a car, please turn to page 3'). Sometimes such instructions are more complex; for instance, respondents may be asked to choose the three most important items from a list and then place these three in order of importance by numbering them 1 (for most important), 2, 3 (for least important). Or an answering key may be provided (2 = very important; 1 = fairly important; 0 = not important at all) which is to be applied to a whole list of items or questions. Due attention must be given to layout, so that the respondent is never in doubt as to how or where a response should be put, how many responses are required, and does not have to zig-zag across the page to find a response box. Serious loss of data can result from ambiguous or inadequate answering instructions which lead respondents to tick several boxes when only one is required, or cross out responses which should be ringed or underlined. All too often questionnaires are sent out with too few answering instructions so that the returns are difficult to process.

Self-completion questionnaires often contain *introductory paragraphs*. These help to set the scene and guide the respondent towards the answering procedures. For example:

*Reasons for drinking*
People give very different reasons for drinking alcoholic drinks. Below are listed 23 reasons given by different people for their drinking. Please look at each one carefully and say whether you think this is a very important reason, a fairly important reason or not an important reason at all by circling the appropriate number.

It doesn't matter at all how often you drink alcoholic drinks. Even if you drink only very rarely, please say what are the important reasons for your drinking when you do. It doesn't matter how many reasons you say are important, you may put as many or as few as you like as being very important or fairly important.'

Such instructions should always be piloted (for example, will respondents be familiar with the word 'appropriate'?).

Quite commonly, *definitions* will be offered, for example 'Often (at least once a week); Occasionally (once or twice a month); Hardly ever, or Never'. Or, 'in counting the number of rooms in your home, include the kitchen but do not count the bathroom and lavatory'. Since respondents generally know how many rooms there are in their home, many of them may well ignore this proffered definition and give a response in line with their own ideas.

Thus, even where a definition is provided, this does not necessarily mean that all respondents will use it! Sometimes definitions become part of the question: 'Do you have some form of denture (removable false teeth or tooth)?' Some research workers like to include instructions to take a break during a self-completion questionnaire, such as: 'You are doing very well; now, take off five minutes to do something else, and then return for the remaining questions.' The main function of all these instructions is to compensate for the absence of an interviewer. They aim at clarifying questions and procedures and at maintaining motivation.

In the case of *interview schedules* the procedural directions, routing instructions, definitions etc. will usually be printed on the schedule itself, and these can be quite complex at times (see Chapter 6). In addition it is essential that interviewers receive a detailed briefing, followed by some training sessions with a new schedule. (We saw earlier that sometimes even interviewers don't agree about the meaning of the word 'week'!) Interviewers should be alerted to possible remaining ambiguities in the wording of some of the questions and should be briefed on ways of overcoming these. Particular attention should be paid to the wording of probes and to methods of verbatim recording.

In addition to a review of definitions and procedural instructions, the briefing of interviewers will generally cover specific matters such as the selection of respondents, number of callbacks, the use of ratings, the distribution of product samples, the handling of show-cards, details of recording techniques and cross-checking procedures, as well as more general instructions about rapport, probing, introducing the purpose of the survey and so on. Many research organizations train their own interviewers and have standard handbooks that cover all routine interviewer problems and procedures.

When computer-assisted interviews are conducted, instructions, definitions and routing directives will usually appear on the screen in the particular code used by the system. Much the same applies to telephone interviewing.

## Non-factual questions
## (see also Workshops II and III, pp. 119 and 123)

Up to now we have been chiefly concerned with the wording of 'factual' questions. We should now note that there are *other types of questions*, each with their own problems of wording. For example, in addition to factual questions, we may distinguish opinion or belief questions, awareness questions, knowledge questions and attitude measures as well as questions about stereotypes, social representations and brand images. Factual questions might seem the easiest to design; after all, they are questions to which there must be a 'true' answer! However, as we have already seen, simple factual questions are often neither simple nor factual.

These other types of question deal essentially with aspects of the state of mind of the respondent and are therefore more difficult to verify and produce less reliable results. They are also much more sensitive to linguistic, situational and other biases. The distinction between factual and non-factual questions has important implications for questionnaire construction. In the case of factual questions we can, quite often, rely on just a handful of questions (about periodical behaviour, ownership, mass media participation, family expenditure and so forth), suitably piloted. An attitude, percept or belief is, however, likely to be more *complex* and multi-faceted than an issue of fact, and so it has to be approached from a number of different angles. There is no external way of *verifying* the answers and the questions and responses are generally much more *sensitive to bias* by wording, by response sets, by leading, by prestige and by contextual effects. For all these reasons, which have been confirmed many times by experimental findings, it is most unwise to rely on single (or just a few) questions when dealing with non-factual topics and we need to develop multiple questions. What we mean precisely by multiple questions will become clearer in the following chapters, when we come to the issue of *scaling*.

Consider, for instance, the attitudinal question:

Do you think that in general the police are fair in their dealings with people?
Yes/No/DK

On its own it is virtually meaningless. The word 'fair' is extremely ambiguous and will mean different things to different people; some of the other words are equally vague, for example 'in general', 'people', 'dealing' and even 'the police' (the local force? the traffic police on motorways? or the police nationwide?). Our hypothetically reasonable respondent ought to refuse to answer such a question on the grounds that it is far too vague, that it asks for impossible generalizations and that brief response categories such as 'Yes' or 'No' fail to do justice to the complex images in the respondent's mind. We might get a quite different distribution of responses if we had substituted words such as 'impartial' or 'honest' for the word 'fair', thus demonstrating how sensitive the question is to the actual choice of words. All three words are strongly 'loaded' which means that the results might be biased in favour of the police, so that this survey would give a misleading impression of people's attitudes to the police; and the entire question is 'leading' because it fails to state alternatives. In addition, such a question is highly susceptible to other biases. Has the respondent recently been burgled, or been given a speeding ticket? Is the interviewer married to a policeman?

Nevertheless people seem able to answer such questions, and survey researchers continue to use the single-question approach to measure attitudes. This is probably because it is simply not possible to develop multiple-item scales for everything. Scaling is an expensive and time-consuming approach to measurement. Within the limitations imposed upon them, many survey workers would reserve the effort of scaling for some of the key attitudinal or other non-factual variables, and would measure the less important variables by means of single questions — less reliable, more open to bias but better than nothing.

## Reliability and validity of questions

As pointed out at the beginning of this chapter, we should think of questions as *measures*; each question has a job to do, and that job is the measurement of a particular variable, as laid down in the questionnaire specification. In trying to assess how well each question, or group of questions, does its job, we shall need to use the concepts of *reliability* and *validity*. These are concepts derived from measurement theory and from psychometrics, where they have long been used in the statistical construction of psychological tests such as measures of aptitude or tests of mathematical ability. (See Chapter 9.)

Reliability and Validity are technical terms, and we have to distinguish between them. This is not always easy because each can have several meanings and can be measured statistically in several ways, while to some extent the two terms also overlap and are interconnected. Validity, for example, may be concerned with the factual here-and-now (this is called *concurrent* validity — is the respondent telling us the truth?); but it might also be concerned with forecasting (will the respondent really buy a new car next year?). This is called *predictive* validity. Let us first of all discuss the general ideas behind these two concepts.

Reliability refers to the purity and consistency of a measure, to repeatability, to the probability of obtaining the same results again if the measure were to be duplicated. Validity, on the other hand, tells us whether the question, item or score measures what it is supposed to measure. For instance, a clock is supposed to measure 'true' time and to do so continuously. If it were to show the wrong time, we would say that it was invalid. If it were sometimes slow and sometimes fast, we would call it unreliable. It is possible to have a measure that is highly reliable yet of poor validity; for instance, a clock that is precisely eighteen minutes fast consistently. The degree of reliability (consistency) sets limits to the degree of validity possible: validity cannot rise above a certain point if the measure is inconsistent to some degree. On the other hand, if we find that a measure has excellent validity, then it must also be reliable. We often have to face these issues in the development of psychological tests, such as measures of intelligence or personality.

By purifying a test we can make it highly reliable so that repeated administrations of the test will give very similar results, but how can we be sure that it really does measure what it sets out to measure? In principle, the answer to this question is not so very difficult if a *criterion* can be obtained. A criterion is an independent measure of the same variable to which the results of our test or questionnaire can be compared. For instance, if our test is a measure of intelligence, then it ought, at the very least, to discriminate between younger and older children. If it is a measure of neuroticism, then we may compare it with psychiatric assessments or show that it distinguishes between 'normals' and patients under treatment in a psychiatric hospital. However, many criteria that might be suggested are themselves unreliable and of doubtful validity; for instance, teachers' ratings or psychiatric diagnoses. Moreover, in a great many instances criteria are not available — a 'true' answer simply does not exist.

### RELIABILITY AND VALIDITY OF *FACTUAL* QUESTIONS

Let us consider, first of all, the somewhat easier case where some sort of criterion is available or could be obtained. Typically, this is most likely to apply to the realm of 'factual' questions. If we ask the respondent: 'How often have you been to the theatre in the last two weeks?' presumably a 'true' answer does exist and could be found — if we were able to take sufficient time and trouble. Therefore, in similar cases, asking the same questions again and again ought to yield consistent results (show high reliability).

To ascertain *reliability* in the case of factual questions we should plan to have a number of internal checks. To avoid annoying the respondent we will probably refrain from asking the same question repeatedly in the same way, but in spite of variations in technique we expect a co-operative respondent to be consistent in factual matters; an inconsistency would point to faults in question wording, serial or contextual effects, or other sources of error. For instance, having asked the above question about theatre attendance, we might, at a later stage, offer the respondent a list of activities such as: 'Could you tell me if you have visited any of the following within the past two weeks: art gallery, theatre, museum, cinema, zoo, exhibition?' followed by a question about frequency. Another form of internal check would be the introduction of phony items such as a non-existent brand name or radio programme; endorsement of such items would suggest guessing or carelessness on the part of the respondents. A more elaborate form of check is the split ballot, which requires that we split our sample into two or more equivalent subsamples and give each of them a slightly different form of wording. (The true answer is usually taken to be the average of the subsamples.) It is probably true to say that internal checks would not detect a respondent who was really determined to mislead.

In some surveys, it is possible to re-interview respondents, for example in panel studies, but we must be careful not to leave too much time between the original question and its repetition, or true changes in behaviour may occur in the meantime.

To ascertain the *validity* of factual questions, a variety of techniques is employed, usually known as external checks, where a second, independent source of information is required, though not often available. Sometimes records can be used to check on certain points of information, for instance hospital records, factory-absenteeism figures, criminal records. Sometimes, the total survey results can be compared with census figures, retail audits or manufacturers' production records, though these may themselves be open to doubt. Occasionally, we may be tempted to use two informants to ascertain the same facts or events, for instance husband and wife (with regard to marital relations or joint financial transactions), parent and teacher (with regard to a child's behaviour). However, there are many reasons why two observers or two participants in the same action may yet report differently on it, so that in cases of disagreement one cannot say who is right and whether or not the criterion is more valid. This applies particularly to different observers reporting on the same individual.

Occasionally, some of the respondents to a mail inquiry are interviewed on the assumption that the interview is more valid (see page 56). In other studies quality checks are made; this means that some of the respondents who have been interviewed in the usual way are re-interviewed by a highly trained group of senior interviewers. This is especially worthwhile where a large number of temporary interviewers has been engaged. The second interviewer is usually allowed more freedom and can often track down a discrepancy, for instance to a simple mistake in recording. In certain instances — in a hospital or supermarket — it is possible to check on the responses with the aid of observations.

We have so far considered mainly the type of questions that deal with facts or behaviour in the past or present. Our test of validity is to compare the respondent's account with what 'actually happened' — assuming that we can verify that by some other means. However, some surveys, such as election polls, are intended to be predictive, and in that case the criterion of validity may be a specified event in the future. This illustrates that a measure can have more than one purpose and thus more than one validity. A pre-election poll may be valid in the descriptive sense if it gives us a true picture of the present political allegiances of the respondents, yet it may show poor validity as a predictor of the popular vote three weeks later. The vote may be affected by any number of variables such as a press campaign, the weather, a political scandal or a domestic disagreement, and therefore a valid description of the present may not be a good predictor of the future. People are often poor predictors of their own behaviour, so that statements of intent often lack validity when compared with subsequent events, though they may well have been valid as statements of hopes, wishes and aspirations. Altogether, we do not often find a one-to-one relationship between attitudes or opinions, and behaviour.

Generally, in the case of factual questions we have the special difficulty that we are not really trying to measure something 'inside' the respondent, but rather that we are using the respondent as an *informant*, observer or reporter about some past event, current status or possession, or future behaviour. The respondent is used as a repository of 'facts', an intermediary between the researcher and the required information. Our skills in question wording can only get us half-way, at best: from the researcher to the respondent and back. The second half — from the respondent to the required information and back — is entirely up to the respondent's ability and willingness to retrieve. When we bear in mind that much of the required information, such as a routine purchasing decision, is of low salience to the respondent and is unlikely to be well remembered, then it seems almost inevitable that major problems of factual validity will remain.

### RELIABILITY AND VALIDITY OF *ATTITUDE* QUESTIONS

Since attitudinal questions are more sensitive than factual questions to changes in wording, context, emphasis and so on, it becomes almost impossible to assess reliability by 'asking the same question in another form'. It will no longer be the same question. For this reason, we should not rely on single questions when we come to measure those attitudes that are most important to our study; we should have sets of questions or attitude scales (see Chapters 9 and 11). Sets of questions are more reliable than single opinion items; they give more consistent results, mainly because vagaries of question wording will probably apply only to particular items, and thus any bias may cancel out, whereas the underlying attitude will be common to all the items in a set or scale. The reliability of a scale can be assessed in the usual way by a correlation coefficient (see page 159) without having to ask the same questions twice.

The assumption underlying these procedures is that there is such a thing as a 'true' attitude, which is also relatively stable, just as in the case of factual questions there are 'true' facts or events. However, since an attitude is more complex than, say, a respondent's method of travelling to work, it is unlikely that a single question will reflect it adequately. Also, the chances are that too much will depend on the actual question form and wording, on context, emphasis and mood of the moment, so that the results will be a compound of the (relatively stable) attitude and of these other (momentary) determinants — hence the poor reliability of the single-attitude question. By using SETS of questions, provided they all relate to the same attitude, we maximize the more stable components while reducing the instability due to particular items, emphasis, mood changes and so on. None of the previously mentioned internal checks can readily be applied to opinion or attitude questions, but split ballots are sometimes used.

It may be helpful to introduce a distinction at this point between relative and absolute consistency. If we need to know what percentage of our sample habitually travels to work by car, then this will be an absolute figure, give or take a margin of error. If we ask the question more than once, we can reasonably hope to get a similar and consistent result. However, if we wish to know what percentage of our sample has a positive attitude to saving, a great deal will depend on how the question is phrased. At what point, on a continuum from unfavourable through neutral to favourable, do we begin to include a respondent in the proportion of those with a positive attitude to saving? What kinds of saving do we ask about? How strong is the respondent's attitude? Suppose we have developed four different techniques (say, a free-response question about the best ways to take care of the future, a checklist, an attitude scale and a projective device using pictures), and that after due consideration of the results we apply a cut-off point to each technique, with the result that we get four different estimates of the proportion of respondents with a positive attitude to saving. Do we now say that the questions are unreliable? Not necessarily. We have to state, of course, that the answer will depend on how one defines and measures positive attitude to saving, but we may find that all four methods intercorrelate quite well, and that group differences between subsamples are consistent. Thus, we may never be able to say what proportion of our sample has a positive attitude to saving in absolute terms, but we may well be in a position to show that the *relative* differences, such as those between middle class and working class, or between older and younger respondents, are in the same direction, irrespective of the technique used, and consistently show that older people, or middle-class people, have a more positive attitude to saving. This type of consistency is well worth stressing, especially if it applies to techniques that apparently tap different 'levels' (see Chapter 12).

The chief difficulty in assessing the *validity* of attitude questions is the lack of criteria. What we need are groups of people with known attitude characteristics (criterion groups), so that we can see whether or not our questions can discriminate among them. Occasionally, such groups can be found, for example the adherents of a particular political party or the members of a particular church, but unfortunately people join groups for many different motives, and there is no reason to suppose that group membership as a reflection of an inner attitude is any more valid than a set of attitude questions. At best, there will only be a rough correspondence between the two indicators. We cannot necessarily predict behaviour from attitudes; nor are attitudes readily inferred from behaviour with any validity, nor is behaviour necessarily a more valid expression of an attitude than a verbal statement. The links between attitudes and behaviour are complex, and group membership may or may not be a valid criterion of a particular attitude. These issues are taken further in Chapter 9.

RESUMÉ

Inadequate question wording and questionnaire construction are not the only causes of poor attitudinal validity. Since so much error and bias arises from irregularities in procedures, changes in wording, faulty recording and failure to maintain rapport we must do all we can in the spheres of interviewer selection, training, briefing and supervision.

However, we also have to admit to a number of theoretical inadequacies. When we sometimes despair about the use of language as a tool for measuring or at least uncovering awareness, attitudes, percepts and belief systems, it is mainly because we do not yet know *why* questions that look so similar actually produce such very different sets of results, or how we can predict contextual effects on a question, or in what ways we can ensure that respondents will all use the same frame of reference in answering an attitude question. We lack strong theories about attitudinal constructs in people's minds, theories that might help us to understand what happens when we use language to trigger or activate such constructs in order to reach and measure them. Without such theories, all our tradecraft leaves us floundering, so that the problem of attitudinal validity remains one of the most difficult in social research and one to which an adequate solution is not yet in sight.

## Selected readings

Schuman, Howard and Presser, Stanley, 1981, *Questions and Answers in Attitude Surveys*, Academic Press, New York.

Belson, William A., 1981 *The Design and Understanding of Survey Questions*, Gower, Farnborough, Hampshire.
A detailed study of question wording and sources of misunderstandings.

Sudman, Seymour and Bradburn, Norman M., 1983, *Asking Questions*, Jossey-Bass, San Francisco.

Converse, Jean M. and Presser, Stanley, 1988, *Survey Questions*, Sage, London.
Some excellent practical advice from two experienced survey researchers.

Belson, William A., 1975, *Juvenile Theft: the Causal Factors*, Harper and Row, London.

Payne, S.L., 1951, *The Art of Asking Questions*, Princeton University Press, Princeton.
An entertaining and still highly relevant book on question wording, with many examples.

### OCCUPATIONAL GRADING

Goldthorpe, J.H. and Hope, K., 1974, *Social Grading of Occupations*, Oxford University Press, London.
Examples and commentary on the status classification of occupations.

### PROBLEMS OF RECALL

Belson, William A., 1962, *Studies in Readership*, Business Publications Ltd, London.

Robbins, Lillian C., 1963, 'The accuracy of parental recall of aspects of child development and of child-rearing practices', *Journal of Abnormal and Social Psychology*, **LXVI**, 261–70.

# 9
# SOME BASIC
# MEASUREMENT THEORY

## Non-factual questions

As we have seen towards the end of the preceding chapter, there are serious objections to the use of single questions to measure such non-factual topics as awareness, percepts, social representations, brand images, opinions, beliefs, attitudes, values and stereotypes. Such issues are usually more complex than questions of fact; they have to do with states of mind, rather than with behaviour or with events in the outside world, and are therefore difficult to measure and to validate; they are generally multi-faceted and have to be approached from several directions; above all, single questions dealing with such sensitive topics are much more open to bias and unreliability due to wording, question format and contextual effects. It is not unusual to find that responses by the same group of subjects to two virtually identical items differ by as much as 20 per cent or more, and we have no guiding principles by which to predict how respondents will react to various forms of wording of what is basically the same question.

Opinion researchers who commonly rely on single attitudinal questions (say, whether or not the prime minister is doing 'a good job') are taking considerable risks. However, they would argue that these risks can be minimized by using the same question in successive surveys, so that an analysis of trends-over-time becomes possible — whatever the question 'means' to respondents. They might also argue that, since they have used this question many times in other surveys, they know a good deal about its properties and correlates with other variables. Also, something depends on what we want to know: perhaps all we need is a quick popularity snapshot of the prime minister, rather than an in-depth analysis of what people mean by 'a good job' and how this percept has been influenced by recent events.

But to the researcher who is hoping to rely on single questions about people's attitudes to their doctor, to animal rights, to immigrants, to Green policies or to a certain brand of washing-up liquid, the unreliability of such single questions will pose a serious problem. As we have indicated, if these variables are at all important to the study, then the way forward may well be through the multiple-question or *scaling* approach. To explain what is meant by scaling, we shall first have to consider some aspects of basic measurement theory; after that we shall look at the linear scaling model in its classical form and then see how this model has been applied to the field of opinion and attitude measurement, and to the measurement of concepts, awareness and other subjective variables.

## The linear scaling model

### WHAT IS A MEASURE?

Let us start with a simple example. Suppose that we wish to know the length of a table; we may take a metal foot-rule, hold it against the longer edge of the table, and read off the answer: say, thirty-eight inches. This measure has, in principle, two components: the 'true' measure and a second component which we may call 'error'. We shall, for the moment, ignore the kinds of errors-of-observation and notation that may arise because we have been a little careless or imprecise, and draw attention to the fact that we have used a *metal* foot-rule. Since we know that metal expands or contracts under different temperature conditions, part of our answer is not a measure of length but a measure of temperature. Since, at this point, we are not interested in temperature, we regard this aspect of the measure as 'error' — in the sense that it is irrelevant to what we need.

In this diagrammatic form, any measure could be represented as shown in Figure 9.1.

Figure 9.1.

The oval shape represents the reading or observation; the true measure is that part of the reading which we want — it is an indicator of an attribute of something or someone, for example length, musical ability, blood pressure; error is that part of the measure which we don't want. The wavy line between the two parts indicates that we are rarely certain about the exact size or location of these components. The diagram is an abstraction; it shows that we know our measure is 'impure' or 'contaminated' but not always by how much or in what way.

### EARLY SCALES IN THE NATURAL SCIENCES

You might argue at this point that the degree of contraction or expansion in a metal foot-rule under normal everyday conditions is very slight and that consequently the amount of error introduced in our measure is negligible — or that we should have used a wooden ruler in the first place! The issue which this example illustrates is, however, a general one which is present in every kind of science.

Let us, by way of another familiar example, look at the ordinary household or medical thermometer. Once again, the measure which we seek is an abstraction: an indicator or an attribute of something or someone. 'Temperature', as such, is an abstraction, a scientific concept invented by humans; we try to measure it by observing the rise or fall of a column of mercury in a glass tube. We cannot say that the position of the mercury *is* the temperature; the mercury is only mercury. We are interested in the position of the mercury in the tube because we have made certain arrangements which will enable us to use it as an indicator of the state of someone (for example, a patient) or something (for example, the air in a greenhouse). These 'arrangements' are important. Some of them have been designed to minimize the kind of error-component which we discussed above. For example, if there were air in the tube above the mercury, then this would make it harder for the mercury to rise, the more so as the mercury nears the top of the tube, and so we would have been measuring both temperature and — to an increasing degree — air pressure. This error would, in other words, have taken the form of a systematic or correlated *bias* because the error gets greater as the readings increase, and vice versa. The error is therefore confounded, rather than uncorrelated or random.

By drawing the air out of the tube above the mercury we usually manage to eliminate this error to a large extent but not altogether. We note further that the mercury moves in a tube made of glass; as the temperature rises, the glass expands, the tube widens and the mercury rises more slowly — another 'confounded' error. We trust and assume that the walls of the tube are smooth and straight on the inside, for if they were uneven this would introduce a random error, and if they were, say, closer together at the top of the tube than at the bottom, we would have another 'confounded' error — though one that works in the opposite direction — yielding an over-estimate rather than an under-estimate.

Another important arrangement with thermometers is that they have a *scale*. In the eighteenth century, when the thermometer was being invented and improved by men such as Celsius, Réaumur and Fahrenheit, it seemed a good idea to think of temperature as a straight line, a linear dimension, and to divide this line into equal intervals (grouped according to the decimal system). The idea of using equal units along a continuum probably came from measures of distance such as miles or leagues, or perhaps from ells or yards or from measures of weight such as pounds or kilograms. However, two difficulties arose: one was the question of the size of the unit or interval, the other was the problem of finding a suitable starting point. After all, with distance, or length, or weight, a zero- or nil-point at the outset seems obvious — but can one think of any point as 'nil temperature', as no temperature at all? There was also the desire to invent something that could be used in a practical way both in the laboratory and in everyday life, covering the *range* of temperatures that were of interest at that time — the idea of measuring the temperature of the sun must have seemed quite out of the question! And so each of the inventors of the thermometer chose a zero-point and a top-of-the-scale point that seemed convenient for range and were thought to be 'anchored in Nature', be it the freezing and boiling points of water, or the temperature of the average healthy adult human body. Fahrenheit actually started his scale at the lowest point he could reach by using a mixture of ice, water and sal ammoniac or salt — this must have seemed like 'absolute zero' at the time. Celsius originally proposed that the steaming point of water should be zero and the freezing point 100°! Réaumur used a spirit thermometer, not a mercury one; instead of taking two chosen points and dividing the distance between them into 100 equal intervals, he considered the rate of expansion of the original volume of spirit as the temperature rose. He defined 1° as an expansion of one-thousandth of the original spirit volume; this led to a scale of eighty degrees or intervals between the freezing and boiling points of water. Today, in the physics laboratory, these early primitive methods of thermometry have been left far behind, but they serve to illustrate the basic problems of measurement that all sciences have to overcome.

We can ask, for example: is it right to think of changes in temperature as lying 'in a straight line'? This is the question of *linearity*, and the answer will lie in a better scientific understanding of the molecular processes that produce changes in temperature in different materials. We can also ask: is it possible to measure 'pure temperature' and nothing else, not even the expansion of the glass? This is the question of *uni-dimensionality* and is closely linked to the earlier notions of error. We know now that water boils at different temperatures at different heights, in accordance with barometric pressures. This, and many similar problems, such as the expansion rate of mercury or of certain gases, raises the problem of *standardization*: how can we be sure that any two or more thermometers will show the same readings under the same conditions? Then there is the question of consistency: can we rely on our thermometer to perform over and over again in the same way, yielding *reliable* readings which we can trust?

Another complex issue is the question of the *units of measurement*. As we have seen, three different inventors produced degrees of different sizes, which may cause us perhaps nothing worse than some irritating conversion problems, but we may ask whether at certain points — say, when something melts, or freezes, or burns, or dies — are there not also *qualitative*, as well as quantitative, differences in temperature? Or, to put it another way, are the units really interchangeable all along the scale? Are, say, the five degrees from 0° to 5°C (which cover thawing) the 'same' as the five degrees from 95° to 100°C (which cover the boiling of water at sea-level pressure)? And what about the beginning and the end, the top and bottom points? Do all measures require a *zero-point*? A maximum? Can they have negative readings? Last but not least, how can we be sure that there is a precise and consistent relationship between the abstract quality we call 'temperature' and the readings we obtain from mercury moving in a capillary tube? This is the problem of *validity* to which we shall have repeated occasions to return.

To sum up then: one answer to the question 'what is a measure?' is to describe the properties of a scale. A scale must satisfy the conditions of linearity and uni-dimensionality; it must be reliable (consistent); it must have units of measurement (not necessarily equal ones); these units will, if possible, be interchangeable; the scale needs some 'anchoring points' obtained through standardization or in relation to fixed, observable events, to give meaning to the scores; and most particularly, the scale must be valid, in the sense that it measures the attribute it sets out to measure. Perhaps surprisingly, the simple yardstick did satisfy all these requirements, once it was standardized (such a standard can still be viewed on the outside wall of the Greenwich observatory).

The basic notions of measurement are not hard to grasp, but they become more difficult to achieve as we move from the natural sciences, through the biological and medical sciences, to the behavioural and social sciences.

## THE PROPERTIES OF A SCALE OF INTELLIGENCE

In the light of these requirements, let us look at a test of intelligence. Will it satisfy the conditions of linearity and uni-dimensionality? Some complex statistical techniques will have to be used to establish this for the particular scale in question, for we are no longer dealing with a simple foot-rule. (Even if uni-dimensionality can be established, how happy are we to think of a complex set of qualities, such as intelligence, in terms of a straight line?) Will it be reliable, in the sense that repeated administration of the test will yield virtually the same results? Leaving practical problems aside, the answer will probably be 'Yes', since we have fairly accurate techniques for assessing the degree of reliability. Will it have units of measurement, and, if so, will they be equal and interchangeable? Here we are on more difficult ground. The test is likely to yield a score in terms of points, which are treated as if they are units of equal interval which are interchangeable in many cases, but this remains a questionable issue.

Can the scores be given meaning, by relating the individual's score to some anchoring points and/or standardized ranges? To this, the answer will be 'Yes' — any test will be published together with its norms for various age groups, ability groups etc., and frequently the test scores will be converted into an Intelligent Quotient which offers, not a zero-point but a mid-point, the 'average' of 100 IQ. It is, however, highly debatable whether IQ points or intervals are equal units and whether they are interchangeable, though they are frequently treated as such.

Finally, will the test be valid? Will it really measure 'intelligence'? The first and crude answer to this will be 'Yes' because the test will have been correlated with some earlier, well-established IQ tests. But this merely moves the problem a stage further back, for how do we know whether *those* tests, the 'criterion measures', are valid? At this point we might have to enter two complex sets of arguments, one having to do with techniques of validation and one with the nature of intelligence. We may note, therefore, that even such a well-tried-out technique as a modern test of intelligence may — from the measurement point of view — have some rather dubious attributes.

## ARE SCALES APPROPRIATE TO OUR DOMAIN?

Of course, it is also possible, indeed desirable, to turn the argument on its head. Instead of asking whether tests of intelligence satisfy the criteria of linear scaling, we might well ask whether the linear-scaling approach is appropriate to the complex set of qualities we call 'intelligence', or can ever hope to do it justice? More broadly, to what extent are the methods of measurement which have been so successful in the physical sciences still appropriate when we have to deal with behavioural and social phenomena? This remains a very controversial question on which the last word will not be spoken for a long time to come.

But if the linear-scaling approach makes demands which are technically hard to satisfy, are there any practicable alternatives? There are many positive answers to this question, but all of them entail losses as well as gains. One type of loss has to do with the richness of human experience. When we describe a rainbow in terms of a spectrum of lightwave frequencies, or motherlove in terms of a score on an attitude scale, we become acutely aware that something important is lost. On the other hand, the richer, more subjective approaches — for example, historical descriptions, diaries, literary accounts, free-style interviews, school reports, group discussions — are less reliable, less valid, less objective and less comparable. In the strict sense of the term they are not data or measures at all. They are rather like statements about hot or cold made by people before the thermometer was invented: subjective, imprecise, not always consistent and with little hope of consensus or comparability. The movement towards making things more 'objective' and 'scientific' is an attempt to get away from subjectivity, to make measures more 'true', more reliable, more precise, more replicable and more comparable even if this does entail certain losses. But it has to be said that the present 'state of the art' in measurement in the human sciences is often so crude and so poorly developed that the losses may well outweigh the gains. It thus becomes a key responsibility of competent research workers to choose the data-generation and -collection techniques which are most appropriate and most likely to 'do justice' to their problem and their subject-matter, a bitter and difficult choice between too much over-simplification for the sake of 'good measurement' and a subtler, more flexible approach which may not yield valid, replicable results. We can only hope that increases in the diversity and sophistication of approaches to measurement will eventually release us from this dilemma.

## Other types of measures

### ORDINAL SCALES

Let us now look at some well-understood departures from the linear scaling model. We have previously seen that, ideally, such a scale should consist of identical, interchangeable units. If at certain points along the continuum we need greater precision or accuracy, we can sub-divide such units and obtain finer-grained readings, but this does not alter the basic principle. However, what if the units are known to be unequal or cannot be shown to be equal? In such cases we look to see if they have a *sequence*, or an ordinal property — in other words, whether they can be *ranked*. In everyday life we quite often use a ranking approach: children may be ranked from top to bottom in a class; athletes, or horses, may be ranked in the order in which they finish a race; the pop charts may rank music recordings in order of their popularity. The important point to note is that an ordinal or ranking scale tells us nothing about the intervals between its points: the winning horse may have been ahead by no more than a neck, whereas the third one could have been trailing by several lengths. So long as we are certain about the ordinal properties of the scale, we can make use of these for the purposes of measurement. There are statistical techniques that will enable us to do this, and ordinal scales — while necessarily less precise than equal-interval ones — should otherwise have most of the other properties of linear scales.

A special sub-variant of ranking scales are scales using the *paired comparisons* method. This can be useful when we have a small number of objects (say, a dozen) and we wish to see how or in what order they should be arranged. For example, we might have a set of pictures, animals, smells or holiday resorts to place in order of preference, if we can. Of course, we might ask each of our respondents to rank the stimulus objects, but a more general method would be to arrange the objects in all possible pairs and present these to each respondent in random order, pair by pair. Instead of having to arrange a dozen pictures, or holiday resorts, in order of preference (which may be very difficult), all that the respondent has to do is to choose between two members of each pair. If there *is* some kind of underlying dimension or continuum on which all the objects can be placed, this will emerge from the statistical analysis, but even so, it will yield not an interval scale, but a rank-order scale as above. This method offers advantages where the dimension is uncertain and ranking would be difficult for the entire set of objects, but with human respondents it can only be used with relatively small sets of stimuli — even twelve objects yield sixty-six paired comparisons to make, and the numbers very soon rise to unmanageable magnitudes.

### NOMINAL MEASURES

We now come to the measurement of nominal or categorical data. These are data which have no underlying continuum, no units or intervals which have equal or ordinal properties, and consequently cannot be scaled. Examples might be: eye colour; the daily newspaper you read; the political party you last voted for; the type of novel you like to read; ownership of consumer durables, such as a car, a home freezer, a motor mower; the brand of cigarette you smoke; your country of birth; and so on. There is no underlying linear scale; instead, there are a number of discrete categories into which the responses can be classified or 'coded', but the categories can be placed in any order and they have no numerical value, nor is there assumed to be an underlying continuum. Essentially, the only possible score for each category is a binary one: yes/no, or present/absent. Thus, if my eyes are brown and I am given a list of eye colours, then my answers will be 'no', 'no', 'no', until I come to 'brown' when I shall give a 'yes' response, and then 'no', 'no', 'no' again to the remainder of the list. There is no order to the categories since no colour is 'better' or 'stronger' or 'bigger' than any other.

### OTHER MEASURES

Beyond this, and in a sense departing still further from the linear-scaling model, are numerous other techniques using multiple items; for example, *perceptual techniques* such as the semantic differential; *sociometry*; various *grid techniques*; and *projective techniques*. These will be discussed in subsequent chapters.

# Statistical treatment

Any accumulation of measures will require some form of management and interpretation, even if this is done in a purely intuitive way. More commonly, the data are subjected to statistical analysis, aided by computers. Typically, the measures for each respondent will be entered into a computer (or, in the case of small-scale manual analysis, on to an analysis sheet laid out in the form of a grid), and thereafter they will be manipulated in a variety of ways. We may calculate various averages, we may compute percentages, we could examine the data for statistical significance, we could work out correlations and we might go on to various forms of multi-variate analysis such as multiple regression or factor analysis. This should enable us to 'make sense of the data'; that is, to test our hypotheses, to compare results for various sub-groups, and so on.

It is very important to realise that the statistical treatment of linear interval scales is quite different from the treatment of nominal or categorical measures. The properties of the linear scale permit us to treat the scores as integers which may be added, subtracted, divided, multiplied and so on. This implies that they can be analysed by means of statistical techniques applicable to interval-type scales. These techniques are quite powerful; they include the familiar 'average' or mean, the variance and the standard deviation, analysis of variance, many types of correlation coefficient and most multi-variate methods. The results can be tested for statistical significance (to check whether the observed findings could have arisen by chance) by means of t-tests, F-tests, Z-tests and others, which many computer programs provide as a matter of course.

Not so with nominal data. Since they lack interval properties and have no underlying continuum, they cannot be added, multiplied or squared. In the initial stages, after entering our data, all we can do is count. For each of our categories (of eye colour, party affiliation or whatever), we shall wish to see *how many* of our respondents endorsed it: how many people in our sample had blue eyes, how many had brown, how many had grey, and so on. No numerical value can be attached to these counts or entries; all we can do is count the frequency of their occurrence. After that, we might wish to compare sub-samples: do men have grey eyes more often than women? Are older respondents more prone to vote for party P than younger ones? To make allowances for differences in sub-sample sizes, we shall wish to convert these frequency distributions into *percentages*, and then study the differences between the groups — but it is not possible, say, to calculate averages or standard deviations.

Distributions of this kind have to be analysed by means of *non-parametric* methods, which are fewer and less powerful than the interval-scale techniques already mentioned. Chief among them is the Chi-squared test (see Appendix II), which allows us to compare our observations with chance expectation, or with expectations based on specific hypotheses. (Warning: the Chi-squared test must *never* be applied to percentages but only to the raw frequencies in our tables.) There will obviously be problems when we try to correlate two nominal measures with each other, or with a scaled variable, though there are some measures of association that can be used, and there are some non-parametric techniques for the multi-variate analysis of nominal or ordinal data. However, in general the statistical management of nominal measures has fewer and less powerful techniques at its disposal than are available for the management of scaled data.

Between the scaled and the nominal measures lie the *ordinal* or ranked measures. These data do not have interval values but are ranked or ordered on an underlying continuum, such as a pupil's position in class or the results of a race, ranked from first to last. There is a special set of statistical techniques which make use of the ordinal properties of such data. The data do not have interval properties but neither are they completely discrete categories, and this has led to the development of measures of rank correlation, tests of significance for ranked data and so forth. However, these techniques are less powerful and relatively limited in number compared to those available for scaled or metric data.

This may explain why researchers frequently 'bend the rules' in order to be able to use parametric techniques of analysis. Take, for example, a five-point classification of socioeconomic status (SES). Strictly speaking, we have five classes or categories in no particular order, with no numerical scale-interval values, and no underlying scale. It follows that we would have to confine ourselves to the use of Chi-squared for significance testing, and we would not be able to use ordinary (product moment) correlation coefficients to relate SES to scaled data such as income, birthweight or holiday expenditure. However, suppose we made the assumption that socioeconomic status is a linear dimension, from low to high in a straight line; and suppose, further, that we made the assumption that each status category is not independent but has a rank, from first to fifth. In that case, we would have an ordinal scale, which would make our analysis easier and more powerful. Better still, suppose we made the assumption that the status categories are not merely ranked but have interval properties; that would be really helpful. Now we can calculate status averages for different occupational groups, we can use correlations to link SES with numerous scaled values such as educational achievement tests, and we can include SES in major multi-variate analyses to show its importance in 'explaining', say, the outcomes of different forms of psychotherapy.

In strict measurement terms this is wrong, and it follows that the parametric techniques for statistical analysis are not applicable. Yet researchers frequently take liberties with the requirements and assumptions on which these statistical techniques are based in the hope that the techniques will prove sufficiently robust to withstand a certain amount of abuse, and that the ensuing results and conclusions will not be too misleading.

One last word about early thermometry, where practitioners seem to have struggled with difficulties not unlike our own. It is obvious now that the original thermometers were rather like pseudo-scales. The units were arbitrary and had different sizes and different meanings according to different measurement systems; the assumption of the linear expansion rate of mercury and of certain gases was not demonstrated until later; there was either no zero-point or there were arbitrary zero-points located to suit human convenience; and for a long time the readings were unreliable because of technical imperfections in the technique of glass-blowing. Also, it took a great deal of international comparative work and organization before universal standards were fixed for the melting points of various metals or for the average temperature of the healthy human body. New, more accurate and more valid measures only began to develop when scientists acquired a better understanding of the underlying processes that determine temperature change.

## The reliability and validity of scaled measures

Up to this point we have been chiefly concerned with two important attributes of scales: *dimensionality* (the presence of a single, linear, underlying continuum) and *equality of intervals* and their statistical treatment. We now turn to a consideration of reliability and validity, two properties which constitute the essence of measurement or data generation of any kind. Each of them is important and, as we have seen previously, they are related to each other.

In the preceding chapter we dealt with reliability and validity in very general terms, and also more specifically in respect of questions dealing with facts and behaviour, and in respect of single questions dealing with attitudes and beliefs. We must now deal more specifically with the reliability and validity of scales and other multi-question approaches.

### RELIABILITY

We shall start with reliability, for adequate reliability is a precondition to validity. Reliability means consistency. We need to be sure that the measuring instrument will behave in a fashion which is consistent with itself; that a very high proportion of the score on every occasion is due to the underlying scale variable, with a minimum of error. If we find differences between readings on the same instrument on two separate occasions, or when applied to two different objects or respondents, we must then be sure that these are 'genuine' differences or changes in the subject of measurement, and not differences which could be attributed to inconsistencies in the measuring instrument or to changes in the attendant conditions. The notion of reliability thus includes both the characteristics of the instrument and the conditions under which it is administered — both must be consistent. In terms of Figure 9.1 (page 151), it is the *error component*, the impurity, which produces the inconsistencies and unreliability which we shall seek to reduce. For instance, when comparing lung X-rays of a patient before and after treatment, the doctor must feel confident that the observed differences are real differences in the patient's lungs and not differences due to imperfections in the emulsion, inconsistent exposure times or postural changes of the patient.

Reliability, or self-consistency, is never perfect; it is always a matter of degree. We express it in the form of a correlation coefficient and, in the social and behavioural sciences, it is rare to find reliabilities much above .90. The square of a correlation coefficient expresses the percentage of shared true variance; thus, a reliability coefficient of .90 means that the two measures have .81 or 81 per cent in common — they overlap, or share a common variance, by just over four-fifths. If the reliability of a scale or other measure drops below .80 this means that repeated administrations will cover less than 64 per cent of the same ground, and that the error component is more than one-third; such a measure will come in for serious criticism and might well have to be discarded or rebuilt.

Reliability may be measured in several different ways: (i) by repeatedly administering the scale to the same sample within a short period (*test-retest* reliability). However, this may produce resistance, as well as a practice effect — in a sense, it will no longer mean that the 'same' test is being administered under the 'same' conditions. To avoid these problems we can use (ii) the *internal consistency* method, usually associated with Cronbach's Alpha coefficient and its variants; (iii) the *split-half* method; and (iv) the *parallel-form* method. All these methods yield reliability measures in the form of correlation coefficients. The parallel form method applies to the situation where the test-building procedure has yielded two equivalent forms of the test, identical in every way except for the contents of the items. Having an alternative form of a measuring instrument can be very useful in a before-and-after design, so that respondents will not receive the same measure twice within a short time period. The split-half method meets the latter problem in a different way: the group of items comprising the measure is divided into two halves at random, and the two halves are then intercorrelated.

The internal-consistency method rests firmly on classical scaling theory. If the scale is expected to measure a single underlying continuum, then the items should have strong relationships both with that continuum and with each other. While we cannot observe the former, a scale will be internally consistent if the items correlate highly with each other — in which case they are also more likely to measure the same homogenous variable. Items are more likely to satisfy these requirements if they are reliable, that is if they have low error-components. Since coefficient Alpha gives us an estimate of the proportion of the total variance that is not due to error, this represents the reliability of the scale.

## VALIDITY

Validity may also be expressed as a correlation coefficient, but this has a different meaning from that of the reliability coefficient. There are other ways of expressing validity, depending on the type of validation being used. In principle, validity indicates the degree to which an instrument measures what it is supposed or intended to measure, but this is a somewhat vague statement, especially since what we usually seek to measure is an abstraction, so that measurement must take place indirectly. Thus, using our previous example of the doctor looking at two X-ray plates, and assuming that the negatives are reliable and are indeed of the same patient before and after treatment, we note that the doctor is not really interested in the differences between two photographic negatives as such, but in changes in the patient's lungs. If the technique is valid, then there will be close correspondence (concurrent validity) between the X-rays and the changes in the lungs. From these, the doctor will try to draw conclusions about further treatment, prognosis and so forth (predictive validity). If the technique had poor validity, this might lead the doctor to draw erroneous conclusions. Note, however, that at best the technique can only reveal changes in the patient's lungs — the rest is inference. Thus we note that each measurement technique can have more than one validity (indeed, potentially an infinite number of validities), depending on the conclusions we want to draw from it — in this instance, the concurrent validity of changes in the lungs and the predictive validity of estimated recovery rate, prognosis and so on (which may be different). We also note that what we want to measure, and what the instrument is 'supposed to measure', may often be an abstract attribute of some kind (for example 'response to treatment', 'likely outcome') for which, at the time, we may have no other, 'true' criterion measure.

Inevitably, these problems are magnified in the social and behavioural sciences. An achievement test in arithmetic may possibly give us a valid measure of *this* child's ability to solve *this* set of problems *today*. In this limited sense it could be said to be 'valid' because it has concurrent validity, but usually we ask such tests to bear a heavier burden. For example, we may want to treat this set of arithmetical problems as representative of all such problems at this level and to predict that this child could solve *another* set of similar problems tomorrow; that is, we may wish to generalize from this score. How valid is such a generalization likely to be? Or we may wish to use this test to assess the success of a new teaching method which is intended to benefit the less-able pupils; would the test be a valid measure by which to assess the efficacy of the new method? And might it also be able to show which pupils would benefit most: does it have predictive validity?

But how do we know that the test is a test of arithmetic? That it measures 'what it is supposed to measure', an abstraction? A common-sense answer would be to examine the contents of the items. This is known, somewhat disparagingly, as 'face validity' and holds many dangers. For example, out of the entire domain of arithmetic, how have these items been selected? What do they represent? For what level of achievement? How well balanced are the items in terms of content? How pure are the items? In addition to knowing some arithmetic, the child must know how to read and write, how to concentrate and solve problems, how to handle language and so on, and these abilities may, in turn, be related to social background factors. Thus, part of the score will show the child's level of achievement in arithmetic, and another part will measure several other skills, which will not merely introduce some random error into the data but a correlated bias, so children from certain backgrounds will tend to have higher scores. We have to satisfy ourselves that these dangers have somehow been minimized by the way in which the test has been constructed.

One method of establishing concurrent validity might be to correlate the scores with an external criterion — with some other, 'truer' measure — but which one? Teachers' ratings or examination results are often used in such contexts but these tend to be unreliable, and anyway, why are they 'better'? Good criterion measures are notoriously hard to find.

There are other ways of approaching the problem of validity. Sometimes we can use *construct validity*. There are times when we have good theoretical grounds for making certain predictions (for example, that children who score higher on an IQ test will also do better at arithmetic), and so we regard the fulfilment of a set of such predictions as evidence of the test's validity. Certainly we should be rather suspicious of an arithmetic test on which the brighter children did less well (always assuming that the intelligence test was reliable and valid in the first place). Finally, we can examine the test's *predictive validity*; for example, high scorers should be able to give change correctly if they are put behind the counter of a shop, they should get higher marks in an arithmetic examination at the end of the year, and they might become more successful bookmakers or actuaries! An aptitude test for motor mechanics might have high validity for predicting examination results at the end of a training course, but may have poor validity in predicting success as a garage owner, and no-one has yet succeeded in designing a test, or a battery of tests, that would predict success in final university examinations. The usefulness of predictive validity, if attained, can be very great — but we may have to wait a long time to achieve it, and even then we must make sure that the criterion measure is sufficiently valid and reliable for our purposes.

To sum up, a measure may be used for a number of distinct purposes, and it is likely to have a different validity coefficient for each of them. There are also different types of validity:

(i) *content validity*, which seeks to establish that the items or questions are a well-balanced sample of the content domain to be measured ('face validity' is not really good enough);

(ii) *concurrent validity*, which shows how well the test correlates with other, well-validated measures of the same topic, administered at about the same time;

(iii) *predictive validity*, which shows how well the test can forecast some future criterion such as job performance, recovery from illness or future examination attainment;

(iv) *construct validity*, which shows how well the test links up with a set of theoretical assumptions about an abstract construct such as intelligence, conservatism or neuroticism.

As we have seen earlier, validity and reliability are related to each other. Above all, reliability is a necessary (though not sufficient) condition for validity: a measure which is unreliable cannot attain an adequate degree of validity — its error component is too great. On the other hand, a measure may be highly reliable and yet invalid. Consider, for example, three radio direction finders who are homing in on the transmissions from a plane, a ship, or a fox that has been radio-tagged. By triangulating their observations and plotting the results on a map, they will obtain a small triangle (or, in the ideal case, a point) from within which the transmissions must have originated. The smaller the triangle, the more reliable the measurement — but by the time the triangle is drawn, the location of the plane, ship or fox is likely to have changed, perhaps by thirty to fifty miles, and so the measure will no longer be a valid indication of position. We can hope to improve on this situation by taking repeated observations, plotting course and speed and thereby *inferring* a valid location (though with a fox carrying a radio collar, this might not work!). Thus we see that, if we can establish good reliability then we are, as it were, 'in business'; we may not yet have much evidence of validity, but there is hope that with further work the scale's validity may become established at an acceptable level.

In general, the more difficult it becomes to find a suitable external criterion, a strong construct system, or some other method of validation, the more researchers will concentrate on content validity and on making their measures reliable. This is particularly the case in the field of attitude scaling (see below and Chapter 11).

## Scores and norms

By itself, a numerical score on a measure will be almost meaningless. To state that someone has scored thirty-two on an ethnic prejudice scale will tell us very little, unless we can place such a score in its *context*. Once a scale has been developed we therefore seek to give it a scoring system and to obtain norms for it. For example, in the case of the test of arithmetical achievement which we mentioned before, we could administer the test to a large number of school children — preferably to representative samples of the relevant age groups — and obtain frequency distributions, percentile curves, means and standard deviations and so on for each school year, and perhaps separately for boys and girls or some other sub-groups of concern. We might also seek to correlate our test with other tests to give more 'meaning' to the scores. Once we have done all this, we can state that a score of, say, forty-nine achieved by a ten-year-old boy is very much below average for children of his age, or that his arithmetic achievement is well below what his IQ test would suggest, so that some remedial work might be needed in order to correct this 'under-achievement'.

In the more complex and multi-faceted domain of attitude measurement we do not generally take such a 'positivist' approach, but it remains necessary to place our scale scores in context, by showing the statistical results of giving the scale to substantial groups (preferably probability samples) of the population of concern.

## Improving the reliability of attitude scales

The traditional method of measuring attitudes is by means of *attitude statements*. In the next chapter we shall see the ways in which these may be composed and assembled into an item pool, but for the moment we shall treat them as any other items that form the raw material of scale building. The purpose of such a scale would be to place each respondent on an attitudinal dimension or continuum, but at the start of our research we may not know whether such a dimension exists, whether it is likely to be linear, or whether it might perhaps break up into several different dimensions.

Though in writing the statements or questions we shall obviously be aiming at content validity, we must be acutely aware that each item may contain a substantial error-component which will make it unreliable as a measure, and that there is no way of 'purifying' single items. Thus, suppose we were building some parental attitude scales and that we were working on items for a rejection scale, a way of finding out whether a parent shows a tendency to reject his or her children. This is obviously a subtle problem, but we might try a permissively phrased item such as: 'If we could afford it, we would like to send our children to boarding school'. But how can we know whether this item really belongs in a rejection scale, for instance whether a mother who responds to this item with

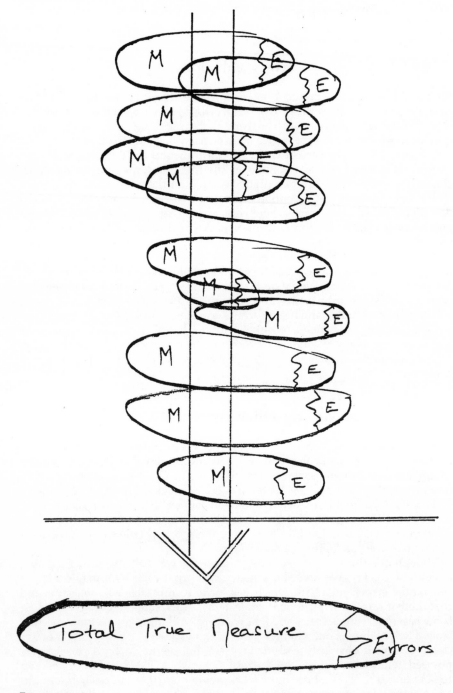

Figure 9.2.

'agree' is actually inclined to reject her children and wants to get them out of the way? For all we know, in her eyes attendance at some famous boarding school opens up a glittering future for her children and so, though she loves them dearly, she is willing to make sacrifices to give them a better future. Conversely, a 'disagree' answer may not mean greater love for the children, it might merely indicate a certain political orientation. If we refer again to Figure 9.1, we can say that in items of this kind the error component is likely to be particularly large and variable, so that a single item will be highly unreliable.

The commonly adopted solution to this problem, though by no means the only one, is to try to apply the linear-scaling model. In principle, the argument can be presented as shown in Figure 9.2.

If we take not one but a set of items all designed to measure the same underlying attribute or continuum in a variety of different ways, and if we score these items and add up the scores for each respondent, then this total score will be a better, more reliable measure because all the M-components of the various items will be added together, whereas the E-components will, the argument suggests, be non-additive and random. In so far as we can accept this argument, it suggests that the more items we use, the higher will be the reliability of the total score. There is, however, a point of diminishing returns (which is probably just as well, or we should be using tests with hundreds of items!), so that most scales tend to consist of no more than a couple of dozen items each.

Figure 9.3.

The argument above is clearly open to question. A lot depends on the construction and weeding-out of the items. There are also serious problems of overlap between the items. If there is too much overlap of the M-components of the items, then there will be redundancy and one-sidedness in the total score. The content area has been 'tapped' but in a limited way, and the underlying dimension will be somewhat lopsided — rather like an intelligence test based principally on space-form and memory items, for example. Even more serious is the possibility of substantial overlap between the E-components of the items. In that case, far from being random, the errors will reinforce each other and create a bias. Suppose that in building an intelligence test we have included quite a few items which, although they approach intelligence in different ways, all require the ability to read rather quickly in order to understand each item, or need some familiarity with coloured blocks making abstract patterns. In such cases children who were fast readers, or who had played a lot with coloured blocks, would have an 'unfair' advantage and the total score would contain an important bias.

In Figure 9.3 we have presented the same problem in a somewhat different way. This drawing suggests that the pool of items or statements should be 'balanced'; that is, it should try to do justice to the multiple facets of an attitude domain. For instance, in Chapter 4 we gave the example of measuring attitudes towards the police. The depth interviews and preliminary conceptual framework might well contain sub-areas to do with uniforms, with law and order, with crossing the road, with domestic crime, with police programmes on television, with motoring, with feelings towards authority and so on. The drawing suggests that items dealing with every one of these aspects, and more, might all have something in common, namely an abstraction which we would call Attitude to the Police, as well as other components each dealing more particularly with burglaries, speeding, or dislike of a particular television programme, as well as error components.

Next, we would need to conduct an *item analysis*: the procedure of statistically 'weeding out' items that do not 'belong' or that have too much error variance. This would help to 'purify' the scale, and to establish its reliability through internal consistency and, as we shall see, there are a variety of methods for achieving this. Ultimately, we might apply a correlational procedure such as factor analysis or principal component analysis (see below) to purify the scale still further and to suggest the underlying dimension. These procedures would also enable us to produce a more precise scoring method.

# Factor analysis

The procedure of factor analysis is an analytic statistical tool which may enable us to find out what (if any) are the chief underlying dimensions of a set of variables, attributes, responses or observations. Suppose, for example, that we want to develop a measure or test that could be used in a secretarial college to measure 'secretarial ability' at the end of a training course. We might assemble a pool of questions, some dealing with keyboard skills, some with office management, some with inter-office communications such as telephones or fax machines, some with minor account-keeping and spread sheets, and some with interpersonal skills. Do all these items have something in common which could be called 'secretarial ability'? And could we refine the item pool so as to yield a smaller number of questions which would enable us to give each student a numerical score on that ability? Or again, suppose we want to grade groups of recruits to the armed services on 'physical fitness' by giving them a number of tests: for endurance, for eyesight, for lung volume, heart rate, doing press-ups, weight lifting and so on. How can we find out whether all these different test procedures have something in common which may be called 'physical fitness' and on which new recruits could be graded? Factor analysis may provide some answers to these questions.

Because of the prodigious amount of calculation involved, the use of a computer is essential, as a rule. We start by creating a *correlation matrix*. This is a square table with all the variables listed both across the top and down the side; each cell in the body of the table contains a correlation coefficient between two variables, so that the matrix as a whole contains every possible correlation between any variable and every other variable. For example, a 20 × 20 matrix would contain 380 correlation coefficients in two identical triangular sets of 190 coefficients each.

Before going further, it is worth giving this matrix some careful inspection. It would be interesting, for example, if we found a group of variables which showed high intercorrelations, for these might have underlying dimension in common. Or we might find a large number of very low correlation coefficients. Does this mean that our data have a 'poor structure', that the variables mostly do not 'hang together' very well? And what if we find some negative correlations? Is this merely a matter of the way some variables have been scored, or do we really have some variables which go down when most other variables go up? If so, do such variables belong in this matrix at all?

Now we must start the factor analysis itself. We need a software package which contains a factor-analysis program (or a variant of factor analysis called a principal-components analysis), which we shall apply to the correlation matrix. The program will take care of the calculations, and of certain transformations which have to precede the analysis, and will produce a set of output tables. The first output table will usually show how much 'structure' there is in the underlying dimensions by giving a measure of the size of each factor. If there is a strong, simple, underlying structure showing that all or most of the variables essentially measure the same dimension (secretarial ability, say, or physical fitness), then the first output table will show a list of one very large percentage value followed by a list of much smaller ones. More typically, the first table will show one fairly large percentage, two or three medium-sized ones and a residual list of smaller percentages which will be ignored. This may be interpreted to mean that the underlying structure is not uni-dimensional but two-dimensional or three-dimensional. Thus, it might show that physical fitness is not a single concept or attribute but requires more than one measure. Sometimes the first output table will show no large percentages at all, merely a set of small ones. This would be interpreted to mean that essentially there is no common dimension. In that case the variables mentioned earlier do not really belong together at all, they should not be added together, and it is not possible to give each subject a single score or grade.

The factor-analysis program will have applied a cut-off point, whereby the remainder of the analysis will be concerned only with underlying dimensions which are substantial. The second output table is likely to show a list of all the tests, measures or attributes in our pool. Next to each of these there will be one or more figures that look like correlation coefficients. These lists will be headed 'Factor I', 'Factor II' etc. If, for example, the analysis has suggested a two-factor structure, then this table will show two lists of coefficients (called 'factor loadings'). Essentially, this is a transformation; what the program has done is to transform most of the variance in our correlation matrix into something simpler and more manageable: a two-factor structure.

This factor structure is, however, not the final stage. The factors produced by this first transformation may be somewhat arbitrary, they may lack meaning and may be difficult to interpret. They are not unlike, say, a grid on a map or a globe. We may draw the zero meridian through Greenwich, or through New Delhi; either way, it will be an arbitrary convention which does not represent any kind of geographical or geological feature or process, and in that sense it is not 'meaningful'. Also, whichever way we choose to draw our grid, this will make no difference to the distances between cities or the location of mountains or other features. If we were to move or rotate the zero meridian to run through New Delhi, this would merely mean that the geographical co-ordinates of any city or mountain would have to be altered. The features themselves would not change, nor would their relative positions.

Various procedures have been developed to help us to identify and interpret the underlying dimensions we may find. These will require the factor-analysis program to engage in 'rotation': the program will make a number of attempts (called 'iterations') to re-align or re-draw the factor loadings in such a way as to produce a more 'meaningful' result, according to certain built-in criteria. When it has done the best it can, the program will produce a third table. This new table will also be a table of factor loadings showing two or more factors, but these will be different — sometimes very different — from the preceding table. This new table constitutes the main results of the factor analysis, and it needs careful scrutiny.

It may be advantageous to turn it into a graphical representation. Two lines crossing at a right angle may be drawn to represent Factor I and Factor II, respectively. For any test or measure there will be two loadings. These can be plotted along the two factor axes, thus locating the measure in a two-dimensional space. When we have thus plotted the positions of all our measures, we should have a graphic representation of their interrelationships. (If we have more than two factors, then this procedure becomes rather cumbersome.)

We now come to the interpretation of the results of the factor analysis. As we have already noted, the first part of the interpretation concerns the overall underlying structure. Is there a single dimension, or are there several, or none? In the second part, we shall seek to give meaning to each factor, as far as we can, and perhaps give it a label. We do this by careful scrutiny of the factor loadings. For example, we might find that the list of Factor I loadings show high loadings for key-board secretarial skills, and low loadings for social or interactive skills, while the Factor II loadings show the opposite pattern. This might suggest that secretarial skills are not all on a single, unitary dimension, but are composed of

Figure 9.4.

Here are some possible reasons for drinking. How important is each one of these to YOU as a reason for drinking?

(For each question place a tick in the appropriate column)

| Not at all important | Slightly important | Fairly important | Very important |
|---|---|---|---|

1. I drink when I am feeling tense.

|  |  |  |  |
|---|---|---|---|

2. I drink to be sociable

|  |  |  |  |
|---|---|---|---|

3. I drink when I am feeling miserable

|  |  |  |  |
|---|---|---|---|

4. I drink because the people I know drink.

|  |  |  |  |
|---|---|---|---|

5. I drink when I have an argument with somebody

|  |  |  |  |
|---|---|---|---|

6. I drink when I am at a lively party

|  |  |  |  |
|---|---|---|---|

7. I accept a drink because it is the polite thing to do in certain situations

|  |  |  |  |
|---|---|---|---|

8. I drink before doing something I feel will be difficult.

|  |  |  |  |
|---|---|---|---|

9. I drink to celebrate social occasions.

|  |  |  |  |
|---|---|---|---|

10. I drink when I just can't cope with things

|  |  |  |  |
|---|---|---|---|

two sets of variables on two separate dimensions: key-board related and social/ interactive, and we might label our factors accordingly.

Often, however, we find more complex results in a factor analysis. For example, there may be one strong, major factor which enters into every variable, and then several more 'specific' factors which are each represented by a cluster of factor loadings. Thus, 'physical fitness' might be one such general factor, followed by a handful of measures that have loadings only on Factor II and which might, on examination, turn out to be tests requiring muscle strength. Another set of loadings might define Factor III — these might have to do with endurance and with recovery from effort; and there might be a fourth factor with loadings derived mainly from sensory performance tests such as visual and auditory acuity.

Various factor analyses can yield different patterns, and the interpretation of the results is a matter of experience and judgement with which a computer cannot help. Sometimes, however, it is possible to apply a different form of rotation, called 'oblique' rotation. Up to now we have assumed that every factor produced by the analysis was *independent* of every other factor. In, say, a two-factor result a person could score high or low on the first factor, but this would not tell us whether that person was likely to score high, or low or somewhere in between on the second factor. The two factors were independent and unrelated to each other. That is why they were drawn at right angles to each other in a graphical representation. However, it sometimes happens that this is not the most meaningful way of representing our data. In that case, we might try an oblique rotation — a solution which assumes that the factors are, or can be, to some extent related to each other.

Factor analysis has a number of uses. As we shall see, the procedure is often employed in scaling and in the development of other kinds of measures. If a respondent is to be given a score on an instrument, then we must make sure that the scale or inventory is uni-dimensional. Otherwise we must either shorten the scale by using only those items that have high loadings on the factor we require, or we must give each respondent two or more scores, depending on the factor solution. We can also use the factor loadings for each test or item to give *weights* to the responses, thus producing refinements in the scoring process.

Perhaps the greatest value of the technique is in showing us the nature of the

| FACTOR | EIGENVALUE | PCT OF VAR | CUM PCT |
|---|---|---|---|
| 1 | 5.16625 | 51.7 | 51.7 |
| 2 | 1.74055 | 17.4 | 69.1 |
| 3 | .61893 | 6.2 | 75.3 |
| 4 | .51339 | 5.1 | 80.4 |
| 5 | .46652 | 4.7 | 85.1 |
| 6 | .39265 | 3.9 | 89.0 |
| 7 | .32205 | 3.2 | 92.2 |
| 8 | .28983 | 2.9 | 95.1 |
| 9 | .26133 | 2.6 | 97.7 |
| 10 | .22850 | 2.3 | 100.0 |

Figure 9.5.

VARIMAX ROTATED FACTOR MATRIX
AFTER ROTATION WITH KAISER NORMALIZATION

|    | FACTOR 1 | FACTOR 2 |
|----|----------|----------|
| 1  | .80006   | .20880   |
| 2  | .21196   | .85585   |
| 3  | .80046   | .21512   |
| 4  | .14687   | .75938   |
| 5  | .81999   | .21028   |
| 6  | .29261   | .81208   |
| 7  | .11888   | .75016   |
| 8  | .74681   | .23221   |
| 9  | .32735   | .80184   |
| 10 | .85535   | .16875   |

Figure 9.6.

dimensional structure underlying our variables, sometimes with revealing or surprising results. Thus, if we have specific hypotheses about our domain of enquiry, for example that *one* score can be used as a summed measure of physical fitness, then we can use factor analysis to test such a hypothesis for construct validity. At other times, perhaps in a new area of research, factor analysis can help us to chart new structures, which may lead to new measures and new theories.

EXAMPLE

Figure 9.4 (on page 169) is an inventory of ten items describing motives for drinking alcohol. The factor-analysis output shows in Figure 9.5 that 51.7 per cent of the variance is accounted for by the first factor, 17.4 per cent by the second factor and that the remaining percentages are negligible. Thus we have essentially a two-factor structure. Figure 9.6 shows the rotated factor loadings for the ten items. To interpret the results, we note that items 1, 3, 5, 8, and 10 have substantial loadings on Factor I; these are all items which express *internal motives* for drinking. The remaining items have high loadings on Factor II and mostly express *external* motives for drinking. The diagram in Figure 9.7 shows a two-dimensional factor plot, with the ten items clustered around the two axes.

# Recapitulation

The classical linear-scaling model requires that a measure shall have four important attributes:

(1) linearity and uni-dimensionality;
(2) at least adequate reliability;
(3) at least adequate validity;
(4) a scoring system, and some statistical norms.

In this chapter we have tried to show how each of these objectives can be achieved by traditional means.

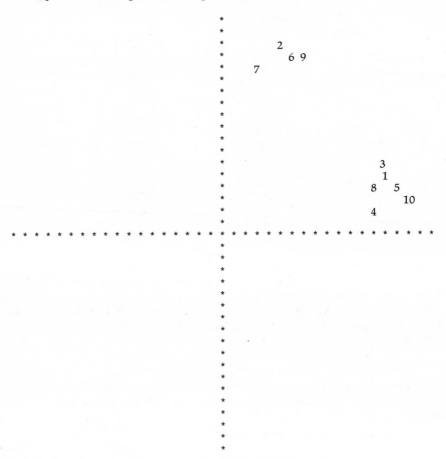

Figure 9.7.

In the following two chapters we shall discuss the various classical scaling methods that have been developed to measure attitudes, and compare these to the linear scaling model. In subsequent chapters we shall deal with less traditional forms of attitude measurement, and with various other multiple-item techniques which diverge from the linear-scaling model.

# Selected readings

Allen, Mary J., and Yen, Wendy M., 1979, *Introduction to Measurement Theory*, Brooks/Cole Publishing Company, Monterey, California.
   A useful, non-mathematical introductory text.

Rossi, P.H., Wright, J.D. and Anderson, A.B. (eds), 1983, *Handbook of Survey Research*, Academic Press, New York.
   See chapter 7.

DeVellis, Robert F., 1991, *Scale Development: Theories and Applications*, Applied Social Research Methods Volume 27, Sage, London.

Torgerson, W.S., 1958, *Theory and Methods of Scaling*, Wiley, New York.
   For advanced students.

Guilford, J.P., 1956, *Psychometric Methods*, McGraw-Hill, New York.
   An older but still very useful text. See especially chapters on psychophysical methods and on rating scales.

Bernstein, I.N., 1976, *Validity Issues in Evaluative Research*, Sage.

Cronbach, Lee J., 1990, Fifth Edition, *Essentials of Psychological Testing*, Harper and Row, New York.
   A classic basic text. See especially on validity and reliability.

Dunn, Graham, 1989, *Design and Analysis of Reliability Studies*, Oxford University Press.
   For the advanced student.


## APPLICATIONS

Streiner, David L. and Norman, Geoffrey R., 1989, *Health Measurement Scales*, Oxford University Press.
   A very useful explanatory text aimed at medical researchers. Deals with reliability, validity, response bias, telephone interviewing and many other relevant topics.

Carley, Michael, 1981, *Social Measurement and Social Indicators*, Allen & Unwin, London.


## FACTOR ANALYSIS

Gorsuch, R.L., 1974, *Factor Analysis*, Saunders, Philadelphia.
   A useful basic text.

Rummel, R.J., 1970, *Applied Factor Analysis*, Northwestern University Press, Evanston, Ill.

Harmon, H.H., 1967, *Modern Factor Analysis*, University of Chicago Press, Chicago.

Kim, Jaeon and Mueller, Charles W., 1979, *Factor Analysis*, Quantitative Applications in the Social Sciences, No. 14, Sage, London.

# 10
# DESIGNING ATTITUDE STATEMENTS

No amount of statistical manipulation will produce a good attitude scale unless the ingredients are right. The most advanced scaling techniques and the most error-free procedures will not produce an attitude scale worth having unless there has first been a good deal of careful thought and exploration, many depth interviews and repeated conceptualizations, and unless the ingredients of the scale — the attitude statements — have been written and rewritten with the necessary care. We shall therefore not approach the topic of attitude scaling at once, as some textbooks do, for in the past too much attention has been paid to the technical and statistical problems of scaling and not enough to the psychological problem of what is being scaled. This chapter is devoted to the writing and selection of attitude statements; the next chapter will deal with the construction of attitude scales.

An attitude statement is a single sentence that expresses a point of view, a belief, a preference, a judgement, an emotional feeling, a position *for or against* something. For example: 'The people in power know best'; 'The police can't be trusted'; 'Children bring a husband and wife closer together'. Attitude statements are the raw material of attitude scales. They should be phrased so that respondents can agree or disagree with the statement. Usually, after the pilot work, a large number of attitude statements (probably somewhere between sixty and 100) is assembled to form an *item pool*. These items will be analysed and submitted to a scaling procedure (see next chapter). If all goes well, the outcome will be a much smaller selection of items (say, between one and two dozen) which together have the properties of an attitude *scale* that can yield a numerical score for each respondent. The analysis will also have thrown light on the topic or dimension which the scale is designed to measure.

## What is an attitude?

The study of attitudes has a long and complex history in social psychology, and this is not the place to engage in elaborate theoretical exposition. Suffice it to say that, for the purposes of verbal measurement, most researchers seem to agree that an attitude is a state of readiness, a tendency to respond in a certain manner when confronted with certain stimuli. Most of an individual's attitudes are usually dormant and are expressed in speech or behaviour only when the object of the attitude is perceived. A person may have strong attitudes for or against foreign travel, but these become aroused and expressed only when some issue connected with travel abroad arises — or when confronted with an attitude questionnaire! Attitudes are reinforced by *beliefs* (the cognitive component) and often attract strong *feelings* (the emotional component) which may lead to particular behavioural *intents* (the action tendency component).

Attitudes, like many other determinants of behaviour, are abstractions — though they are real enough to the person who holds them. There is no limit to the topics about which people may have attitudes — from war and peace, God and eternity, to toy trains, roses, or frozen fish. It would be possible to argue persuasively that in the final analysis everything in life depends on people's attitudes. Since attitudes are so important in domains such as politics, marriage, religion, food preferences, social change, education, fashion, child rearing, ethnic prejudice, communication and many others, it is not surprising that social psychologists have devoted much time and ingenuity to finding ways of measuring them. We become particularly aware of the strength and pervasiveness of attitudes when we try to change them — through the processes of communication, advertising, education, conversion, propaganda, military drill, alcohol consumption, brainwashing, and others.

Most attitudes are given labels such as liberalism, pacifism, feminism, anti-Moldavianism, authoritarianism, strictness, vegetarianism, and others. Such labels should be regarded with caution, for it is of vital importance to know what the attitude measure is supposed to be about. This is more easily said than done, for most attitudes are parts of a wider compound of values, beliefs and feelings and are themselves made up of several components or sub-areas. It is only too easy to impose a preconceived framework (which may or may not be misguided) on an attitude, but this could result in unintentionally measuring the wrong attitude, or only part of an attitude, or too many attitudes all at once.

Nor do attitudes necessarily 'hang together' in a logical way. There are, for example, no *logical* reasons why people who favour capital punishment should also be against homosexuality and against socialized medicine, but in favour of restrictions on immigration, yet research has shown that these are all part of a much wider orientation to many social issues.

Our thinking on the nature of attitudes has been rather primitive. Most of the time we tend to perceive them as straight lines, running from positive, through neutral, to negative feelings about the object or issue in question. Our attempts at measurement then concentrate on trying to place a person's attitude on the straight line or linear continuum in such a way that it can be described as mildly positive, strongly negative, and so on — preferably in terms of a numerical score or else by means of ranking. There is no proof, however, that this model of a linear continuum is necessarily correct, though it does make things easier for measurement purposes. For all we know, attitudes may be shaped more like concentric circles or overlapping ellipses or three-dimensional cloud formations.

The model of the linear continuum or dimension is not always easy or appropriate. For instance, the positive part and the negative part may or may not be linear extensions of each other. In studying the attitudes of mothers to their children we have found that rejection is not the exact opposite of acceptance (as measured by two separate attitude scales); apparently, a variety of other components enter into the attitude of a rejecting mother that are not present in a loving and accepting mother. Moreover, it is possible for some respondents to be ambivalent and to score highly both on acceptance and on rejection. It would clearly have been a mistake to assess these attitudes by means of a single acceptance–rejection continuum. Again, the degree of differentiation at one end of an attitude continuum may be very different from that at the other end. Thus, if we considered how we felt about peace, we would find it easy to deal with the negative end — statements about the benefits of war, courage and the will to fight, and national unity — but at the positive end we would very soon run short; there is not all that much that one can say about love for peace. Does this mean that the units or intervals will be smaller, or more numerous, at one end of the scale than at the other? One is tempted to divide the dimension into units of some kind. Such units, while not strictly 'legitimate', may help us to compare groups of people with one another, but they are not comparable from one scale to another.

Attitudes have many attributes. So far, we have talked mainly about their *content* — what the attitude is about. An attitude, however, also has *intensity*. It may be held with greater or lesser vehemence. To some people, the exploitation of animals may be but of passing interest or concern, whereas to others it may be of great importance and propel them to leading positions in the animal liberation movement. We might expect the latter to agree or disagree more strongly than the former would to a series of statements dealing with the treatment of animals. This attribute of intensity can be very important in understanding how attitudes function.

Some attitudes are more enduring than others. For instance, a man's political beliefs may be fairly stable throughout his lifetime, whereas his attitudes to tennis or to gambling may undergo multiple changes. Similarly, some attitudes go much deeper than others and touch upon a person's fundamental philosophy of life, while others are relatively superficial. Again, some attitudes seem to be more embracing than others; they lie at the base of more limited or specific attitudes and beliefs, thus predisposing individuals in a certain way toward new attitudes and experiences that may come their way. For ease of understanding, social psychologists make a rough distinction between these different levels, calling the most superficial one 'opinions', the next one 'attitudes', a deeper level 'values' or 'basic attitudes', and a still deeper level, 'personality'. These rather vague distinctions between different levels of attitudes must be thought of as more versus less enduring, deeper versus more superficial; relatively stable versus relatively changeable; and more general versus more specific. Furthermore, these levels must not merely be thought of as the different layers of a cake; there are relationships and patterns of connection between these layers, rather like what is sometimes called 'the tree model' (see Figure 10.1).

This diagram should not be taken too literally. Its chief function is to warn against treating opinions and attitudes too much as isolated units, and to illustrate the problems we face in trying to bring about a change in anyone's attitudes. At the most specific level, that of opinions, change is relatively easy to bring about so long as the underlying attitude is not involved. Thus, it may not be too difficult to convince a man with strong anti-Mexican views that he is

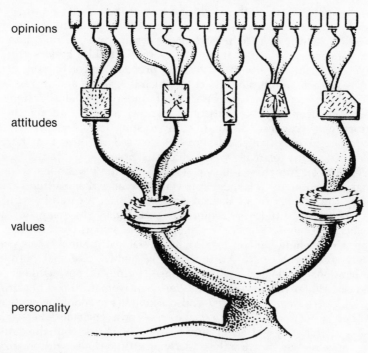

opinions

attitudes

values

personality

Figure 10.1.

wrong in his opinion that Mexicans have a high crime rate; but his underlying anti-Mexican attitude remains unaltered, and he will soon find some other belief with which to bolster his hostile attitude.

Typically, attitudes do not exist in isolation within the individual. They generally have links with components of other attitudes and with the deeper levels of value systems within the person. For instance, suppose we are having dinner with a friend in a restaurant and suggest to him that he might like pork chops, which are on the menu. Our friend declines. At this point, we might say to ourselves that we are dealing with an opinion, with a relatively superficial and not immutable food preference of the moment. However, suppose we started questioning our friend. We might find that he is a vegetarian, a Jew or a Muslim, and that his refusal to eat pork chops has to do with a more general and deeper underlying attitude to pigs and other animals as food. This in turn may be linked to an underlying value system that has to do with the role of humans *vis-à-vis* other creatures, with religious proscriptions concerning 'clean' and 'unclean' animals, or possibly with other taboos. An apparently simple matter of food preference may in fact be a key to the individual's fundamental philosophy of life.

So far, we have talked about relationships in terms of depth. However, attitudes are also related to each other 'horizontally', at the same level. Some of the most interesting research contributions in social psychology have been concerned with such interrelationships. We find, for instance, that racial prejudice against one minority group is usually associated with prejudice against several other groups, and with the glorification of the individual's own group. The word 'ethnocentrism' has been coined to reflect such as underlying predisposition, which in turn is part of a personality syndrome known as authoritarianism and which contains many other attitudes besides ethnocentrism. We are dealing here with the difficult problem of isolating one attitude from a considerable number of others to which it is linked and correlated and which, in their turn, may also be part of underlying value systems and personality syndromes. It is difficult to know where to draw the line. Exploratory work suggests all kinds of interesting links and patterns with neighbouring and underlying fields, but we also need, for measuring purposes, a scale covering some relatively well-demarcated area.

Interrelations such as these follow no logic except the 'psycho-logic', the logic of feelings and emotions. It is most important to realize that attitudes are only very rarely the product of a balanced conclusion after a careful assembly of evidence. As a rule, attitudes are acquired or modified by absorbing, or reacting to, *the attitudes of others*. We like to maintain the fiction of rationality and impartiality in reaching our conclusions, but, in fact, attitudinal predispositions play a very considerable part. Attitudes can be highly emotional, both in the sense of irrational or illogical and in the sense of arousing powerful needs and ego defences. When we ask a highland Peruvian woman to boil her drinking water to kill germs, we are, in her eyes, also asking her to adopt the white man's magic, to betray her ancestors and to make a fool and a renegade of herself in her village. To us this may not seem very reasonable at first, but this is where research can help — by showing the underlying attitude links, with their strong emotional connections.

## Measurement problems

After studying the literature on the subject we must begin with a series of depth interviews, the essential purpose of which is two-fold: (1) to explore the origins, complexities, and ramifications of the attitude areas in question, in order to decide more precisely what it is we wish to measure (conceptualisation); (2) to get vivid expressions of such attitudes from the respondents, in a form that might make them suitable for use as statements in an attitude scale.

Suppose we are asked to construct a scale to measure people's attitudes toward vitamins. We may well find, in exploratory interviews, that almost everyone is favourably disposed toward them; accordingly, a pro–con scale concerning vitamins would show little differentiation. This often happens: the pilot work causes a change in the aim of the scale, and possibly in the aim of the investigation. Next, we propose to build a scale dealing with 'vitamin conscious-ness' or 'vitamin-salience' — dealing with the extent to which considerations of vitamin content enter into people's minds when they shop, cook, self-medicate and so on. At first, it would seem that this attitude is directly related to people's knowledge about vitamins; and we shall find it comparatively easy to differen-tiate between the more knowledgeable and the less knowledgeable on the basis of a few well-chosen factual knowledge questions. Further exploration may show, however, that many people with little correct knowledge about vitamins nevertheless are very interested in them and are influenced by advertising claims concerning vitamin content. We begin to find various links; health-consciousness is one, of which vitamin-consciousness may be a part, though a rather unruly one. Child care may be another link, associated especially with women and with small babies. A general tendency towards self-medication, toward taking pills and tablets of all kinds, may represent yet another connection. There may also be a link with health foods and an interest in alternative medicine. And we could continue. This is a part of social psychology where clinical acumen, intuition and a capacity for 'listening with the third ear' are invaluable and where chairbound, preconceived frameworks may constitute a real hindrance.

We must next decide, after doing perhaps thirty or forty preliminary interviews, what it is we wish to measure, and we will then be in a position to draw up a conceptual sketch of the attitude clusters in question, with their likely linkages and possible undercurrents. We should also have some idea of the function that our scale is to play within the context of the research as a whole. This may tell us how general or specific, and how deep or superficial, our scale should be and what sub-areas it should include or leave out. As a rule, the more aspects of a particular attitude can be included, the more likely it is that scores will be obtained that will mean something in terms of that underlying attitude, rather than in terms of one or two particular aspects of it. But it must be remembered that the same attitude may express itself in different ways in different people, while some people may have no such attitude at all.

Using a Sentence Completion technique (see Chapter 4) can also be helpful at this stage.

## Writing attitude statements

Having decided on the general pattern which our attitude scale should have, we may now compose the *item pool*, the collection of attitude statements from which the scale will be built. Perhaps the best guide to the writing of attitude statements is to say that they should be meaningful and interesting, even exciting, to the respondents. There are many attitude scales which falter because the items have been composed in the office according to some theoretical plan and fail to arouse much interest in the respondents.

How can we tell whether or not we are producing useful attitude statements? We are on the wrong path when many of our pilot work respondents start to quibble or want to change the items or add to them; when there are many 'uncertain' or 'don't know' responses; when items are skipped or crossed out; when respondents do not seem interested in discussing the scale or, if they want to discuss it, do so chiefly in order to explain how it fails to cater to their own attitudes. We are on the right path when respondents seem to recognize the statements ('I'll bet you got that from my brother-in-law; he's always saying things like that'); when they make free use of the 'strongly agree' or 'strongly disagree' response categories; when they seem excited or angered by some of the statements that they disagree with, or show signs of satisfaction that their own views are well represented; when they seem eager to provide us with more examples or more information along the lines of certain statements; and, of course, when there are few signs that they reject the items by making amendments or deletions, skipping, giving 'Don't know' responses and so on.

Remembering that attitudes are emotional, we should try to avoid a stilted, rational approach in writing attitude statements, and select from the depth interviews some of the more contentiously worded statements of opinion; we must not be afraid to use phrases relating to feelings and emotions, hopes and wishes, hates, fears and happiness.

In writing attitude statements we should generally bear in mind the question-wording principles set out in Chapter 8. We should, for example, avoid statements that are too long, that are double-barrelled, that use colloquialisms, proverbs, acronyms or double negatives. Slogans or well-known sayings are also best avoided. Attitude statements are better when they have a certain freshness, forcing respondents to pause for a moment and take a stand (see Workshop VI).

Paradoxically, however, it does not always pay to make the statements too clear and unambiguous, nor to ask the respondent to think very hard. Often, a statement that is, strictly speaking, almost meaningless, works very well because pilot work has shown that respondents invest it, in their own way, with the meaning that our context requires. For example, the statement 'if you're not firm, children will try to get away with anything' is far from exact or unambiguous; yet it works very well with parents, and correlates acceptably with other indicators of strictness. As to careful thought, of course we want respondents to be attentive, but we want them to think and express themselves as they do habitually; we don't want them to think out a new philosophy of life on the spot or to start ruminative doubts with every item. This is one more reason for using language that will be familiar.

We may not always want the purpose of our inquiry to be obvious. There are many ways of accomplishing this, one of which is to avoid statements that are too direct, in favour of more indirect or oblique statements. Suppose that we are trying to measure the feelings of readers toward a library. A very direct statement might be: 'I hate going to the library', whereas a more indirect statement would be: 'I often wish the library did not have so many silly rules and regulations.' Research has shown that the two statements correlate well with one another; they express the same underlying dislike for the library but in the second case a little more subtly, so that respondents can agree with it without fully realizing what they are saying. Or again, instead of: 'I don't always trust the doctors in this hospital,' try: 'I wish my own doctor could look after me here.' Of course, one cannot tell in advance whether a more oblique approach will work; only careful item-analysis and correlation studies can show when and where it is justified.

All this illustrates that the writing of successful attitude statements demands careful pilot work, experience, intuition and a certain amount of flair. Later on, the scaling procedures will separate the wheat from the chaff. Listening to the depth interview tapes is essential.

One way of looking at the composition of an item pool is to regard it as a sampling process. Out of the total number of sub-areas within the attitude cluster we wish to measure, only a limited number can be represented in our scale; and within each sub-area the actual statements we compose will represent but a fraction of the almost unlimited number of hypothetical statements that might have been written. Since we do not yet know which sub-areas will have the most powerful correlations with the remainder of the attitude cluster and which are more peripheral, it would be wise to include items dealing with most of them. In other words, without being too rigid about it, we must try to keep the item pool reasonably *balanced*. We will want to have roughly equal numbers of items dealing with each main aspect of the attitude; we will want items covering the attitude from one extreme to the other, but we won't want too many extremes; and we need roughly equal proportions of positive and negative items. As we will see, this balancing of the item pool is particularly important in the case of the Likert scaling procedure (see Chapter 11). If we wish to include some long shots — items which, though seemingly unrelated, may correlate well as indirect measures — we must be particularly careful that they do not upset or unbalance the rest of the pool.

Finally, before we use them, the items have to be scrambled, by putting them more or less in random order; we might also put a few innocuous items at the beginning, to get the respondents used to the answering procedure.

## Response sets (see also Chapter 8)

A few words should be added here concerning different response sets, the tendency to reply to attitude-scale items in a particular way, almost irrespective of content. One such set has been identified as 'social desirability'; this is the tendency to reply 'agree' to items that the respondents believe reflect socially desirable attitudes, in order to show themselves in a better light. Another response set has been described as 'acquiescence', a general tendency toward assent rather than dissent, especially when the statements are in the form of plausible generalities. Some aspects of rigidity, dogmatism and authoritarianism may also lead to certain response tendencies. The incorporation of both positively and negatively worded items dealing with the same issue goes only part of the way towards overcoming these problems because some response sets are largely independent of content. More research is needed into response styles, since they affect some scales and some kinds of respondents more than others, and there seems to be no easy way either of detecting their influences or of neutralizing them.

---

WORKSHOP VI: EDITING ATTITUDE STATEMENTS

Here are some attitude statements designed to form part of an item pool to measure sexism, chauvinism and androgyny. Part of the problem was that these topics had not yet crystallized along well-established lines; consequently there were uncertainties about the dimension or dimensions which the scale was supposed to measure. The item pool contains various sub-dimensions such as gender-role differentiation, male chauvinism, occupational and social sexism, gender differences in presentation of self, in emotional expression, in child-rearing and aspects of social equality.

(A) 'It is important for men to look masculine.' (Though this item may seem meaningless, people do say such things in interviews and the statement seems likely to be effective.)

(B) 'I do not have any hesitation in trusting a woman doctor.' (This statement may 'work' very differently for male and for female respondents: the issue of same-sex/different-sex doctor may get mixed up with the purpose of the scale: here, to measure occupational sexism. Also, the word 'trusting' might have to be replaced.)

(C) 'There is a right and a wrong way of expressing emotions for a man and for a woman.' (Clumsy wording.)

(D) 'Men who wear scented aftershave are disgusting.' (Wording may be too strong, may yield poor frequency distribution. Perhaps take out 'scented'? Does the statement tap the issue of equality between the sexes, or is it measuring something else as well?)

(E) 'Public toilets should be made unisex.'

(F) 'I like to see men carrying babies.' (This might be misunderstood to mean that men might, one day, be able to get pregnant. Otherwise, a good, personalized expression of view.)

(G) 'I should like to see more male secretaries.'

(H) 'Men should be the breadwinners.' (This looks like a good statement, but some exploration may be needed of the term 'breadwinner'.)

(I) 'Men and women are different but for most things irrelevantly so.' (Double-barrelled. What would a 'disagree' response mean?)

(J) 'I see no reason why a woman should not propose marriage to a man, if she wants to.' (Could be shortened. May produce problems with double negatives — best rephrase it to get rid of the 'no'.)

(K) 'I like to see men pushing prams.' (A nice, colloquial phrasing.)

(L) 'I would have less confidence in a woman professional than in a male one.' (This is probably better than statement B above, but it is so general that it may prove unreliable: different respondents may give very different meanings to the term 'professional'.)

(M) 'Boys who play with dolls should be firmly discouraged.' (Likely to 'work' very well.)

(N) 'Jobs like changing the baby's nappy could be done as well by the father as by the mother.' (Clumsy wording. Also, some respondents may take it literally: the issue is not really how competently it is done but about gender differences in the parenting role.)

(O) 'All-male clubs/societies are a good thing.' (May need some rephrasing, but should work well.)

(P) 'Women drivers aren't as good as male drivers.' (This statement may well be effective, but as a rule we should avoid statements in the form of general observations (for example 'dogs foul the pavement'), on the grounds that it tells us too little about the respondent's own feelings.)

(Q) 'One thing I do not like in the way young persons are dressed nowadays is that you cannot distinguish easily the male from the female.' (Too long, too clumsy, dangers of double negatives. Content seems appropriate; needs rewording.)

(R) 'The father should be the only one who spanks a child.' (Problem: will this get mixed up with attitudes to corporal punishment? It assumes that a child will be spanked.)

(S) 'A woman's place is in the home.' (This is a widely used item in many scales, especially those measuring political conservatism. Should we avoid it?)

(T) 'No real man would want to help with housework.' (Probably a useful statement; the phrase 'real man' nicely worded to provoke.)

(U) 'A man who wears makeup must be a homosexual.' (Two problems: (1) will the homosexuality issue get mixed up with the gender equality issue? (2) again, a general observation, which tells us little about the respondent's own views — it is possible to disagree with the statement, yet still to feel that men should not wear makeup. See statement P above.)

The above comments illustrate some of the issues that arise in selecting and editing attitude statements for an item pool. We need items that are clear, personalized expressions of feelings, containing not more than one issue. The main topic addressed by the item must be part of the object of our scale, and the items must be relevant to the issue being measured. Descriptive observations are best avoided. If a person agrees, say, that 'most old people live in the past', this does not tell us whether the respondent likes or dislikes old people (unless we are prepared to make the assumption that living in the past is something of which the respondent disapproves, but such an assumption would be risky). After reading each statement, try to 'translate' it into 'I like/dislike' whatever the statement is about. If this is not clear, then the statement may be too vague or too neutral, and it will be impossible to score the responses. Try to ensure that the item pool is reasonably balanced. In the item pool referred to in Workshop VI, there would have been perhaps a dozen sub-areas (gender equality at work; dress and makeup; and so on), each of which would have to contain at least half-a-dozen statements, in roughly equal numbers of 'pro' and 'con' items. Thus, an item stating that men are better drivers than women would have to be balanced, if possible, by items stating that there are good and bad drivers among either sex, or that women are better drivers than men. At the end of the day, the item analysis and scaling procedures will sort out the good items from the bad ones and will show whether the whole area can be represented by a single, uni-dimensional scale or will need several scales or sub-scales.

One problem with attitude scales is that they have a limited life span. Sometimes the cause is obvious: the objects of concern have changed or disappeared. For instance, scales built to measure attitudes to the Vietnam War or to the Soviet Union can no longer be used in their original form. At other times, the debate has moved on. For example, it seems likely that in most countries and in most periods there will be a political dimension of radicalism–

conservatism (perhaps called by different names, such as left-wing versus right-wing, Labour versus Tory, Social Democrat versus Christian Democrat) in the electorate. However, the issues that define this dimension will change over time. For example, issues such as corporal punishment, abortion, homosexuality, women's suffrage or premarital sex probably no longer divide the voters in most Western countries in the way they once did; other issues have come to the fore, and the same dimension will have to be re-defined. Sometimes, too, social mores and attitudes change, to make many of the scale items irrelevant. Here, for example, are some items from a 1959 chivalry scale (Nadler and Morrow, 1959) developed in the United States:

A gentleman should remove his hat and hold it in his right hand when a lady enters the elevator in which he is a passenger.

It is inexcusable when a man escorting a lady fails to help her on with her coat.

No right-thinking person would question the sanctity of motherhood.

In accompanying a lady anywhere at night, a gentleman should never fail to offer his arm.

The same considerations apply when we take a scale from one country to another: we must not assume that, after translation, it will measure the same 'thing' in both countries; we have to make sure that it does (usually by means of factor analysis). Translation can subtly alter the meanings and overtones of an attitude statement, or the same statement may have a changed significance in a different social context.

There are accessible collections of questionnaire items and attitude scales in several countries (see Selected Readings). These can be a useful input when we are building a new scale, but existing attitude scales should never be uncritically applied in a different country or in a changed social context.

Some attitude scales are crude and obvious in their purpose, giving rise to the notion that scales cannot be subtle or sensitive and can only deal with the banal and the obvious. This is far from true, as has been illustrated in Workshop VI where the items were designed to uncover an emergent attitude or set of attitudes.

It is even possible to develop complex attitude scales for use with school children, provided extensive pilot work has ensured that the children are aware of the topics of concern, and that they do have opinions about them. (With children, it is helpful to have answering categories such as 'I have not heard or thought about this' and 'I have no opinion', in addition to agree/disagree.) Some years ago a cross-national study of political socialization and civic education (Torney *et al.*, 1975) was undertaken in ten countries, which included Finland, Iran, Germany, Italy and the United States. Within each country, representative samples of children were drawn from either two or three age groups (ten to eleven-year-olds, fourteen to fifteen and seventeen to nineteen-year-olds) — twenty-two sub-samples and over 30,000 children in all (some countries did not collect data for some age levels). Despite differences in ages and languages, it proved possible to develop attitude scales and other measures which were shown to have near-equivalent factor structures in all twenty-two sub-samples, though the measures dealt with such complex topics as civil liberties, ethnic equality, war and peace, political participation, equal rights for women and attitudes to local government. This study illustrates that, with sufficient care in the pilot work and much pre-testing in different countries, it is possible to develop attitude measures which meet the requirements of scaling, which are comparable across countries and age groups, and which deal with complex and subtle issues as understood by children and adolescents.

---

## WORKSHOP VII: UNSCALED ATTITUDE STATEMENTS

The following attitude statements appeared in a questionnaire that was sent out to a sample of married women. They were designed to assess women's attitudes to detergents, soap flakes and the polluting effects of detergents. There were no other attitude statements.

'Regular soap flakes cannot be used in a washing machine.'
'All detergents are equally good.'
'Enzymes in detergents should be outlawed.'
'Soap flakes get clothes as white as detergents.'
'Detergents make clothes cleaner than soap flakes.'
'I would buy a more expensive soap if it was non-polluting.'
'If we continue to use detergents we will harm our lakes and rivers.'

We could criticize these statements for their clumsy wording and poor grammar and for the fact that they seem to be trying to measure two or three quite different issues, but more important is the fact that these statements *do not form a scale*. This means that each statement stands on its own, like any other single attitudinal question, with all the attendant risks of unreliability and poor validity. Such a set of statements looks like a short scale, and it may impress the uninitiated, but it will not yield a combined score. Each item could be analysed separately (though, as we have seen, this would be most unwise), but that would defeat the purpose of using attitude statements. As they stand, these seven statements are misleading and of little use: they give the superficial impression of being 'scientific', but they do not constitute a measure. Unless they are to form part of a much larger item pool and will be subjected to item analysis and scaling procedures, they should be abandoned.

# Selected readings

## ATTITUDE THEORIES AND MEASUREMENT

Fishbein, Martin (ed.), 1967, *Readings in Attitude Theory and Measurement*, Wiley, New York.
This very useful collection contains many classical papers dealing both with measurement and with theory.

Fishbein, Martin and Ajzen, Icek, 1975, *Belief, Attitude, Intention and Behaviour*, Addison–Wesley, Reading, Massachusets.
A well-known general text on attitude theory and the links between attitudes, intentions and actions.

Pratkanis, Anthony R., Breckler, Steven J. and Greenwald, Anthony G. (eds), 1989, *Attitude Structure and Function*, Lawrence Erlbaum Associates, Hove, East Sussex.
Deals with more recent developments in attitude theories.

Adorno, T.W., Frenkel-Brunswik, Else, Levinson, D.J. and Sanford, R.N., 1950, *The Authoritarian Personality*, Harper, New York.
A classic study of prejudiced attitudes, showing the development of concepts and scales from depth interviews as well as the links between different ethnic prejudices, ethnocentrism and authoritarianism.

Nadler, R.B., and Morrow, W.R., 1959, 'Authoritarian attitudes toward women and their correlates', *J. Social Psychol.*, 49, 113–23.
Source of the chivalry scale cited in the text.

Torney, Judith V., Oppenheim, A.N. and Farnen, Russell F., 1975, *Civic Education in Ten Countries*, Wiley.

## WRITING ATTITUDE STATEMENTS

Edwards, Allen L., 1957, *Techniques of Attitude Scale Construction*, Appleton–Century–Crofts, New York.

# 11
# ATTITUDE SCALING

This chapter is devoted to an account of the classical methods of measuring attitudes through the use of attitude scaling. Other methods of measuring attitudes will be discussed in the following chapters.

Attitude scales consist of from half a dozen to two dozen or more items — usually attitude statements — with which the respondent is asked to agree or disagree. In previous chapters we have noted the dangers that attach to the use of single questions to measure attitudes, and we have discussed the generation and composition of a pool of attitude statements, preparatory to the construction of an attitude scale. However, more important than the number of attitude statements used is the fact that they have been *scaled*: they have been selected and put together from a much larger number of statements according to certain statistical scaling procedures. Because of this, we must not judge the relatively small number of attitude statements in a finished scale at their face value; they are the outcome of a complicated process of item analysis and represent a synthesis of all the preliminary thought and work described in Chapters 4, 5 and 10.

Attitude scales are relatively overt measuring instruments designed to be used in surveys, and we must not expect too much of them. They are not designed to yield subtle insights in individual cases and should not be used as clinical instruments. Their chief function is to divide people roughly into a number of broad groups with respect to a particular attitude, and to allow us to study the ways in which such an attitude relates to other variables in our survey. They are techniques for placing people on a continuum in relation to each other, in relative and not in absolute terms.

## Principles of measurement

The traditional methods of attitude measurement are best viewed and evaluated in relation to the linear-scaling model (see Chapter 9). This model has the following requirements:

1. *Uni-dimensionality* or homogeneity — the scale should be about one thing at a time, as uniformly as possible. This means that the items should be internally

cohesive, they should 'hang together' to measure the same dimension with as little extraneous variance as possible.
2. *Reliability* — the indispensible attribute of consistency. Traditional scaling methods are often strong in this respect.
3. *Validity* — the degree to which the scale measures what it sets out to measure. As we have seen, at present it is often impossible to find a sufficiently reliable and valid external criterion against which to validate an attitude scale.
4. *Linearity* and equal or equal-appearing intervals — to make quantitative scoring possible.

To these requirements a fifth has been added later, namely:

5. *Reproducibility* — when we say that a man weighs 150 pounds, we mean that the pointer on the scales will move from zero to 150 but will cover none of the remainder; in other words, the figure of 150 refers, not to just any 150 pound units, but to the first 150 pounds on the scale. From the 'score' of 150, we can reproduce exactly which units on the scale were covered and which were not. This is not an essential requirement when we are dealing with constant and interchangeable units, such as kilograms or inches; but if we were dealing, say, with the symptoms of the different stages of an illness, it would be helpful if they could be ordered or scaled in terms of their degree of seriousness in such a way that the presence of symptom D would mean that the patient also must have symptoms A, B, and C. Similarly, a score on an attitude scale might show us, by means of a single figure, with which statements the respondent agreed and with which he or she disagreed, thus telling us the respondent's place on the attitude continuum. This is a requirement that in practice is difficult to achieve, for many attitude pools are not amenable to this kind of cumulative or progressive scaling — partly because they may not be uni-dimensional.

Apart from these main requirements, there may be others. For instance, it is helpful to have norms or standards derived from the scores of large numbers of respondents, enabling us to compare an individual's score with those of others and interpret its meaning.

In the following sections we will discuss the four best-known methods of attitude scaling, namely the Bogardus, Thurstone, Likert and Guttman scales. One might ask why more than one method is needed. This has come about because, since the 1920s, different research workers have developed methods of scale-building in which they have laid particular stress on one or another of the above requirements, and have paid less attention to the others. One method has concentrated on uni-dimensionality, another on finding equivalent scale units, a third on obtaining reproducibility and so on. There does not seem to be a method that combines the advantages of them all, and it is therefore very important that we understand their respective aims and the differences between them.

It follows that, for the present, it is impossible to say which method is best. Each has important desirable features, but each is also open to criticism. The best method for any enquiry is the one which is most appropriate to the particular problem. If we wish to study attitude patterning or to explore theories of attitudes, then probably the Likert procedure will be the most relevant. If we wish to study attitude change, or the hierarchical structure of an attitude, then Guttman's method might be preferable. If we are studying group differences, then we shall probably elect to use the Thurstone procedures. Each type of scale does one thing well, and, if this is what our research needs, then this is the type of scale we will want to use.

## Social-distance scales

In 1925, Bogardus brought out a social-distance scale, subsequently revised, that has been widely used in the United States and illustrates some of the problems in scale construction.

*Directions:* According to my first feeling-reactions, I would willingly admit members of each race (as a class, and not the best I have known, nor the worst members), to one or more of the classifications which I have circled.

|  | To close kinship by marriage | To my club as personal chums | To my street as neighbours | To employment in my occupation | To citizenship in my country | As visitors only to my country | Would exclude from my country |
|---|---|---|---|---|---|---|---|
| Canadians | 1 | 2 | 3 | 4 | 5 | 6 | 7 |
| Chinese | 1 | 2 | 3 | 4 | 5 | 6 | 7 |
| English | 1 | 2 | 3 | 4 | 5 | 6 | 7 |
| French | 1 | 2 | 3 | 4 | 5 | 6 | 7 |
| Germans | 1 | 2 | 3 | 4 | 5 | 6 | 7 |
| Hindus | 1 | 2 | 3 | 4 | 5 | 6 | 7 |
| etc. | | | | | | | |

Apart from the rather complicated instructions, at first sight there seems little to criticize in this scale. The idea of expressing ethnic prejudice as 'social distance' seems reasonable, and by analogy we may think of a straight road with the seven classifications as milestones along it. Early large-scale investigations did show a fairly regular progression in the proportions of Americans endorsing each position. Usually, there is a 'hump' somewhere in the middle — suggesting neither extreme hostility nor complete acceptance, depending on the 'race' or nationality in question.

How well does this scale satisfy the five requirements outlined before? Concerning uni-dimensionality, we have little evidence. It is quite possible that, underlying these various categories, there is a single, pure attitude, but then again, such categories as 'marriage', 'neighbours', 'exclude', and others may bring in many extraneous influences. Criticism has been directed against the scale's questionable linearity and its unequal intervals. For some respondents, admission to occupational membership signifies a greater degree of closeness than 'to my street as neighbours', and so on. This would require a different (or perhaps non-linear) ordering of the steps — though in large samples this might only apply to a minority. As for equality of intervals, there is no evidence that the social distance between, say, 2 and 3 is in any way equivalent to the distance between 5 and 6 and so on. The scoring is thus completely arbitrary. Reliability of the scale has reached beyond .90 and must be regarded as satisfactory. There is, at least, some positive evidence of the validity of the scale in comparison with other types of scale. Until lately, the question of reproducibility had not been raised, but more recent inquiries have shown that this can be surprisingly good.

If we disregard the scoring and consider the results merely as a way of ordering individuals or groups with regard to their ethnic attitudes, then useful comparisons can be made, but a good deal of caution is required in the interpretation of such results.

## Thurstone scales

Thurstone's chief preoccupation was with the problem of equal or, rather, equal-appearing intervals. Part of his reasoning stemmed from experiments in psychophysics, where various methods have been developed to scale the judgments of individuals with regard to various physical properties such as weight. The smaller the true difference in weight between two objects, the fewer people will be able to distinguish correctly between them (see Guilford, 1956 for an exposition of various psychophysical methods). In much the same way, Thurstone attempted to devise attitude scales by getting people to compare attitude statements two at a time and deciding which of each pair was the more positive or the more negative.

This method, known as the paired-comparisons technique, becomes very cumbersome when more than fifteen or twenty items are involved, as is frequently the case. A less precise, but also less laborious, method was therefore proposed by Thurstone, known as the method of equal-appearing intervals.

The first step in this and every other scaling procedure is to design and collect a pool of items (see Chapter 10) from the literature and from pilot interviews. After that, we need a group of 'judges'. While in the past university students were often used as judges, it is preferable to have the judgments made by people who are similar to those to whom the finished scale will be applied. To give some rough idea of numbers: one might have 100–150 statements and 40–60 judges, though as many as 300 judges have been used.

Next, the items are reproduced individually on cards or slips of paper, and each judge is given, in random order, a complete set of items. The judges are told what the scale is 'about', and a hypothetical scale is set up, running from 'most favourable' through a neutral point to 'least favourable'. The scale is divided into a fixed number of sections, usually eleven, and it will be the task of the judges to consider each item and to place it in one of these eleven sections or piles. In pile No. 1 should go only the extremely favourable items, in pile No. 2 the slightly less favourable ones and so on through pile No. 6, which should contain only neutral items. Slightly unfavourable items go into pile No. 7, and so forth; the extremely unfavourable items will go into pile No. 11. The intervals between the categories should be regarded as subjectively equal. It is most important that the judges ignore their own agreement or disagreement with the item; their job is merely to place the item in a particular category according to its meaning. Irrelevant, ambiguous or poorly worded items will have been eliminated beforehand. At the end of the judging process, each judge will record on each statement the number of the pile in which it has been placed.

Next, we assemble all the judgments for each statement. If we consider a hypothetical statement, No. 95, we will no doubt find that most judges have placed it in, say, category 8, while some have placed it in 7 or 9, and a few in 6, 10, or 11. We are now going to consider the distribution of judgments for each item in order to select, from our total pool of items, those two dozen or so that will form a scale.

First of all, we consider the *spread* of judgments. The wider the spread, the more ambiguous the item is. Ambiguous items will cause unreliability and have no place in our scale; we therefore wish to eliminate them. Almost any measure of spread (range, variance, standard deviation, semi-interquartile range) will do, but the last is probably the simplest and quickest, and at the same time it allows us to read off the median.

We need the *medians* in order to examine item position or scale value. After eliminating the items with excessive spread, we will probably still have a considerable number of statements left, and their medians or scale values will be unevenly distributed along the hypothetical continuum of our scale, so that we may get medians reading 1.7, 1.8, 2.2, 2.2, 2.9, 3.0, 3.1, 3.1, 3.2, 3.2, 3.4, 3.5, and so on. (Medians are used because in psychophysics a 'just noticeable difference' between two stimuli has traditionally been defined as one that could be distinguished by 50 per cent of the respondents. Thus, for example, if the median calculated for one statement is 4.0 and for another 3.0, then the two statements may be said to lie *one* just noticeable difference apart on a psychological continuum.) We have to decide how long our scale is going to be and how many items we need to select. Twenty or twenty-two items would be common practice, but longer and also much shorter scales exist; or we may decide to build two *parallel forms* of the scale, if the available items permit this.

The detailed steps of the Thurstone scaling procedure are as follows:

1. On the enclosed paper slips you will find a set of statements concerning ———. The statements are in no particular order, but they range from extremely favourable to extremely unfavourable. Before starting the judgment process, read through all the items carefully.
2. Note that there is only one item on each slip, that the item number is on the left, and that the space for recording your judgment is on the right.
3. Sort out the items into eleven piles. In pile No. 1, you should put those items that, in your opinion, would reflect the most favourable attitude to ———. In pile No. 2 will be those items that you would regard as slightly less favourable to ———. Thus each successive group of statements should be slightly less favourable than the preceding one, until you reach pile No. 6, which should

contain those statements that show a neutral attitude. In pile No. 7 would go those items which you regard as slightly unfavourable and so on until you reach pile No. 11, which should reflect only the most rejecting and hostile attitudes in the item pool.

4. Your own agreement or disagreement with these items must be disregarded.
5. Write on each item slip, in the space provided, the number of the pile in which you put it.
6. Feel free to use any of the eleven points on the scale, but do not attempt to put the same number of slips in each pile.
7. After recording your judgments, put all the slips together into an envelope.

### INSTRUCTIONS FOR CALCULATION OF MEDIANS AND Q'S

1. The median and the semi-interquartile range may either be calculated, or can be 'read off' from a cumulative-frequency graph. In the latter case, proceed as follows.
2. Sort all the items returned by the judges according to their item numbers. Put all the item slips bearing the same number together.
3. For each group, sort the item slips into piles, according to the written judgments recorded on each slip. You will find most often that you will need from four to six piles — occasionally more.
4. Draw up a frequency distribution for each item by writing down the pile numbers from 1 to 11 and recording the number of slips in each pile. If there are no slips for some pile numbers (categories), record a zero.
5. Add up the total number of frequencies, i.e. the total number of slips you have for this item. Convert the frequencies for each category into percentages of this total.
6. The distribution may now be made cumulative, by adding the percentages successively to one another. When the last percentage has been added, the cumulative percentage frequency should read 100. Table 11.1 may clarify this process.
7. Draw up a cumulative graph for the cumulative-percentage frequencies. The eleven categories are placed along the bottom line, while the percentages are indicated along the side. Find the approximate point directly above each category *value* that corresponds to the correct cumulative percentage for that category. Draw lines to connect these percentage points. This will give a steeply rising curve of cumulative-percentage frequencies.
8. Lines should be drawn across the page for the median (50 per cent of the total frequencies) and the two quartiles (25 per cent and 75 per cent respectively). Their corresponding scale values may be read off by noting the points at which these lines cross the cumulative-percentage curve and dropping perpendiculars to the base-line at those three points (see Figure 11.1).
9. Record the median from the value of the central perpendicular. Calculate Q = the semi-interquartile range as follows: record the scale value of the third perpendicular; subtract from it the value of the first perpendicular; halve this difference to obtain Q.

Table 11.1.

| Pile No. | Frequency | Percentage | Cumulative percentages |
|---|---|---|---|
| 1 | 0 | — | — |
| 2 | 0 | — | — |
| 3 | 0 | — | — |
| 4 | 0 | — | — |
| 5 | 0 | — | — |
| 6 | 2 | 4% | 4% |
| 7 | 2 | 4% | 8% |
| 8 | 10 | 20% | 28% |
| 9 | 11 | 22% | 50% |
| 10 | 15 | 30% | 80% |
| 11 | 10 | 20% | 100% |
| | 50 | 100% | |

10.  For the example in Table 11.1, the following values have been found:

median = 9.0
$$Q = \frac{1}{2}(9.8 - 7.8) = 1.0.$$

The actual selection of the items will be in terms of the intervals between them. This might be one whole scale point, half a point or any other distance. If we decide, for instance, that we want about twenty items, then we may want to choose those items whose medians are nearest to scale points 1.5, 2.0, 2.5, 3.0, 3.5, 4.0, and so on. In this way we build up a scale with equal-appearing intervals. In exceptional cases, we may wish for finer discrimination on a particular part of the scale than on the remainder, and we may choose items which lie closer together on that section.

Our scale is now ready for administration. The statements will be printed in random order, without their scale values. Respondents will only be asked either to agree or to disagree with each statement. Subsequently, we look up the scale value of each agreed statement, and the median of these constitutes the respondent's score. If all goes according to plan, our respondent should only agree with a very few statements. If, let us say, he is a male with a mildly positive attitude, then he should disagree with items that are strongly positive, neutral or negative. In fact, ideally, he should agree only with the one or two items that best reflect his particular attitude.

Although, as we have seen, Thurstone's procedure is primarily concerned with locating items at points on a hypothetical scale, we must be careful when treating these scale values as actual numbers, as intervals that are additive and interchangeable on a linear continuum. We are dealing not with equal, but with equal-*appearing* intervals, with psychological rather than numerical units, which may or may not be equal. Moreover, since the division of the continuum into eleven units is arbitrary, we should not think of a score of eight as numerically

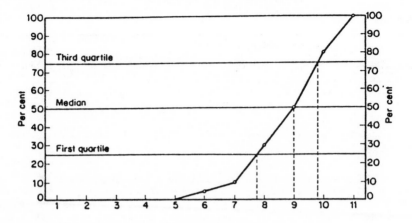

Figure 11.1. Cumulative-frequency graph for item no. ——
median =
Q = ½ (third quartile minus first quartile) =

twice as high as a score of four, and so on. In any case, in scale construction it is often felt that more units would be preferable on one side of the neutral point than on the other; some attitudes seem more differentiated at one end of the scale, or go further or deeper, and judges often make finer discriminations at the extremes of a scale than in the middle. Doubts have also been cast on the comparability of scores from one scale to another in a battery of several attitude scales.

What can we say about the uni-dimensionality of Thurstone scales? Our first guide here, apart from the care taken in the composition of the item pool, is the elimination of the more ambiguous items, the ones with high semi-interquartile ranges. Items on which general agreement exists among judges have an *a priori* claim for inclusion, but this is still quite removed from proven uni-dimensionality. We can, however, go further and administer our newly developed scale to a sample of respondents, with instructions to tick the statements with which they agree. Next, we can analyse the results to check on the internal consistency of the items. If respondents who agree with one particular statement also tick other statements with widely differing scale values, the statement has to be rejected since it obviously contains large elements that are irrelevant to the attitude that the scale should measure; if only statements with roughly similar scale values have been ticked, the statement can be retained. (See also discussion of factorial scales later in this chapter.)

The reliability of Thurstone scales tends to be adequate, and they have the additional advantage that often a parallel form emerges from the item analysis; this is particularly useful when studying attitude *change*. Reproducibility (in the technical sense) would, presumably, be good in the ideal case where a respondent endorses only a single item, but since this happens very rarely the scales may be criticized on this account. The validity of these scales has occasionally been demonstrated with the aid of criterion groups whose attitudes were allegedly known (because of their membership in certain organizations, their comments in an interview, or their responses to essay-type questions), but since these other measures may be less reliable than the scale that is being validated, or may refer to different attitude facets, doubts must remain.

Judges should be similar to those on whom the scale will be used. However, do different groups of judges produce the same scale values? For instance, would black judges produce the same scale values as white judges for an item pool dealing with ethnic prejudice? By and large, experimental investigations have shown that the scale values obtained from such widely differing groups of judges correlate highly with one another so long as judges with extreme views are excluded. Judges with strong 'pro' or 'anti' feelings concerning the particular attitude in question tend to bunch the items toward the opposite end of the scale; thus, judges with strong pro-black attitudes tend to displace items toward the anti-black end of the scale and to place few items in the middle (neutral) categories. In practice, judges who place more than one-third of the items in the same category should be excluded; inevitably, all judges will be influenced by their own attitudes, but in most cases the effect will be small and will barely affect the order of the items.

Caution is also required when scales are applied cross-culturally and when some of the older scales are reapplied today — issues, words, and stereotypes sometimes undergo subtle changes (see p. 183).

## Likert scales

The construction of a Thurstone scale always means a lot of work, and it is often difficult to obtain an adequate group of judges. The Likert procedure may have its disadvantages, but it is certainly less laborious, and this — together with the experimental finding that Likert scales correlate well with Thurstone scales — has helped to make it the most popular scaling procedure in use today.

Likert's primary concern was with uni-dimensionality — making sure that all the items would measure the same thing. He also wanted to eliminate the need for judges, by getting subjects in a trial sample to *place themselves* on an attitude continuum for each statement — running from 'strongly agree' to 'agree', 'uncertain', 'disagree', and 'strongly disagree'. These five positions were given simple weights of 5, 4, 3, 2, and 1 for scoring purposes (or sometimes 4–0), after more complex scoring methods had been shown to possess no advantage.

To produce a Likert scale we proceed as follows: first, as usual, we compose an item pool. However, for the Likert procedure it is best not to have many neutral items or many extreme items at either end of the continuum. Next, we need a sample of respondents on whom to try out the entire pool of items together. Probably 100 respondents would suffice for most purposes, but numbers of the order of 250 or 300 are not unusual. Each respondent will be asked, not merely whether he/she agrees or disagrees with each statement, but to tick one of the five positions given above. Respondents should be similar to those on whom the scale will be used.

Next, we score the record of each respondent. To do this, we must decide whether we want a high scale score to mean a favourable or an unfavourable attitude. It does not matter what we decide, but from then on we must be consistent. If we decide that a high score on the scale will mean a favourable attitude, then favourable statements must be scored 5 for 'strongly agree', down to 1 for 'strongly disagree' — and unfavourable statements must be scored 1 for

| | Strongly agree | Agree | Uncertain | Disagree | Strongly disagree |
|---|---|---|---|---|---|
| | 5 | 4 | 3 | 2 | 1 |
| (1) Children bring a husband and wife closer to each other. ____ | | | ✓ | | |
| (2) It is fun showing children how to do things. ____ | | ✓ | | | |
| (3) Children need some of their natural meanness taken out of them.____ | | | | | ✓ |
| (4) A mother with young children badly misses adult company and conversation.____ | ✓ | | | | |
| (5) On balance, children are more of a blessing than a burden. ____ | | ✓ | | | |
| (6) It is often difficult to keep one's temper with a child.____ | | | | ✓ | |
| (7) Looking after children really demands too much of me. ____ | | | | ✓ | |
| (8) If we could afford to do so, we would prefer to send our children to a boarding school.____ | | | ✓ | | |
| (9) When things are difficult, children are often a great source of courage and inspiration.____ | | | | ✓ | |
| (10) If I had my life to live over again, I should again want to have children.____ | ✓ | | | | |

Figure 11.2.

'strongly agree' up to 5 for 'strongly disagree'. If we decide that a high score will mean an *un*favourable attitude, then the opposite system of scoring will apply. It helps, therefore, if we have few neutral items, making it easy to tell from the wording of the statement whether it is positive or negative. But if we feel uncertain about some statements, we can score them arbitrarily from 1–5 or from 5–1; the correlations will subsequently show us whether we are right. Research workers often get into difficulties over this problem of scoring reversals, so it is important to be meticulous about it from the start.

Having scored each item from 1–5 or from 5–1, we next add up the item scores to obtain a total score. For instance, if we have 132 items in our pool, then the possible range of total scores will be from 132 to 660 (5 × 132) for each subject. Figure 11.2 illustrates some items from a scale for mothers, dealing with acceptance or rejection of children. It becomes obvious, on reading through the items, that some of them express greater or lesser acceptance, others express degrees of hostility or rejection, and one or two may not fit on this particular dimension. Thus, agreement with statement (2) 'It is fun showing children how to do things' would seem to imply positive feelings for children; agreement with statement (3) 'Children need some of their natural meanness taken out of them' would seem to indicate hostility to children on the part of the respondent; while the implications of statement (8) 'If we could afford to do so, we would prefer to send our children to a boarding school' are unclear: agreement might signify rejection of the children, or it might mean the desire to lavish money on them in order to give them a better education (which could, however, be a form of overcompensation for unconscious feelings of rejection) (see page 163).

We now come to the problem of scoring. If we decide that a high scale score is going to mean a positive attitude to children, then agreement with the statements that imply love of children should be scored 5 or 4, and agreement with statements that imply rejection of children should be scored 1 or 2 — in other words, the scoring of these latter statements is *reversed*. If, on the other hand, we decide that a high scale score will mean a negative attitude to children, then the scoring on the items that imply positive feelings toward children (items 1, 2, 5, 9 and 10) should be reversed. The important thing is to be consistent. We must also make sure that we write our scoring instructions correctly, and that in the case of computer analysis of each statement, we know whether the respondents' ticks were entered as given or were reversed, where necessary, before data entry.

In Figure 11.2 we have given but ten items, and we have shown the responses of one particular mother. Just glancing at her responses we get the impression of a mother with a mildly positive attitude toward children (items 2, 5, 7 and 10) who is able to express some moderately negative feelings (items 4 and 9) but shies away from extreme hostility (item 3) or inspired love (item 9). She also expresses some doubts (items 1 and 8); this may be because she is uncertain of her feelings, or uncertain of the implications of the items. Perhaps these items do not belong in this scale because they contain other powerful attitude components (to marriage, to social class, to boarding schools, to separation) besides acceptance or rejection of children. Item analysis would show us whether these items should be retained.

How should this mother's response be scored? Let us assume that we have decided that a high scale score shall mean a positive attitude to children. In that case, all the positive items can be scored as they stand:

5 = strongly agree
4 = agree
3 = uncertain
2 = disagree
1 = strongly disagree.

The scoring for items 3, 4, 6, 7 and 8 will, however, have to be reversed as follows:

1 = strongly agree
2 = agree
3 = uncertain
4 = disagree
5 = strongly disagree.

Note, by the way, that the scoring of 'uncertain' is the same (namely 3) in both cases. We can now give a numerical score to each tick (or program the computer to do so) and calculate a total score, as follows:

```
    item   1 =  3
           2 =  4
           3 =  5
           4 =  1
           5 =  4
           6 =  4
           7 =  4
           8 =  3
           9 =  2
          10 =  5
total score   35
```

Since there are ten items, we have a maximum possible score of 5 × 10 = 50, and a necessary minimum score of 1 × 10 = 10. A score of 35 is thus a little above the midway point toward the positive end of the scale — which confirms our earlier impression of someone with mildly positive attitudes towards children.

Now we shall want to carry out an item analysis to decide which are the best statements for our scale. Ideally, the item analysis should take place by correlating each item with some reliable outside criterion of the attitude that it is supposed to measure, and retaining only the items with the highest correlations. Such external criteria are, however, almost never available. It would not be safe to infer from the fact that a woman has children that she necessarily loves them; nor can we be sure that people who vote for a certain political party necessarily occupy a given position on a political spectrum; or that professional military men are necessarily more war-minded. In other words, it is dangerous to infer people's attitudes from their behaviour or from their group membership. We must therefore say to ourselves that, for the moment at least, the best available measure of the attitude concerned is *the total item pool* that we have so carefully constructed. By purifying this, the items will at least be consistent and homogeneous — they will all be measuring the same thing — and the scale may possibly also be valid.

If we are prepared to make this assumption, then the rest is plain sailing. We simply work out correlation coefficients for each item with the total score and retain those with the highest correlations. This is an internal-consistency method of item analysis, since no external criterion is available. We should not really use the total score, but the total score minus the score for the item in question. This means that, for each item in turn, we will have a slightly different set of total scores. However, this subtraction procedure will not often make much difference, especially if the item pool is at all large; many research workers do not bother with it.

Here is an example. Suppose we are concerned with the analysis of Item 5 from the item pool in Figure 11.2. We have the scores of ten respondents on the pool as a whole, on Item 5, and on the pool as a whole minus their score on Item 5 (see Table 11.2).

We can now calculate the relationship between Item 5 and the total score (or rather, between Item 5 and the total score minus the scores for Item 5). This relationship is very strong ( r = .96), and we should probably wish to retain this item if such results had been obtained on the basis of a much larger sample and a large item pool.

Our final scale will consist of, let us say, eighteen items. They have no scale values such as we find in the Thurstone procedure; all the items carry equal weight. The respondents, as before, are asked to indicate their degree of agreement, and these responses are subsequently scored 1–5, remembering that scoring for some of the items may have to be reversed. After that, the eighteen item scores are added up for a total score, which is the respondent's score on our scale.

Table 11.2.

| Respondent | Total score | Score on item 5 | Total score minus item 5 |
|---|---|---|---|
| A | 45 | 5 | 40 |
| B | 42 | 5 | 37 |
| C | 35 | 4 | 31 |
| D | 35 | 4 | 31 |
| E | 20 | 1 | 19 |
| F | 39 | 4 | 35 |
| G | 33 | 3 | 30 |
| H | 40 | 4 | 36 |
| I | 22 | 1 | 21 |
| J | 27 | 2 | 25 |

Some investigators have used a seven-point degree-of-agreement score rather than the more usual five points. Others prefer to use some other index, rather than correlation coefficients, for item selection. In the psychometric literature there are methods of item analysis, many of which could be applied to attitude scaling.

Reliability of Likert scales tends to be good and, partly because of the greater range of answers permitted to respondents, is often higher than that of corresponding Thurstone scales; a reliability coefficient of .85 is often achieved. The scale makes no pretence at equal-appearing intervals but by using the internal-consistency method of item selection it approaches uni-dimensionality in many cases. The number of items in a Likert scale is arbitrary but is sometimes very small.

The most serious criticism levelled against this type of scale is its lack of reproducibility (in the technical sense): the same total score may be obtained in many different ways. This being so, it has been argued that such a score has little meaning or that two or more identical scores may have totally different meanings. Often, for this reason, the pattern of responses becomes more interesting than the total score.

Another criticism has been that since the scale offers no metric or interval measures and lacks a neutral point, we do not know where scores in the middle ranges change from mildly positive to mildly negative. As against this, it should be pointed out that percentile norms or standard-deviation norms can be calculated if a sample of sufficient size is available; certainly, Likert scales will effectively separate people within the same group. With regard to the neutral point on the scale, we must agree that this is not necessarily the midpoint between the two extreme scale scores. Moreover, scores in the middle region could be due to lukewarm response, lack of knowledge or lack of attitude in the respondent (leading to many 'uncertain' responses) — or to the presence of both strongly positive and strongly negative responses which would more or less balance each other. With such different possibilities, the neutral point would be difficult to locate and even more difficult to interpret.

In practice, if we remember that equal score intervals do not permit us to make assertions about the equality of underlying attitude differences, and that identical scores may have very different meanings, the Likert scales tend to perform very well when it comes to a reliable, rough ordering of people with regard to a particular attitude. Apart from their relative ease of construction, these scales have two other advantages. First, they provide more precise information about the respondent's degree of agreement or disagreement, and respondents usually prefer this to a simple agree/disagree response. Second, it becomes possible to include items whose manifest content is not obviously related to the attitude in question, enabling subtler and deeper ramifications of an attitude to be explored. These 'long shots', such as the item about sending children to boarding schools in our earlier example, which are unlikely to be included in the Thurstone procedure, enable us to make use of the links that an attitude may have with neighbouring areas and to uncover the strands and interconnections of its various components.

## Factorial scales (see Chapter 9)

Internal-consistency methods of item analysis provide some safeguard against the inclusion of unrelated items in a scale, but clearly a better way of ensuring uni-dimensionality would be through the use of factor analysis. In the case of a set of attitude items or statements, when we are looking for a single score to express an individual's position on an attitude continuum, we will want to use factor analysis for scale-building purposes, in order to eliminate items that do not belong and to keep items that have high 'loadings' on the factor (attitude) that we want to measure. Sometimes, however, we can use factor analysis to show how a seemingly homogeneous attitude complex in fact 'breaks down' into several independent factors. A person's political orientation, for instance, has been shown by Himmelweit *et al.* (1981) to consist not merely of a left-wing/right-wing dimension, but of several other independent dimensions. Parental childrearing attitudes have similarly been shown to have at least two independent components (see also the androgeny scale items, p. 181).

Factor analysis is a laborious technique unless one has a computer available. Often, therefore, we find factor analysis applied not to the original item pool but to finished scales. When applied to a single scale, it can throw light on its uni-dimensionality after all the individual items have been intercorrelated. When applied to a battery of scales all given to the same respondents, it can reveal similarities and differences between the scales as well as some of the underlying attitudes or value systems. Factor analysis then becomes a tool for theoretical investigation and new discoveries. In this connection, the problem of rotation and naming of factors remains a source of difficulties (see p. 170).

Factor analysis opens the way to other possibilities. In the rare instances where an external criterion is available, validation and purification will obviously lead to a very high-quality scale. More refined scoring might sometimes be useful, by weighting the items according to their factor loadings. Factor analysis, even more than the original Likert scaling procedure, enables us to show the common attitudinal basis for some widely diverse issues. For example, it has been shown that opinions on sovereignty, abortion law, corporal punishment and religious education have a common underlying attitude structure (Eysenck, 1954).

The factor analysis of attitude scales also opens the way to cross-national comparisons. As a rule, these present problems because of the difficulties of translation and 'equivalent meaning', and because one never knows whether the attitude concerned is structured in the same way in another country. However, if scales are translated and factor-analysed in several countries and continue to produce similar factor pictures, then this strongly suggests similarity of attitude structure and opens the way to cross-national comparisons (see page 184).

## Scalogram analysis

The chief concerns of the method of scalogram analysis, developed by Guttman and his associates, are the twin problems of uni-dimensionality and reproducibility. The method enables us, from a respondent's score, to know exactly which items he or she has endorsed, with not more than 10 per cent error for the sample as a whole. This is, of course, in marked contrast to the Likert scale scores, which can be arrived at in a number of different ways. The method can be used with items other than attitude statements, such as neurotic symptoms or the possession of consumer durables.

The items in a Guttman scale have the properties of being ordinal and cumulative. For instance: lead, glass, and diamond are ordered according to their cumulative degrees of hardness; addition, multiplication and the extraction of square roots are arithmetical operations ordered according to their cumulative degree of difficulty (it is highly likely that anyone who can multiply can also add and that anyone who can extract square roots can both add and multiply). If we think of a dozen or more degrees of hardness or difficulty, ranked in order, then many respondents will endorse the early ones — indicating that they know how to add, subtract, multiply and so on — but, sooner or later, they will 'cross over' and fail to endorse such remaining items as solving differential equations or carrying out integrations. This cross-over point is their individual score. From it, we know precisely which items they must have endorsed.

Another illustration might be a social-distance scale. If it has been constructed with the aid of scalogram analysis, then the individuals' scores will tell us which items they have endorsed, since the score tells us at what point they have crossed over to a negative attitude.

Over the years, many Guttman scales have been developed successfully, some in the socio-political field, others in psychiatry, in consumer research and so on (see, for example, Marsh, 1977).

Guttman set great score by the property of reproducibility, which, as we have seen, is a useful but by no means necessary attribute for most scales. The

Table 11.3.

| Respondent | Item 1 | Item 2 | Item 3 | Item 4 | Item 5 | Item 6 | Item 7 | Item 8 | *Score* |
|---|---|---|---|---|---|---|---|---|---|
| 1 | yes | yes | yes | yes | yes | — | yes | — | 6 |
| 2 | yes | — | — | — | yes | — | yes | yes | 4 |
| 3 | yes | yes | — | — | yes | — | yes | yes | 5 |
| 4 | — | — | — | — | yes | — | yes | — | 2 |
| 5 | yes | — | — | — | yes | — | yes | — | 3 |
| 6 | yes | — | — | — | yes | — | yes | yes | 4 |
| 7 | yes | yes | — | yes | yes | yes | yes | yes | 7 |
| 8 | yes | — | — | yes | yes | — | yes | — | 4 |
| 9 | yes | yes | — | yes | yes | yes | yes | yes | 7 |
| 10 | yes | yes | — | yes | yes | — | yes | yes | 6 |
| 11 | — | — | — | — | — | — | — | yes | 1 |
| 12 | — | — | — | — | — | — | yes | — | 1 |
| 13 | yes | yes | — | yes | yes | — | yes | yes | 6 |
| 14 | yes | — | — | — | yes | — | yes | yes | 4 |
| 15 | yes | — | — | — | yes | — | yes | — | 3 |

procedures of scalogram analysis are designed to test a given universe of content or, at any rate, a group of items for 'scalability' by seeing whether they will yield a scale with a satisfactory coefficient of reproducibility (in practice, a coefficient of .90 or over is accepted). Of course, not all areas of content will scale, especially not if they are rather wide and heterogeneous, and one cannot know beforehand whether the attempt at scale construction will be successful. The procedure has been criticized for this and for a tendency to produce scales covering a very narrow universe of content (because wider areas often do not scale).

The procedure of scalogram analysis is designed to enable us to see how far our items, and people's responses to them, deviate from the ideal scale pattern. Suppose that we start out with a set of social-distance items and that we have given these (as yet unscaled) items to several hundred respondents. A tabulation of the results for the first fifteen cases might look like Table 11.3.

Note that we have given each respondent a score equal to the number of yes-answers given. Let us now rearrange the table, by placing the *rows* (respondents) in order of their scale score. The result is shown in Table 11.4.

Next, let us rearrange the *columns* (items) in the table, by putting them in order of the number of yes-answers given to each item, as shown in Table 11.5.

We have now produced a scalogram pattern that is very nearly perfect and has very high reproducibility. A score of 3 clearly means a yes-response to items 7, 5, and 1 (and not to *any* three items, as would be the case in a Likert scale); a score of 6 means a yes-response to items 7, 5, 1, 8, 2 and 4; and so on. The lowest item on the scale is item 7, to which nearly everyone agrees; the highest or, in this case, most intimate one is item 3, to which almost no one agrees. Note the

Table 11.4.

| Respondent | Item 1 | Item 2 | Item 3 | Item 4 | Item 5 | Item 6 | Item 7 | Item 8 | *Score* |
|---|---|---|---|---|---|---|---|---|---|
| 7 | yes | yes | — | yes | yes | yes | yes | yes | 7 |
| 9 | yes | yes | — | yes | yes | yes | yes | yes | 7 |
| 10 | yes | yes | — | yes | yes | — | yes | yes | 6 |
| 1 | yes | yes | yes | yes | yes | — | yes | — | 6 |
| 13 | yes | yes | — | yes | yes | — | yes | yes | 6 |
| 3 | yes | yes | — | — | yes | — | yes | yes | 5 |
| 2 | yes | — | — | — | yes | — | yes | yes | 4 |
| 6 | yes | — | — | — | yes | — | yes | yes | 4 |
| 8 | yes | — | — | yes | yes | — | yes | — | 4 |
| 14 | yes | — | — | — | yes | — | yes | yes | 4 |
| 5 | yes | — | — | — | yes | — | yes | — | 3 |
| 15 | yes | — | — | — | yes | — | yes | — | 3 |
| 4 | — | — | — | — | yes | — | yes | — | 2 |
| 11 | — | — | — | — | — | — | — | yes | 1 |
| 12 | — | — | — | — | — | — | yes | — | 1 |
| | 12 | 6 | 1 | 6 | 13 | 2 | 14 | 9 | |

Table 11.5.

| Respondent | Item 7 | Item 5 | Item 1 | Item 8 | Item 2 | Item 4 | Item 6 | Item 3 | *Score* |
|:---:|:---:|:---:|:---:|:---:|:---:|:---:|:---:|:---:|:---:|
| 7 | yes | yes | yes | yes | yes | yes | yes | — | 7 |
| 9 | yes | yes | yes | yes | yes | yes | yes | — | 7 |
| 10 | yes | yes | yes | yes | yes | yes | — | — | 6 |
| 1 | yes | yes | yes | — | yes | yes | — | yes | 6 |
| 13 | yes | yes | yes | yes | yes | yes | — | — | 6 |
| 3 | yes | yes | yes | yes | yes | — | — | — | 5 |
| 2 | yes | yes | yes | yes | — | — | — | — | 4 |
| 6 | yes | yes | yes | yes | — | — | — | — | 4 |
| 8 | yes | yes | yes | — | — | yes | — | — | 4 |
| 14 | yes | yes | yes | yes | — | — | — | — | 4 |
| 5 | yes | yes | yes | — | — | — | — | — | 3 |
| 15 | yes | yes | yes | — | — | — | — | — | 3 |
| 4 | yes | yes | — | — | — | — | — | — | 2 |
| 11 | — | — | — | yes | — | — | — | — | 1 |
| 12 | yes | — | — | — | — | — | — | — | 1 |

triangular pattern of the responses — this is the pattern that scalogram analysis aims to produce.

We should observe several further points. First of all, Table 11.5 is a 'rigged' example for demonstration purposes; in practice we may have to rearrange the order of items and of respondents not once or twice, but many times, until we have obtained the nearest approximation to a scalogram pattern. This procedure becomes very tedious and fraught with errors, especially if we deal, not with fifteen respondents, but with a hundred or more, and with dozens of items instead of a mere eight. However, modern statistical software packages frequently contain a scalogram analysis program. These should make Guttman scaling more accessible. The researcher can also quickly see whether or not a particular domain will 'scale', in Guttman terms.

Looking again at Table 11.5, we note that it is not absolutely regular. For instance, respondent 8 has given a yes-response to item 4 instead of to item 8. Similarly, respondents 1 and 11 show slight deviations from the perfect scale pattern, and to this extent they make reproducibility less certain. Such deviations are called 'errors' in this context. The formula for calculating the reproducibility coefficient is as follows:

$$R = 1 - \frac{\text{no. of errors}}{\text{no. of responses}}$$

(The number of responses is the number of items multiplied by the number of respondents.) If reproducibility is below 0.9 then the scale is considered unsatisfactory. In that case, we might have to give up the scaling attempt altogether, or we might — as with the other scaling procedures — get rid of a number of items and then rescore and rescale the remaining responses, and recalculate the coefficient of reproducibility. In the above example, for instance, we might wish to drop item 8 (which contains one error, and has two gaps caused by other errors), and item 3 (which is so extreme that it fails to differentiate, and also because it contains one error).

Scalogram analysis is usually carried out on one or more samples of a hundred cases each. The number of items might initially be several dozen that, after repeated attempts at scaling, might be whittled down to perhaps eight or ten items which form a scale. Such a scale might sometimes be much narrower in content than the original item pool; at other times, seemingly unrelated items are unexpectedly easy to scale — there is no way of forecasting the outcome. If we have many respondents, it would be advisable to repeat the scaling operation on several samples of one hundred, to reduce the possibility that a scale pattern is improved by a combination of chance variables. We must also guard against spuriously high estimates of reproducibility by first omitting all items to which almost everyone or almost no one agrees; usually, therefore, items with less than 20 per cent or more than 80 per cent endorsement are omitted from a scalogram analysis at the start.

So far, we have assumed all the items to be dichotomous. However, we might have items with multiple responses such as degrees of agreement, or frequency of a symptom. Many investigators would probably fix a cut-off point for each item and turn them into dichotomies. However, the place of the cut-off point will affect the scale position of the item, and a certain amount of trial and error may be necessary before we find the cut-off point that produces the least number of scale errors. It is also possible to treat each of the multiple responses as a single dichotomous item; thus, if we had two items, one with three response positions and another with five response positions, we might treat these as eight separate items and try to scale them as before. Or we might wish to group the response positions by turning, say, five responses into three. Obviously, this kind of analysis will increase the amount of work involved in the scaling operation.

Guttman has been criticized for his insistence on reproducibility, and for regarding cumulative reproducibility as the chief criterion for a 'true' scale; other writers have felt that these are valuable but not essential properties. He has also been criticized for his somewhat arbitrary standards, such as the lower limit of 0.9 for coefficients of reproducibility. His procedures are laborious, and there is no certainty that, in the end, a usable scale will result. On the other hand, scalogram analysis will prevent us from building a single scale for a universe of content that really demands two or more separate scales; in other words, it offers the important safeguard of uni-dimensionality.

Scalogram analysis can produce some short yet highly effective scales. The problem of validation remains and depends largely on the manifest content of the items; also, the scales do not have equal or equal-appearing intervals, but as a rule they are highly reliable.

## The problems of validation

In Chapter 8 we noted the difference between factual and attitudinal measures and the greater difficulty of validating the latter because of their abstract and indirect nature, and because of the absence of suitable criteria. Attitude scales share this problem with other forms of mental measurement. The literature contains but a small number of attempts at direct validation against a criterion, and we may well ask whether the measures employed as criteria were themselves valid. Such attempts have included the use of essay-type questions, experts' judgments, membership in groups with known policies or interests, pictorial material, interviews and case studies, judgments by friends or co-workers, self-ratings, political votes, and such overt behaviour as church attendance. New scales are often correlated with older, well-known scales which, however, may themselves be of questionable validity. Scales are often given names or labels that help to create a spuriously high impression of validity. The very fact that they look like tests and can be scored may create expectations of validity and exactitude that may not be well-founded.

It may be helpful to remind ourselves of the different approaches to the problem of validity. We have repeatedly pointed out the weaknesses in the criterion-group approach, sometimes known as pragmatic validation. As we saw in Chapter 9, for more theoretically oriented research the concept of construct validity has been developed, which hinges on the relationship of our scale to other measures. We also saw that much depends on the quality of the attitude statements and the feelings that they arouse in the respondents; in this sense, validity depends on the respondents' candour and willingness to cooperate and the absence of stereotyped answers or 'façade' responses. Some investigators simply state that what the scale measures is indicated by the manifest content of the items; others rely on groups of judges for ascertaining what the items measure. Of particular importance is predictive validity, usually in the sense of predicting some future aspect of behaviour such as voting (see Himmelweit *et al*, 1981, for a sophisticated approach to this problem). We can see from this that a great deal depends on our purpose in building a scale. It is one thing to require a purely descriptive device, which can roughly divide our sample into several groups with regard to a given attitude, but quite another to ask for a technique that will predict people's actions at some time in the future. Speaking very generally, many of our scales will probably do an adequate descriptive job, as long as not too much precision is required, but the problems of predictive validity are a long way from being solved.

## General comments and evaluation

Most of the theoretical underpinnings of attitude scaling go back to before World War II, and they owe more to psychometrics and educational testing traditions than to modern social psychology. In theoretical as well as practical terms, these early techniques, and the linear-scaling model itself, have been outstripped by subsequent developments in attitude theories, qualitative measurement, social-representations theory, ethnomethodology, studies of intentionality and so on. These later developments try to do better justice to the subtlety and complexity of many attitudes, to their oblique yet powerful links with the many interactive forces that produce overt behaviour, and to their distinctive place among the components of human personality.

Yet attitude scales still have many uses, at least until some better methods come along. The advent of modern computer software packages has given attitude scales an extended life-span. Where, in the past, researchers sometimes shied away from scaling procedures because of the monumental amount of tedious arithmetic involved, they can now rely on tireless computers to carry out internal consistency checks, to produce correlation matrices and factor analyses, and to attempt scalogram analyses in even the most recalcitrant domains. This has generally improved the quality of survey research, and the Likert five-point format has become widely accepted. Many researchers will, however, not follow the Likert procedures step by step, but will use whatever techniques of item analysis they find convenient. They will probably assemble their item pool under several area headings or sub-domains, each dealing with a different aspect of the topic under investigation; they will probably not bother with item–total score correlations but will go straight on to do a large factor analysis. This will enable them to discard unwanted items and will produce a scale with high reliability. It will also reveal some of the interconnections between the various aspects or sub-domains, some of which may be useful for future research. Should time pressures make it impossible to carry out the necessary scaling work before the main field work, then some researchers will administer the entire item pool to the full survey sample (at some cost, no doubt), in the knowledge that the scaling can be done by the computer subsequently, and will be all the more reliable for being based on larger numbers.

Where computers offer no short-cuts is in the preliminary work of conceptualization, depth interviewing, pilot work and pre-testing. Now that for many investigators the scaling calculations present few problems, it is this preliminary research investment which rightly remains the crucial requirement of a good attitude scale.

## Selected readings

### On attitude scaling theories

Dawes, Robyn M., 1972, *Fundamentals of Attitude Measurement*, Wiley.
    An introductory text, see especially sections on the Bogardus scale and on the semantic differential.

Fishbein, Martin (ed.), 1967, *Readings in Attitude Theory and Measurement*, Wiley.
    This very useful collection contains many classical papers dealing both with measurement and with theory.

Edwards, A.L., 1957, *Techniques of Attitude Scale Construction*, Appleton–Century–Crofts, New York.

Cronbach, Lee J., 1990, Fifth Edition, *Essentials of Psychological Testing*, Harper and Row, New York.
    Standard text on measurement and test construction. See discussion of item analysis and scale construction, percentiles, reliability measures and validation.

McKennell, Aubrey C., 1974, *Surveying Attitude Structures*, Elsevier, Amsterdam.
    For the specialist.

## SOCIAL-DISTANCE SCALES

Bogardus, E.S., 1933, 'A social-distance scale', *Sociological and Social Research*, **XVII**, 265–71.
Source publication for the Bogardus scales.
See also Fishbein (above), chapter 9.

## THURSTONE SCALING

Thurstone, L.L. and Chave, E.J., 1929, *The Measurement of Attitudes*, University of Chicago Press, Chicago.
Source book for Thurstone scales.
See also Fishbein (above), chapter 10.

Guilford, J.P., 1956, *Psychometric Methods*, McGraw-Hill, New York.
An older reference book, but see especially chapters 4–7 on psychophysical methods.

## LIKERT SCALING

Likert, R., 1932, *A Technique for the Measurement of Attitudes*, Columbia University Press, New York.
Source book for Likert scaling.
See also Fishbein (above), chapter 11.

## FACTORIAL SCALES

Eysenck, Hans J., 1954, *The Psychology of Politics*, Routledge & Kegan Paul, London.
An early factor-analytic approach to attitude scaling.

Torney, Judith V., Oppenheim, A.N. and Farnen, Russell F., 1975, *Civic Education in Ten Countries*, Wiley.
Shows the uses of factorial attitude scales in cross-national research with children.

## GUTTMAN SCALING

Guttman, Louis, 1950, 'The basis for scalogram analysis' in Stouffer, Samuel A. (ed.), 1950, *Measurement and Prediction*, Princeton University Press, Princeton.
The main source book for the Guttman scaling technique and its theoretical background.
See also Fishbein (above), chapter 12.

Marsh, Alan, 1977, *Protest and Political Consciousness*, Sage Library of Social Research, Vol. 49 Sage, London.
Developed a Guttman-type scale of Protest Potential.

## VALIDATION PROBLEMS

Ajzen, Icek, 1988, *Attitudes, Personality and Behaviour*, Open University Press, Milton Keynes.
Deals with attitudinal consistency, prediction of behaviour and action intentions.

Himmelweit, Hilde T., Humphreys, Patrick, Jaeger, Marianne and Katz, Michael, 1981, *How Voters Decide*, Academic Press.
Detailed attempt to predict voting behaviour.

## COLLECTIONS

Shaw, M.E. and Wright, J.M., 1967, *Scales for the Measurement of Attitudes*, McGraw-Hill, New York.
An older collection, containing many Thurstone and Likert scales from the 'thirties and 'forties, as well as a description of scaling methods.

ESRC Survey Archive, University of Essex, Colchester, Essex CO4 3SQ, Great Britain.
Has extensive computerized holdings of British and some European survey materials. These include the General Household Survey from 1973, and a major series of the Eurobarometer, the comparative polls held in the European Community member countries.

Social and Community Planning Research, annual, *British Social Attitudes*, Gower, Aldershot, Hants.
Regular series of detailed reports on British political and social attitudes.

Young, Copeland H., Savola, Kristen L. and Phelps, Erin, 1991, *Inventory of Longitudinal Studies in the Social Sciences*, Sage, London.
Source book of longitudinal studies in the United States and Canada going back sixty years.

Robinson, John P., Rusk, Jerrold G. and Head, Kendra B. (eds), 1969, *Measures of Political Attitudes*, Survey Research Center, ISR, University of Michigan, Ann Arbor, Mich.

Robinson, John P. and Shaver, P.R., 1973, *Measures of Social Psychological Attitudes*, Survey Research Center, University of Michigan, Ann Arbor, Mich.

Stewart, B., Hetherington, G. and Smith, M., 1985, *Survey Item Bank*, MCB/University Press, London.

Sudman, Seymour, and Bradburn, Norman M., 1983, *Asking Questions*, Jossey-Bass, San Francisco.
Lists the major US archives of survey data and questionnaires in chapter 1.

# 12
# PROJECTIVE TECHNIQUES IN ATTITUDE STUDY

Attitude scales rely for their effectiveness on the cooperation and frankness of the respondent. This may have its disadvantages. For one reason or another, a respondent may try to fake or give a great many 'uncertain' responses. Fear, misunderstanding, the desire to place oneself in a more favourable light, social taboos, dislike for the research worker and other motives may all play a part in distorting the results and may lead to outright refusal. This has led to the development of methods of attitude measurement whose purpose is less obvious to the respondent.

Sometimes, by means of indirect methods, we can approach a deeper level in the respondent than we can with attitude scales alone. For this reason, we may wish to use both methods in the same inquiry to obtain data on the same attitude-complex at several different levels. It is important to plan such an investigation with great care, or the results will tend to be contradictory instead of complementary.

## When to use projective techniques

In planning our investigation, one of the first things we will have to decide is how deeply we need to probe. If we can stay at a relatively superficial level, then direct techniques for attitude measurement such as the various types of attitude scales, ratings and rankings, grids and indices (see Chapter 13) can be used with advantage and will yield quantitative results. If, however, we have to penetrate deeper, perhaps below the level of conscious awareness or behind the individual's social façade, then indirect, projective techniques have to be used. Projective techniques can be particularly useful in evoking and outlining stereotypes, self-images and norm-percepts; for instance, ideas connected with 'the good husband' or 'the single parent'.

The best way to find out whether or not we will need to probe in depth is to carry out a series of careful depth interviews to explore the origins, complexities, motivational links and ramifications of the behaviour and attitudes in question, to enable us to conceptualize them. Extended interviews will most likely yield a number of promising lines for investigation which may be studied by means of attitude scales and other direct techniques, but which may also call for projective devices. Such techniques should be used at first in a purely exploratory way; later, they may be built and utilized to test specific hypotheses emerging from the depth interviews.

## What projective techniques can do

When suitably designed, projective techniques can help to penetrate some of the following barriers:

1. *The barrier of awareness* People are frequently unaware of their own motives and attitudes and cannot give us the answers we need, even with the best will in the world. For instance, very submissive people may keep dogs in order to exercise their desire for dominance and control; lonely people may keep cats as some kind of substitute for children; but these respondents might be quite unaware of such needs and motives.

2. *The barrier of irrationality* Our society places a high premium on sensible, rational, and logical behaviour. Most of us tend to rationalize a lot of the time: we stress or invent sound, logical reasons for actions whose origins are far from rational. For instance, if a sample of motorists is asked to rank the ten most important characteristics of a new car, they will generally put 'reliability' and 'safety' high on the list, with 'styling' or 'appearance' toward the bottom. However, if they are asked to state which characteristics their friends or neighbours regard as important, 'styling' jumps to third or second place. The average male driver is not aware of the extent to which he actually is influenced by appearance — he likes to think that his choice is determined by such rational aspects as safety, performance, reliability and economy.

   In an experiment carried out at an exhibition, people were asked to choose between two cameras in terms of quality. A considerable majority chose camera B. Actually, the two cameras were identical, but camera B had a small weight concealed inside it. Feeling the extra weight, people tended, subconsciously, to think of that camera as a more 'solid job', with 'better materials' and so forth. Yet if they had been asked for their reasons, they would no doubt have spoken of shutter speeds, lens quality or flash synchronization, and any suggestion that weight played a part in their decision would have been regarded as preposterous.

3. *The barrier of inadmissibility* Our society sets many norms and expectations for all of us, and we find it difficult to admit to a stranger, or even to ourselves, that we sometimes fail to meet such standards. Ideally, we ought always to pay our fare on the bus, share our sweets, never buy pornography, tell only innocent jokes and drop our litter in litter-baskets — yet we sometimes fall short of these ideals, and this produces guilt feelings and a desire to 'cover up'. For instance, when passing around a box of assorted sweets, many people have some kind of strategy that will prevent their favourite flavour from being picked by someone else — but one would need indirect techniques to find this out.

4. *The barrier of self-incrimination* This is really a variant of the barrier of inadmissibility. It concerns those aspects of behaviour and feelings that might

lower the respondent's self-esteem, such as ethnic prejudice, violation of sexual taboos, irrational fears, or alcoholic overindulgence. For instance, when men's toiletries (such as after-shave lotions and deodorants) were first introduced, many men had the secret fear that they would be considered homosexuals if they used these products. People about to undergo an operation are sometimes extremely afraid that they will 'say terrible things' while under the anaesthetic. People do not admit such secret fears because they are afraid to make themselves look silly, childish, deficient or prejudiced, but projective techniques can often help us to uncover such feelings, attitudes or emotions.

5. *The barrier of politeness* People often prefer *not* to say negative, unpleasant or critical things unless they have specific complaints. They tend to say that most things are 'all right', and present a rather bland façade. Thus, projective techniques could help to show us whether, say, a given newspaper was considered rather vulgar by certain groups of respondents.

It follows that whenever the pilot work shows us that any of these barriers exist with respect to the problem in hand, then the use of projective techniques should be considered in the survey that is being designed.

# How indirect techniques work

There are four commonly used approaches, which overlap to some extent:

1. *Association* The 'say-the-first-thing-that-comes-into-your-mind' approach is based on the assumption that a fast response to a stimulus word, picture or question will be less 'guarded' and therefore more revealing of underlying attitudes and motives.

2. *Fantasy* The respondents are asked to guess, or tell a story, or discuss a picture in imaginary terms. In doing so, they have to use their own attitudes and experience as 'building blocks' and this will give us an insight into some of the deeper levels of their personality. For instance, we might show a rather vague picture of a man with a worried face leaving a bank. The respondents' task is to tell us what the man is feeling, and why, and what has taken place in the bank. In doing this, the respondents are likely to reveal some of their own attitudes and feelings toward banks and to saving, borrowing and financial problems generally.

3. *Ambiguous stimuli* All perception involves a certain amount of projection and interpretation on the part of the respondent — the more so when the stimulus is indefinite and ambiguous. The term 'projection' is not used here in the strict Freudian sense; rather, it refers to the fact that whenever subjects are asked to respond to a relatively ambiguous stimulus they will reveal something about themselves when making their responses. Usually, the subjects are not aware that the stimulus is ambiguous; to them, it has but one clear meaning, and they proceed to respond accordingly. However, in imposing their particular connotation on the stimulus they have already told us something about themselves. For instance, we might ask a group of prison

officers: 'Why are uniforms worn?' Now, it is not at all clear whether the question refers to the uniforms of the wardens, or the uniforms of the prisoners or any other uniforms. Nor is it always clear what is meant by a uniform; in some prisons, wardens wear ordinary clothes, made to a standard pattern inside the prison, and these may or may not be considered 'uniforms'. When respondents begin to answer such a question, they will almost unwittingly assign a particular meaning to it, and in so doing they have revealed their particular way of looking at the issues involved.

4. *Conceptualizing* We can find out something about respondents' attitudes by the way in which they name things, order things or group things. For instance, is insurance regarded as part of the concept 'investment'? Are Asian people regarded as 'black'? We can give respondents various labels or objects to 'sort in whatever ways you think they belong together' and question them about the grouping afterward.

All these approaches have certain elements in common. They all rely on spontaneity of interpretation, on the fact that the respondent (and often the interviewer) must not know the purpose behind the task or the questions. They all rely on a greater or lesser degree of ambiguity in the task, or in the stimulus, so that the respondents have to provide their own interpretations. They should always be as nondirective as possible, in order not to bias the responses. And they all require the making of inferences on the part of the research worker.

In dealing with projective material, we are almost inevitably involved in interpretation of the responses; that is, we do not necessarily take them at their face value but impose some significance or categorization of our own on them. For instance, a small boy of ten was given a set of incomplete sentences to finish, among them the sentence beginning: 'In the dark . . .'. This is what he wrote: 'In the dark I am never, NEVER afraid!' Now it is clear that we should not simply accept this young man's doubly underlined assurances; indeed, we may well feel that he 'doth protest too much' and that he is probably very fearful in the dark, though he denies this. We have here a problem in interpretation, and much depends on how far we are prepared to go. At the completely 'objective' level, we should classify the response as 'not afraid' — which would probably be nonsense; at a more interpretative level, we might classify it as 'denial of fear'; at a deeper level still, we might simply classify it as a 'fear response'. The deeper we go, and the more we indulge in such interpretations, the less objective we become — and probably reliability (consistency between interpreters) also suffers. In the construction and use of projective techniques we seek, therefore, some kind of half-way house: a system of coding, scoring, classifying or interpreting that satisfies the demands of consistency and of objective scoring criteria, yet one that permits us to go some part of the way beneath the *prima facie* value or meaning of the responses.

There is often a painful conflict between the demands of objectivity, scientific method and rigour, on the one hand, and the desire to get the fullest flavour of meaning and significance out of such self-revealing responses, on the other. We have not yet acquired methods that will allow us to do both. In making the choice of 'level', the social scientist faces a difficult task requiring judgment and complex analysis. Small wonder, then, that some of us build our half-way houses a little further down the slope than others.

## Types of techniques

Indirect or projective techniques have a long history in the field of clinical psychology, and some of the devices to be discussed in this chapter are simply applications or offshoots of early clinical tests. However, systematic attempts to make such tests valid, reliable and scorable have met with such great difficulties that most of them have fallen into disuse. Some remain valuable in the clinical field, where one is dealing with individual cases and where the test material can be used to gain further insight into the patient's problems, even if it does not meet the demands of objectivity. In group situations, however, or where we have no supportive sources of information, such tests are found wanting.

Projective devices often present respondents with an ambiguous stimulus, which they have to interpret; in doing so, they reveal to us something of their perceptual world, their fantasies, their characteristic modes of responding, their frames of reference. Some stimuli, however, are more ambiguous than others. One could imagine a gradient, all the way from such highly ambiguous stimuli as a cloud, a blank page or an inkblot, through rather more structured but still largely ambiguous stimuli such as incomplete sentences or uncaptioned cartoons, to highly structured stimuli that leave the respondent little latitude. It has been suggested that such a gradient would roughly correspond to greater or lesser 'depth' within the person; the more ambiguous the stimulus, the deeper the level of personality that it reveals — but the interpretation also becomes more difficult and the problems of objectivity and validity are greater. In social research we have tended, therefore, to work with techniques of moderate degrees of ambiguity; many of our problems do not require the exploration of the deeper levels of personality, and by using stimuli that retain some of their structure we can usually devise ways of making them suitable for large-scale investigations.

Before discussing some of these techniques in detail, it may be necessary once more to stress the need to plan in advance what use will be made of them and the way the analysis is to take place. Will the results contradict other data? Will they be used to interpret the results of more direct methods of questioning? At what 'level' do we want to explore our respondents? What relative importance do we intend to give to 'rational' and 'irrational' factors? Careful pilot work should make it possible to answer most of these questions; failure to plan in advance will often result in large quantities of unanalysable or contradictory information.

SENTENCE COMPLETION (see also Pilot Work, Chapter 4)

As the name suggests, this device consists of a number of incomplete sentences — sometimes just a single word — which the subjects are asked to complete, usually in writing, with the first thing that comes to mind. In clinical psychology there are standard sets of sentence openings with standard scoring methods.

However, in social research we tend more often to deal with *general* attitudes, values, beliefs and feelings. For this reason, social investigators usually compose their own incomplete sentences, tailored to the needs of their particular problems.

It should be realized that sentence beginnings can vary greatly in their ambiguity. Compare, for instance: 'if only . . .' and 'the nicest cigarette of the day . . .' It is clear that responses to the first item could range very widely indeed, whereas responses to the second item are limited to smoking and probably to the mention of a particular time or occasion during the day.

Sentence beginnings can also differ in subtlety. Some of them approach the problem in a highly predetermined way and obtain useful but rather narrow results. Others are more 'open' and their aim is less obvious; as a consequence the results may produce more spontaneous and more revealing information. Often it is best to have items of both types in a judicious mixture. Extensive pilot work is essential to make sure that the desired results are obtained.

In all social-research techniques, and in sentence completion in particular, the effects of *context* should be kept in mind. For instance, if a respondent had been asked a lot of questions about smoking habits and had been given a series of incomplete sentences dealing with cigarettes, the inclination would be to complete the sentence 'If only . . .' with some comment about smoking. In this way, contextual influence can be a help or a hindrance, depending on our intent. If we had wanted to explore the respondents' more general worries and regrets, not only those linked to smoking, then the context would have produced a rather misleading restriction, making it appear as if their chief concern in life was with cigarettes and smoking. On the other hand, we can sometimes utilize contextual influences of this kind to guide the responses into certain areas, but this will have to be taken into account when we interpret the results.

In sentence-completion techniques we are looking particularly for spontaneity. When we seek to test a particular hypothesis or explore a certain problem, we tend to have greater confidence in a set of responses given to items that do not reveal our purpose. For instance, suppose we were conducting an investigation into the fears and worries of hospital patients about to undergo surgery. We might wish to obtain some idea of the methods that patients favour in trying to cope with anxiety, in particular whether they find that talking to other patients is helpful or important. To begin with, we might use a fairly 'open' item, as follows:

*The best way to overcome fear is. . . .*
    say a prayer
    don't think about it
    ask for help from above
    to forget it
    pray
    to try to face up to it
    get to know your doctor
    not to think of it
    write down these fears and examine them
    to admit to it. No one is fearless

to keep up your heart
to try and believe that you will get better
to take a lesson from others
share it if possible
I don't know
to try and help other people who are frightened
to screw up courage

We note only three or four responses that concern communication with other patients. We can acquire a further understanding of people's feelings about this by setting a much more specific item:

*Talking to others about your coming operation. . . .*
    I don't
    you find things out
    is not one of my pet subjects, better try and forget
    doesn't worry me — I like to sympathize
    is very good
    helps one to feel happier about having them
    no use
    does not really appeal to me
    one can dispel fear
    pointless, they cannot understand it

Thus, each type of item has its function, and this has to be kept in mind when the sentence beginnings are designed. Pilot work is most helpful here, for some items yield quite unexpectedly varied results, whereas others produce very stereotyped responses. After a time, one acquires a flair for writing good sentence beginnings.

How is this type of data to be quantified? With the more direct kind of item the results can usually be coded or classified much as one would code the results of an open-ended question (see Chapter 14). The same approach, in principle, is adopted with the subtler items, but a more 'interpretative' coding frame is often required. For instance, suppose that we had given the following item (among others) to three groups of married women — middle-class, working-class and socially mobile women: '*I feel embarrassed and uncomfortable when . . .*' Here are some of the results:

WORKING-CLASS
    I am wrongly dressed
    I have lost my temper
    a visitor calls and I have an empty cupboard
    my child repeats something about somebody we have been discussing
    my four-year-old daughter makes loud remarks about deformed persons

MIDDLE-CLASS
    I can't hear properly
    other people's children climb on my furniture
    my husband introduces me to his female business associates

I am given gifts
my husband and my mother argue
I am complimented profusely

SOCIALLY-MOBILE
in the company of people of a higher-income group
I have to visit my children's school and talk with their teacher
my husband loses his temper in public
I am laughed at
I am asked to entertain strangers
my children misbehave in company

Rather than have specific categories, such as 'dress', 'temper', 'visits', 'strangers', one might try a slightly more ambitious category such as 'social defeats'. From the few cases we have here, it would seem that embarrassment over 'social defeats' is more common among the upwardly mobile respondents.

As with open-ended questions here, too, one may be led to a particular form of categorization by the need to explore a particular hypothesis, or by the data themselves — as in the above example. When developing such categories, usually on a pilot sample, it is often helpful to divide the respondents into the sub-groups of concern. We can then start building the coding frame by asking: in what ways do these groups of people differ in their responses to this item?

Here is a further example in which the results are more readily and more meaningfully classified after they have been subdivided according to the respondents' background. They were obtained in an inquiry carried out among nurses in a psychiatric hospital. Observe the nature of the differences between student nurses, and nurses with twelve or more years of experience, to the following item:

*I wish that doctors . . .*
STUDENT NURSES
would sometimes be more understanding
had more time to teach and discuss with staff
were a little more unbending sometimes
were more considerate
had more time to discuss why they are doing certain kinds of treatment
would sometimes show more humour

NURSES WITH TWELVE OR MORE YEARS OF EXPERIENCE
would come to the ward on time
would have patience with their patients
were more ready to appreciate nursing experience
would occasionally discuss patients with staff
would find out from the nurses the condition of certain patients
would spend more time on the wards
took more notice of nurses' knowledge
would discuss more fully with staff

There seems to be a general desire for more and better communication with the medical staff, but the tone of the younger nurses is more sad than angry, more eager than cross, whereas the older nurses feel passed by and are evidently critical of the doctors.

Perhaps these examples also illustrate what we mean when we say that projective techniques can be revealing without the respondents being aware of this and also permit greater depth and subtlety.

Here are some rich, though unclassified, responses of university students to the item:

*If my father . . .*

had more respect for others' intelligence, my mother would be happier

had received a better education, he might have got further than he has

had a quieter temperament he would be happier

has so many hobbies, he isn't able to look after his family

had not left home, things would have been easier

had loved me less, he would have disciplined me less

had not remarried a woman with a son of 19, life might have been less complicated

had been as much a friend as my mother, home would have been happier still

were not as he is, I would have disliked him

did not adore me so, I should not be so spoiled

had been a rational person, life would have been easier.

For items of this kind, the responses can usually be reliably classified as positive; neutral or mixed feelings; negative; factual/descriptive. However for some purposes, different and more insightful schemes could be devised, though these might be less reliable.

## Objective scoring of projective materials

Here is an example of a sentence-completion device that was designed to find out to what extent school children are aware of sexism and gender barriers in the world of work. A dozen items were drafted, each using an occupation which was predominantly associated either with men or with women. In each of the 'stories' the name of the speaker suggested a child's gender, and the names were so juxtaposed with the chosen occupations that gender barriers might be experienced. However, the wording of the items merely suggested that there might be 'difficulties' and it was up to the respondent to indicate what these difficulties might be. Three of the items follow:

WHEN I GROW UP

'When I grow up I want to become a pilot,' said Anne, 'but it may be difficult for me because ................................................................................................................

................................................................................................................................

................................................................................................................................

'When I grow up I want to become an engineer,' said Mary, 'but it may be difficult for me because ...................................................................................................
...............................................................................................................................
...............................................................................................................................

'When I grow up I want to become a nurse,' said John, 'but it may be difficult for me because ...................................................................................................
...............................................................................................................................
...............................................................................................................................
...............................................................................................................................

There were twelve items altogether, and these were mixed with a number of other items using occupations which in Western societies are usually held by men and women more or less equally, so as to conceal the purpose of the questionnaire from the children. When piloting the items, some occupations had to be replaced by others, but essentially the technique worked well and the children readily 'projected' themselves into the person of the speaker in each item.

Obviously, the results produced qualitative information about the ways in which jobs are perceived by boys and girls still at school. It also proved possible to give each child an objective score indicating 'awareness of sexism' by counting the frequency of responses such as 'because I'm a girl, and girls don't usually go in for this kind of job' (whether the respondent was male or female). This shows that, with a little ingenuity, we can make projective devices yield objective scores.

## CARTOONS

Here the respondent is presented with a picture or a drawing such as one might find in comics or in cartoon strips, with 'balloons' indicating speech. However, one of the balloons is empty and the respondents' task is to fill it. They will read and study the cartoon, then place themselves in the situation of the character with the empty balloon and answer accordingly.

Figure 12.1 (overleaf) shows an example that was used in a study with adolescents. The drawing has deliberately been left rather vague and schematic to facilitate self-identification. As with the sentence-completion technique so here, too, the answers can be classified 'projectively', according to the attitudes, frames of reference and role perceptions that they reflect. In our example, the results would show us a good deal about the respondents' attitude to authority, and there might well be social-class or other group differences in their reactions.

There is almost no limit to the types of problems that this technique can be made to explore, and it is readily adaptable to all kinds of consumer research. It can and has been used in ordinary field interviews. A suspected disadvantage is that the respondents may occasionally fail to identify with the character in the cartoon and therefore give an answer that tells us very little about their likely reactions in a similar situation. Careful pilot work, to make sure that the pictures are perceived as intended, is essential.

It is possible to apply this technique without the use of pictures or drawings. The respondent is asked to imagine the situation from the words of one of the

Figure 12.1.  Teacher catches adolescent boy arriving late for class

characters (shopkeeper to lady customer, 'I'm sorry you are returning this vacuum cleaner, madam. Can you tell me what seems to be the matter?') and responds accordingly. Even multiple-choice answers may be provided. The cartoon technique is perhaps at its best when dealing with perceptions of human relations such as authority, social class, queuing, games, buying and selling.

It would be a mistake to assume that subjects would necessarily react to such situations in real life in the way that their responses might suggest. The responses reflect attitudes and feelings, but their behavioural expression will depend on the actual situation.

### PICTURE INTERPRETATION

This technique, too, has its origins in a clinical device, the well-known Thematic Apperception Test. The test consists of twenty cards, one blank and nineteen with various vague drawings on them. The drawings represent, for the most part, human figures in situations that the respondent is asked to describe and to interpret in the form of a story.

In social research, one or more TAT cards may be borrowed, or more likely some pictures or drawings will be created that relate to the problem at hand. Figures 12.2 to 12.5 (on pages 222–3) are some pictures that were used by Caudill (1958) to explore attitudes and social relationships in a psychiatric hospital; the pictures were shown to both patients and staff.

In social research our aims are general, not personal or clinical. We will probably want to gain an understanding of the attitudes of a large number of people toward a particular problem or relationship. Therefore, we will probably use fewer pictures, and they will be focused on our specific research problem. Caudill, in his exploration of relationships inside a psychiatric hospital, used pictures dealing with typical (though still ambiguous) hospital scenes. His results did not enable him to do a character analysis of each of his respondents, but he learned a good deal about their attitudes and feelings from the way they perceived and interpreted the pictures.

The technique has been widely used to measure ethnic prejudice, and achievement motivation. A typical example of its use in the commercial field might be some pictures showing a motorist at a garage or talking to a mechanic, situations that could prompt various fears, frustrations, authority problems and other attitudes. It has been shown, for instance, that some motorists regard the mechanic as a friend; others treat him more like a servant; and to a third group he is a mixture of doctor and magician.

As the purpose of the test becomes less broad and fundamental, so the type of analysis will become more specific. We may no longer require our respondents to tell a story but, instead, ask them to answer a number of questions about the picture, or to rate it on a number of characteristics. Such questions or ratings need to be so designed that they will seem quite reasonable to the respondents, yet require them to interpret the picture and to use their imaginations, thereby revealing their own attitudes. For instance, we may show a picture of a baby with a rubber dummy in its mouth, followed by a series of questions including some about the baby's mother (who is not shown in the picture). We may ask respondents to guess her age, her social background, the number of other children she has, and so on, in order to see whether the practice of giving a baby a dummy to suck is thought of as something that is done only in certain social classes, or only in large families where the mother is very busy, or only by young and inexperienced mothers. Such questions will need to be embedded in groups of other questions, and a control sample should be shown the same picture but without the dummy.

People are surprisingly willing to guess. In an investigation of attitudes towards types of alcoholic drinks (beer, whisky, wines, cocktails) one can show respondents pictures of many kinds of people, and guesses about their favourite drinks will be readily forthcoming. A picture of a loaded carrier bag will produce 'character sketches' of the good and the bad shopper, the bargain hunter, the buyer of convenience foods, the boutique addict, and others, according to the type of goods displayed. The need for control samples and control pictures must be borne in mind, to find out which cues respondents are using to arrive at their guesses.

Pictorial techniques are particularly useful with young children. For instance, a picture-inset test has been designed to test attitudes to skin colour among three-year-old children.

Figure 12.2.  A patient at the front door of the hospital (either entering or leaving)

Figure 12.3.  Evening on the open ward

Figure 12.4.  The night nurse making rounds on the open ward

Figure 12.5.  A patient in seclusion

## STORIES

Stories are most commonly used when we wish to test one or more specific hypotheses. The respondents are presented with a brief account of some events, and at the end they are asked to make a choice, say, between two characters in the story, or to state which course of action they themselves would have adopted, or how the motivation of one character in the story can be explained. Often, therefore, the story technique, though projective, resembles the 'closed' type of question.

For instance, here is a story that has been used to examine the attitudes of adolescent boys toward saving:

> *Tim uses his pocket money to go to the cinema, to sports events, to buy sweets, books and so on. It gives him a lot of enjoyment now, but he hasn't got anything put away for the future. Jack saves as much of his pocket money as he can. He will have money if he needs it in the future, but he goes without many pleasures now.*
> Which of the boys is using his money in a better way?
> 1. . . . Tim
> 2. . . . Jack

Note the care taken in the wording of the question so as to make neither alternative overwhelmingly more attractive.

For a more complex and subtle example, we may turn to a study of the attitudes of doctors. General practitioners are sometimes asked to help with all kinds of social problems, which may or may not be regarded as part of a doctor's job. Some of these involve them in a semi-psychiatric role. To find out how doctors feel about such problems, a sample of general practitioners was asked to respond to a set of case vignettes from which the following examples are taken:

> *A married woman complains that she cannot go on looking after her widowed mother who lives with her. The latter has a hemiplegia and obviously needs care but seems cheerful and fairly alert. The daughter however is tearful and agitated and insists that 'something must be done'.*

1. I would not regard this as a medical problem.
2. I would treat the patient symptomatically (ie, with sedatives and/or anti depressant drugs) but make it clear that I would not intervene in the social situation.
3. I would feel the most important thing here would be to give the patient some relief from her burden. I might try to get a geriatric bed for the old lady for a few weeks or alternatively arrange for a daily home-help.
4. I would spend some time with the patient trying to bring out the underlying emotional difficulties. If indicated, I should continue with psychotherapy.
5. I would refer this patient to a psychiatrist.

*A ten-year-old boy, with no previous history of disturbed behaviour, is brought to you by his mother because, since they moved to the district, he has been difficult about school attendance. He has taken to malingering and playing truant and seems generally 'nervy'. Physical examination is negative.*

1. I would not regard this as a medical problem.
2. I would treat the boy symptomatically (for example, with sedatives) but would make it clear that his school attendance was a matter for the school to deal with.
3. I would regard this as a case for firm reassurance and positive advice (for example, I would counsel the mother on how she should handle the problem; in addition, I might get in touch with the head of the boy's school to ensure proper management of the boy at school).
4. I would spend some time with the boy and afterward his mother, trying to bring out the underlying emotional difficulties; if indicated I would continue with psychotherapy.
5. I would refer this patient to a child guidance clinic or psychiatrist.

Sometimes the story technique can be combined with the use of incomplete sentences. Here are some examples from a story that has been used successfully with adolescent boys, together with one set of responses:

THIS IS A STORY ABOUT A BOY CALLED JOHN

1. *John came to a new school. He had hardly been there a few days when he already made friends because . . .* he was the sort of boy who attracted everyone's attention for no reason.
2. *Coming home from school one day, he happened to hear his father and mother talk about him in the other room. His father said: . . .* 'I wish John could do better at school.'
3. *And his mother said . .* 'But you know that he is not very good at learning.'
4. *In the evening, after he was in bed and the lights were out, he was thinking of girls. He thought: . . .* 'There's that horrible Sharon down the road always running after me, can't she leave me alone?'
5. *John had a friend he liked very much. Next day he said to his friend: 'I want to tell you something which you must not tell anybody. The secret is: . . .* You know that somebody put a drawing pin on Mike's chair, well, I did it.'
6. *After tea, in the evening, the family was sitting together. John was looking at his mother and said to himself: . . .* I think she understands me more.
7. *John thought: I love my parents very much, but . . .* it isn't my fault if I don't do so good at school.
8. *John thought of his future. He said to himself: When I am a man I'll . . .* be blowed if I'm going to do the job Dad wants me to do.

Analysis of the results can take place in two stages: for each item separately and then, in a more thematic way, for the story as a whole.

## PSEUDO-FACTUAL QUESTIONS (see p. 58)

Under this heading comes a variety of techniques in which people are asked seemingly innocuous questions of knowledge or belief which can be analysed projectively. A very simple example might be the question: 'What percentage of the people in this town are foreigners?' Here, the true percentage is probably quite small, yet there will be a wide variety of estimates, and the size of the estimate has been found to correlate positively with anti-foreigner prejudice scores on attitude scales and similar overt techniques.

If people are asked to estimate the results of public-opinion polls, they will tend to show a bias in favour of their own opinions. Similarly, estimates of the average pay of directors and workers, or of profit percentages, will reflect political attitudes. The analysis of the results need take no account of the true answer, if there is one; the distribution of the high and low scores within the sample can be used.

The inclusion of one or two fictitious items among objects to be rated can be very successful. Suppose we are holding an 'immigration' survey asking respondents to say whether people from various other countries or of different races or religions should be allowed to come to this country, or should be kept out, or sometimes be kept out. We might insert among these the names of one or two fictitious groups ('Danireans', for instance, has been used successfully). When respondents come to such a name, referring to a group of people of whom they have never heard, they will almost never admit this. They will feel that a response is expected of them, and they will proceed to engage in argument with themselves, along the following lines: 'Danireans? Hmm, never heard of them. I suppose they are all right; I've not heard anything said against them. Let's have some in and see what they are like'; or else 'Danireans? Hmm, never heard of them. Who knows what they might be like? Better be safe than sorry, we'll keep them out.' Unwittingly, therefore, the respondents tell us what their attitude is and what kind of world they live in: a world in which other people are dangerous and potential enemies until proven to be friendly; or a world in which most people are probably all right, unless there is some evidence to the contrary. Such projective responses correlate well with other prejudice scores.

The '*guess who*' device is another seemingly factual approach that can be used projectively (see p. 113). We may ask: 'These are the people who have too much power in our community. Who are they?' or 'These are the people you can never be sure of, you never know what they are thinking. Who are they?' And so on. The items may be suitably varied to fit our own particular problem, and they may deal with the more stereotypical level or with deeper feelings. The illusion of a 'general knowledge test' can be kept up by having a few items at the beginning and at the end that are innocuous.

In many of these techniques the respondents are under some degree of subtle pressure. The 'rational' answer to many of these questions would be 'I don't know,' or 'the question is meaningless to me,' but since the question is part of a survey, printed on a form, presented by a sane and competent interviewer, who apparently expects a simple answer to a simple question, the respondents feel that they must say something; and since there usually is no true, factual knowledge on which they can base their answers, they delve into their attitudes, stereotypes, prejudices and feelings. In interpreting the data later on, we must take into account the fact that the subjects have been 'forced' to some extent.

Apparently simple questions asking for some obvious explanation — questions so simple that they provoke respondents a little — can be most fruitful. In the previously mentioned inquiry into the attitudes of hospital staff, the nurses were asked to imagine that they were taking a visitor around the wards and had to answer a number of questions: for instance, 'Why are uniforms worn?' As we noted earlier, this is a rather ambiguous question, since it is not clear whether the question refers to the wearing of uniforms by doctors, patients, nurses, or attendants and since it is not always clear whether, say, a suit of hospital clothes is a 'uniform'. Most nurses referred to the uniforms worn by hospital staff, but their attitudes were very different; some spoke of the practical side, keeping clothes clean and safeguarding hygiene; some said it helped confused patients to know whom to approach; some said it was a mark of distinction and ensured respect and authority; others thought the uniform was just 'traditional' and created a psychological barrier between themselves and the patients; still others said that a uniform helped the nurse to feel secure. When such responses were classified, clear differences emerged in the attitudes of different grades of staff — yet to the nurse-respondents the question seemed not attitudinal but factual.

## PLAY TECHNIQUES

With children, and even with adults on occasion, certain play techniques can be used. In an interview, various objects are shown to the respondents to get them talking; they may then be asked to do something with them; for instance, build a miniature house with blocks and furniture, which may reveal their attitudes via different spatial relationships (such as the proximity of parents' and children's bedrooms, or the size of their own room versus that of others). In the psychiatric clinic, doll-play techniques are used both for diagnosis and for therapy.

A useful device, which could easily be adapted to other purposes, is the Bene–Anthony Family Relations Test (Bene and Anthony, 1959). The child is asked to state who are the members of his or her family, and for each person a cardboard cut-out figure and a 'post box' are provided. The child is then given (or has read aloud) a number of 'messages' such as 'I wish I could keep this person near me always,' or 'I want to do things just to annoy this person in the family,' and the task is to 'post' these messages. Provision is made for messages that apply to more than one person and for a 'Mr Nobody', who receives messages that apply to no-one in the family. The test can readily be scored to show affection, ambivalence and hostility to different family members, and can be used with children up to the age of adolescence. Adults can be asked to complete the test in accordance with the way they remember their childhood feelings.

Getting respondents to *sort* objects or cards with labels on them and questioning them non-directively afterwards can be immensely revealing. People can be asked to sort or group almost anything: various kinds of pets, children's misdemeanours, holiday resorts or chocolate bars; first, spontaneously, in whatever way they like and in an unlimited number of groups and then, perhaps, with some direction such as 'now put together all those that would not be suitable for young children'. This may be repeated several times, with different directions. In this way we obtain, first of all, the respondents' frame of reference, the way they see things: for instance, do they group holiday resorts geographically or according to distance, according to the type of facilities they offer, according to prestige associations and likely cost, or in terms of their suitability for children? We also obtain some idea of the importance to them of specific points such as the name of a product's manufacturer, the intention that may lie behind a child's misbehaviour, or the small differences in price between chocolate bars. Non-directive sorting tests can show how often such criteria are used spontaneously as classificatory principles, and by what kinds of respondents. Sometimes, this can lead to the development of multi-dimensional scaling techniques.

# Selected readings

Campbell, Donald T., 'The indirect assessment of social attitudes', chapter 19 in Fishbein, M. (ed.), *Readings in Attitude Theory and Measurement*, Wiley, New York, pp. 163–79.

SENTENCE COMPLETION TECHNIQUES

Hoeflin, Ruth and Kell, Leone, 1959, 'The Kell–Hoeflin Incomplete Sentences Blank: Youth–parent relations', *Monographs of the Society for Research in Child Development*, XXIV No. 72.

PICTORIAL TECHNIQUES

Atkinson, John W. (ed.), 1958, *Motives in Fantasy, Action and Society*, Van Nostrand, New York.
   A series of studies using pictures from the TAT to measure needs such as achievement, affiliation and power, complete with scoring systems.

Caudill, W., 1958, *The Psychiatric Hospital as a Small Society*, Harvard University Press, Cambridge, Mass.

PLAY TECHNIQUES

Bene, Eva, and Anthony, E.J., 1959, *The Family Relations Test*, manual published by the National Foundation for Educational Research, Slough, Bucks.

# 13
# VARIETIES AND APPLICATIONS

It is not always possible, within the constraints of time and resources, to apply the full rigour of the linear-scaling model (see Chapters 9 & 11) to every technique we use in our survey. There are times when a 'quick and dirty' approach is the only way open to us. However, if we bear in mind the basic requirements of measurement, it soon becomes obvious that some methods are 'dirtier' than others. As a general guideline, when there is no opportunity for depth interviewing, detailed conceptualization, pre-testing, validation exercises and so on, we should first and foremost strive for *reliability*. This means that it is better to have a group, or several groups, of items rather than a single item, and that we should apply some form of item analysis to achieve *internal consistency*; that is, reliability. If we can show that the items 'measure the same thing' then it may be possible, later on, to attain some form of validity; or we may be able to apply factor analysis to the data set to discover the underlying components of our instrument. There may not be time or opportunity to apply such statistical techniques during the pilot work and pre-testing, and we may have to administer the entire group of items to all our respondents. In that case the internal consistency analysis can take place later. So long as we have not tried to measure attitudes, beliefs, awareness, knowledge or percepts by means of single items, we should be fairly safe.

Surveys have come a long way from the early days of biased samples and crude techniques. Nowadays survey researchers are often asked to tackle subtle and complex issues such as the determinants of voting for a political party, people's images or stereotypes about another country, children's perceptions of social institutions such as trades unions, or people's feelings of control over their own health (the health locus-of-control model). Survey researchers are thus frequently required to exercise great ingenuity and creativity in designing new types of techniques and adapting them to fieldwork conditions. In this chapter we shall consider a variety of such alternative techniques, most of which are elaborations of the 'closed' type of question; that is, they do not require the respondent to write anything but only to tick the appropriate response categories. Usually such techniques aim at generating some kind of score; they are suitable for postal and group-administered questionnaires and can also be used in standardized face-to-face interviews, perhaps with the help of show cards for the respondent.

Before going into detail it may be helpful to make a rough-and-ready distinction between 'objective' and 'subjective' measures. When an interviewer is asked to assess the socioeconomic level of the respondent's dwelling area, the intention is to obtain an 'objective' rating of the neighbourhood (though, inevitably, such a rating will also contain subjective elements, which we shall strive to keep to a minimum). If, however, we ask the respondent about the brand image of a particular soft drink, then we intend to use this information 'subjectively', to tell us something about the respondent rather than about the drink. In this case we are not interested in what is 'out there' but in what is 'inside'. However, this distinction between 'objective' and 'subjective' measures is not always clear-cut. For example, when dealing with subjective responses we shall want to collect these and add them up, to form collective images, profiles, representations, percepts or stereotypes. But, once we assmble a considerable number of subjective impressions they almost cease to be subjective and come to represent some kind of 'objectified subjectivity'. This, in turn, can be related to what is 'out there' and thus becomes a perceptual attribute. For example, objective economic indicators may show that a certain country is 'rich', yet survey research may show that many potential holiday visitors subjectively perceive it as 'poor' and, since behaviour is more often determined by subjective impressions than by 'objective facts', this has important implications for tourism.

# Ratings

Rating gives a numerical value to some kind of assessment or judgment. Familiar examples are school marks or grades, and proficiency reports on personnel in industry which attempt to give an objective assessment of an individual's performance. Usually, a set of assumptions is made about equality of the intervals on a rating scale.

We may apply ratings to almost anything — to individuals, to objects, to abstractions and to ourselves. The task is usually to give 'so many marks out of so many', or some percentage equivalent. Sometimes, graphic rating scales are used in which the response consists in making a mark on a line running between two extremes.

The use of ratings invites the gravest dangers and possible errors, and in untutored hands the procedure is useless. Worse, it has a spurious air of accuracy, which misleads the uninitiated into regarding the results as hard data. For instance, hospital nurses are often rated by their ward supervisors on such attributes as practical ability, appearance, neatness, cleanliness, emotional stability, professional deportment, conscientiousness, reliability, punctuality, self-reliance, common sense, physical stamina and so on. The ratings may run from 1–5, or from 1–10, or any other intervals. These ratings are taken into account when matters arise concerning promotion and transfer or the provision of references. Yet in a typical investigation, if the same supervisor rates the same nurses on two occasions, the correlations between the first and second rating will be very low and will only occasionally reach statistical significance. The correlations with assessment of these nurses by other supervisors, and with examination results, will be similarly low. The procedure here is, in fact, meaningless. It assumes that we know which traits are important, that these traits are unitary and not complex entities, that the trait names or labels mean the same things to different people at different times, or to one person on repeated occasions, and that the raters have the necessary information. This type of rating is of doubtful validity and suffers from gross unreliability. Here is an example from a student project.

### Example 13.1.

ASPECTS OF THE LIBRARY

Please give a rating from 0–10 (10 = good) on the following:

|  | Rating |
|---|---|
| 1. Provision of seats | |
| 2. Heating and ventilation | |
| 3. System of classification of books on the shelves | |
| 4. Catalogue system | |
| 5. Colour schemes and decoration | |
| 6. Quietness | |
| 7. Attitude of staff | |
| 8. Lighting | |
| 9. Hours of opening | |
| 10. Table space | |

Part of the problem here is with the various items or dimensions and their meaning: different respondents will probably have something very different in mind when they assess, say, 'attitude of staff'. Another problem concerns the use of numbers. Respondents have been provided with an arbitrary range (0–10) and told which is the favourable end (10 = good; often even this elementary precaution is omitted, so that some respondents use '1' for 'best', while others use '10'), but have otherwise been left to their own devices. Just what would be the meaning of, say, a '4' on quietness? And would respondents use such ratings consistently with themselves (across the items) and with each other? A third problem is somewhat subtler and is known as the 'halo effect'. Instead of assessing the library on its merits regarding each item separately, respondents let themselves be influenced by their *general* feelings of like or dislike.

A different form of the halo effect expresses itself in a response set. If the rating scales are arranged one underneath the other and always with the 'good' (socially desirable) end on the left-hand side and the 'bad' end on the right, then the respondents — having once made up their minds that they are favourably disposed toward the object of the ratings — may run down the page always checking the position on the left, or vice versa, without actually reading the items or giving each of them separate thought. To counteract this, we try to randomize the direction of the scales, so that the socially most desirable end falls sometimes on the left and sometimes on the right.

Having the rating scales on separate pages further helps to offset the halo effect and is also useful in combating the logical error, the tendency to give an object or a person similar ratings on two attributes that are thought to be correlated, such as intelligence and emotional stability, or price and quality. We must also make sure that our raters have the necessary information: we should not ask them to rate Greek grammar or the work of an electroencephalographer if they have no relevant knowledge.

Perhaps the chief danger of ratings lies in the ease with which they can be influenced, often by variables of which the rater is unaware. For instance, suppose we asked a schoolboy's mother and his teacher to rate him on various attributes such as irritability, shyness, obedience and so forth. We would probably find differences between the two sets of ratings, not only because the child may behave differently at school and at home, but also because the teacher compares him with other children of the same age and sex, whereas his mother probably compares him with the others in the family and with a few children in the neighbourhood. In other words, the two raters have different *frames of reference*. This is a problem that frequently affects our perceptions and evaluations and can lead to much misunderstanding. It is most important, therefore, when we ask for a set of ratings, to indicate the frame of reference that the raters are expected to use. The label or title of the set of ratings will have an influence, too; in the preceding example, a title such as 'neuroticism scale' would probably yield quite different ratings from a title like 'Child Development Scale'. It should be recognized that the respondents are also influenced by what they think is the purpose of the rating procedure. If we do not tell them what the purpose is (by offering a title or a frame of reference), then they will try to guess what the purpose might be, and since different respondents may guess very differently, their ratings may diverge more than they might have done.

Ratings can be used in various ways: (1) as objective assessments — for instance, a rating of the quality of fixtures and furnishings in a home during or after an interview; (2) in a subjective, projective way to tell us something about the rater's percepts and attitudes; (3) as self-ratings of personality traits or attitudes. Each of these types of rating scales requires a somewhat distinct interpretation, and different aspects have to be stressed in their design and quantification.

In constructing an *objective* rating scale, perhaps the first step is to define the dimension that is being rated. It should be possible to describe it so that it will have approximately the same meaning to all the raters involved in the investigation. This may be relatively easy when a food product is being rated on 'sweetness', but it becomes more difficult when, say, we want to rate a family on the 'extent to which the family supports the child in conflicts with the outside world'.

The number of steps in a rating scale tends to vary from four or five to perhaps ten. Raters are unable, in most instances, to make discriminations that are finer than ten points or so. Many research workers favour an uneven number of steps, especially when there are only three or five, in order to have a neutral category or midpoint, to one side of which lie the favourable categories and to the other side the unfavourable ones. This is also because raters are a little afraid of using the extreme categories — a phenomenon known as the *error of central tendency*. We can try to make our extreme categories sound less extreme to encourage their use, or we may reconcile ourselves to the inevitable and decide afterwards to combine, say, the two or three extreme categories at each end — in which case something like a ten-point scale would seem desirable. Although steps on a rating scale are often used as if they had numerical values and as if the intervals were equal, we usually lack the evidence to justify such assumptions.

After deciding the number of steps in our scale, we have to define the extremes, or better still, define each step. If we have a seven-point scale of 'punctuality' then we must say when, or by what criteria, a person is to be rated five, or one, or three and so on. Is a person who is frequently late by a few minutes to get the same rating as someone who is never late, but who has been very late on a single occasion? Is earliness rated the same way as lateness? On

### Example 13.2.

*Fels Parent-Behaviour Rating Scale No. 3.15*
Democracy of Regulation and Enforcement Policy (Democratic-Dictatorial)

Rate the parent's tendency to share with the child the formulation of regulations for the child's conduct. Does the parent give the child a voice in determining what the policy shall be? Or does the parent hand down the established policy from above?

Disregard immediate issues not covered by policy. Rate independent of justification of policy to child, and independent of restrictiveness of regulations. Include both overt consulting with child and considering child's expressed wishes. Dictatorial policies may be wise or foolish, benevolent or selfish.

---

☐ Endures much inconvenience and some risk to child's welfare in giving child large share in policy forming. Consults with child in formulating policies whenever possible.

☐ Attempts to adjust policies to child's wishes wherever practicable. Often consults child.

☐ Deliberately democratic in certain safe or trivial matters, but dictates when there is a sharp conflict between child's wishes and other essential requirements.

☐ Neither democratic nor dictatorial, deliberately. Follows most practical or easiest course in most cases.

☐ Tends to be rather dictatorial, but usually gives benevolent consideration to child's desires. Seldom consults child.

☐ Dictatorial in most matters, but accedes to child's wishes occasionally when they do not conflict with own convenience or standards.

☐ Dictates policies without regard to child's wishes. Never consults child when setting up regulations.

## Example 13.3.

How would you rate the mother on these scales?
(Check appropriate space on each scale)

| Warmhearted | —————————\|—\|—\|—\|—\|—\|—\| | Coldhearted |
| Overprotective toward her children | —————————\|—\|—\|—\|—\|—\|—\| | Takes good care of her children |
| Unselfish | —————————\|—\|—\|—\|—\|—\|—\| | Selfish |
| Patient | —————————\|—\|—\|—\|—\|—\|—\| | Impatient |
| Competent mother | —————————\|—\|—\|—\|—\|—\|—\| | Incompetent mother |
| Lively | —————————\|—\|—\|—\|—\|—\|—\| | Quiet |
| Very like myself | —————————\|—\|—\|—\|—\|—\|—\| | Not at all like myself |
| Scatterbrained | —————————\|—\|—\|—\|—\|—\|—\| | Sensible |
| Self-assured | —————————\|—\|—\|—\|—\|—\|—\| | Always worried |
| Unhappy by nature | —————————\|—\|—\|—\|—\|—\|—\| | Happy by nature |
| Bad at housekeeping | —————————\|—\|—\|—\|—\|—\|—\| | Good at housekeeping |
| Takes good care of her children | —————————\|—\|—\|—\|—\|—\|—\| | Pampers her children |
| Would like to have as a friend | —————————\|—\|—\|—\|—\|—\|—\| | Would not like to have as a friend |

what occasions is punctuality to be assessed? Over what period? These and many other questions have to be given unambiguous answers, and we have to give all raters full and clear instructions. Unless we do this, two raters rating the same person or object will have conflicting results.

By way of illustration, an excerpt from the Fels scales for the assessment of child-rearing by means of home visits is reproduced in Example 13.2. Note that each step, as well as the general dimension, has been described in some detail. When objective assessments are wanted, it is dangerous to give such labels as 'frequently', 'moderately', 'often', 'occasionally' and so on to the different grades, since they can be interpreted differently by the various raters.

We often use rating scales when an attitude or a personal impression is wanted in *subjective* rather than objective terms. For instance, suppose we wished to employ an actress in a half-minute advertising film concerning baby foods. Our choice may have been narrowed down to three or four candidates whose photographs (with babies on their laps) may be shown to an audience of mothers. To find out how the audience perceives these 'mothers' we might ask

**Example 13.4.**

Here are some reasons European students give for dissatisfaction with their conditions in this country. Please indicate how important each has been for *you*.

| | Of very great importance | Of great importance | Of some importance | Of no importance |
|---|---|---|---|---|
| 1. Absence of parents, family | | | | |
| 2. Absence of close friends | | | | |
| 3. Separation from wife, husband, children | | | | |
| 4. Missing your own language, books, magazines etc. | | | | |
| 5. Missing the festivals, celebrations, social functions etc. | | | | |
| 6. Food difficulties | | | | |
| 7. Discomforts of working in a household | | | | |
| 8. Long period of absence from home | | | | |
| 9. Boredom and monotony of present life | | | | |
| 10. General sense of psychological (emotional) depression | | | | |
| 11. Other reasons (please specify) | | | | |

a group of women to fill out the graphic rating scales that are shown in Example 13.3.

Here, where only a rough, personal impression is required and where the differences between the candidates are more important than the absolute figures, only the extremes of each scale have been indicated. Note, however, that the 'favourable' extreme is sometimes on the right and sometimes on the left, to try to counteract response set and halo effect. The scales are deliberately contrived to encourage guessing, to obtain attitudes and first impressions. We must be very clear in our own minds that we are not getting an 'objective' assessment but rather a snap judgment and sometimes a wild guess — for our present purpose, that is what is required.

Sometimes, rating scales are used to tell us something about the rater rather than about the object of the ratings. The work of Osgood (see below) on the semantic differential is important, particularly in the clinical field. For instance, suppose we take again the set of mother-rating scales discussed above and ask a woman to rate herself, her own mother and also the 'ideal' mother on each of the scales. From the results, we might be able to see how she perceives her own mother, how far she looks upon herself as similar to her mother, to what extent her image of her mother and the 'ideal mother' overlap and where she feels that she herself falls short of the ideal. For such an investigation we would no doubt wish to add other variables and change some of the existing ones (see Selected Readings).

Example 13.4 gives a simple set of self-assessment ratings from an inquiry by Postlethwaite (1962) into the problems of continental students living in Great Britain.

It is really a scale of subjective importance applied to each item in turn, and each respondent supplies his or her own frame of reference. Such scales of subjective importance can be applied to many kinds of persons, objects and hypothetical or actual situations. They yield attitudes rather than objective assessments, and a crude total 'unhappiness score' could be calculated. With more items, balanced and grouped into different areas, the technique may be made to yield sub-scores and profiles, provided that internal consistency can be demonstrated. A factor analysis might be attempted, if suitable computing facilities are available.

## The semantic differential and the repertory-grid techniques

The semantic-differential technique was originally developed by Charles E. Osgood (Osgood *et al.*, 1957) and his colleagues as part of their quantitative study of meaning. It consists essentially of a number of seven-point rating scales that are bipolar, with each extreme defined by an adjective: examples might be wise/foolish, strong/weak, excitable/calm. The respondent is given a set of such scales and asked to rate each of a number of objects or concepts on every scale in turn. It is possible to submit sets of such ratings to factor analysis, in a search for the basic dimensions of meaning. Osgood has shown the importance of three factors (evaluation, potency and activity), though other factors (such as tautness, novelty and receptivity) may also play a part.

As we saw above, there are risks in using rating scales; for instance, are we justified in basing our calculations on the assumption of equality of intervals, both within each scale and between different scales? Osgood offers valuable evidence on the validity, reliability and sensitivity of his scales and, in any case, some of the most interesting types of analysis permitted by this technique refer not to assessments by groups of respondents, but to the subjective semantic worlds of single individuals.

If the semantic differential is simply regarded as a set of rating scales, it can be used to obtain the percepts of various political personages, different national or ethnic groups or any other subject matter. If we are willing to average sets of ratings given by groups of respondents, then we can compare the results produced by different groups for the same concept or object. Thus, we can show, for example, that women, on average, regard a given brand of cigarettes as less mild (stronger) than men do.

Example 13.5 illustrates the use of the semantic differential technique. It shows a set of rating scales developed for research with players in international crisis simulation games, to obtain their percepts of different countries. Previous pilot work on a much larger number of scales had shown, with the aid of factor analysis, that these percepts were determined by five underlying factors. In the final instrument each of these was defined by six semantic differential scales, making thirty rating scales in all.

The following factors were obtained:

Factor I: General 'niceness'; liking;
Factor II: Western/Oriental or developed/underdeveloped;
Factor III: Tough/gentle;
Factor IV: Volatile/equable;
Factor V: Crude/sophisticated.

In this way we can obtain, for each respondent, five reliable subjective scores expressing his or her perception of a given country, or of several countries, and the percepts of groups of respondents may be compared country by country.

Note that the S–D scales deal not only with 'factual' aspects, such as 'Western/ Oriental' or 'secular/religious' (which often are very much a matter of opinion, anyway) but also with images and feelings, for example 'warm/cold', 'hard/soft', 'masculine/feminine'.

The same approach can be used to obtain brand images of products, or the public images of well-known firms or personalities. Each time extensive pilot work, pre-testing and factor analysis must precede the choice of the final set of scales.

Research has shown that S–D scales with seven intervals are usually optimal. However, some investigators prefer to use five-point or three-point scales for particular purposes.

The technique really boils down to a selection of rating scales made up for the particular purpose at hand, on the basis of pilot interviews. In setting up these scales, the location of the positive end should be randomized, so as to try to counteract any halo effect (see p. 231). If several concepts have to be rated, it is best to have a separate rating sheet for each one; thus, the same set of scales can

**Example 13.5.**          About: _____
                                             (country name)

| | | |
|---|---|---|
| 1. | Kind : ___ : ___ : ___ : ___ : ___ : ___ : ___ : | Cruel |
| 2. | Trustworthy : ___ : ___ : ___ : ___ : ___ : ___ : ___ : | Untrustworthy |
| 3. | Malevolent : ___ : ___ : ___ : ___ : ___ : ___ : ___ : | Full of good will |
| 4. | Basically peace-minded : ___ : ___ : ___ : ___ : ___ : ___ : ___ : | Basically war-minded |
| 5. | Break bargains : ___ : ___ : ___ : ___ : ___ : ___ : ___ : | Fulfil bargains |
| 6. | Cold : ___ : ___ : ___ : ___ : ___ : ___ : ___ : | Warm |
| 7. | Backward : ___ : ___ : ___ : ___ : ___ : ___ : ___ : | Advanced |
| 8. | Western : ___ : ___ : ___ : ___ : ___ : ___ : ___ : | Oriental |
| 9. | Rich : ___ : ___ : ___ : ___ : ___ : ___ : ___ : | Poor |
| 10. | Autocratic : ___ : ___ : ___ : ___ : ___ : ___ : ___ : | Democratic |
| 11. | Influenced by Western powers : ___ : ___ : ___ : ___ : ___ : ___ : ___ : | Not much influenced by Western powers |
| 12. | Illiterate : ___ : ___ : ___ : ___ : ___ : ___ : ___ : | Literate |
| 13. | Hard : ___ : ___ : ___ : ___ : ___ : ___ : ___ : | Soft |
| 14. | Weak : ___ : ___ : ___ : ___ : ___ : ___ : ___ : | Strong |
| 15. | Hesitant : ___ : ___ : ___ : ___ : ___ : ___ : ___ : | Decisive |
| 16. | Active : ___ : ___ : ___ : ___ : ___ : ___ : ___ : | Passive |
| 17. | Masculine : ___ : ___ : ___ : ___ : ___ : ___ : ___ : | Feminine |
| 18. | Cowardly : ___ : ___ : ___ : ___ : ___ : ___ : ___ : | Brave |
| 19. | Feels secure : ___ : ___ : ___ : ___ : ___ : ___ : ___ : | Feels insecure |
| 20. | Holds a grudge : ___ : ___ : ___ : ___ : ___ : ___ : ___ : | Forget grudges |
| 21. | Shortsighted policies : ___ : ___ : ___ : ___ : ___ : ___ : ___ : | Longsighted policies |
| 22. | Greatly concerned with prestige and saving face : ___ : ___ : ___ : ___ : ___ : ___ : ___ : | Not much concerned with prestige and saving face |
| 23. | Quick to escalate : ___ : ___ : ___ : ___ : ___ : ___ : ___ : | Slow to escalate |
| 24. | Deliberate : ___ : ___ : ___ : ___ : ___ : ___ : ___ : | Impulsive |
| 25. | Rigid : ___ : ___ : ___ : ___ : ___ : ___ : ___ : | Flexible |
| 26. | Guided by domestic considerations : ___ : ___ : ___ : ___ : ___ : ___ : ___ : | Guided by foreign considerations |
| 27. | Looks to the past : ___ : ___ : ___ : ___ : ___ : ___ : ___ : | Looks to the future |
| 28. | Secular : ___ : ___ : ___ : ___ : ___ : ___ : ___ : | Religious |
| 29. | Strong leadership : ___ : ___ : ___ : ___ : ___ : ___ : ___ : | Weak leadership |
| 30. | Spends heavily on arms : ___ : ___ : ___ : ___ : ___ : ___ : ___ : | Spends little on arms |

be given over and over again, each time with a different concept at the top of the page. Care should be taken that the two descriptors at the extremes really are opposed and do define some kind of scale or dimension between them. Some extremes have more than one opposite (for instance, sweet/bitter or sweet/ sour), while others have none (for instance, burning), so that instead of having two extremes we really have one extreme and a neutral end (in terms of our example, burning/not burning). It is possible and often useful to obtain responses to rating scales that seem inappropriate to the concept under consideration, such as masculine/feminine (with respect to a brand of cigarettes), or rough/smooth (with respect to Socialism). By their more imaginative approach, such scales can be used to cover aspects that respondents can hardly put into words, though they do reflect an attitude or feeling.

The value of the technique depends largely on a suitable choice of concepts and rating scales. Since the scales will be applied to all the concepts, the problem of relevance or applicability must be carefully considered: can we, for instance, apply calm/excitable to certain foods? Another issue is the scales' factorial composition, which is often not available. We are less restricted in our choice of objects, which may well be largely determined by the nature of the investigation However, only pilot work will show whether more imaginative objects, such a 'my ideal self' or 'the good housewife' can fruitfully be used.

As part of his broader theoretical framework, Kelly has proposed the repertory-grid technique, which has been taken further by Bannister and others in several investigations (see Selected Readings). The technique is essentially an individual approach, though it can be adapted for group sessions. Its purpose is to supply a 'map' of the respondent's 'personal constructs' and their interrelationships or changes over time. It is an attempt to find out how people 'see' their world, or at least that part of their world with which the investigation is concerned, such as their family members, certain objects or abstractions, brand names, other nations or groups, consumer durables and so forth. Repertory-grid testing is not a single test but a highly flexible technique which can be evolved afresh for each new investigation.

To begin with, it is probably best to let a respondent, say, a thirty-five-year-old male, supply his own constructs. In accordance with Kelly's theoretical approach, *a construct is a way in which two things are alike and in the same way different from a third*. We therefore start by getting the respondent to look at sets of three objects, photographs, persons and so on and ask him to say in what way two of these are alike, and in that way different from a third. For instance, the respondent may be shown pictures of three men, and he may say that two of them are 'Jewish-looking', while the third is not. Thus we find out what are, to him, meaningful attributes of the stimulus material; these are his 'constructs'. Such constructs are incorporated in a grid, down the left-hand side. Across the top will appear the 'objects', the things, persons, photographs, nationalities, or other stimulus material, to each of which the construct is to be applied, now that it has been produced. Each construct is regarded, not as a matter of degree, but as a dichotomy: as an attribute, it is either present or absent. In the above example, the respondent may now be shown a series of photographs of men, and in each case he has to say whether or not the person is 'Jewish-looking'. The investigator takes the respondent through the grid step by step, in each case placing a tick underneath each object that is said to possess the construct in question. (See Example 13.6 for an example of this.) Inspection now allows us to make certain inferences; for example, two constructs that go together (both being ticked, or left unticked, all along the two rows) have similar or subsumed meanings to our respondent; in the example below, 'intelligent' and 'Jewish-looking' go together in this way. Similarly, we may infer that two objects, in whose columns the patterns of ticks and blanks are closely matched, are perceived as similar by the respondent.

The most important aspects of the repertory-grid technique are the constructs (attributes) and the objects (cards, persons, photographs) to be included. These depend entirely on the purpose of the investigation and should flow directly from it. Such purposes can, in turn, be classified as being concerned with *objects* (to find out which person, things, photographs and so on are seen as similar or in what ways objects are said to differ), with *structure* (to find out how the meaning of different constructs hangs together, to study the individual respondent's 'construct map') or with *change* (for instance, as a result of psychotherapy or advertising). Variations in the technique are often introduced. We may, for instance, ask the respondent to produce his own objects such as 'my best friend,' 'the most intelligent person I know,' 'My favourite uncle.' Or we may offer certain constructs to the respondent, rather than letting him suggest them. This latter procedure has the advantage that it turns the repertory grid into a group technique, enabling many respondents to fill in the same grid, and factor analysis as well as other statistical techniques can be applied.

The repertory-grid technique is extremely flexible, allowing studies at the personal level (for instance, of schizophrenic thought) as well as at the group level. It has been employed in such diverse inquiries as the study of social-class differences in language and thinking habits, group differences in value systems and the perception of different kinds of houses. The assumption underlying each variant of the technique is that we can usefully infer the way a person 'sees' the world from patterns of associations between constructs and objects. Kelly's theoretical framework is not strictly necessary in order to make use of the

### Example 13.6.

| Constructs | Photo A | Photo B | Photo C | Photo D | Photo E |
|---|---|---|---|---|---|
| Intelligent | — | ✓ | — | ✓ | ✓ |
| Tough | ✓ | — | ✓ | — | — |
| Jewish-looking | — | ✓ | — | ✓ | ✓ |
| Likable | — | ✓ | — | ✓ | — |
| Selfish | ✓ | — | ✓ | — | — |

technique, but for studies of change, in particular, it would well repay a detailed consideration.

An especially valuable use of the repertory-grid technique is in conjunction with the development of a set of semantic-differential scales. In a sense, the concepts can be used as pilot work for a set of S–D scales. For example, in research on the ways in which people choose a new dwelling when they move home, the successive deployment of both techniques can show us how people perceive their own homes, how they initially conceptualize the home they are looking for, how they prioritize various attributes, and how these percepts and priorities gradually change after viewing a succession of dwellings. Both techniques have also found favour among social geographers (see Selected Readings).

## Inventories and checklists

An inventory is essentially a list that respondents are asked to mark or tick about themselves. It may consist of a list of interests, and the task may be to 'tick those things that interest you a lot'. It may be a list of small social misdemeanours, and the respondent is asked to tick various columns to say 'how bad' each is. It may be a list of personality traits or emotional feelings, and people are asked to tick which of these apply to them. It may be a list of spare-time activities, in which one has to tick the activity engaged in most often, and so on.

Inventories resemble subjective rating scales, except that they are designed to yield two or more scores. The items — though commonly presented in random order — can be grouped in specified ways and scores can be computed for each respondent on a number of such groups of items, or on the inventory as a whole. In the better types of inventory, in particular those that can be properly described as personality tests, the items are selected after careful pilot work, and the grouping into areas is done on a statistical basis, by means of factor analysis, so that those items that are scored together really belong together. However, since there are always problems for which no inventory has been devised, many people construct inventories and group items together largely on an *a priori* basis. In this way, they obtain a quick, relatively crude but useful set of measures, with reasonable reliability because of the use of area scores rather than single questions.

Here is one set of items, from an inventory dealing with the (perceived) effects of television. The items refer to 'stimulation of activities':

(a) I have copied the way people dress on television.
(b) I have tried to cook something after it has been shown on television.
(c) I have made things after they have been shown on television.
(d) I have tried to read a book after it has been talked about on television.
(e) I have gone to a museum or art gallery after seeing it on television.

The items are ticked as 'true' or 'untrue', and in the actual inventory they were mixed in with many other items. Note that the item referring to cooking may inflate the total area score for women; depending on the purpose of the

## Example 13.7.

Almost everyone at one time or another is worried about some things. Different people are worried about different things. Read through the list and for each thing tick to show whether it worries you a lot, a little or does not worry you.

Tick what is right for you.

| | Worries me *a lot* | Worries me *a little* | *Hardly ever* worries me |
|---|---|---|---|
| Not getting along well with other children _____ | | | |
| Not being popular _____ | | | |
| Feeling that some children would not like to come to my home _____ | | | |
| Feeling left out of things _____ | | | |
| Other children making fun of me _____ | | | |
| Being called names _____ | | | |
| Feeling that some children look down on me _____ | | | |

inventory, the relative balance of the items in each area should be kept in mind.

Inventories have a wide variety of uses; they can be constructed with various purposes in mind or to test particular hypotheses. Taboo items, inadmissible problems or antisocial forms of behaviour can readily be inserted; respondents who see such items in print often respond to them more readily than to an open question. Example 13.7 is a set of seven items from an inventory of 'worries' used with schoolchildren. This particular area covers feelings of rejection by other children; it could be used, for instance, to explore the feelings of youngsters from a minority group going to an ethnically mixed school.

The scoring is 3–2–1, or 2–1–0, or some other arbitrary scores, and the items are given equal weight. Note the careful wording of the instructions.

Inventories can sometimes be made to perform at a fairly subtle level. In a study of the attitudes of psychiatric nurses, a successful attempt was made to discriminate between those with rather autocratic and repressive tendencies, and those with a more psychotherapeutic orientation. Example 13.8 is part of the inventory that was used. Note the permissive way in which some of the items have been worded, ('Find that you have to be firm . . .' instead of 'be firm with . . .') Also note the category 'it would depend', which was hardly ever used by the more autocratic kind of nurse. However, psychiatrists, who were also given this inventory to fill in, made frequent use of 'it would depend', partly because they were less aware of the nursing 'ethos'.

It is possible to use factor analysis to determine the underlying components of

## Example 13.8.

HOW BAD IS IT? HOW GOOD IS IT?

How good or bad would it be, in your opinion, if a psychiatric nurse like yourself on your present ward did any of the following things? (Please put a tick in the right column.)

| *How bad is it if you*<br>*How good is it if you* | Very bad | Bad | Would not matter | Fairly good | Very good | It would depend |
|---|---|---|---|---|---|---|
| Spend a good deal of time talking to patients? ___ | | | | | | |
| Let some patients remain untidy? ___ | | | | | | |
| Sometimes show that you are in a bad mood yourself? ___ | | | | | | |
| Appear to the patients to be very busy and efficient? ___ | | | | | | |
| Forget to put on a clean uniform? ___ | | | | | | |
| Avoid discussion of personal problems of a patient with him because you feel that the doctor should do this? ___ | | | | | | |
| Take special pride in having patients who are quiet and do as they are told? ___ | | | | | | |
| Talk about a patient when the patient is present, acting as though the patient was not there? ___ | | | | | | |
| Get deeply involved with what happens to particular patients? ___ | | | | | | |
| Find that you have to be very firm with some patients? ___ | | | | | | |

**Example 13.9.**

Imagine that you had to explain what a good citizen is or what a good citizen ought to do. Please read each sentence, then put a tick (✓) under the heading 'Good Citizen' if that is what *you* mean by a good citizen. If the sentence does NOT help to explain what you mean by a good citizen, put a tick under 'Other'. If you are not sure, put a tick under the question-mark ('?').

| A GOOD CITIZEN: | Good Citizen | ? | Other |
|---|---|---|---|
| 1. Obeys the law | | | |
| 2. Is always polite | | | |
| 3. Loves his/her parents | | | |
| 4. Votes in every election | | | |
| 5. Is loyal to his/her family | | | |
| 6. Goes to church regularly | | | |
| 7. Is loyal to his/her country | | | |
| 8. Cares about other people's troubles | | | |
| 9. Is good at sports | | | |
| 10. Takes an interest in the way the country is run | | | |
| 11. Works hard | | | |
| 12. Joins a political party | | | |
| 13. Knows a good deal about how our tax money is spent | | | |
| 14. Has good table manners | | | |
| 15. Studies hard to pass an examination | | | |
| 16. Pays his/her taxes regularly | | | |
| 17. Minds his/her own business | | | |
| 18. Keeps up with what is happening in the world | | | |
| 19. Tries to change things in the government | | | |
| 20. Gets other people to vote in elections | | | |
| 21. Is liked by most people | | | |
| 22. Knows his/her rights | | | |
| 23. Is willing to serve on a jury | | | |

| A GOOD CITIZEN: | Good Citizen | ? | Other |
|---|---|---|---|
| 24. Knows that his/her country may sometimes make mistakes | | | |
| 25. Gives presents to the police in the hope of getting favours in return | | | |
| 26. Stands up when the National Anthem is played | | | |
| 27. Shows respect for a funeral | | | |
| 28. Belongs to a trade union | | | |
| 29. Tries to make the government change its mind | | | |
| 30. Demands his/her rights if they are threatened | | | |
| 31. Knows a good deal about art and music | | | |
| 32. Helps to keep the streets and parks tidy | | | |

a checklist or inventory, so that internally consistent scales or sub-scales can be obtained.

Example 13.9 shows a checklist concerned with the description or attributes of a 'good citizen' in a number of countries. There are three simple answer categories and thirty-two items, culled from pilot interviews in different countries; each item has been mentioned by at least *some* respondents as being an important attribute of a good citizen.

Factor analysis has consistently shown that the inventory has an underlying structure comprising three 'factors' or 'dimensions'. Each factor describes one of three distinct types of good citizen, characterized by different sets of items: the *active* good citizen (who joins a political party, always votes, and takes an interest in public affairs); the *passive* good citizen (who pays taxes, obeys the law and is loyal to his/her country); and the *disengaged* good citizen (who expresses citizenship in non-political forms such as hard work, respect for a funeral, and family loyalty). A score for an individual's perceptions of each of the three types of citizen can be obtained by summing the scores on the items that comprise it. Thus a respondent who endorsed all the items relating to 'the active good citizen' would see a good citizen as active in a large number of ways, while a respondent who did not endorse any of them, would reject the notion that 'the good citizen' is 'active' altogether. After piloting and factoring, the inventory can therefore be shortened to contain just sufficient items to identify the different percepts of a good citizen and yields three scores per subject, of adequate reliability. The items have been so worded that they can and have been used with adults, but also with children from the age of ten years upwards. The inventory can be included in any research project to which it might be relevant and which uses self-administered questions. Translations (which have themselves also been independently factor analysed) are available in half-a-dozen languages (see Torney, Oppenheim and Farnen, 1975).

**Example 13.10.**

How do you think AIDS is transmitted?

Yes   No

1  ☐☐ Don't know

2  ☐☐ A healthy person cannot get AIDS in any way

3  ☐☐ By touching the body of a person with AIDS/AIDS virus

4  ☐☐ By travelling on the same bus, taxi, etc, with a person with AIDS/AIDS virus

5  ☐☐ By kissing a person with AIDS/AIDS virus

6  ☐☐ By living in the same room/house with a person who has AIDS/AIDS virus

7  ☐☐ By sharing food or eating utensils with a person with AIDS/AIDS virus

8  ☐☐ By injection, using needles used by a person with AIDS or AIDS virus

9  ☐☐ By innoculation/vaccination

10  ☐☐ By having sex with prostitutes

11  ☐☐ By sharing needles/syringes/blades with a person who has AIDS/AIDS virus

12  ☐☐ By shaking hands with a person with AIDS/AIDS virus

13  ☐☐ By having sex with many people

14  ☐☐ By having sex with a man who has AIDS/AIDS virus

15  ☐☐ By having sex with a woman who has AIDS/AIDS virus

16  ☐☐ By using public toilets

17  ☐☐ By being bitten by a mosquito or other blood-sucking insect

18  ☐☐ By donating blood to a person who has AIDS/AIDS virus

19  ☐☐ By blood transfusion/receiving blood from a person who has AIDS/AIDS virus

20  ☐☐ By having sex with a person who has AIDS/AIDS virus

21  ☐☐ Other (specify) _____

KNOWLEDGE AND AWARENESS

In some surveys, such as those preceding a public information campaign, we need to find out how much knowledge people already have about the issue in question. Example 13.10 is a checklist designed to discover how much people know about the ways that HIV, the AIDS virus, can be transmitted. In other surveys, we may require an estimate of each respondent's intelligence or IQ. For that, we may use a standardized *Word Knowledge Test*; such tests are usually highly correlated with verbal intelligence quotients.

With children (and sometimes with adults, too) we may be interested in tapping *'awareness'* rather than knowledge of the strict true/false variety. At other times, accurate knowledge of the subject may not exist or may not be available, and so we build instruments to reveal *percepts*. Example 13.11 is part of an international inventory of superstitions.

To find out to what extent school children are aware of political differences in their society, the inventory in Example 13.12 was designed.

# Grids

A grid is an elaboration of the usual type of inventory — more like a two-way inventory (Example 13.13). It is a very simple and straightforward means by

## Example 13.11.

|  | Tick if True |
|---|:---:|
| 1. Walking under a ladder brings bad luck. | |
| 2. A black cat crossing your path brings bad luck. | |
| 3. You have to be more cautious on Friday the 13th. | |
| 4. Seeing only one magpie brings bad luck. | |
| 5. It is bad luck to leave your shoes/slippers overturned. | |
| 6. Putting shoes on a table means a snake will come into the house. | |
| 7. Opening an umbrella indoors brings bad luck. | |
| 8. Handing over a knife to someone (ie hand to hand) means that you are going to have a fight with that person. | |
| 9. Throwing away spilled salt brings bad luck. | |
| 10. A rabbit's foot brings good luck. | |
| 11. It is bad luck to cut your own hair. | |
| 12. It is bad luck to own peacock feathers. | |
| 13. You should avoid walking on cracks in the pavement to avoid bad luck. | |

## Example 13.12.

Will grown-ups generally agree about what our government should do, or do they sometimes disagree? Below you will find different groups of people in each question: please tell us how well *you* think they agree with each other about what the government should do, by putting a tick (✓) in the right column. At the top of the columns you will find the following headings:

Mostly agree  
Agree about half of the time  } ABOUT WHAT THE GOVERNMENT  
Disagree most of the time  SHOULD DO  
I don't know  

| | Mostly agree | Agree about half of the time | Disagree most of the time | I don't know |
|---|---|---|---|---|
| | about what the government should do | | | |
| 1. Men and women | | | | |
| 2. Business leaders and trade-union leaders | | | | |
| 3. The newspapers and the people in Parliament | | | | |
| 4. Middle-class people and working-class people | | | | |
| 5. Older people and younger people | | | | |
| 6. Left-handed people and right-handed people | | | | |
| 7. People of different religions | | | | |
| 8. Husbands and their wives | | | | |
| 9. Well-to-do people and poor people | | | | |
| 10. Different political parties | | | | |
| 11. People in the northern parts and people in the south of our country | | | | |
| 12. People in towns and people in villages | | | | |
| 13. Married people and single people | | | | |
| 14. Farmers and factory workers | | | | |
| 15. Radio or TV commentators and the people in Parliament | | | | |

which one can quickly collect information without having to ask a great many questions, and the data can be analysed in several different ways. Particular hypotheses can be explored in a way that does not make them obvious to the respondent.

The over-all frequency tabulation will immediately show which is the preferred method of treatment for, say, a dry throat. It will also show under what circumstances a particular remedy, such as a syrup, will be applied. Next, the maladies can the grouped — comparing, for instance, all the types of coughs

## Example 13.13.

Here are some well-known remedies that can be used to give relief with different types of complaints and illnesses. For each of these illnesses or complaints, please tick those remedies that you think are best:

| | Nose drops | Chest rub | Gargle | Inhalants | Throat sprays | Syrup | Throat pastilles | Throat tablets | Cough medicine |
|---|---|---|---|---|---|---|---|---|---|
| Chest cough | | | | | | | | | |
| Dry cough | | | | | | | | | |
| Smoker's cough | | | | | | | | | |
| Severe cough | | | | | | | | | |
| Sinus pains | | | | | | | | | |
| Common cold | | | | | | | | | |
| Sore throat | | | | | | | | | |
| Infected tonsils | | | | | | | | | |
| Dry throat | | | | | | | | | |
| Catarrh | | | | | | | | | |
| For a lost voice | | | | | | | | | |
| Bad taste in mouth | | | | | | | | | |
| Help to sleep | | | | | | | | | |
| Indigestion | | | | | | | | | |
| Bronchitis | | | | | | | | | |
| Asthma | | | | | | | | | |

with all the various throat disorders. Or we may wish to make a detailed comparison of the profile shown by throat pastilles with that shown by throat tablets. We can group respondents by age, or sex or in some other way to show whether older people are more inclined toward the 'traditional' remedies, or whether there is a sex difference in preference for chest rubs, and so on. Quite likely the grid has some items in it that are aimed at particular hypotheses; for instance, will harsher remedies be advocated for a smoker's cough because it is 'your own fault'?

## Ranking (see also Chapter 9)

Ranking means arranging in order, with regard to some common aspect. We can rank children in terms of their school performance, soldiers in terms of their leadership potential, lettuces in terms of freshness, or paintings in order of merit. There are practical limitations to the number of rankings most people can be expected to carry out; under normal survey conditions, to put ten objects in rank order is probably as much as can be asked. Ranking tells us nothing about the differences between ranks; the 'distance' between ranks two and three may be very large, but between five and six it may be minute — ranking tells us the order or sequence, but the size of the rank intervals is unknown and unlikely to be equal. This has led to the development of Spearman's Rho and Kendall's Tau (the special correlation co-efficients for two rank orders) and to numerous other statistical devices, none of which requires any knowledge of the size of the rank intervals. Indeed, we would not use the ranking technique if such knowledge were available (or if suitable assumptions could be made about equality of scale intervals); we would use some form of rating or scaling, instead.

Before setting a ranking task we must be very clear about the results needed. For instance, to rank paintings in order of 'merit' may produce very confusing findings because merit is a very vague term compounded of a liking for the subject matter, colours, expressiveness, evaluation of technical skill, size, fame of the painter and so on. But everything depends on the purpose to which the rankings will be put. Sometimes, a fairly vague ranking can be useful, such as to rank jobs in order of 'prestige'. Also, a ranking on a vague dimension may be used as a first step in an exploratory sequence of questions; when we follow it up with various probes and 'why' questions we obtain a clearer idea of the criteria used by the respondent in assigning ranks. But these are exceptions; mostly, we should state as clearly as possible on what basis the ranking is to be carried out.

Ranking is a very common process in our society. Among familiar forms of ranking are those by teachers of their pupils. We commonly rank the finishers in a sporting event or in any other competition. We rank many goods in terms of quality and price. We grade farm produce, coffee and tobacco. We rank books and pop records according to their sales. The idea of ranking is familiar, but the basis for ranking in any particular case is not always clear.

For ranking of large numbers of objects we sometimes use *classed ranks*. We place together all those to whom we assign the first rank, then all those to whom we assign the second rank, and so on. This procedure resembles rating, but it differs from rating in that no statements or assumptions are made about the intervals between classes or ranks — ranking is less precise. The commonly used prestige rankings of occupations are of this kind.

Mention should be made of *paired comparisons*. Here, the objects to be ranked are presented two at a time, and the respondent has to choose between them. To obtain a rank order from this procedure, all possible combinations of pairs have to be presented, preferably in random order. For ten objects this requires forty-five paired comparisons ($\frac{1}{2}N(N-1)$), and the number of comparisons rises very steeply when the number of objects is increased. For this reason, paired comparisons are not used much in social research; the method comes more into its own in the laboratory (see Chapters 9 and 11).

Ranking can be used projectively in a useful and revealing way to tell us something about the respondent rather than about the objects being ranked. Teachers, for instance, may reveal a social-class bias when ranking pupils on 'popularity'. Nurses may identify themselves so closely with doctors that they tend to up-grade the prestige of their own job as compared to the way nursing is ranked by the general population.

### Example 13.14.

What are, in your views, *the most important* causes of poor living conditions in under-developed countries? (Please tick not more than three, and number them, 1, 2, 3 in order of importance.)

_____ The results of colonialism

_____ The people not trying hard enough

_____ Freak weather patterns

_____ Lack of government planning and foresight

_____ Lack of natural resources

_____ Exploitation by the developed countries

_____ Corrupt local politicians

_____ Wars and civil wars

_____ The West buying too much of their food

_____ The West putting tariff barriers in the way of products from such countries

_____ Excessive population growth

_____ Unwillingness to adapt to modern conditions

_____ Lack of medical facilities

_____ Racial prejudice against non-whites

_____ Other causes (please explain):

An alternative to asking respondents to rank a substantial number of items or responses is to ask for a *partial ranking*, that is for a ranking of the three or four preferred responses (see Example 13.14).

Note that an 'Other (please specify)' category is almost always needed and that a 'Don't know' category should have been added. Observe also the carefully worded answering instructions, which will make the statistical analysis more precise.

# Diaries

The diary technique refers to a daily record kept by the respondent at the research worker's request — not to a document containing intimate personal confidences. The intention is to obtain, as accurately as possible, a daily or even hourly record of certain of the respondent's activities. Since the technique is expensive, difficult to design and to place, and hard to analyse, it should only be used when the necessary estimates cannot be obtained in any other way. Moreover, there is the danger that the respondents' interest in writing up the diary will cause them to modify the very behaviour we wish them to record. If, for instance, they are completing a week's diary of their television-viewing behaviour, this may cause them to engage in 'duty viewing' in order to 'have something to record', or they may view 'better' types of programmes in order to create a more favourable impression.

Most commonly, diaries deal with behaviour rather than with attitudes, interests or emotions. Mass-media consumption patterns are a frequent topic, along with many other spare-time activities, illnesses, visiting and being visited, the use of various forms of transport and so on. Diaries cover a given time span, such as a week or a fortnight, or sometimes a much longer period. The limited time span is then regarded as a sample from which weekly, monthly or annual rates can be calculated. This raises the question of the representativeness of such a time sample; how 'typical' was the respondent's behaviour in that particular week? Will the typical and the atypical 'average out' when we collect large numbers of diary records? Is the activity with which we are concerned subject to fluctuations? (Compare, for instance, newspaper reading, which shows fluctuations between weekdays and the weekends but is fairly stable over the year, with gardening, which will show wide seasonal variations as well.) Much depends on the degree of generalization required; the figures may be typical for a given week or month but not for the year as a whole. For these reasons the dates or spread of dates for diary placement should be chosen with great care.

As we have seen (see Chapter 8), there are various types of questions from which we may derive estimates of respondents' behaviour. Here are some examples (1) 'Within the past seven days, how often have you . . .'; (2) 'Within the past seven days, have you done any of the following: (Tick all that are right for you) (a) (b) (c) (d) (e) (f)'; (3) 'How long ago is it since you last . . . ?';(4) 'How many times a week do you usually . . . ?' The type of question used will depend on the purpose of the research. For instance, the second question enables one to conceal the purpose of the study, while the last one asks the respondent, in effect, to ensure that the answer is 'typical'. All these questions present problems with regard to validity and selective recall and tend to yield *under*estimates. Daily checklists, on the other hand, may yield *over*estimates; here the respondent is daily given or sent a list of magazines, radio programmes, social activities or other relevant materials, with a request to fill in a list for that day. The diary technique, used with proper safeguards, can yield results that are probably nearest the 'true' frequency for a given period, but a good deal of comparative research is needed to make sure of this.

The diary technique presents so many difficulties that it will only be used when our requirements can be met in no other way. What are some of these requirements? One of them might be the timing of activities within the day, when an hourly record is needed. Another is the summing of certain activities over a period of a week or longer for the same respondent, such as time spent in outdoor leisure activities, weekday/weekend contrasts or the reciprocity of visiting behaviour. A third requirement might concern such unobservable behaviour as dream records. Sometimes better data might be obtained by specially stationed observers or by mechanical means — for instance, the daily tasks of teachers, or television channel-switching habits — but observational or mechanical methods present their own difficulties. Diaries come into their own particularly when we are dealing with information that is not likely to be remembered accurately for a period of time and needs to be recorded immediately.

The design of a diary form will follow the same lines as any other self-completion device. We will have to pay a good deal of attention to definitions (for instance, in a health diary, what details pertaining to disease, malaise, self-medication or medical consultation are to be recorded) and to the problem of time intervals (daily, hourly, minute-by-minute). In setting out the form, more attention than usual must be given to making it clear, providing adequate space and making it look interesting and important. As always, careful pilot work using alternative diary layouts is vital; it is, for instance, not at all easy to find out if the diary form is *failing* to obtain certain information. A frequent problem is the difference between weekdays and weekends in the patterning of many activities.

A diary will need to be accompanied by written instructions. These should generally cover the need for accuracy and frankness, the danger of allowing the diary to influence the respondent's behaviour, and the importance of filling in the diary at the requested intervals and not at the end of the period. Among other topics, we may also deal with the respondent's feeling that a given diary period may be atypical.

Next, there are the problems of placement and collection, and the sampling problems allied to these. Diary samples are often small, and the difficulties in placement increase the danger of volunteer bias. Many investigators stress the need for a personal touch, suggesting that an interviewer should spend time persuading the respondents, instructing them in the details of the recording process, perhaps calling in or telephoning once or twice during the diary period, and personally collecting the diary and thanking the respondents. If co-operation can be obtained, school children can be asked to fill out diaries about their previous day's activities for a week, under the (non-directive) supervision of their class teacher, during the first period of every school day. They can even be asked to keep notes of their activities over the weekend for entry in Monday morning's diary. Some schools regard this as very useful practice for their pupils. It is important, in such cases, to brief the teacher personally, to maintain the children's interest by means of letters or visits and to make it very obvious to the children that their diary records are being collected by the research worker and will not be seen by the school.

In some studies it is possible to have one informant in a family who keeps a diary for the whole household; for instance, in respect of leisure activities in the home or in respect of illnesses and medical needs. Care must be taken, however, that the chosen informant really is in a position to give full information on others and is not absent from the home for crucial periods or unaware of the activities of some persons in the family. Other members of the family should also be warned against letting the diary-keeping affect their behaviour.

Since diaries often continue for periods of a week or longer, we have the problem of sustaining motivation. It often happens that, as the diary period wears on, less and less information is recorded. Ways of preventing or reducing this 'falling off' effect include encouraging letters, personal visits or telephone calls, where possible. Others include varying the colours of the daily pages or by adding extra questions now and then on separate slips of paper. The important thing is that whatever the method of encouragement, we make the respondents feel that we realize how much work we are asking for, that we are very grateful for their assistance and that the data really are important for the purpose of our research. Perhaps, in the final analysis, how the respondents feel about the stated purpose of our study will be more important than personal encouragement or financial inducements.

Diaries are among the most arduous techniques to code and process. They provide rich illustrative material but, in addition, we usually need to abstract certain data for tabulation. Let us take a very simple example: bedtimes. If we have a week's diary for each respondent, then we have seven bedtimes available. We may code and process each of these separately to show mean differences of bedtimes between different days of the week, and between weekdays and weekends. However, we shall also want to develop codes covering seven days together for each respondent. For instance, we may want to develop a 'regularity' code to show how much the bedtimes fluctuate in the course of a week. These are simple tally codes; things become more complex if we have to assess, say, the 'sociability' of a family on the basis of a week's diaries, or their tendency toward eating health food, or the 'richness' of a person's dreams. We must bear in mind also that the diary is often part of a larger survey and that the diary results must be linked to other data. Given the difficulties of design, placement, completion and processing, it is not surprising that diaries are often given to only part of a sample.

## Sociometry

The sociometric technique enables us to obtain a visual picture of the pattern of likes and dislikes among people in a group. The name J.L. Moreno has long been associated with the development of this technique and with its application in many now classic investigations. One of his earliest researches dealt with a holiday camp community of adolescent girls. The girls lived in fourteen cottages, and there was a good deal of squabbling and unco-operative behaviour both among girls sharing the same cottage and among girls in different cottages. Moreno asked each of the girls to state — on a short, confidential questionnaire — the names of the girls in the camp with whom she would most like to share a cottage and the names of those with whom she would least like to share. By sorting the names into groups of individuals who were mutually attracted and gradually rehousing the girls accordingly, the disharmony in the camp was greatly reduced.

This early application of the technique contains its most important ingredients, though a good deal has been added subsequently. Let us examine it in some detail. First of all, the technique can only be applied to a group, although we may ultimately arrive at scores or descriptions for each individual in a group. The group should be closed, in the sense that each member of the group can both make and receive nominations, that each member knows at least some others in the group and that nominations outside the group are not permitted. The nominations express positive feelings of some kind (liking, admiration, utility, wish-fulfilment), and the technique is often elaborated by asking also for nominations expressing negative feelings (with whom would you least like to be?). The number of nominations is usually limited (three is a common number) and is the same for every respondent. The questionnaire should specify a situation or criterion that the respondents should bear in mind when making their nominations. A criterion could be, as we have seen, sharing the same dwelling, or doing homework together, or belonging to the same club and so on. It is often suggested that better validity is obtained if the criterion is real, so that the respondents know that some social action will follow the analysis of the choice patterns, such as the reassignment of boarders to different dormitories. It is also important that the responses be given privately.

In its original form the technique is extremely simple. All that is required from each respondent is a slip of paper giving his or her name and the names of the choices. The situation to which the choices refer should also appear on each slip. If these data are available for each member of the group, and no choices have gone to persons outside the group by mistake, then the investigator is in a position to draw a visual representation of the pattern of likes and dislikes within that group. Probably the easiest way to start doing this is to draw as many small circles as there are members in the group and arrange these in the form of an oval. Taking each completed questionnaire in turn, we may draw arrows from the chooser to the chosen — using only first preferences, for a start (see Figure 13.1). The first attempt will not be very satisfactory, since it will show too many lines criss-crossing each other. The next step is to break the oval pattern and to rearrange the results in a more meaningful way. For instance, we might start with the most popular individual — the one receiving the largest number of choices. We may put him or her in the centre and arrange around this person little circles of all the respondents who have chosen him or her and also the person he or she has chosen. Next, we take another very popular individual and plot their choosers. After that, we draw around the periphery those who have chosen one of the individuals surrounding these very popular persons and so on.

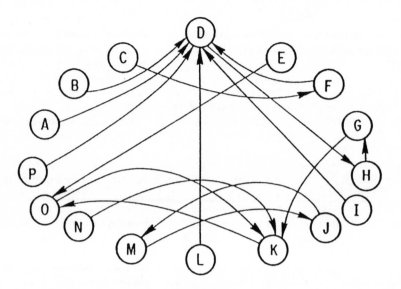

Figure 13.1.

Not surprisingly, a specialized terminology has grown up around these sociometric configurations; for instance, very popular group members are often referred to as 'stars'. In any group, we are likely to find a few individuals who are chosen by no one or by hardly anyone; they are referred to as 'isolates'. Then we may find 'pairs', two persons who have given each other's names, whose choices have been reciprocal. There may be gangs or subgroups or 'chains', as they are called in sociometry — groups of perhaps half-a-dozen respondents who give only each other's names. Of course, there may be all kinds of other patterns.

We will now make the picture more elaborate by bringing in the second and third choices, or as many as have been allowed, and further, by bringing in the negative choices. It will soon become obvious that, even with numerous attempts at redrawing, and even with the help of coloured inks and a variety of symbols, the complexity of the data obtained from a group of more than, say, two dozen individuals is too great to permit pictorial representation in this way. This has led to the development of index-analysis and matrix-analysis methods. Index analysis involves the calculation of various ratios for each individual or for the group as a whole. For each individual, we find the total number of choices and rejections and, dividing these by (N–1) to allow for comparisons across groups, we may calculate a choice status and a rejection status; we may also subtract these two indices from each other to enable us to distinguish individuals who are frequently liked from those who are frequently liked by some but disliked by others. For the group as a whole, we may calculate such indices as *group cohesion* (the proportion of mutual pairs), *group integration* (the proportion of isolates) and other common-sense ratios. There are ways of making such indices comparable across groups. If more than one choice per person has been permitted, then the indices have to take this into account as well.

Matrix analysis starts by setting up a square of rows and columns with the names or numbers of the group members both across the top and down the side. Customarily, the latter represent the choosers. In the row opposite each name we may now plot this person's choices and rejections in the relevant columns. First, second, and third choice may be indicated by entering the numbers 3, 2 and 1 in the appropriate cells (or some other weighting or notation may be employed); rejections may be similarly entered, preceded by a minus sign, or a separate rejection matrix may be composed. Some of the data for index construction may be readily compiled by adding up the entries in each column representing the incoming choice patterns. For some purposes, we now proceed to rearrange the matrix, by changing the order of the individuals simultaneously and in the same way both in the rows and columns, aiming to bring as many

## Example 13.15.

|  |  | CHOSEN | | | | | | | | | | | | | | | |
|  |  | Middle Class | | | | | | | | Working Class | | | | | | | |
|  |  | A | B | C | D | E | F | G | H | I | J | K | L | M | N | O | P |
| CHOOSING — Middle Class | A |  |  |  | X |  |  |  |  |  |  |  |  |  |  |  |  |
|  | B |  |  |  | X |  |  |  |  |  |  |  |  |  |  |  |  |
|  | C |  |  |  |  |  | X |  |  |  |  |  |  |  |  |  |  |
|  | D |  |  |  |  |  |  |  | X |  |  |  |  |  |  |  |  |
|  | E |  |  |  |  |  |  |  |  |  |  |  |  |  |  | X |  |
|  | F |  |  |  | X |  |  |  |  |  |  |  |  |  |  |  |  |
|  | G |  |  |  |  |  |  |  |  |  |  | X |  |  |  |  |  |
|  | H |  |  |  |  |  |  | X |  |  |  |  |  |  |  |  |  |
| CHOOSING — Working Class | I |  |  |  | X |  |  |  |  |  |  |  |  |  |  |  |  |
|  | J |  |  |  |  |  |  |  |  |  |  |  |  | X |  |  |  |
|  | K |  |  |  |  |  |  |  |  |  |  |  |  |  |  | X |  |
|  | L |  |  |  | X |  |  |  |  |  |  |  |  |  |  |  |  |
|  | M |  |  |  |  |  |  |  |  |  | X |  |  |  |  |  |  |
|  | N |  |  |  |  |  |  |  |  |  |  | X |  |  |  |  |  |
|  | O |  |  |  |  |  |  |  |  |  |  | X |  |  |  |  |  |
|  | P |  |  |  | X |  |  |  |  |  |  |  |  |  |  |  |  |
|  |  | — | — | — | 6 | — | 1 | 1 | 1 | — | 1 | 3 | — | 1 | — | 2 | — |

positive choices as possible near the diagonal, while moving rejections away from the diagonal (see Example 13.15). This will reveal cliques, leadership patterns and group cleavages; but the clerical work involved is tedious unless a computer program is available.

The x's represent the first choices of a group of schoolboys, divided according to their social background. Although we have not yet plotted their second and third choices nor their rejections, we can already see the beginnings of certain trends. For instance, eleven out of the sixteen choices are 'within class', and only five are 'across class'; this suggests that social background might be important to these boys in deciding with whom to make friends. We also note that boy D is outstandingly popular; interestingly enough, all the 'across-class' choices of the working-class boys go to him (although his own best friend, H, is a middle-class boy). Could this mean that working-class boys are basically more inclined to stick to their own class, unless an outstandingly attractive middle-class person, such as boy D, happened to be in the same group? We note further, that there are eight boys who have received no first choices. Are these boys, in fact, isolated or rejected? To answer such questions we shall need to plot the second and third choices and the patterns of rejection, and the study will have to be repeated in a number of groups before more general conclusions can be drawn.

In Figure 13.2, we see the same pattern of first choices drawn as a diagram. The 'class-barrier' runs across the page. As we have seen, boy D is very popular, and there are five choices across the 'class-barrier'. We now also note another interesting phenomenon, namely, that among the working-class boys there are two 'pairs' (reciprocated choices). This might, if repeated in further analyses,

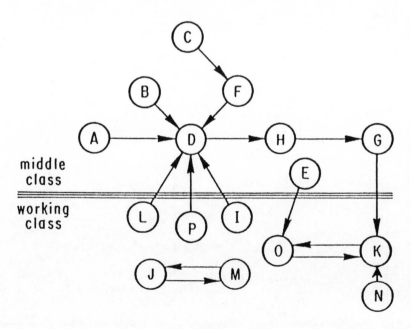

Figure 13.2.

strengthen the evidence for the greater group cohesion of the working-class boys.

In many investigations we have other information available to us about each individual, besides the sociometric choice data. For instance, we may have social class, sex, age, ethnic group and so on. This will enable us to group the respondents in a meaningful fashion and to study the extent to which such a grouping accounts for the choice/rejection patterns, with the aid of matrix analysis. We can distinguish various kinds of in-groups and out-groups, and we can calculate the extent to which choices are restricted to the in-group and rejections to the out-group, and how many choices take place across subgroup barriers. For instance, very young children in a mixed group will choose each other without regard to sex; later on, boys and girls will only choose their own sex, but toward adolescence there will be some choices across the sex line. Similarly, the degree of integration of minority-group members can be studied and compared.

The sociometric technique can also be used to focus attention on certain individuals. Thus, we may wish to identify the qualities that make for popularity or leadership in certain groups, or the effects of isolation or rejection; sociometry will enable us to pick such individuals for more intensive questioning. In industry or in the armed forces, 'buddy ratings' have been used to study the relationship between leadership and popularity or to identify people who are powerful and influential.

It is possible to construct a sociogram on the basis, not of questionnaire responses, but of observations of frequency and duration of contact between members of a group. It is also possible to use the sociometric approach projectively: the respondent has to answer such questions as: 'who do you think would choose to work with Mr A?' and 'whom do you think Mr A would choose?' thus giving us a consensual percept of relations existing between members of the group.

Sometimes, no limit is placed on the number of names permitted; this enables us to calculate a measure of social expansiveness of each individual. We can also vary the criterion, for instance by asking first, 'who are your best friends?' then, 'with whom would you rather be, if you had to join the army?' and next 'whom would you like to take home to tea?' This may tell us something about the qualities that our respondent considers necessary in a friend, in a fellow soldier and in a visitor to take home to the family.

This last elaboration raises the question of validity. Some investigators have suggested that sociometric questionnaires are of doubtful validity unless the respondent knows that the results will be used for a restructuring of the group. Many others, however, have freely used hypothetical criteria in ways analogous to an attitude questionnaire.

Network analysis (see Knoke and Kuklinski, 1982) is a technique which, in many ways, is analogous to sociometry. It is used to study the relations and communication patterns within and between members of various groups. Epidemiologists, for example, find it useful for the modelling of disease-transmission patterns.

# Selected readings

## RATINGS

Guilford, J.P., 1954, *Psychometric Methods*, McGraw-Hill, New York.
Arguably the best discussion on rating scales is still in Chapter 11 of this book. For paired comparisons see chapter 7.

Postlethwaite, T.N., 1962, *Young Europeans in England*, Political and Economic Planning Foundation, London.


## SEMANTIC DIFFERENTIAL AND REPERTORY GRID

Osgood, C.E., Suci, C.J. and Tannenbaum, P.H., 1957, *The Measurement of Meaning*, University of Illinois Press, Urbana, Ill.
The main source book for the semantic differential technique and its various applications.

Fransella, Fay and Bannister, Donald, 1977, *A Manual for Repertory Grid Technique*, Academic Press, London.
Has become a standard text on the repertory grid.

Kelly, George A., 1955, *The Psychology of Personal Constructs*, W.W. Norton, New York.
Volume I contains the basic theory and the development of the repertory grid test.

Bannister, Donald and Mair, J., 1970, *The Evaluation of Personal Constructs*, Academic Press, London.
Entertaining early text. Useful on reliability and validity of repertory grids.


## SOCIOMETRY

Moreno, J.L., rev. ed. 1953, *Who Shall Survive?*, Beacon House, Washington DC.
This has long been the chief source book of the sociometric movement and a recognized classic.

Moreno, J.L., 1960, *The Sociometry Reader*, The Free Press, Glencoe, Ill.
A source book of sociometric research.

Knoke, D., and Kuklinski, J.H., 1982, *Network Analysis*, Sage.

# 14
# DATA PROCESSING

At the beginning of the study we should explore what data-processing facilities will be available to us and what computer programs and equipment we shall be using. Certainly it would be most unwise to leave such considerations till after the fieldwork, for by then it will almost always be too late. It is best, therefore, to seek advice on data processing, and on computers and computer software, at a very early stage so that the data-processing requirements can be incorporated from the outset, thus enabling the analysis to proceed as smoothly as possible.

It is wise to anticipate the data-processing requirements also during the pilot stage. If it is intended, for example, to place data-processing indications and numbers in the right-hand margin of each questionnaire page, perhaps in a column headed 'for office use only', then this layout should be introduced during the pilot work to check that it does not unduly distract the respondents. As we have seen (see Chapter 4), such data-processing indications should be placed close to, and aligned with, the answer categories or boxes to minimize transfer errors. For some questionnaires it is possible to generate bar codes for each response category, or to make the responses machine-readable in some other way, so that the data can be directly entered into a computer.

During the quantification stage of our survey we have to face up to the fact that, however subtle our questions and however thoughtful and cooperative our respondents have been, the main purpose of the questionnaire, and of the survey as a whole, is *measurement*. The final product is likely to consist of a series of tabulations and statistical analyses; these, together with a few illustrative quotations from the raw data, will be turned into a report showing in what ways our findings bear on the hypotheses with which we began. During the quantification stage the words that were spoken or written by our respondents will be processed; they will be turned into figures and symbols that can be counted and added up. In this way we obtain the entries for the tables that we need in order to draw conclusions.

How is this to be done? How are these bundles of questionnaires or interview records to be transformed into meaningful figures which can be used for tabulation?

Essentially the processing routine will be determined by the nature of the data collection techniques, though something will depend on the size of the survey, the composition of the questionnaire, the processing facilities available and the requirements of the computer software package that will be used. If the questionnaire consists (almost) entirely of 'closed', pre-coded questions and some scales or inventories, and if all the categories have been assigned numerical values which have been printed on the questionnaires, then there should be very little delay in entering the data into the computer. Indeed most of the work will already have been done during the fieldwork and data-collection stage. Respondents will have ticked answer categories in multiple-choice questions, attitude scales, grids, inventories and other 'closed' techniques, or the interviewers will have listened to the responses and then field-coded these by ticking prepared answer boxes. When such completed questionnaires are returned to the research office, they are almost ready for processing.

The task will be more difficult in the case of free-response or 'open' questions, follow-up probes, projective techniques, or recorded responses to interview questions. Here the data reach the survey office in the form of words and sentences written either by the interviewer or by the respondent, or perhaps in the form of tape recordings, and before we can start any kind of statistical analysis we first have to convert the data into numerical form. Usually we do this with the aid of a classification system, and the process of classifying responses in this way is known as *coding* (see below).

Difficulties arise in the case of 'mixed' questionnaires, which contain both 'open' and pre-coded techniques. Usually in such cases the questionnaires are first given to the coders, who will enter the numerical codes for the 'open' items in the margin. Once all the 'open' questions have been coded there should be a complete set of numerical symbols next to every question on all the questionnaires.

Data entry of each completed questionnaire can now take place at the computer keyboard, or by other means, because there is now a numerical value for every response. Supervision and checking are of the greatest importance here, for it is only too easy to make clerical mistakes. For this reason special data-entry-management computer programs have been developed; such programs can be of great help in minimizing errors from the start.

The need for checks and double-checks cannot be over-emphasized. Some years ago a clerical error crept into a major cross-national survey of several countries with many thousands of respondents, and the error was eventually traced to a point even before the data-processing stage. When the analysis was being prepared, it was noticed that some of the statistical results for country Y seemed to differ quite markedly from those of the other participating countries. Many theories were advanced, based on psychological insights or alleged 'national character' indicators, to explain these differences. However, it was discovered subsequently that a minor error had occurred during the printing of the question booklets: the questions were supposed to have been numbered consecutively, but somehow a number was left out, so that the numbering sequence ran from fifteen to seventeen, omitting sixteen. As a result, all subsequent question numbers were wrong, in that they did not tally with the numbering system used by the other countries. So when, for example, all the results for question 94 were being compared, the data from country Y were actually the results of question 95!

It took a costly and time-consuming rescue operation to rectify this small piece of carelessness and it left a lot of people with red faces. The moral is twofold: endless checks and cross-checks are a vital part of data processing; and before producing speculative interpretations of 'interesting' findings, check that they are not due to some slip in the data processing.

## Assembling the code book

Every survey should conduct its data processing and statistical analysis with the aid of a *code book*. A code book is essentially an assembly of three components: the text of the original questionnaire complete with filter questions, probes and pre-codes, together with the numerical values that have been allocated to every answer category; the variable allocation document (see below); and the coding frames (see page 267). The code book should be written before the start of the data entry phase.

As soon as practicable, a *variable allocation document* should be produced. Essentially this is a list which tells us what variable numbers have been allocated to each question or item. A computer can handle any number of variables, each scored numerically in a variety of ways, for each respondent. But how do we know what each variable *is*; that is, what question it represents? For this we need some sort of shortened labelling system (see below) for each question, plus an agreed allocation of questions to variables (which represent spaces in the computer's memory), so that everyone on the survey team will know that, for example, question 39 (TRAVTWRK=journey to work) has been allocated to variable 176.

The variable allocation document has to be prepared with great care (often while resisting considerable time pressure) and will become part of the code book. On it we can see the text and the label of every question and every answer category (with their code values) as well as the variable number which has been allocated to it. In due course it will be merged with the code book.

The code book *must* be error-free. It will be needed by everyone: by the data processors first of all, but also by those who are doing the statistical analysis, by the coders, by the supervisors and team leaders, and by the writers of the report. If the project is small, and most of these functions are carried out by a handful of people, or even by just one researcher, there is always the temptation not to be systematic, not to write things down, to make changes without telling anybody and to assume that everyone will know and will remember. These are dangerous assumptions which can have wasteful and costly consequences. The meticulous care that has to go into the production of a code book will pay dividends many times over, even for a small project.

The first aim of the data-processing phase of our study is to get to the point where all the responses to a questionnaire can be turned into numbers. As we shall see, when we are dealing with 'open' questions, these numbers are provided by the coding frame; that is, by the classification system which we have to develop for dealing with the responses. But how do we deal with the 'closed', multiple-choice questions?

In principle we shall have to allocate a number to each answer category, either during the pilot work leading up to the printing stage or (if unavoidable) during the data-processing stage. The procedure is straightforward enough, but it helps to observe some systematic data-processing conventions. Let us take, as our first example, a very commonly asked factual question:

Are you [TICK ONE]

(a) Married ....................................... [  ]
(b) Single ......................................... [  ]
(c) Separated or divorced ........... [  ]
(d) Widowed .................................... [  ]

Here we would probably assign numbers quite straightforwardly as follows:

Response category (a) = 1
                   (b) = 2
                   (c) = 3
                   (d) = 4

and the question will now look like this:

Are you [TICK ONE]

(a) Married ....................................... [  ]  1
(b) Single ......................................... [  ]  2
(c) Separated or divorced ........... [  ]  3
(d) Widowed .................................... [  ]  4

To enter any of these four responses into a computer, the keyboard operator simply keys in the number printed alongside the box that has been ticked. In addition, there will have to be an instruction about *missing data*, that is where the respondent has not ticked any of the boxes, has ignored the boxes and has written something else, or has defaced the questionnaire. Since this problem may occur with any question, it would be good practice to use the same number throughout the survey to indicate 'no answer' to a question, for example '9' or '999', or any other.

The above question concerns a nominal variable, so these numbers are a purely symbolic means of entering the responses. They are not integers; that is, response (d) is not twice as large as response (b). We might equally well have chosen a=3, b=1, c=4 and d=3; or a=16, b=39, c=4 and d=22 or any other numbers, as long as no two categories have the same number. This point is important because in the case of interval measures or ranked data we assign numbers which *do* have a numerical value or else indicate a rank order. For example, responses to a question about bedrooms in the home, or number of children, might be entered as 'real' numbers. Attitude scale responses ranging from strongly agree to agree, then uncertain, followed by disagree and strongly disagree might be entered as 5, 4, 3, 2 and 1, which are taken to indicate a matter of degree on a pro–con dimension.

Usually we also need to give each variable or question a short *name* or *label*, for example marital status, which will be used in the variable allocation document and in the code book. Some computer programs require a label of not more than eight letters, so we might call this variable MRTLSTAT, or MARSTAT, or

MARITALS or whatever we like. To avoid confusion, we should try to generate labels which are easily understandable by fellow researchers.

## The data base

The final results of the data-entry phase should enable the computer (or, in the case of a small classroom survey, the manual data processor, for example the teacher) to produce a simple two-way matrix of variables versus respondents. This is the *data base*. With the aid of the code book, it now becomes possible to enter the next phase: the statistical analysis of the data.

You *must* make one or more copies of your data base (on diskettes, or on tape or by whatever means available) and keep such copies in some other locations to guard against the risks of electrical power failure, fire, theft or malfunction. You would also be well advised never to carry out any manipulations on your original data set. If you wish to create new scores, or do correlations, or re-name certain variables or deal with certain data subsets, it is far safer to copy or transfer the data to another file, diskette or other storage medium, in order to carry out your manipulations without disturbing the original data base.

## Serial case numbering

Each individual in the sample will need an identifying case number. This is essential if one person's responses are not to get mixed up with those of another, but there are added reasons for having case numbers. For example, we may be conducting a follow-up study, so we shall probably need to calculate any changes or differences in each individual's responses after an interval of time. To do this, it will be necessary to compare the set of responses given by each individual at the first point of data collection with any subsequent ones. These sets of responses can be found and compared with the aid of their serial or case numbers. Another reason for having case numbers may arise if we want to add existing records (for example medical records, examination results) to our survey data. After collecting such additional information according to a list of names, we shall need to add the appropriate case number to each name, to enter the information in the computer, and then to 'merge' these data with our survey responses by means of their case numbers.

To make such operations possible we must devise a numbering system which can be related to names, or names and addresses. Usually this is not difficult; however, if we have drawn an *anonymous* sample, then our case number will be the only means of giving a unique identity to each returned questionnaire. And if our sample is not anonymous but *confidential*, then the existence of a list of names and addresses linked to case numbers could constitute a danger to our respondents. Suppose, for example, that our data contain confidential health information, or self-disclosures about illegal drug use or about sexual or delinquent activities, then an office burglary or a raid by the police might cause some of our respondents to be blackmailed or arrested. In studies of this kind it is essential that we take added precautions to preserve anonymity; for example, by using a double-blind procedure or by lodging the only existing list of names linked to case numbers with a colleague abroad.

Use can be made of the identifying case numbers for classification purposes, by linking them to the sampling frame in some suitable way. Suppose, for instance, that we have a sample of children selected through their schools. We may decide to give each child a six-figure case number: the first digit might indicate sex (1, or 2, meaning girl or boy); the second digit might indicate district or area (assuming there are not more than ten districts represented in our sample); the third digit will indicate the school that the child attends (assuming that we sample not more than ten schools in each district); the fourth digit might be used to indicate the form or level within the particular school; and the last two digits will identify any given child within his or her class. Thus, case number 279513 would mean, to the initiated, a fifth-form boy in school 9, in district 7, identifiable as number 13 on the list of names in his class. Such a system would also enable us to bring together all the third-formers in our sample, or all the children from area 4, or all the girls from school 81 (meaning school 1 in district 8) and so forth. There is no need to insist on numbering all cases consecutively; if there are, say, only three school districts represented in the sample, then the remaining numbers in that variable will be left unused.

It is often wise not to leave the design of a case-numbering system until the data-processing stage. For example, postal surveys often put case numbers on outgoing questionnaires (unless we have promised our respondents complete anonymity); interviewers are also sometimes given sets of case numbers to assign to respondents. The design of a case-numbering scheme will force us to think about the intended statistical analysis, and will help to keep track of the questionnaires during the data-processing phase. The case numbering system we adopt should appear in the code book.

## Coding frames

Each free-response question, probe, sentence-completion item, or other 'open' technique in our questionnaire will require its own classification scheme. Only rarely can we use a scheme devised for some other inquiry. Our first task will therefore be the design of all the classification schemes, usually known as 'codes' or 'coding frames', required for our particular study. Quite possibly we have already given this matter some thought during the pilot stages, and perhaps we have produced some tentative drafts for coding frames. However, the coding frames proposed during the pilot stage will have been based on the raw data obtained from pilot samples, and since the responses of such samples may differ markedly from those of the main sample, we must always construct our coding frame with the aid of responses from the main sample.

It is very tempting to start the design of our coding frames as soon as the first returns from the fieldwork arrive back at the office. However, since these are likely to be unrepresentative, it is advisable to wait until all the returns, or a substantial part of them, are in. Otherwise, we run the risk that the coding frames will turn out to be a poor fit, requiring amendment, perhaps several times, in the course of the coding operation. It is always undesirable to have to amend a coding frame in midstream, since amendments produce errors and are wasteful because they require re-coding of questionnaires that have been coded already.

How do we set about designing a coding frame? Probably the first step should be the examination of a representative sample of responses. In practice, we select a convenient number of questionnaires (say, fifty or sixty cases) on a representative basis and copy all the responses to a particular question on to sheets of paper, or on to a word processor. At the top of each page will be the text of the question as it appeared in the questionnaire, and below that will be copied all the various answers given to that question by our subsample of fifty or sixty cases, each answer preceded by the case number. Where answers are few, for instance if the question applied to only part of the sample, more cases will be needed, until we have a sufficiently large and varied selection of answers. When we come to design the coding frame of the next free-response question, we go through the entire batch of selected questionnaires again, copying all the responses to that particular question together, so that we can look at them.

From this point on we must bear in mind very clearly what it is that we are trying to do. By imposing a set of classificatory categories, perhaps eight or ten in number, on a very much larger and probably very varied set of responses, we are inevitably going to *lose information* (see Chapter 7). Bearing in mind the aims and hypotheses of the survey and the particular purpose of the question under consideration, we must so design the coding frame that this loss of information will occur where it matters least, enabling us to run our comparisons or test our hypotheses with the greatest accuracy. This means that our set of categories will not necessarily be designed simply 'to do justice to the responses'; other considerations may apply, and compromises often have to be made.

For a start, how many categories should we have? If there were no constraints, and we were anxious not to cause any distortion, we might like to have almost as many categories as there are responses, grouping under one heading only those responses that are identical. This is obviously not a practical proposition. Even if we could afford to design so elaborate a coding scheme, we would probably find during the statistical analysis that each category contained only one case or a very few cases. Therefore, *the number of categories we can afford to have will in part be determined by the number of cases in the sample and the number of statistical breakdowns we shall use*; a category that will, in the final analysis and after subdivision of the sample, hold fewer than two or three dozen cases must usually be regarded as a luxury. However much it offends our sensibilities, we must realize that it is pointless to retain a category that is used by too few people.

There is an exception to this argument. It sometimes happens that we have a hypothesis about a certain type of response being absent or very rare. In that case we might reserve a category for it, in order to show just how rare it is. For instance, suppose we had asked people why they had changed from one brand of cigarettes to another, and suppose, further, that we wished to test the specific hypothesis that people very rarely admit to reasons of economy in answering such a question. In such a case we would make up a coding frame suitable to the distribution of the answers we get but, come what may, we should reserve one category for 'economic reasons' or something like that.

Most survey practitioners try to keep their coding frames down to twelve to fifteen categories, though they may go beyond this number occasionally. Since we will require categories for 'miscellaneous', 'don't know' and 'no answer', this would leave us effectively with nine to twelve categories. This number may, at first sight, seem impossibly small when the variety of responses is being considered, yet it is surprising how often one starts off with a much more ambitious scheme only to find that up to a dozen categories will suffice after all, with the added advantage of increased frequencies in each category.

What other considerations guide us in the composition of coding frames? Let us take, for example, a question asking for the respondent's favourite film star. Let us assume that we have copied the replies of five dozen people and that we are now faced with the problem of classifying these responses. One approach might simply be by frequency. We allot, say, seven categories to the seven names occurring most often and lump the remaining names in one or two other categories. Or perhaps we wish to expand the frame; we could have dozens of categories, each with one film star's name, if we chose. Or we might decide to group the names under different labels, such as 'romantic', 'Western', 'musical' and so on, according to the type of role with which such film stars are associated. Then again, we may decide to have two coding frames, one for male and one for female film stars. Or we may wish to group together those stars who also appear on other mass media, and those who do not. We may classify stars by their ages, or by their ethnic background, or by the number of divorces they have had. So we see that it is often not a simple matter to design a coding frame that will 'do justice to the data' and, moreover, the type of coding frame we need will depend on what we wish to find out.

Suppose, for instance, that we wish to examine the hypothesis that men will most often admire female film stars, whereas women will more often mention male film stars. In that case, all we need to do, strictly speaking, is to classify the responses by sex into just two categories, male stars and female stars. This would tell us all we needed to know — though it would not enable us to go very much further. On the other hand, suppose we had the hypothesis that a lot depends on the star's age in relation to the respondent's age, with younger respondents admiring a somewhat older and more mature actor or actress, while middle-aged respondents prefer a younger star. In that case we would need a fairly complex coding frame giving categories of age differentials, up or down from the respondent's own age, and to do the coding we would need to know both the respondent's age and that of his or her most admired film star.

When we copy out the responses, it is helpful to group the respondents in terms of one or more variables of concern, such as sex, age, social mobility and so on. This often suggests differences in content, flavour or expression between subgroups, and a coding frame can be designed to highlight these. For this reason, the copied responses must not merely be regarded as a try-out; they should be most carefully studied and perused.

Usually, the order of the categories is unimportant, and the categories are quite independent of each another (they form a *nominal* variable). Sometimes, however, we may need a coding frame that is more like a rating scale. For instance, we may use some of our categories to indicate the degree of favourableness with which the respondent views a certain person or object. Some responses would be classified as 'highly favourable', others as 'moderately favourable' or as 'favourable with reservations', and so on. Sometimes the coding frame requires a *logical* structure; the classification of favourite subjects at school might be an example. Here we would perhaps wish to use two linked frames. The first frame would have broad categories such as (1) 'languages', (2) 'numerical subjects', (3) 'natural history' and so forth, while the second frame would be different for each of the broader categories and would contain the subcategories, so that, say, code 14 might be French, code 26 might be trigonometry and code 36 could stand for geology.

For some questions, typically those used for classificatory purposes, there are probably some well-designed and elaborate coding frames available ready-made. A classification of occupational prestige might be one example. When using prepared coding frames one should follow the coding instructions most carefully, and, of course, the original question(s) should be the same, if comparability is desired with the results of other investigations using the same coding frame. Occasionally, too, we may have asked the same question in 'open' and in 'closed' form; in that case there may be something to be said for using at least some of the pre-codes of the 'closed' question as categories in the coding frame of the 'open' question.

Every coding frame is likely to need two or three categories that are standard, namely 'miscellaneous', 'don't know' and 'no answer' or 'not ascertained', though the latter two categories are frequently grouped together. On the other hand, sometimes it is important to know how many respondents said that they did not know the answer, or which ones refused to commit themselves; these two categories may not just be 'waste categories'. Into 'miscellaneous' go all those responses that cannot readily be fitted into one of our prepared categories. In cases of doubt, it is better practice to classify a response as 'miscellaneous' than to force it into another category. One reason for this is that it is best not to blur the limits of the categories. Another is that if such doubtful responses occur with unexpected frequency, then at some point they can be 'rescued', by making the decision to amend the coding frame by introducing a new category. In that case we merely have to look again at the responses coded 'miscellaneous' with a view to reclassification, instead of having to recode every response category. Such a course of action should be seriously considered if the frequency of 'miscellaneous' responses rises above, say, 15 per cent or so.

It should be realized that code categories can always be *combined*, for example by putting together all the male film stars, or all the favourable plus moderately favourable responses, or all the respondents doing manual labour of any kind. This is sometimes necessary when we are dealing with small sub-analyses, where the lack of cases is making itself felt.

Each category in a coding frame should be designated in the clearest possible way. It should be described in words, or given a label, and it is always helpful to give many illustrative examples taken from actual responses. Suppose we have asked people a question about the platform of a given political party, and that we wish to classify the answers in terms of the amount of knowledge revealed by the respondents. In such a case it would not be enough to set up a coding frame with categories such as 'very good', 'adequate', 'poor' and so forth. Obviously, this would lead to inconsistencies among the coders and might not be clear to our readers. We have to set up definite criteria such as: 'very good: gives at least three different items of party policy correctly', together with some examples of actual responses. This is particularly important when numerous coders will be engaged on the same survey, in order to ensure consistency and reliability. Even where the investigator does all his or her own coding, the categories should be as clear and as unambiguous as possible, for it is only too easy to change standards as one goes on. It is also necessary that the reader know what is the precise meaning of each category; often categories are ambiguous, but examples can make the meaning clear.

In the entire coding operation it is important to introduce frequent checks, for statistics based on inconsistent coding can be very misleading. Some coding frames are relatively objective and merely require consistency and attention to detail on the part of the coder for instance, the coding of favourite school subjects. Other coding frames, however, require a certain amount of interpretation on the part of the coder; for instance, coding the job dissatisfactions of teachers, or the reasons people give for not travelling abroad more than they do. We then have to face the delicate problem of designing a coding frame that goes 'deep' enough, yet one that can be used consistently by the coding staff available, bearing in mind their training and experience. In some investigations it is necessary to check every coded response, or to have two coders working independently on the same data and then discussing and resolving the differences between them. The primary aim must be consistency and the elimination of ambiguities; a coder who 'stretches' a category, in order not to have to classify a response under 'miscellaneous', or one who 'improves' a category from one day to the next, or who 'knows' what the respondent 'really meant', merely does the study a disservice. The better and clearer the coding frame, the fewer such occasions will arise.

We may now turn to some examples of coding frames. Here, first, is a very simple code that enables us to classify a man's army service rank:

1   no military service
2   private
3   noncommissioned ranks, below sergeant
4   noncommissioned ranks, sergeant and above
5   commissioned ranks up to and including captain
6   commissioned ranks, major and above
7   special service troops, marines
8   navy or air force, merchant navy
99  no answer, not ascertained, rank not specified
0   don't know, can't remember etc.

Obviously this is a fairly crude code, designed for a particular purpose — chiefly, that of ascertaining the highest army rank attained by the respondent. Most of the categories are, therefore, prestige levels, and the categories are ordered, though this is not strictly necessary here. Note that, for special reasons, a separate category has been reserved for private; also, that most of the other categories cover a range (from — to) of ranks, so that the highest and lowest rank have to be specified. Thus, if we had worded category 3 as 'noncommissioned ranks up to sergeant', this would not have made it clear whether the rank of sergeant was or was not to be included in that category. Clearly, for other purposes one would code the material differently, in terms of home service versus various overseas theatres of service, or in terms of army, paratroopers, air force or marines, and so on. For some purposes we can make use of a special marker, say, for all those with any kind of overseas service. Such a marker code would enable us quickly to locate those respondents who had served abroad. Note, finally, that this is also an example of a logical code, which could largely have been anticipated except for the cut-off points for each category.

Next, we look at a somewhat similar example. Here is a coding frame, from a student survey, for the answers to the question: 'During the past seven days, how many hours have you spent reading newspapers?':

1   none
2   less than 1 hour
3   1 hour to 2 hours 59 minutes
4   3 hours to 4 hours 59 minutes
5   5 hours to 6 hours 59 minutes
6   7 hours to 8 hours 59 minutes
7   9 hours to 10 hours 59 minutes
8   11 hours and over
99  no answer, not ascertained
0   don't know, can't remember etc.

Here we have another ordinal code, going up in regular steps of two hours. Obviously, the actual categories have been determined from a sample of responses. How else would we know that intervals of two hours would be the most appropriate, or that very few students read newspapers for more than eleven hours a week? A 'miscellaneous' category is not, of course, required, but note that 'none' has been given a separate category on its own — to show which students had not read any newspapers at all.

We also note the special care that has been taken to create *non-overlapping categories* (as was the case with the preceding example). *All code categories must be non-overlapping.* Beginners frequently make the mistake of creating categories that overlap, in part. This becomes most obvious in numerical codes such as the one above, or in the following age categories: 20–30, 30–40, 40–50 etc. (The problem is: how should a respondent aged 30, or 40, be coded?) In non-numerical codes, the problem of overlap is less obvious, but the danger is always there, and can lead to inconsistency among coders.

In the same survey of student reading habits, some questions were asked about the most recent textbook that the student had read in the college library. One of the questions was 'What system did you follow in reading this book?' to which the following coding frame was applied:

1   miscellaneous
2   chapter headings
3   skim chapter by chapter, then make notes
4   read from cover to cover
5   skim and make notes

6   concentrate on one section only
7   use index, look up pages
8   read chapter summaries
10   just read conclusions
11   introduction only
12   read various sections thoroughly
99   don't know, no answer, not ascertained

We observe that the categories for 'don't know' and for 'no answer; not ascertained' have been grouped together. We also notice that the categories are described in somewhat abbreviated style; this is liable to lead to misunderstandings. Likewise, it is not clear how categories 3 and 5 differ from each other; this kind of ambiguity should be avoided, and it should certainly be one of the points to be discussed with the coders before they start. The code is obviously based on the study of a sample of responses; it is neither ordinal nor logical, in our sense. To some extent, the makers of the frame were also guided by the knowledge of what the teaching staff regarded as good practice in getting the most out of time in the library. Last but not least important, this is a *multiple-mention* code: a student can obviously use two or more of these systems in reading a book, and we must so devise our code that we can cope with multiple answers (see below).

Also in the same study of student reading habits were questions about the most recent extra-curricular book read. These books were coded as follows:

0   miscellaneous
1   biography, autobiography
2   travel and geography
3   crime, detection, Westerns, mysteries
4   poetry
5   essays and short stories
6   humour
7   plays
8   books about art, music, ballet, theatre etc.
10   theology, religious books
11   novels (see next column also)
99   no answer, not ascertained, don't know

NOVELS CODE

1   modern, romantic
2   modern, historical
3   modern, novel of ideas (social message)
4   modern, other
5   between wars, romantic
6   between wars, historical
7   between wars, novel of ideas (social message)
8   between wars, other
9   classical, romantic
10   classical, historical
11   classical, novel of ideas (social message)

12 classical, other

0 no novel mentioned

(NB: Classical meant that the book was published before 1914.)

This is an example of a double code, and an example of a grouped code as well. To begin with, a relatively crude classification was made of the main types of books mentioned by students — a classification that cannot bear comparison to the elaborate systems of classification employed by librarians, but that sufficed for the purpose at hand. It then became evident from the study of a sample of responses that novels were by far the most popular type of extra-curricular reading. It was therefore decided to do a more detailed, but separate, classification of this kind of fiction. Any respondent who mentioned a novel was given 11 on the first coding frame, and coded once more on the second frame. In the second frame we have, first, three broad groupings (modern, between wars, and classical), and then, within each of these, four categories (romantic, historical, novel of ideas, and other). The relative crudeness of both these frames illustrates once again the inevitable compromise between the degree of refinement in which one can indulge and the constraints of sample size, number of statistical breakdowns, quality of coders and so on. Both frames also illustrate the need for examples: in the actual coding operation lists were kept of names of books that occurred frequently, together with their date of publication and agreed classification by content. Even so, there would obviously be much room for discussion and need for checking and cross-checking. In the end, if it seemed as if a particular book could fit into more than one category, it would be necessary to lay down a ruling, however arbitrary, in order to maintain consistency among the coders.

We now come to a more difficult kind of code. In an attitude study of teachers, the following question was put: 'In these days, what qualities in children do you think a teacher should encourage most?' This question is obviously very wide indeed, and the answers covered a considerable range. Here is the frame that was finally developed:

1 religion

2 ambition, striving

3 *self-development and happiness:* spontaneity, happiness, curiosity, creativity, self-reliance, active and open personality, originality

4 *rational use of energies for the attainment of educational and work goals:* industry, efficiency, perseverance

5 *active adjustment to social situations:* sociability, co-operativeness, comradeship

6 *inhibitory adjustment to social situations:* self-control, self-discipline, correct manners, cleanliness, orderliness

7 *inhibitory adjustment to authority figures:* respect for authority, deference to teachers and elders, obedience

8 *self-assertive adjustment to social situation:* competitiveness, toughness

10 *goodness, kindness, love, tolerance, generosity*

11 *adherence to enduring values, personal integrity:* truthfulness, honesty, sense of justice, sincerity, sense of honour, dignity, courage

0 other

99 no answer, not ascertained, don't know

This coding frame requires a good deal of interpretation of the responses before they can be classified. The coders would have to think and discuss quite carefully; inevitably, coding this kind of material is slow. Note that often a broad verbal label has been given, followed by some examples. We observe that this, too, must be a multiple-mention code (see below).

Finally, here is an example of a *frame-of-reference code*. The question asked was: 'Taking all things into account, what would be the most likely cause for another world war? I don't mean the things that happen just before a war, but the real cause.' Here is the coding frame:

99   no answer; there will be no war
 0   don't know
 1   military preparations as such
 2   a specific nation or group of nations is mentioned as responsible
 3   conflicting economic interests
 4   power conflicts, tendencies for nations to want to expand, get more control
 5   economic and social needs of underprivileged peoples
 6   ideological conflicts, differences in political belief systems
 7   human nature in general, man's aggressive tendencies, reference to 'instincts' etc.
 8   moral-ethical problems, breakdown of values, loss of religious influence
10   people's mistrust of each other, misunderstandings due to different social traditions and experiences, cultural differences
11   miscellaneous other

As we see, here we do not code the contents of the responses, but rather the framework within which the respondents seem to be thinking, their frame of reference. This kind of code places quite a heavy burden of interpretation on the coder and requires a special effort to ensure reliability. The results, however, can be quite revealing and may make the effort worthwhile.

It is worth mentioning that the analysis of sentence-completion items and other projective devices proceeds in much the same way as outlined above.

For the content-analysis methods applied to written documents, radio broadcasts, case histories, propaganda, etc. the reader should refer to the Selected Readings.

## The coding process

The first thing we should do after designing all the coding frames is to draw a second small sample of completed questionnaires and try out the new codes. After making any necessary amendments, the coding frames may now be finally typed or duplicated and, in due course, assembled in the *code book* that is distributed to every coder, together with coding instructions. The coding instructions should lay down some general principles, such as how to deal with queries, the case-numbering system, the method of coding multiple-answer questions and even such details as the type and colour of the pen or pencil to be used. In large survey organizations there may be a separate coding department dealing, perhaps, with several surveys at a time, and obviously some control arrangements have to be made in order to regulate the various responsibilities and the flow of work. In particular, there should be a standard procedure for keeping track of each questionnaire from the moment it comes into the coding section, for it is very easy for questionnaires to get lost, if they happen to become query cases, or part of a try-out sample, or if they get mixed up with a batch of questionnaires from another survey.

Usually, it is best to let each coder work right through each questionnaire, going from question to question and from code to code until the final page, to gain an over-all picture of the respondent and to check on any apparent inconsistencies. Sometimes, however, there may be a good reason for allotting one question or one batch of questions to one particular coder, who will code those questions and nothing else. This may happen, for instance, if a particularly elaborate code is used, in which case it saves time and reduces inconsistencies if one coder becomes thoroughly familiar with the coding frame and codes no other questions.

In most coding operations, the first hundred or so cases will be the slowest and will give rise to the largest proportion of queries. The coders, though they have been carefully briefed and though the codes have been made as explicit as possible, will inevitably differ in their coding of certain responses, and there are also likely to be weaknesses in the coding frame. From the start, therefore, we must organize a procedure for dealing with queries, a procedure for regular discussion of difficult cases, a procedure for making amendments in the codes or the establishment of special rulings, and a checking procedure. In any but the smallest surveys there should be a coding supervisor, whose job it is to organize and implement these procedures, to do some of the check-coding and to decide whether or not a code will be amended. Earlier, when we discussed the 'miscellaneous' category, we saw that amending a code is something that is not to be done lightly, since it will involve recoding. By resisting the temptation to 'stretch' categories and by classifying all doubtful responses under 'miscellaneous', we can reduce the work of recoding if, at a later stage, we should decide to make a new category for some of the cases hitherto classified as miscellaneous. In any case, it is always best to keep the meaning of each category as clear as possible; this will cause fewer doubts when we come to interpret the findings.

The life of the coder is greatly eased if, throughout the survey, we keep to certain consistencies in designing the coding frames. For instance, we may decide always to code 'miscellaneous' or 'other' as category 0, 'no answer' or 'not ascertained' as category 9 or 99, and so on. If we use gradings or ratings, we should try to make them all follow the same direction, for example from positive to negative.

One useful refinement in the coding process is to instruct the coder to 'record', in the case of certain questions. This instruction means that the coder is to copy out verbatim what the respondent or the interviewer has written, together with the identifying case number. For instance, in an election study we may ask our coders to 'record' any references to the XYZ party, in order to study their particular contents more closely. Sometimes we may give this instruction because we wish to look at certain selected cases or to use their answers as illustrative quotations in our report.

## Multiple-mention codes

We have several times made reference to multiple-mention codes. This is one solution to the problem that arises when the respondent gives, or is asked to give, more than one answer to a question. Suppose we have asked: 'What do you mostly do in your spare time?' and that we have developed a broad set of nine categories. We can arbitrarily decide to allot, say, three variables to this question, one each for the first, second and third answer. We may even wish to assume that the order of the answers indicates the importance they have for the respondent, so that the first variable will contain the most important answers — though many would question this assumption. We will also have to ignore all fourth and subsequent answers, while having to cope at the same time with the problem that not everyone has given three answers, or even two. Moreover, when it comes to the statistical analysis, we will have to treat each set of answers independently, and since the frequency distribution of the first answers may well be very different from that of the second and the third answers, how are we to interpret these results? In issues such as these it may be better to have a different wording for the question, for instance: 'What are the three things you most enjoy doing in your spare time? Please put them in order of their importance to you.' Now we have a reasonable assurance that most respondents will produce the same number of answers; we have done away with any possible fourth or fifth answers; and we can feel fairly sure that the first answer really is the most important one. Furthermore, if we find that the frequency distribution of this answer differs from that of the other two, then we can make use of their relative importance to say, for example, that photography usually merits first place among older men, whereas younger men only mention it as a second or third choice.

There is, however, another solution to this problem that can be applied when phrasing the question in the above way is not suitable, or would 'force' the answers too much. Let us consider again the example given earlier from a student-readership survey, concerning the different systems used in reading a textbook in the college library. We saw then that many students might use more than one system while working from the same book. What would happen if we coded these responses on, say, three variables (or more), using the same code for each answer, and merged the responses? From the statistical point of view, we must find a way of coping with the problem of having more answers than we have respondents. There are no difficulties in tabulating such data and turning them into percentages, even though such percentages will add up to more than 100 per cent. Similarly, if we wish to study group differences, we can compare such percentages — but the problem of assessing statistical significance presents a difficulty because the data are not independent.

Let us take this problem a little further. Suppose that we had obtained, in the above example, the data contained in the list below for 200 men and 50 women students:

|  | | Men (N = 200) | Women (N = 50) |
|---|---|---|---|
| 1 | miscellaneous | 10 % | 8 % |
| 2 | chapter headings | 11 | 14 |
| 3 | skim chapter by chapter, then make notes | 18 | 16 |

| 4 | read from cover to cover | 10 | 36 |
| 5 | skim and make notes | 25 | 30 |
| 6 | concentrate on one section only | 3 | 12 |
| 7 | use index, look up pages | 30 | 30 |
| 8 | read chapter summaries | 3 | 2 |
| 10 | just read conclusions | 36 | 34 |
| 11 | introduction only | 10 | 10 |
| 12 | read various sections thoroughly | 10 | 14 |
| 99 | don't know, no answer | 8 | 8 |

We might be tempted to raise the general question: Are reading systems related to the respondent's gender? However, this would require us to calculate a 12 × 2 Chi-squared test of significance on the raw frequencies from which these percentages are derived, and this is not possible since Chi-squared assumes that the entries in the cells are independent — an assumption that is not justified where more than one answer comes from the same individual. What we might do, however, is to test each category against all the others put together, in a series of 2 × 2 Chi-squared tests (see under statistical comments, page 286). If we look again at these percentages we notice a substantial sex difference for category 4 ('read from cover to cover'): 10 per cent for men versus 36 per cent for the women (or, in raw frequencies: 20 out of 200 men and 18 out of 50 women). We can now test all those who responded in terms of category 4 against all those who did not (all non-4 responses), that is 180 men and 32 women, with the aid of an ordinary 2 × 2 Chi-squared test. This reduces the problem of lack of independence. It allows the respondents to give up to three (or more) answers, which can all be coded and used, and it makes no assumptions about their relative importance to the respondent. Note that we do the Chi-squared tests on the total number of *cases* in each sample, not the total number of responses. This, then, is a way in which we can deal with the statistical analysis of multiple-mention codes.

## Problems of coder reliability

One of the major problems of data processing is the problem of consistency between coders. As we have noted before, our concern is less with occasional slips or lapses which may produce a certain amount of random error, but rather with the consistently divergent use by some coders of certain code categories, which may produce a hidden systematic *bias*. As we have seen, precautions against this must be taken by designing the code categories as unambiguously as possible and with no overlap between them; by training the coders both in general and in respect of our particular coding frames; by close supervision and frequent checks; and by check-coding of batches of questionnaires. But even by adopting all these approved practices, how reliable is the coding of open-ended questions likely to be?

There is a prior question to this: how should we express inter-coder reliability? If we were to conduct a coding experiment, we might be tempted to think that the results can be expressed in terms of percentage agreement among coders. However, we have to take into account that a certain amount of agreement between any two coders would occur anyway, purely by chance, and especially in respect of relatively short coding frames. This has led to development of coefficients of concordance, which make allowance for chance expectations; for example, coefficient Kappa (see Selected Readings).

Using this coefficient, some experimental research (Kalton and Stowell, 1979; Collins and Kalton, 1980) suggests typical Kappa coefficients of around 70 per cent, averaged over dozens of questions and coded by a number of reputable research organizations. Around 12–15 per cent of all the coding frames were found to have reliability coefficients of under 50 per cent, making the data almost useless. A good deal depends on variations in complexity between coding frames. Moreover, these are not random inconsistencies: at least a quarter of the coding frames produced correlated coder variance or bias, significant at the 1 per cent level. The proportion of disagreements between coders was, in these experiments, far higher than would normally be detected by check-coding or by a supervisor. Clearly there is cause for much concern here: the more 'qualitative' and revealing the question, the more complex the coding frame will need to be, and hence the greater the risks of inconsistency and bias in the coding of the responses.

# Selected readings

Hedderson, J., 1991, *SPSS/PC+ Made Simple*, Chapman & Hall, London.

Krippendorf, K., 1981, *Content Analysis*, Sage, London.
    Deals with content analysis of interviews and documents. Helpful in studying the creation of coding frames.

Rossi, P.H., Wright, J.D., and Anderson, A.B. (eds), 1983, *Handbook of Survey Research*, Academic Press, New York.
    See chapter 11.

### ON RELIABILITY OF CODING

Dunn, Graham, 1989, *Design and Analysis of Reliability Studies*, Oxford University Press, New York.
    Practical guide. Deals also with correction for chance probability of agreement (coefficient Kappa). For the advanced student.

Kalton, G. and Stowell, R., 1979, 'A study of coder variability', *J. Roy. Stat. Soc.*, Applied Statistics Series, Vol. 28, 276–89.

Collins, M. and Kalton, G., 1980, 'Coding verbatim answers to open questions', *J. Market Res. Soc.*, **22**, No. 4, 239–47.

# 15
# STATISTICAL ANALYSIS

## Cleaning the data set

Before the start of the statistical analysis of our survey, and whether or not this is to take place on a computer, a series of checking operations should be performed on the complete data set. This is necessary in order to try and eliminate some of the more obvious errors that may have crept in during the preceding stages. Each data set will suggest its own checking procedures, but typically we may start by running frequency distributions on our main sampling variables. Thus, if the fieldwork records suggest that we should have 241 females and 456 males in our sample, are they actually there, in the data set? And what about the distributions for socioeconomic class, or by geographical area?

Next, we should run *range-checks* for each variable. Thus, if we have some five-point attitude-scale items, all coded 1–5 plus 9 for no answer/don't know, then there should be no entries for 6, 7, 8 or 0. Some data-input software programs come provided with such checking facilities.

After cleaning up whatever errors were found in the range-checks, we should run a selection of *internal consistency checks*. These ought to pick up probable inconsistencies, such as ten-year olds coded as married or a chartered accountant who has not completed primary school. Other inconsistencies might concern, say, a filter question to which a respondent has answered 'no' and has then gone on to answer the following questions as if the response to the filter question had been 'yes'. We may never get a completely 'clean' data set, but it is far easier to anticipate and rectify errors at this stage than later, after we have engaged in some complex statistical manipulations.

## Missing data

During the pilot work and at the research design stage we shall have given some attention to the problem of missing data. Now is the moment when we must make firm decisions about these and take appropriate action. Sometimes there will be gaps in an otherwise complete individual record. For example, some respondents will have missed out or mutilated certain questions (for instance, the ethnicity question in a census). Sometimes a respondent (or an interviewer) may have missed out one or two whole pages, or stopped part of the way through the questionnaire. But in addition there may be many *non-respondents*; that is, people who are missing from our data set altogether, perhaps because they could not be interviewed or because they did not return a postal questionnaire.

Every survey researcher will be confronted by the need to take some uncomfortable decisions about missing data. Obviously the best way to minimize such problems is by making every effort to prevent them — by reducing the non-response rate to the lowest possible figure. However if, despite our best efforts, many respondents have refused, or been unable, to answer a certain question, should we discard it? If a person has done the first part of our questionnaire but has left the rest uncompleted, what should we do? Are there any steps we can take to retrieve missing respondents? In thinking about such issues we should be less concerned with reduced sample size than with the ever-present risk of *bias* (see page 106): are people who have drinking problems less, or more likely to refuse to be interviewed about their alcohol consumption and related topics? Is our political postal questionnaire more likely to be discarded by the followers of a particular party? We must remember (see page 106) that even a very high response rate is no guarantee against bias.

In principle, we need to satisfy ourselves as best we can (see below) that the reasons or causes for non-response or missing data are unconnected with the topics in our questionnaire, so that there are no *'correlated biases'*. Our numbers may be down because people were away on holiday, or in hospital, or had friends staying with them, and we may think that our non-response rate will therefore be randomly distributed — but nevertheless there will be a bias in the returns if our questionnaire happened to deal with shopping habits, say, or with TV viewing or with social visiting.

It may be helpful to distinguish here between *listwise deletion* and *pairwise deletion*. Listwise deletion refers to the deletion of all the data of an entire case from the analysis because it is in some way(s) incomplete. Pairwise deletion refers to the temporary deletion of a case from the analysis only in respect of those items for which that particular case has no entries. The case is 'resuscitated' for the remainder of the analysis, provided entries are present. (It is called 'pairwise' because the problem usually arises when we try to generate a cross-tabulation between two items or questions. If an entry is missing for the first item, then it cannot be 'paired' with the second item, so that both members of the pair are lost to the calculation.) Discarding incomplete cases altogether (listwise deletion) should never be done lightly, not only because of the inadvertent creation of possible bias but also for some good, practical reasons. Consider, for example, the issue of *inter-correlations*. If we intend, in due course, to calculate a correlation coefficient between any two variables in a sample of, say, 200 cases, and if there are nineteen 'missing data' cases on the first variable, and twelve on the second, then this may leave us, at worst, with only 169 cases on which to do our calculation — which in turn might affect the value of the correlation coefficient, its level of statistical significance and perhaps even some of our conclusions. If we intend to engage in some multi-variate analysis, such as regression or factor analysis (see Chapter 9), then we might prefer a strategy of pairwise deletion, but this will create some major computational problems, as well as problems of statistical significance. Multi-variate analysis is likely to require the creation of a correlation *matrix*; that is, a square table containing the correlation of each variable under consideration with every other variable in that set (in other words, two identical triangles, so that every correlation coefficient appears twice). This may call for some complex pairwise deletions. Let us imagine, for example, that we intend to do some factor-analytic scaling (see Chapter 11) on a couple of dozen attitude statements. This will require the calculation of 276 correlation coefficients ($24 \times 23$ divided by 2), each of which may be subject to sample 'shrinkage' (pairwise deletion), and a changing sample size N, to a different degree!

Ideally, we should want to have an 'all-completed' data set for the entire sample but, if that is not possible, then we need to make sure that our statistical software package can cope with varying case numbers. If the loss of cases is not substantial and the possibility of introducing a bias is small, then we could, with the aid of listwise deletion, create a sub-sample which contains only cases that have completed every item in the questionnaire, but there is always the possibility of introducing an inadvertent bias.

## The plan of analysis

While each survey analysis has different requirements, which in turn are set by the nature of the research design, the analysis of a typical survey will usually have to go through several predictable stages:

a. univariates;
b. bivariates;
c. multivariates;
d. special sub-group studies.

As the name suggests, *univariates* are total sample distributions of one variable at a time; for example, the over-all distribution by region, or party-political preference, or belief in astrology, in our sample. In practice, sampling or classifying univariates are usually required first, because we want to know 'where we are and what we have' by comparing our achieved sample with our designed sample, and begin to consider likely biases in the return rates and possible follow-up strategies. Presumably we shall have some population parameters in terms of age, gender, geographical location and so forth; our achieved sample parameters can now be compared to these and attention paid to any significant discrepancies.

At this stage we can also see how often a much-discussed code category has actually been used, or how many twins there are in the sample, or whether it contains enough users of product X to make comparisons possible with the users of other products. Despite our earlier efforts at cleaning and checking our data set, it is still likely that some remaining errors will be detected.

We also need the univariates in order to plan the subsequent stages of the analysis. If our study is, say, a political poll on a representative sample, then these univariates, especially those on voting intent, may be almost the only distributions we require, and any further tables will be mainly in the nature of elaborations. But if we are dealing with a more complex, analytic research design, then the real interest of the survey analyst will lie in the interrelationships between certain variables, and the over-all distributions will chiefly be used to plan the study of these interrelationships more carefully.

In the case of a simple random sample, sampling errors and confidence limits of estimates based on the whole sample (say, of the proportion of respondents whose preference is for party P) can now be calculated. If interest focuses on differences between sub-groups (say, on the proportions of men and women who prefer party P), then estimates of the sampling errors of such observed differences need to be calculated (see page 43), since these are likely to be higher. As we know (see page 159) such estimates are further influenced by measurement unreliability and by response bias.

For the study of *bivariates* (including cross-tabulations, breakdowns and different measures of association between two variables) we must turn to our design. We should remind ourselves which are our dependent and our independent variables and set up some kind of groupings within the sample that will enable us to determine the relationships between them. Perhaps we should first of all like to satisfy ourselves that we have a robust, reliable and valid dependent variable; for example, achievement in mathematics (adding up marks for arithmetic, geometry, algebra and so forth and calculating each student's average over several semesters), or a social adjustment index (similarly a composite score with several sub-domains). In more complex investigations there will be more than one dependent variable; it can also happen that a dependent variable in one context becomes an independent variable in another part of the analysis.

After that, we shall essentially be engaged in making comparisons between fairly stable sets of sub-groups in our sample (for example those with a high social adjustment score versus those with a low one) in relation to each independent variable, in accordance with our theoretical expectations as embodied in the research design. A carefully devised basic plan is therefore needed for the generation of statistical 'production runs'. Of course, the better and tighter our research design is, the more readily the analysis will 'run itself'. If, for example, we have a factorial design or one using multiple regression, then the main classifying variables are known from the start. Or, if we have employed a control group, then a matching operation will have to take place and group univariates compared, after which comparisons between experimental and control groups can proceed. Similar preparatory operations will be required to set up a run of comparative tabulations in the case of a before-and-after type of design. If we are doing, for example, a quality-of-life study on a group of patients before, and some months after an operation, then we shall first need to compare the second ('after') set of data with the first, to see how many cases have been 'lost' in the sense of 'cannot be traced'. Next, we shall need to compare the 'lost' cases with the remaining ones on some of the most important variables in the first ('before') data set to ascertain bias in the remaining sample of responders. After that we shall need to create a definitive data set which will include only those cases for which we have complete follow-up responses, as well as a complete set of responses from before the operation. Only then can we proceed to plan our before-versus-after set of comparisons.

Many statistical analyses will go no further, but with some studies a *multi-variate* stage will need to follow — or may be needed at an earlier stage. In a multi-variate analysis we try to explore the patterns of relationships among our variables not just in two-way, cross-tabulated form (for example, income level versus possession of a video recorder) but in more complex ways, using many variables. To follow the above example, and perhaps having found a relatively weak association between income level and owning or hiring a video recorder, we may cast our minds wider and start to wonder about income level and the possession of consumer durables generally (for which we would have to calculate a composite index), about income level and materialistic life-style in other ways (for example a second home, holidays abroad) and even about income level and 'materialism' as an attitude or value construct (assuming we have, or can create, a measure of the latter). We are now embarking upon a more exploratory stage of data analysis. Statistical techniques do exist to make such a multi-variate analysis possible (for example multiple regression, principal-components analysis), but it would be best to plan these at the research design stage; that is, at the beginning of our study, not at the end.

In educational research, to take another example, we may try to 'explain' why some children do better at a given school subject (say, mathematics) while others do less well. Our dependent variable would be a set of maths test results for each child, but our independent variables would be many: perhaps a measure of intelligence, a measure of homework supervision, the number of children in the class, availability of teaching and computing equipment, parental occupation (for example, parents with maths-related jobs), maths and other qualifications of the teacher, the child's intended career and further education, possession of an electronic calculator, and so on. All of these, and many other measures, could be *simultaneously* related to achievement in mathematics, and we could ascertain both the relative contribution of each variable to the child's achievement and their various combined 'effects'. In particular, since many of these variables overlap with each other, we could show which ones contribute relatively little to the 'explained variance' once others have been included in the pattern, and which ones still contribute independently. We could also combine these variables into groups, or blocks (for example, family variables, classroom variables) to show the relative importance of each group of variables compared to that of other groups. Obviously such an analysis will require a great deal of thought and planning.

Part of a multi-variate analysis may involve us in 'building up' rather than 'breaking down' the data. Carrying out a principal-components analysis or developing a new scale or a composite index would come under this heading. Quite often such newly generated variables will then require us to undertake new 'production runs' to show how these new variables are related to responses to other parts of our questionnaire. Before doing so, it is essential to calculate the reliability of any scale or index (see page 159) to make sure that it is at least adequate; if the reliability coefficient falls below .80 then further work using this variable must be regarded as of dubious value. The generation of new variables at this stage is likely to present us with serious problems of interpretation, but at least we can hope to replicate these new measures in subsequent studies.

The fourth and final stage of statistical analysis is difficult to plan. This is the analysis of *special sub-groups*. It comes after the main results of the survey have been tabulated and digested, and have begun to give rise to new research questions. At this point we shall very likely wish to undertake a series of additional breakdowns, cross-tabulations or correlational studies that were not part of the main analysis. Often such cross-tabulations require the identification of a particular sub-sample (for example, people who are self-employed and are working from home; people who never vote; people who used to buy a particular product but have ceased to do so) for special study. Or we may wish to explore a pattern of relationships within several graded sub-samples, for example studying the relationship between family size and maternal strictness within each social class in turn. This kind of analysis will require us to 'hold constant' other variables, or to engage in the compilation of matched sub-samples.

This part of the analysis is both interesting and time-consuming, and in a sense there is no end to it, for there always seem to be further interesting possibilities just over the horizon. Most surveys are never 'analysed-out' completely; the analysis stops for lack of money or lack of time.

As we have seen in Chapter 2, unless this kind of detailed sub-group analysis is planned for from the beginning and the sample collected accordingly (for example, by over-sampling the sub-groups of concern), we tend very soon to run out of cases. Perhaps this is just as well, for there are distinct disadvantages in going on a 'fishing expedition'. The chances are that we shall end up with a great many wasted tables, with a few substantial and interesting differences that we will be unable to interpret, and with a large number of small trends that may whet our curiosity but are unlikely to emerge again in subsequent surveys. We might find, for example, in a study of airport noise, that the people most likely to complain about aircraft noise are those with marital problems. This looks interesting but, unless we can say how such an association has come about and thus derive a new explanatory variable that might have wider applications, such results are of doubtful value. Up to a point such exploratory analyses are useful and may yield important supplementary findings, but they need to be 'theory-driven' and we must learn to curb the urge to do too many. We should also remember that at, say, the 5 per cent level of statistical significance, one in every twenty cross-tabulations will be 'statistically significant' by pure chance.

It is often the case that the over-all plan of our analysis will also determine the shape of the final report, and so it is perhaps worth mentioning that only a small fraction of all our tabulations will eventually be published, perhaps less than 5 per cent. This 'wastage' is inevitable; many results can be summed up in a few words, quoting perhaps one or two figures for illustrative purposes, without publishing an entire set of tables. This is especially true if the findings are negative. If we have a questionnaire with 114 questions and we wish to find out which of these are related to the respondents' religion, then this will require 114 tables, none of which will be published if the results are altogether negative; such findings are likely to be summarised in a few words, unless they are of special importance. When writing a report we must constantly ask ourselves: 'Is this table really necessary?'; otherwise the reader will not be able to see the wood for the trees.

# Statistical comments

Competence in statistics is a necessary requirement for the research worker in any field; readers who are uncertain of their skill in this respect may try the test in Appendix I. There is no shortage of textbooks in this field, covering probability theory, tests of significance, and correlational and multi-variate techniques. A variety of computer software packages both for PCs and for mainframes are available, the most helpful of which will also be interactive; that is, tables can be generated, inspected, changed and printed on line. Often such packages will automatically apply several tests of significance and measures of association to each table (not always appropriately). The facilities for creating and re-shaping two-way tables would be one of the criteria by which to judge the suitability of a statistical package for our proposed analysis.

Statistical techniques are like excavation tools and building blocks: they help us to 'dig' into the data and mine them for precious findings, and enable us to summarize and compose these into a meaningful structure, but, depending on the nature of the data, different statistical tools will have to be used for different purposes.

When planning the statistical analysis of a survey, an important distinction will have to be made between metric or interval-type data, and nominal or categorical data (see Chapter 9), since they require different statistical treatments. *Interval-type* data have additive properties and equal intervals along a continuum. In social surveys variables such as age, family size, income, years of residence and number of cigarettes smoked per day are all examples of interval scales. The statistical techniques applicable to them are means, standard deviations, t-tests and F-tests, regression methods, analysis of variance, product moment correlation coefficients, and so on. *Nominal* data are not measured along a continuum; they lack additive or even ordinal properties and can best be thought of as frequencies in discrete categories, placed in no particular order. Nominal data in social surveys might be marital status, place (state/country) of birth, eye colour, religious affiliation, daily paper read most frequently, favourite school subject, or the reasons for liking/disliking any specific product. Applicable statistical techniques are percentages, Chi-squared tests and other non-parametric devices (see page 157). In addition, between the interval measures and the nominal classifications lie variables that have *ordinal* properties such as ranking data, measures of relative interest or preference, orderings of priority or prestige, and others (155). A number of statistical techniques such as Spearman's Rho and Kendall's Tau have been specially developed to use with ordinal data.

It should be stated that the *parametric* techniques of statistical analysis applicable to interval scales have considerably greater power and versatility, and can make fuller use of the information contained in our data, than *non-parametric* techniques.

A typical social survey is likely to contain a mixture of interval measures and nominal data, and these will have to be treated in different ways. This fundamental distinction will greatly affect the production of the tables in our statistical analysis. For example, suppose we want to know whether religious affiliation is related to alcohol consumption. We cannot answer this question by calculating a single measure of strength of association, such as a correlation coefficient, because in the case of the usual product-moment correlation *both* variables must be metric, whereas in our example one variable (alcohol consumption) is metric but the other (religion) is not. So how, by what means, could we explore and present this relationship (if any), and what instructions shall we give to our computer? Having drawn attention to the general problem of trying to relate metric to non-metric data, we can say that some possible solutions are available. For instance, there are various types of correlations other than the product–moment coefficient; one of these, the point-biserial correlation coefficient, might be applicable to this example. This coefficient is designed to express the relationship between a metric measure and a dichotomy. Our nominal variable — in this case, religion — could be regarded as a series of dichotomies, that is Protestant/non-Protestant; Roman Catholic/non-Catholic; Muslim/non-Muslim and so on. Each of these dichotomies could be related to our interval scale — in this case, alcohol consumption — and a series of point-biserial correlation coefficients could be calculated. (Warning: if we follow this procedure for a number of variables we shall greatly increase the number of correlation coefficients, to the point where some of them might be statistically significant purely by chance.)

Or we could approach the problem in another way, by calculating the average or mean alcohol intake (assuming that we have an interval-type measure of this) for each religious group and then performing a one-way analysis of variance and an F-test on the data. This would tell us whether, in our sample, the average alcohol intake differs significantly according to the respondent's religion. Perhaps further analysis might show that one religious group drinks significantly more, or less, than most of the others. But whatever approach we use, we cannot generate a single summary coefficient to describe the overall strength of this association. This is the type of analytic and presentational problem that arises in the case of 'mixed' categorical and interval scale data.

To try to avoid some of these cumbersome procedures when we try to inter-relate variables of different types, we sometimes engage in data *transformation*. In our first example we showed how some data can be transformed (in that case from nominal to dichotomous). Other transformations are possible. For example, groupings of jobs or occupations can be regarded as purely nominal categories of economic activity in no particular order, or they can be placed in a prestige hierarchy (see page 269) and used as a ranking of socioeconomic background with perhaps half-a-dozen levels, that is they will have been transformed into an ordinal scale. Some researchers would go farther, and turn these ranks into an interval scale, with numerical values such as 5 or 2 given to every occupation. Researchers are driven to such dubious transformations by the desire to apply parametric techniques of analysis (such as ANOVA, correlations, and regression methods), since these are more powerful and more versatile than non-parametric methods such as the Chi-squared test.

However, while such transformations may be useful, they require us to make certain assumptions. Are we, for instance, willing to assume that occupations can be reliably placed into a prestige hierarchy? A single hierarchy? In which culture? For women, too? And are we then willing to turn them into an interval scale? Or what about five-point Likert scale items in attitude scales (see Chapter 11)? Is it justifiable to treat these as metric variables? And how can we justify making similar assumptions in the case of semantic differential items (see Chapter 12), or inventories (see Chapter 13)? The temptation to do so is often strong because the statistical 'mining' tools for metric variables are more versatile and more powerful.

Sometimes, however, we prefer to carry out transformations in the opposite direction; that is, from ordinal or metric measures into categorical ones. For instance, ordinal data can also be analysed, though with some loss of information, with the aid of the non-parametric techniques applicable to nominal data (percentages and Chi-squared tests). This latter approach is often used for the sake of uniformity and simplicity, though it takes no account of the ordinal attributes of the data.

It is also worth pointing out that interval measures can readily be transformed into categorical data (albeit with some loss of information) by arranging them into frequency distributions. Thus, instead of calculating the average age of a sub-sample, we may say that 24 per cent were over forty-five years old. Since this involves considerable loss of information, why would we do this? Suppose we have obtained age in terms of date of birth, and we wish to create a table in which age is related to another variable, a nominal one, for example to brand preferences of a particular product. Imagine how such a table would look: across the top we have, say, eight different brands: Brand A, Brand B and so on, heading eight separate columns; and down the side we have age, calculated from each respondent's date of birth — running, say, from eighteen years three months down to sixty-five and over! Such a table would require many print-out pages and would be quite unmanageable. Obviously, before asking for such a table, we would transform the age variable into, say, half-a-dozen class intervals. Now we have a table of eight columns and six rows, which is much more intelligible, even though we have turned the metric variable 'age' into a much cruder ordinal classification.

However, as we have seen, nominal data cannot be turned into ordinal or interval ones unless we are willing to make certain assumptions; for example, about the nature of social class or about the response categories of attitude items. When tempted to indulge in some data transformation of a dubious nature, it might therefore be useful to carry out the analysis several times, each time using a different assumption. Such a procedure might well show that making some radical data transformations is not really necessary and that almost equally clear results can be obtained by more conservative means.

A final statistical comment refers to the exact nature of the question we want to ask of our data. We may, for example, find a statistically significant pattern of associations between certain variables, but this tells us little about either *strength* or *direction* (which 'causes' which) of the associations, nor anything about their *predictive* powers. Thus, we may find a significant association (for example a Chi-squared test result which significantly departs from chance) between political party allegiance and a measure of ethnic prejudice, but we cannot calculate a coefficient to indicate its strength. Without doing much further research we do not know its direction (which came first, choice of party or ethnic prejudice?);

nor can we tell its power to make causal predictions of, say, voting behaviour. So what exactly is the question to which we hope that our data analysis will provide an answer?

Furthermore, we must always remember that statistical significance does not indicate social significance or practical usefulness. If our sample is large enough, a difference between average scores of 23.8 and 24.2 on an attitude scale may be statistically significant, but is it meaningful, or socially relevant?

# Finally

There is no end to statistical argumentations, but perhaps two more issues from among many may be singled out for discussion.

The first is the problem of *difference scores* or change scores. These arise in longitudinal studies (for example, how stable are people's preferences, over time, for product X, or for certain types of music or health foods?) and in before-and-after experiments (for example, the impact of a TV programme on certain attitudes, or the effects of a new teaching method in schools). (For longitudinal studies, see Chapter 2.) To create an oversimplified example, suppose that just before an election we find that 40 per cent of our sample would vote for party P and that, when we go back to the same respondents six months later, we find again that 40 per cent express a voting intention for party P. Does this indicate that there has been no change? Not necessarily for, theoretically, it is possible that every respondent has changed political allegiance and that none of those who intended to vote for party P on the first occasion still intends to do so on the next! And what if the figures had been, say, 35 per cent on the first occasion, and 50 per cent on the next — does this prove that party P has broadened its support by holding on to its original adherents while capturing an additional 15 per cent of the vote? Again, not necessarily; it is theoretically possible that party P has lost all its original supporters and that its current adherents are all new recruits. Thus, total-sample statistics can mask, or under-estimate, underlying change. What is necessary is the calculation of a *change score for each individual* in the sample. Where the dependent variable is more complex than simple party preference, such calculations can become quite demanding; for example, studying shifts in readership of a daily newspaper in a city that has six. Moreover, the statistical treatment of the results, especially if the variable is a categorical one, becomes a permutational ordeal; and there are problems, too, with the assessment of reliability and of statistical significance. So it is as well to be aware of these problems and, as far as possible, to anticipate them before undertaking longitudinal research.

The second issue also has to do with comparisons, but not with comparisons over time. The problem arises when we have used more than one technique to measure the same attribute or variable. Suppose that we have asked a number of questions to measure attitude to abortion, and that on our first question we have found 62 per cent of middle-class respondents to be 'in favour'. By itself, this figure is very nearly meaningless. It only acquires some meaning when we can compare it, say, to a response of 48 per cent 'in favour' among working-class respondents. But perhaps if we look at the results of a differently worded question on attitudes to abortion, we might find a different result. Perhaps now we will find 53 per cent of our middle-class respondents giving a favourable reply. Again, let us look at the working-class figures; quite likely we shall find them running at around 32 per cent in favour for our second question. In other words, it is often impossible to say, in absolute terms, how many respondents have a particular attitude to a given extent, because so much depends on the wording of the question (see page 148). Nevertheless, the *relative* differences (between classes, age groups, sexes or some other variable of concern) may well be quite stable and consistent in their direction, no matter how the question is phrased. In social research we have few absolute measures, but relative differences are well worth having if they are consistent. They constitute a 'real' finding and can give us an indication of relationships between underlying variables.

# Selected readings

## STATISTICS TEXTS

Rossi, P.H., Wright, J.D. and Anderson, A.B. (eds), 1983, *Handbook of Survey Research*, Academic Press, New York.
See chapters 11–16.

Wright, George and Fowler, Chris, 1986, *Investigative Design and Statistics*, Penguin Books.
A practical and instructive basic text.

Zeisel, Hans, 1957, *Say It With Figures*, Harper, New York.
Still a very useful and approachable text, with good advice on cross-tabulations, on Don't Know responses and on panel studies.

Howell, D.C., 1989, *Fundamental Statistics for the Behavioural Sciences*, 2nd edition, Chapman & Hall, London.

Healy, J.F., second edition, 1990, *Statistics: A Tool for Social Research*, Chapman & Hall, London.

Skinner, C.J., Holt, D. and Smith, T.M.F., 1989, *Analysis of Complex Surveys*, Wiley, Chichester, Sussex.
For the advanced student.

O'Muircheartaigh, C.A. and Payne, C., 1977, *The Analysis of Survey Data*, 2 vols, Wiley, Chichester, Sussex.
More advanced methods of data exploration and model fitting.

## SPECIAL TOPICS

Neave, H.R. and Worthington, P.B., 1988, *Distribution-free Tests*, Unwin Hyman, London.
Introductory text on non-parametric methods, a successor to Siegel's book (see below) of 1956.

Siegel, S., 1956, *Nonparametric Statistics for the Behavioural Sciences*, McGraw-Hill, New York.
A widely used and very intelligible text.

Dunteman, George H., 1989, *Principal Components Analysis*, Quantitative Applications in the Social Sciences No. 69, Sage, London.

Kalton, G., 1983, *Compensating for Missing Survey Data*, Institute for Social Research, University of Michigan.
   Careful treatment of the problems of missing cases and missing items, advising on weightings, estimates and other possible adjustments.

Rubin, D.B., 1987, *Multiple Imputation for Nonresponse in Surveys*, Wiley, New York.
   For the specialist.

Himmelweit, Hilde T., Humphreys, Patrick, Jaeger, Marianne and Katz, Michael, 1981, *How Voters Decide*, Academic Press.
   A sophisticated statistical treatment of causality.

Everitt, Brian S. and Dunn, Graham, 1991, *Applied Multivariate Data Analysis*, Edward Arnold, Hodder & Stoughton, Sevenoaks, Kent.
   Deals with problems of dimensionality, MDS, cluster analysis, regression, factor analysis and discriminant analysis. For advanced students.

# Appendix I
## STATISTICS TEST

If you get more than one answer wrong, you should not embark on survey research without a refresher course in statistics.

1. Imagine that you had asked a group of men and a group of women: 'What kind of music do you like best of all?' How would you find out whether there is a significant gender difference in the type of music preferred?

(a) Calculate the means and use the t-test to test for statistical significance;
(b) use the F-test to test for statistical significance;
(c) construct two frequency distributions and apply the Chi-squared test for statistical significance;
(d) calculate the standard deviation for each gender and compare;
(e) none of the above.

2. Suppose you had been involved in the evaluation of an experimental slimming diet. You have available the weights of forty-six subjects who had each been weighed before and after taking part in the experiment. How would you check whether there had been a significant change in weight following the experiment?

(a) For each subject, calculate the gain or loss in weight and apply the Chi-squared test;
(b) calculate the product-moment correlation between the two sets of weights;
(c) calculate a regression coefficient based on the weights before the start of the experiment, and test its significance;
(d) calculate the means of the two sets of weights and apply the formula for t-test for related samples;
(e) none of the above.

3.                              Belief in life after death

|                      | Yes  | No   |
| -------------------- | ---- | ---- |
| Aged under 65        | 23%  | 47%  |
| Aged 65 and over     | 77%  | 53%  |
|                      | 100% | 100% |

On the basis of the above table, which of the following conclusions would you accept?

(a)  Younger people are less afraid of death;
(b)  belief in an afterlife causes people to live longer;
(c)  older people have had a more religious upbringing;
(d)  older people are less afraid of death;
(e)  none of the above.

4.  Suppose we have the average digestion time of a typical meal for a sample of horses, a sample of cows, a sample of dogs and a sample of rabbits. The results of an over-all ANOVA are significant at the 5% level. Does this mean:

(a)  that such a result would occur by chance 1 in 20 times?
(b)  that grass eaters eat more slowly?
(c)  that smaller animals have faster digestions?
(d)  that 5% of the animals have above-average digestion rates?
(e)  none of the above?

5.  If we find a statistically significant correlation of −.64 between speed and accuracy on a simple clerical task, does this mean:

(a)  that the faster subjects were more accurate?
(b)  that the slower subjects were often more accurate?
(c)  that 64% of the subjects made mistakes?
(d)  that the faster subjects made fewer mistakes?
(e)  none of the above?

ANSWERS:

Question 1: (c).
These are nominal, not interval data.

Question 2: (d).
These are not independent but related samples.

Question 3: (e).
We can accept *none* of these conclusions: first, because all we have are the percentages and we do not know the number of cases in the two samples, so we cannot test the data for statistical significance; and second, because we have no evidence of causality, or of the direction of causality, or of the possible presence of a third variable which might affect both the others.

Question 4: (a).
Since the means are not given, we cannot say which animals have faster or slower digestions. We can say nothing about relative digestion speeds except that they differ significantly. This over-all difference was found to be significant at the 5% level, which means a chance probability of 1:20.

Question 5: (b).
Since the correlation is *negative*, the two variables are inversely related. This means that lower times (ie faster performance) are associated with higher numbers of mistakes (ie lower accuracy); and conversely, that higher times (slower performance) are associated with lower numbers of mistakes (ie higher accuracy). Since the correlation is of medium strength, it will not necessarily apply to *all* subjects equally.

# Appendix II
## NOMOGRAPHS FOR THE TESTING OF STATISTICAL SIGNIFICANCE OF DIFFERENCES BETWEEN PERCENTAGES

In order to facilitate the inspection of results, most surveys produce their findings in the form of large numbers of percentages. Eventually, we have to determine the statistical significance of differences between percentages, and usually this can only be done by going back to the raw frequencies and calculating Chi-squared values. If we are dealing, for instance, with the differences between men and women in response to one particular multiple-mention question with, say, seven answer-categories, then we shall probably wish to test for the sex difference in respect of one or two specific answer-categories. In principle this means 'collapsing' the 2 × 7 into a 2 × 2 table, or several 2 × 2 tables, and testing for the statistical significance of one answer-category (or several answer-categories combined) against the remainder. The procedure has been outlined in Chapter 15.

In 1939, Joseph Zubin published a nomograph in Volume 34 of the *Journal of the American Statistical Association* (pp. 539–44) which has been recalculated and adapted for inclusion in the present text. It has the great advantage that we do not have to go back to the raw frequencies but can determine the significance of different proportions directly from the percentage figures. All we need is a ruler (preferably transparent), and the three charts that follow. All three nomographs are 'read' in the same way, namely by placing the ruler at our two observed values on the left-hand line and right-hand line, and reading off on the middle line. The first chart enables us to find a 'significant value', which will depend on the two sample sizes; if we place the ruler as accurately as we can against the two sample sizes (such as the number of men and the number of women, in the above example) on the left and on the right, then we shall be able to read off the significant value where the ruler crosses the centre line. This value has to be *reached* or *exceeded* on one of the next two charts, or both, if the difference is to be statistically significant at one of the customary levels of probability. One chart has, on its centre line, significance values for the 10 per cent and the 5 per cent levels; the next chart has the values for the 1 per cent and the 0.1 per cent levels. Thus, if we find that a difference between two percentages is significant at the 5 per cent level, it may be worthwhile checking on the next chart whether it will reach the 1 per cent or even the 0.1 per cent level.

It may be worth repeating that, ordinarily, Chi-squared cannot be calculated from percentages but only from the raw frequencies. In the case of the present nomographs, however, we can utilize percentages directly because our first chart takes the respective sample sizes into account in establishing our 'significant value'. This is particularly helpful in survey work, where we often have to test large numbers of percentages for statistical significance, but where such percentages are based on sample sizes that remain stable throughout the length of the questionnaire. Having once looked up our significant value on the first chart, we need henceforth concern ourselves only with the second and the third charts — unless we come to deal with a different set of sub-samples.

Inevitably, nomographs are somewhat lacking in precision, so that for the more important differences, where these border on the limits of significance, the necessary calculations should also be carried out. The same applies to instances where the sample sizes are very low. Note also that a given difference (say, fifteen percentage points) may be significant at the extremes, where one of the percentages approaches zero or one hundred, but not in the middle ranges; if we merely observe the magnitude of the difference, without considering its place in the percentage range, we are likely to produce errors. Where one of the percentages is very small (say, below 5 per cent) or very large (say, above 95 per cent), the nomograph tends to give an overestimate of statistical significance, and calculations again become necessary.

Perhaps the most helpful way to use this nomograph is to think of it as an aid to inspection, a simple device that will enable us to focus attention on the more important differences and sort the grain from the chaff.

EXAMPLES

(1) $N_1 = 125$    $N_2 = 164$    significant value = 0.119
Percentages: 61 and 50, significant at the 10 per cent level.

(2) As above, percentages 81 and 70 significant at the 5 per cent level.
(NB: the difference between the two sets of percentages is the same, but the significance is greater when approaching extreme values 0 or 100.)

(3) $N_1 = 350$    $N_2 = 600$    significant value = 0.068
Percentages: 75 and 66, significant at the 1 per cent level.

(4) As above, percentages 12 and 5, significant at the 0.1 per cent level.

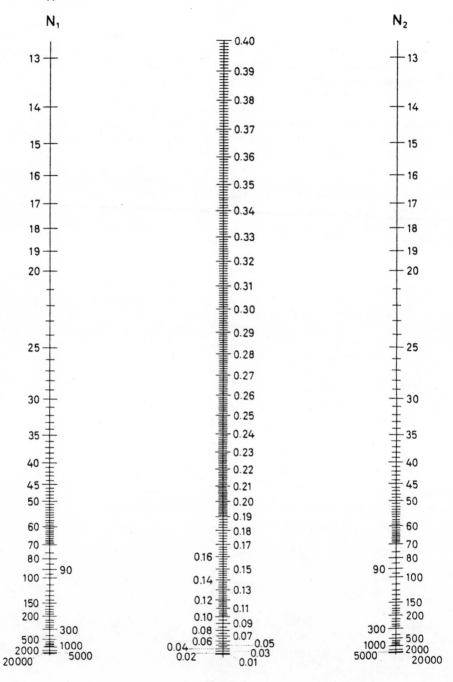

**Chart 1**

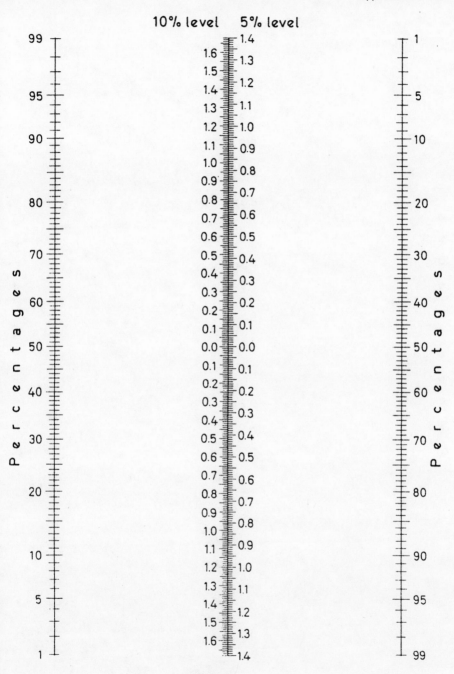

**Chart 2**

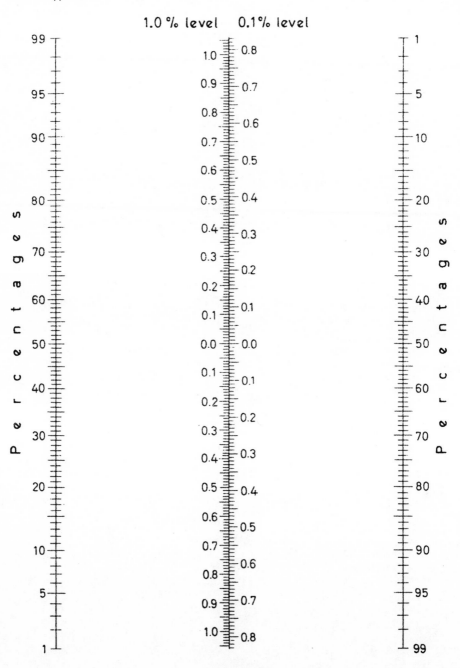

**Chart 3**

# INDEX